THE
PORTABLE MBA
IN ENTREPRENEURSHIP

The Portable MBA Series

THE
PORTABLE MBA
IN ENTREPRENEURSHIP

Third Edition

William D. Bygrave and

Andrew Zacharakis, Editors

WILEY

John Wiley & Sons, Inc.

Chapter 2 is excerpted from *New Venture Creation: Entrepreneurship for the Twenty-First Century* by Jeffry A. Timmons. Burr Ridge, IL: Irwin/McGraw-Hill, 1999. This material is used with permission. All rights reserved.

Exhibit 12.12: Amazon.com is the registered trademark of Amazon.com, Inc.

ISBN 0-471-27154-3

Printed in the United States of America.

10 9 8 7 6 5 4 3 2 1

CONTENTS

v

PREFACE

The decade that has passed since we published the first edition of this book has been one of the most remarkable periods in the annals of entrepreneurship in the United States. The crucial role that entrepreneurs play in keeping the U.S. economy dynamic, vibrant, and growing has become more and more apparent.

In the introduction to the first edition we stated that the U.S. economy would have to create 21 million new jobs by the year 2000 just to keep pace with the number of people entering the workforce for the first time. As it turned out, 23.5 million new jobs were generated. It is estimated that small businesses and the entrepreneurs who run them accounted for more than two-thirds of those new jobs. Today, U.S. small businesses—firms with 500 or fewer staff—employ slightly more than 50% of the labor force and generate approximately one-half of the nonfarm private gross domestic product (GDP). If the small-business sector of the U.S. economy were a nation, its GDP would rank third in the world behind the non-small-business sector of the United States and the entire economy of Japan and ahead of the entire economies of Germany, the United Kingdom, France, and Italy.

Not only are small businesses the engine for job creation, they are also a powerful force for innovation. They employ 39% of all high-tech workers and produce approximately 14 times more patents per employee than large firms. Consider just one example—the World Wide Web. That was barely a blip on the radar screen when the first edition of this book was published. The Web was invented by Tim Berners-Lee to make the Internet more easily accessible for his colleagues at CERN, the European high-energy laboratory in Geneva. The possibilities of the Web immediately fired up the imagination of entrepreneurs who created a multitude of new products and services. A 23-year-old University of Illinois computer programmer, Marc Andreessen, led the Web revolution with Netscape browser. Not far behind were Jeff Bezos with Amazon.com, David Filo and Jerry Yang with Yahoo, and Pierre Omidyar with eBay. Those daring entrepreneurs and many others like them changed forever the way we work, live, and play—in ways that we never dreamed of less than 10 years ago.

Entrepreneurship is what America does best. No other advanced industrial nation comes close. U.S. entrepreneurial companies created the personal computer, biotechnology, fast food, and overnight package delivery industries; transformed the retailing industry; overthrew AT&T's telecommunications monopoly; revitalized the steel industry; invented the integrated circuit and the microprocessor; founded the nation's most profitable airline; and the list goes on.

Is it any wonder that more and more people are choosing to be entrepreneurs? Entrepreneurship courses and programs have proliferated in the past 10 years. It is estimated that 61% of U.S. colleges and universities have at least one course in entrepreneurship. It is possible to study entrepreneurship in certificate, associates, bachelors, masters, and PhD programs. All business students, regardless of their career plans, need to understand the role of entrepreneurship in the economy. Today, a business education without an entrepreneurship component is as incomplete as medical training without obstetrics.

The Portable MBA in Entrepreneurship is a book for would-be entrepreneurs, people who have started small firms and who want to improve their entrepreneurial skills, and others who are interested in entrepreneurship, such as bank loan officers, lawyers, accountants, investors, and consultants—indeed, anyone who wants to get involved in the birth and growth of an enterprise. The chapters are written by leading authorities on new business creation, including professors, entrepreneurs, and consultants with extensive experience teaching the art and science of starting and growing a venture. These authors practice what they teach. They have started businesses, served on boards of venture capital funds, boards of directors, and boards of advisors of entrepreneurial companies; raised startup and expansion capital; filed patents; registered companies; and, perhaps most important of all, created new products and many new jobs. They are tireless champions of entrepreneurship, and they believe that entrepreneurs are crucial to America's economic well-being.

WILLIAM D. BYGRAVE
ANDREW ZACHARAKIS

Arthur M. Blank Center for Entrepreneurship
Babson College

ABOUT THE EDITORS

William D. Bygrave, MA, DPhil (Oxford University), MBA (Northeastern University), DBA (Boston University), honorary doctorate University of Ghent, honorary doctorate Glasgow Caledonian University, is the Frederic C. Hamilton Professor for Free Enterprise and visiting professor at the London Business School. He was director of the Arthur M. Blank Center for Entrepreneurial Studies at Babson College (1993–1999) and visiting professor at INSEAD (the European Institute of Business Administration, 1992–1995).

Bygrave teaches and researches entrepreneurship, especially financing of startup and growing ventures. He spent the 1992 to 1993 academic year at INSEAD where he led a pan-European team from eight nations that studied entrepreneurs' attitudes toward realizing value and harvesting their companies. One of the outcomes of that research was the initiative that led to the founding of EASDAQ (now merged with Nasdaq). In 1997, he and Michael Hay at the London Business School started the Global Entrepreneurship Monitor (GEM), which examines the entrepreneurial competitiveness of nations. The principal investigator is Paul Reynolds. Reports on the GEM studies can be read and downloaded at www.gemconsortium.org.

Bygrave founded a Route 128 venture-capital backed high-technology company, cofounded a pharmaceutical database company, and was a member of the investment committee of a venture capital firm. His company won an *IR100* award for introducing one of the 100 most significant new technical products in the United States in 1977.

He is co-author or co-editor of *Venture Capital at the Crossroads, Realizing Enterprise Value,* the *Venture Capital Handbook, The Portable MBA in Entrepreneurship, The Portable MBA in Entrepreneurship Case Studies,* and *Frontiers of Entrepreneurship Research.*

Andrew Zacharakis, PhD, is the acting director of the Arthur M. Blank Center for Entrepreneurship and Paul T. Babson Term Chair in Entrepreneurship. Zacharakis' primary research areas include the (1) venture capital process and (2) entrepreneurial growth strategies. The editors of *Journal of Small Business Management* selected his article, "Differing Perceptions of New Venture Failure" as the 1999 best article. Zacharakis' dissertation *The Venture Capital Investment Decision* received the 1995 Certificate of Distinction from the Academy of Management and Mr. Edgar F. Heizer recognizing outstanding research in the field of new enterprise development.

Zacharakis has been interviewed in newspapers nationwide including the *Boston Globe,* the *Wall Street Journal,* and *USA Today.* He has also appeared on the *Bloomberg Small Business Report* and been interviewed on *National Public Radio.* He has taught seminars to leading corporations, such as Boeing, Met Life, Lucent, and Intel. He has taught executives in countries worldwide, including Chile, Australia, China, and Germany. Zacharakis received a BS (finance/marketing), University of Colorado; an MBA (finance/international business), Indiana University; and a PhD (strategy and entrepreneurship/cognitive psychology), University of Colorado.

Zacharakis is the program chair for the Entrepreneurship Division of the Academy of Management. He consults with entrepreneurs and small business startups. His professional experience includes positions with The Cambridge Companies (investment banking/venture capital), IBM, and Leisure Technologies.

1 THE ENTREPRENEURIAL PROCESS
William D. Bygrave

This is the entrepreneurial age. It is estimated that as many as 460 million persons worldwide were either actively involved in trying to start a new venture or were owner-managers of a new business in 2002.[1] More than a thousand new businesses are born every hour of every working day in the United States. Entrepreneurs are driving a revolution that is transforming and renewing economies worldwide. Entrepreneurship is the essence of free enterprise because the birth of new businesses gives a market economy its vitality. New and emerging businesses create a very large proportion of innovative products and services that transform the way we work and live, such as personal computers, software, the Internet, biotechnology drugs, and overnight package deliveries. They generate most of the new jobs. For example, from 1990 to 1994, small, growing firms with 100 or fewer workers generated 7 to 8 million new jobs in the U.S. economy, whereas firms with more than 100 workers destroyed 3.6 million jobs. In 1998 to 1999, the last period for which data are available, small business accounted for two-thirds of the 2.6 million net new jobs.

There has never been a better time to practice the art and science of entrepreneurship. But what is entrepreneurship? Early this century, Joseph Schumpeter, the Moravian-born economist writing in Vienna, gave us the modern definition of an entrepreneur as the person who destroys the existing economic order by introducing new products and services, by creating new forms of organization, or by exploiting new raw materials. According to Schumpeter,

1

that person is most likely to accomplish this destruction by founding a new business but may also do it within an existing one.

Very few new businesses have the potential to initiate a Schumpeterian "gale" of creation-destruction as Apple computer did in the computer industry. The vast majority of new businesses enter existing markets. In *The Portable MBA in Entrepreneurship,* we take a broader definition of entrepreneurship than Schumpeter's. Our definition encompasses everyone who starts a new business. Our entrepreneur is the person who perceives an opportunity and creates an organization to pursue it. And the entrepreneurial process involves all the functions, activities, and actions associated with perceiving opportunities and creating organizations to pursue them. Our entrepreneur's new business may, in a few rare instances, be the revolutionary sort that rearranges the global economic order as Wal-Mart, FedEx, and Microsoft have done, and Amazon.com, eBay, and Expedia.com are now doing. But it is much more likely to be of the incremental kind that enters an existing market.

- An *entrepreneur* is someone who perceives an opportunity and creates an organization to pursue it.
- The *entrepreneurial process* involves all the functions, activities, and actions associated with perceiving opportunities and creating organizations to pursue them.

Is the birth of a new enterprise just happenstance and its subsequent success or demise a haphazard process? Or can the art and science of entrepreneurship be taught? Clearly, professors and their students believe that it can be taught and learned because entrepreneurship is the fastest growing new field of study in American higher education. A study by the Kauffman Foundation in 2002 found that 61% of U.S. colleges and universities have at least one course in entrepreneurship. It is possible to study entrepreneurship in certificate, associates, bachelors, masters, and PhD programs.

That transformation in higher education—itself a wonderful example of entrepreneurial change—has come about because a whole body of knowledge about entrepreneurship has developed during the past two decades or so. The process of creating a new business is well understood. Yes, entrepreneurship can be taught. However, we cannot guarantee to produce a Bill Gates or a Donna Karan, any more than a physics professor can guarantee to produce an Albert Einstein or a tennis coach a Serena Williams. But give us students with the aptitude to start a business, and we will make them better entrepreneurs.

CRITICAL FACTORS FOR STARTING A NEW ENTERPRISE

We begin by examining the entrepreneurial process—the personal, sociological, and environmental factors that give birth to a new enterprise (Exhibit 1.1). A person gets an idea for a new business either through a deliberate search or a chance encounter. Whether or not he decides to pursue that idea depends on factors such as his alternative career prospects, family, friends, role models, the state of the economy, and the availability of resources.

There is almost always a *triggering event* that gives birth to a new organization. Perhaps the entrepreneur has no better career prospects. For example, Melanie Stevens was a high school dropout who, after a number of minor jobs, had run out of career options. She decided that making canvas bags in her own tiny business was better than earning low wages working for someone else. Within a few years, she had built a chain of retail stores throughout Canada. Sometimes the person has been passed over for a promotion, or even laid off or fired. Howard Rose had been laid off four times as a result of mergers and

EXHIBIT 1.1   A model of the entrepreneurial process.

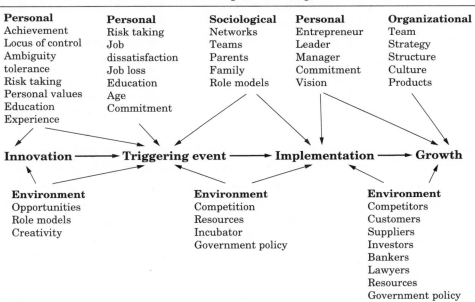

Source: Based on Carol Moore's model, presented in "Understanding Entrepreneurial Behavior," in J. A. Pearce II and R. B. Robinson, Jr., eds., *Academy of Management Best Papers Proceedings*, Forty-sixth Annual Meeting of the Academy of Management, Chicago, 1986.

consolidations in the pharmaceutical industry, and he had had enough of big business. So he started his own drug packaging business, Waverly Pharmaceutical. Tim Waterstone founded Waterstone's bookstores after he was fired by W. H. Smith. Ann Gloag quit her nursing job and used her bus driver father's $40,000 severance pay to set up a bus company, Stagecoach, with her brother. They exploited legislation deregulating the U.K. bus industry.

For other people, entrepreneurship is a deliberate career choice. Sandra Kurtzig was a software engineer with General Electric who wanted to start a family and work at home. She started ASK Computer Systems Inc., which became a $400 million-a-year business.

Where do would-be entrepreneurs get their ideas? More often than not it is through their present line of employment or experience. A 2002 study of the *Inc. 500*—comprising America's [500] fastest growing companies—found that 57% of the founders got the idea for their new venture in the industry they worked in and a further 23% in an industry related to the one in which they were employed. Hence, 80% of all new high-potential businesses are founded in industries that are the same as, or closely related to, the one in which the entrepreneur has previous experience. That is not surprising because it is in their present employment that they get most of their viable business ideas. Some habitual entrepreneurs do it over and over again in the same industry. Joey Crugnale, himself an *Inc. 500* Hall of Famer and an *Inc. 500* Entrepreneur of the Year, became a partner in Steve's Ice Cream when he was in his early twenties. He eventually took over Steve's Ice Cream, and created both a national franchise of some 26 units and a new food niche, gourmet ice creams. In 1982, Crugnale started Bertucci's where gourmet pizza was cooked in wood-fired brick oven and built it into a nationwide chain of 90 restaurants. Then he founded Naked Restaurants as an incubator to launch his innovative dining concepts. The first one, the Naked Fish, opened in 1999 and brought his wood-fired grill approach to a new niche: fresh fish and meats with a touch of Cubanismo. The second restaurant, Red Sauce, opened in 2002, serves moderately priced authentic Italian food somewhat along the lines of Bertucci's.

Others do it over and over again in related industries. In 1981, James Clark, then a Stanford University computer science professor, founded Silicon Graphics, a computer manufacturer with 1996 sales of $3 billion. In April 1994, he teamed up with Marc Andreessen to found Netscape Communications. Within 12 months, its browser software, Navigator, dominated the Internet's World Wide Web. When Netscape went public in August 1995, Clark became the first Internet billionaire. Then in June 1996, Clark launched another company, Healthscape, to enable doctors, insurers, and patients to exchange data and do business over the Internet with software incorporating Netscape's Navigator.

Much rarer is the serial entrepreneur such as Wayne Huizenga, who ventures into unrelated industries: first in garbage disposal with Waste Management, next in entertainment with Blockbuster video, then in automobile sales with AutoNation. Along the way he was the original owner of the Florida Marlins baseball team, which won the World Series in 1997.

What are the factors that influence someone to embark on an entrepreneurial career? As with most human behavior, entrepreneurial traits are shaped by *personal attributes* and *environment.*

Personal Attributes

Two decades ago, at the start of the entrepreneurial 1980s, there was a spate of magazine and newspaper articles that were titled "Do you have the right stuff to be an entrepreneur?" or words to that effect. The articles described the most important characteristics of entrepreneurs and, more often than not, included a self-evaluation exercise to enable readers to determine if they had the right stuff. Those articles were based on flimsy behavioral research into the differences between entrepreneurs and nonentrepreneurs. The basis for those exercises was the belief, first developed by David McClelland in his book *The Achieving Society,* that entrepreneurs had *a higher need for achievement* than nonentrepreneurs, and that they were moderate risk takers. One engineer almost abandoned his entrepreneurial ambitions after completing one of those exercises. He asked his professor at the start of an MBA entrepreneurship course if he should take the class because he had scored very low on an entrepreneurship test in a magazine. He took the course, however, and wrote an award-winning plan for a business that was a success from the very beginning.

Today, after more research, we know that there is no neat set of behavioral attributes that allow us to separate entrepreneurs from nonentrepreneurs. It turns out that a person who rises to the top of any occupation, whether it be an entrepreneur or an administrator, is an achiever. Granted, any would-be entrepreneur must have a need to achieve, but so must anyone else with ambitions to be successful.

It does appear that entrepreneurs have a *higher locus of control* than nonentrepreneurs, which means that they have a higher desire to be in control of their own fate. This has been confirmed by many surveys which have found that entrepreneurs say that independence is their main reason for starting their businesses.

By and large, we no longer use psychological terms when talking about entrepreneurs. Instead we use everyday words to describe the characteristics found in most entrepreneurs (see Exhibit 1.2).

EXHIBIT 1.2   The 10 Ds.

Dream	Entrepreneurs have a vision of what the future could be like for them and their businesses. And, more important, they have the ability to implement their dreams.
Decisiveness	They don't procrastinate. They make decisions swiftly. Their swiftness is a key factor in their success.
Doers	Once they decide on a course of action, they implement it as quickly as possible.
Determination	They implement their ventures with total commitment. They seldom give up, even when confronted by obstacles that seem insurmountable.
Dedication	They are totally dedicated to their business, sometimes at considerable cost to their relationships with their friends and families. They work tirelessly. Twelve-hour days, and seven-day work weeks are not uncommon when an entrepreneur is striving to get a business off the ground.
Devotion	Entrepreneurs love what they do. It is that love that sustains them when the going gets tough. And it is love of their product or service that makes them so effective at selling it.
Details	It is said that the devil resides in the details. That is never more true than in starting and growing a business. The entrepreneur must be on top of the critical details.
Destiny	They want to be in charge of their own destiny rather than dependent on an employer.
Dollars	Getting rich is not the prime motivator of entrepreneurs. Money is more a measure of their success. They assume that if they are successful they will be rewarded.
Distribute	Entrepreneurs distribute the ownership of their businesses with key employees who are critical to the success of the business.

Environmental Factors

Perhaps as important as personal attributes are the external influences on a would-be entrepreneur. It's no accident that some parts of the world are more entrepreneurial than others. The most famous region of high-tech entrepreneurship is Silicon Valley. Because everyone in Silicon Valley knows someone who has made it big as an entrepreneur, role models abound. This situation produces what Stanford University sociologist Everett Rogers called "Silicon Valley fever." It seems as if everyone in the valley catches that bug sooner or later and wants to start a business. To facilitate the process, there are venture capitalists who understand how to select and nurture high-tech entrepreneurs, bankers who specialize in lending to them, lawyers who understand the importance of intellectual property and how to protect it, landlords who are experienced in renting real estate to fledgling companies, suppliers who are willing to sell goods on credit to companies with no credit history, and even politicians who are supportive.

Role models are very important because knowing successful entrepreneurs makes the act of becoming one yourself seem much more credible.

Would-be entrepreneurs come into contact with role models primarily in the home and at work. If you have a close relative who is an entrepreneur, it is more likely that you will have a desire to become an entrepreneur yourself, especially if that relative is your mother or father. At Babson College, more than half of the undergraduates studying entrepreneurship come from families that own businesses. But you don't have to be from a business-owning family to become an entrepreneur. Bill Gates, for example, was following the family tradition of becoming a lawyer when he dropped out of Harvard and founded Microsoft. He was in the fledgling microcomputer industry, which was being built by entrepreneurs, so he had plenty of role models among his friends and acquaintances. The United States has an abundance of high-tech entrepreneurs who are household names. One of them, Ross Perot, was so well known that he became the presidential candidate preferred by one in five American voters in 1992.

Some universities are hotbeds of entrepreneurship. For example, Massachusetts Institute of Technology has produced numerous entrepreneurs among its faculty and alums. Companies with an MIT connection transformed the Massachusetts economy from one based on decaying shoe and textile industries into one based on high technology. According to a 1997 study by the Bank of Boston, 125,000 jobs in Massachusetts were MIT-related.[2] Nationwide in 1996, 733,000 people working in more than 8,500 plants and offices held jobs that originated with companies founded by MIT graduates. The 4,000 or so firms that MIT graduates founded accounted for at least 1.1 million jobs worldwide and generated $232 billion in revenues. If MIT-related companies were a nation, it would be the 24th largest economy in the world. The neighborhood of East Cambridge adjacent to MIT has been called "The Most Entrepreneurial Place on Earth" by *Inc.* magazine. According to *Inc.*, roughly 10% of Massachusetts software companies and approximately 20% of the state's 280 biotechnology companies are headquartered in that square mile.

It is not only in high-tech that we see role models. Consider these examples:

- It has been estimated that half of all the convenience stores in New York city are owned by Koreans.
- It was the visibility of successful role models that spread catfish farming in the Mississippi delta as a more profitable alternative to cotton.
- The Pacific Northwest has more microbreweries than any other region of the United States.

- In the vicinity of the town of Wells, Maine, there are half-a-dozen secondhand bookstores.

African Americans make up 12% of the U.S. population, but owned only
4% of the nation's businesses in 1997.[3] One of the major reasons for a relative
lack of entrepreneurship among African Americans is the scarcity of African-
American entrepreneurs, especially store owners, to provide role models. A
similar problem exists among Native Americans. Lack of credible role models
is also one of the big challenges in the formerly communist European nations as
they strive to become entrepreneurial.

Other Sociological Factors

Besides role models, entrepreneurs are influenced by other sociological factors. *Family responsibilities* play an important role in the decision whether to
start a company. It is, relatively speaking, an easy career decision to start a
business when a person is 25 years old, single, and without many personal assets and dependents. It is a much harder decision when a person is 45 and
married, has teenage children preparing to go to college, a hefty mortgage, car
payments, and a secure, well-paying job. A 1992 survey of European high-
potential entrepreneurs, for instance, found that on average they had 50% of
their net worth tied up in their businesses. And at 45 plus, if you fail as an entrepreneur, it is not easy to rebuild a career working for another company. But
despite the risks, plenty of 45-year-olds are taking the plunge; in fact, the median age of the CEOs of the 500 fastest growing small companies, according
to *Inc. 500* in 2000, was 40.[4]

Another factor that determines the age at which entrepreneurs start
businesses is the trade-off between the *experience* that comes with age and
the *optimism* and *energy* of youth. As you grow older, you gain experience,
but sometimes when you have been in an industry a long time, you know so
many pitfalls that you are pessimistic about the chance of succeeding if you
decide to go out on your own. Someone who has just enough experience to feel
confident as a manager is more likely to feel optimistic about an entrepreneurial career. Perhaps the ideal combination is a beginner's mind with the experience of an industry veteran. A beginner's mind looks at situations from a new
perspective, with a can-do spirit.

Robert Swanson was 27 years old when he hit upon the idea that a company
could be formed to capitalize on biotechnology. At that time, he knew almost
nothing about the field. By reading the scientific literature, Swanson identified
the leading biotechnology scientists and contacted them. "Everybody said I was
too early—it would take 10 years to turn out the first microorganism from a

human hormone or maybe 20 years to have a commercial product—everybody except Herb Boyer." Swanson was referring to Professor Herbert Boyer at the University of California at San Francisco, coinventor of the patents that, according to some observers, form the basis of the biotechnology industry. When Swanson and Boyer met in early 1976, they almost immediately agreed to become partners in an endeavor to explore the commercial possibilities of recombinant DNA. Boyer named their venture Genentech, an acronym for genetic engineering technology. Just seven months later, Genentech announced its first success, a genetically engineered human brain hormone, somatosin. According to Swanson, they accomplished 10 years of development in seven months.

Marc Andreessen had a beginner's mind that produced a vision for the Internet that until then had eluded many computer industry veterans, including Bill Gates. When Andreessen's youthful creativity was joined with James Clark's entrepreneurial wisdom, earned from a dozen or so years as founder and chairman of Silicon Graphics, it turned out to be an awesome combination. Their company, Netscape, distributed 38 million copies of Navigator in just two years, making it the most successful new software introduction ever.

Before leaving secure, well-paying, satisfying jobs, would-be entrepreneurs should make a careful estimate of how much *sales revenue* their new businesses must generate before they will be able to match the income that they presently earn. It usually comes as quite a shock when they realize that if they are opening a retail establishment, they will need annual sales revenue of at least $600,000 to pay themselves a salary of $70,000 plus fringe benefits such as health care coverage, retirement pension benefits, long-term disability insurance, vacation pay, sick leave, and perhaps subsidized meals, day-care, and education benefits. Six hundred thousand dollars a year is about $12,000 per week, or about $2,000 per day, or about $200 per hour, or $3 per minute if they are open 6 days a week, 10 hours a day. Also they will be working much longer hours and bearing much more responsibility if they become self-employed. A sure way to test the strength of a marriage is to start a company that is the sole means of support for your family. For example, 22.5% of the CEOs of the *Inc. 500* got divorced while growing their businesses. On a brighter note, 59.2% got married and 18.3% of divorced CEOs remarried.[5]

When they actually start a business, entrepreneurs need a host of *contacts*, including customers, suppliers, investors, bankers, accountants, and lawyers. So it is important to understand where to find help before embarking on a new venture. A network of friends and business associates can be of immeasurable help in building the contacts an entrepreneur will need. They can also provide human contact because opening a business can be a lonely experience for anyone who has worked in an organization with many fellow employees.

Fortunately, today there are more organizations than ever before to help fledgling entrepreneurs. Often that help is free or costs very little. The Small Business Administration (SBA) has Small Business Development Centers in every state; it funds Small Business Institutes; and its Service Core of Retired Executives provides free assistance to entrepreneurs. Many colleges and universities also provide help. Some are particularly good at writing business plans, usually at no charge to the entrepreneur. There are hundreds of incubators in the United States where fledgling businesses can rent space, usually at a very reasonable price, and spread some of their overhead by sharing facilities such as copying and FAX machines, secretarial help, answering services, and so on. Incubators are often associated with universities, which provide free or inexpensive counseling. There are numerous associations where entrepreneurs can meet and exchange ideas. In the Boston area, for example, the 128 VC Group provides a place where entrepreneurs, financiers, accountants, lawyers, and other professionals meet each month for a two-hour breakfast.

EVALUATING OPPORTUNITIES FOR NEW BUSINESSES

Let's assume you believe you have found a great opportunity for starting a new business. How should you evaluate its prospects? Or, perhaps more importantly, how will an independent person such as a potential investor or a banker rate your chances of success? The odds of succeeding appear to be stacked against you because, according to small business folklore, only 1 business in 10 will ever reach its tenth birthday. This doesn't mean that 9 out of 10 of the estimated two million businesses that are started every year go bankrupt. We know that even in a severe recession, the number of businesses filing for bankruptcy in the United States has never surpassed 100,000 in any year. In an average year, the number is about 50,000. In 2001, for instance, there were slightly fewer than 40,000. So what happens to the vast majority of the ones that do not survive 10 years? Most just fade away: They are started as part-time pursuits and are never intended to become full-time businesses. Some are sold. Others are liquidated. Only 700,000 of the two million are legally registered as corporations or partnerships, which is a sure sign that many of the remaining 1.3 million never intended to grow. Hence, the odds that your new business will survive may not be as long as they first appear to be. If you intend to start a full-time, incorporated business, the odds that the business will survive at least eight years with you as the owner are better than one in four; and the odds of its surviving at least eight years with a new owner are another one in four. So the eight-year survival rate for incorporated startups is about 50%.

But survival may not spell success. Too many entrepreneurs find that they can neither earn a satisfactory living in their businesses nor get out of them easily because they have too much of their personal assets tied up in them. The happiest day in an entrepreneur's life is the day doors are opened for business. For unsuccessful entrepreneurs, an even happier day may be the day the business is sold—especially if most personal assets remain intact. What George Bernard Shaw said about a love affair is also apt for a business: Any fool can start one, it takes a genius to end one successfully.

How can you stack the odds in your favor, so that your new business is successful? Professional investors, such as venture capitalists, have a talent for picking winners. True, they also pick losers, but a startup company funded by venture capital has, on average, a four in five chance of surviving five years— better odds than for the population of startup companies as a whole. By using the criteria that professional investors use, entrepreneurs can increase their odds of success. Very few startup businesses—perhaps no more than one in a thousand—will ever be suitable candidates for investments from professional venture capitalists. But would-be entrepreneurs can learn much by following the evaluation process used by professional investors.

There are three crucial components for a successful new business: the opportunity, the entrepreneur (and the management team, if it's a high-potential venture), and the resources needed to start the company and make it grow. These components are shown schematically in Exhibit 1.3 in the

EXHIBIT 1.3   Three driving forces.

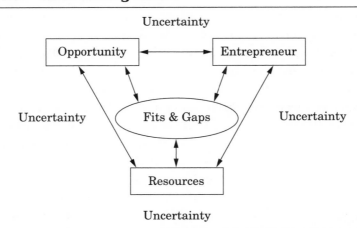

Source: Based on Jeffry Timmons' framework, as presented in Jeffry A. Timmons, *New Venture Creation* (Homewood, IL: Richard D. Irwin, 1990).

basic Timmons framework. At the center of the framework is a business plan, in which the three basic components are integrated into a complete strategic plan for the new business. The parts must fit together well. There is no point in having a first-rate idea for a new business if you have a second-rate management team. Nor are ideas and management any good without the appropriate resources.

The crucial driving force of any new venture is the lead entrepreneur and the funding management team. Georges Doriot, the founder of modern venture capital, used to say something like this: "Always consider investing in a grade A man with a grade B idea. Never invest in a grade B man with a grade A idea." He knew what he was talking about. Over the years, he invested in about 150 companies, including Digital Equipment Corporation (DEC), and watched over them as they struggled to grow. But Doriot made this statement about business in the 1950s and 1960s. During that period, there were far fewer startups each year; U.S. firms dominated the marketplace; markets were growing quickly; there was almost no competition from overseas; and most entrepreneurs were male. Today, in the global marketplace with ever-shortening product life cycles and low growth or even no growth for some of the world's leading industrial nations, the crucial ingredients for entrepreneurial success are a superb entrepreneur with a first-rate management team and an excellent market opportunity.

> The crucial ingredients for entrepreneurial success are a superb entrepreneur with a first-rate management team and an excellent market opportunity.

Frequently, I hear the comment that success in entrepreneurship is largely a matter of luck. That's not so. We do not say that becoming a great quarterback, or a great scientist, or a great musician is a matter of luck. There is no more luck in becoming successful at entrepreneurship than in becoming successful at anything else. In entrepreneurship, it is a question of recognizing a good opportunity when you see one and having the skills to convert that opportunity into a thriving business. To do that, you must be prepared. So in entrepreneurship, just like any other profession, *luck is where preparation and opportunity meet.*

In 1982, when Rod Canion proposed to start Compaq to make personal computers, there were already formidable established competitors, including IBM and Apple. By then literally hundreds of companies were considering entering the market or had already done so. For instance, in the same week of May 1982 that DEC announced its ill-fated personal computer, four other companies introduced PCs. Despite the competition, Ben Rosen of the venture capital firm Sevin Rosen Management Company, invested in Compaq. Started initially to make transportable PCs, it quickly added a complete range of high-performance PCs and grew so fast that it soon broke Apple's record for the fastest time from founding to listing on the *Fortune* 500.

What did Ben Rosen see in the Compaq proposal that made it stand out from all the other personal computer startups? The difference was Rod Canion and his team. Rod Canion had earned a reputation as an excellent manager at Texas Instruments. Furthermore, the market for personal computers topped $5 billion and was growing at a torrid pace. So Rosen found a superb team with a product targeted at an undeveloped niche, transportable PCs, in a large market that was growing explosively. By 1994, Compaq was the leading PC manufacturer with 13% of the market.

> In entrepreneurship, as in any other profession, luck is where preparation and opportunity meet.

The Opportunity

Perhaps the biggest misconception about an idea for a new business is that it must be unique. Too many would-be entrepreneurs are obsessed with finding a unique idea. Then, when they believe they have it, they are haunted by the thought that someone is just waiting to steal it from them. As a result, they become super secretive. They are reluctant to discuss it with anyone unless that person signs a nondisclosure agreement. That in itself makes it almost impossible to evaluate the idea. For example, many counselors who provide free advice to entrepreneurs refuse to sign nondisclosure agreements. Generally speaking, these super-secret, unique ideas are big letdowns when the entrepreneur reveals them to you. Among the notable ones I have encountered were "drive-through pizza by the slice," "a combination toothbrush and toothpaste gadget," and "a Mexican restaurant in Boston." One computer programmer telephoned me and said that he had a fantastic new piece of software. Eventually, after I assured him that I was not going to steal his idea, he told me his software was for managing hairdressing salons. He was completely floored when I told him that less than a month previously another entrepreneur had visited my office and demonstrated a software package for exactly the same purpose. Another entrepreneur had an idea for fluoride-impregnated dental floss. Not three months later, on a visit to England, I found the identical product in Boots—Britain's largest chain of drugstores and a major pharmaceutical manufacturer.

I tell would-be entrepreneurs that almost any idea they have will also have occurred to others. For good measure, I point out that some of the most revolutionary thoughts in the history of mankind occurred to more than one person almost simultaneously. For instance, Darwin was almost preempted by Wallace in publishing his theory of evolution; Poincaré formulated a valid theory of relativity about the same time Einstein did; and the integrated circuit was invented in 1959 first by Jack Kilby at Texas Instruments, and then independently by Robert Noyce at Fairchild a few months later. The idea per se is not what is important. Ideas are a dime a dozen. Developing the idea, implementing it, and building a successful business are the important aspects of entrepreneurship. Alexander Fleming discovered penicillin by chance but never developed it as a useful drug. About 10 years later, Ernst Chain and Howard Florey unearthed Fleming's mold. They immediately saw its potential. Working in England under wartime conditions, they soon were treating patients. Before the end of World War II, penicillin was saving countless lives. It was a dramatic pharmaceutical advance that heralded a revolution in that industry.

> The idea per se is not what is important. Ideas are a dime a dozen. Developing the idea, implementing it, and building a successful business are the important aspects of entrepreneurship.

Customer Need

Many would-be entrepreneurs call me telling me that they have an idea for a new business and that they want to come to see me. Unfortunately, it is impossible to see all of them, so I have developed a few questions that allow me to judge how far along they are "with their idea." The most telling question is, "Can you give me the names of prospective customers?" Their answer must be very specific. If they have a consumer product—let's say it's a new shampoo—I expect them to be able to name buyers at different chains of drugstores in their area. If they are unable to name several customers immediately, they simply have an idea, not a market. There is no market unless customers have a real need for the product—a proven need rather than a hypothetical need in the mind of a would-be entrepreneur. In a few rare cases, it may be a revolutionary new product, but it is much more likely to be an existing product with improved performance, price, distribution, quality, or service. Simply put, customers must perceive that the new business or product will be giving them better value for their money than existing businesses or products.

> Would-be entrepreneurs who are unable to name customers are not ready to start a business. They have only found an idea and have not yet identified the market.

Timing

Time plays a crucial role in many potential opportunities. In some emerging industries, there is a window of opportunity that opens only once. For instance, about 25 years ago, when VCRs were first coming into household use in the United States, there was a need for video stores in convenient locations where viewers could pick up movies on the way home from work. Many video retail stores opened up in main streets and shopping centers. They were usually run by independent store owners. Then the distribution of videos changed. National chains of video stores emerged. Supermarket and drugstore chains entered the market. Today, the window of opportunity for starting an independent video store is closed. There are simply too many big competitors in convenient locations.

In other markets, high-quality restaurants for example, there is a steady demand that, on average, does not change much from year to year, therefore, the window of opportunity is always open. Nevertheless, timing can be important, because when the economy turns down, those kinds of restaurants are usually hit harder than lower quality ones, so the time to open one is during a recovering or booming economy.

If the window of opportunity appears to be very brief, it may be that the idea is a consumer fad that will quickly pass. It takes a very skilled entrepreneur to make money out of a fad. When Lucy's Have a Heart Canvas of Faneuil Hall Market in Boston introduced shoelaces with hearts on them, they flew off the shelves. Children and teenagers could not get enough of them for their sneakers. The store ordered more and more of them. Then demand suddenly dropped precipitously. The store and the manufacturer were left holding huge inventories that could not be sold. As a result, the store almost went out of business.

Most entrepreneurs should avoid fads or any window of opportunity that they believe will be open only for a very brief time, because it inevitably means that they will rush to open their business, sometimes before they have time to gather the resources they will need. Rushing to open a business without adequate planning can lead to costly mistakes.

The Entrepreneur and the Management Team

Regardless of how right the opportunity may seem to be, it will not make a successful business unless it is developed by a person with strong entrepreneurial and management skills. What are the important skills?

First and foremost, entrepreneurs should have experience in the same industry or a similar one. Starting a business is a very demanding undertaking indeed. It is no time for on-the-job training. If would-be entrepreneurs do not have the right experience, they should either go out and get it before starting their new venture or find partners who have it.

Some investors say that the ideal entrepreneur is one who has a track record of being successful previously as an entrepreneur in the same industry and who can attract a seasoned team. Half of the CEOs of the *Inc. 500* high-growth small companies had started at least one other business before they founded their present firms. When Joey Crugnale acquired his first ice cream shop in 1977, he already had almost 10 years in the food service industry. By 1991, when Bertucci's brick oven pizzeria went public, he and his management team had a total of more than 100 years experience in the food industry. They had built Bertucci's into a rapidly growing chain with sales of $30 million and net income of $2 million.

Without relevant experience, the odds are stacked against the neophyte in any industry. An electronics engineer told me that he had a great idea for a chain of fast-food stores. When asked if he had ever worked in a fast-food restaurant, he replied, "Work in one? I wouldn't even eat in one. I can't stand fast food!" Clearly, he would have been as miscast as a fast-food entrepreneur as Crugnale would have been as an electronics engineer.

True, there are entrepreneurs who have succeeded spectacularly with no prior industry experience. Anita Roddick of The Body Shop and Ely Callaway of Callaway Golf are two notable examples. But they are the exceptions that definitely do not prove the rule.

Second to industry know-how is *management experience*, preferably with responsibility for budgets, or better yet, accountability for profit and loss. It is even better if a would-be entrepreneur has a record of increasing sales and profits. Here, we are talking about the *ideal* entrepreneur. Very few people measure up to the ideal. That does not mean they should not start a new venture. But it does mean they should be realistic about the size of business they should start. Fifteen years ago, two 19-year-old students wanted to start a travel agency business in Boston. When asked what they knew about the industry, one replied, "I live in California. I love to travel." The other was silent. Neither of them had worked in the travel industry, nor had anyone in either of their families. They were advised to get experience. One joined a training program for airline ticket agents; the other took a course for travel agents. They became friends with the owner of a local Uniglobe travel agency who helped them with advice. Six months after they first had the idea, they opened a part-time campus travel agency. In the first six months, they had about $100,000 of revenue and made $6,000 of profit but were unable to pay themselves any salary. They acquired experience at no expense and at low risk. Upon graduation, one of them, Mario Ricciardelli, made it his full-time job and continued building the business and gaining experience at the same time. In 2001, after many bumps in the road, the business had sales revenue of $22.1 million and was one of the largest student travel businesses in the world.

Resources

It's hard to believe that Olsen and Anderson started DEC with only $70,000 of startup capital and built a company that at its peak ranked in the top 25 of the *Fortune* 500 companies. "The nice thing about 70,000 dollars is that there are so few of them, you can watch every one," Olsen said. And watch them he did. Olsen and Anderson moved into a 100-year-old building that had been a nineteenth-century woollen mill. They furnished it with second-hand furniture, purchased tools from the Sears catalog, and built much of their own equipment as cheaply as possible. They sold $94,000 worth of equipment in their first year and made a profit at the same time—a very rare feat for a high-tech startup.

Successful entrepreneurs are frugal with their scarce resources. They keep overheads low, productivity high, and ownership of capital assets to a minimum. By so doing, they minimize the amount of capital they need to start their business and make it grow.

Entrepreneurial frugality includes:

- Low overhead
- High productivity
- Minimal ownership of capital assets

DETERMINING RESOURCE NEEDS AND ACQUIRING RESOURCES

To determine the amount of capital that a company needs to get started, an entrepreneur must determine the minimum set of essential resources. Some resources are more critical than others. The first thing an entrepreneur should do is assess what resources are crucial for the company's success in the marketplace. What does the company expect to do better than any of its competitors? That is where it should put a disproportionate share of its very scarce resources. If the company is making a new high-tech product, technological know-how will be vital. Its most important resource will be engineers and the designs they produce. Therefore, the company must concentrate on recruiting and keeping excellent engineers, and safeguarding the intellectual property that they produce, such as engineering designs and patents. If the company is doing retail selling, the critical factor is most likely to be location. It makes no sense to choose a site in a poor location just because the rent is cheap. Choosing the wrong initial location for a retail store can be a fatal mistake, because it's unlikely that there will be enough resources to relocate.

When Southwest Airlines started up 32 years ago, its strategy was to provide frequent, on-time service at a competitive price between Dallas, Houston, Austin, and San Antonio. To meet its objectives, Southwest needed planes that it could operate reliably at low cost. It was able to purchase four brand-new Boeing 737s—very efficient planes for shorter routes—for only $4 million each because the recession had hit the airlines particularly hard and Boeing had an inventory of unsold 737s. From the outset, Southwest provided good, reliable service and had one of the lowest costs per mile in the industry. Today, Southwest is the most successful domestic airline, while two of its biggest competitors when it started out, Braniff International and Texas International, have gone bankrupt.

Items that are not critical should be obtained as thriftily as possible. The founder of Burlington Coat, Monroe Milstein, likes to tell the story of how he obtained estimates for gutting the building he had just leased for his second store. His lowest bid was several thousand dollars. One day he was at the building when a sudden thunderstorm sent a crew of laborers working at a nearby site to his building for shelter from the rain. Milstein asked the crew's foreman what they would charge for knocking down the internal structures that needed to be removed. The foreman said, "Five." Milstein asked, "Five what?" The foreman replied, "Cases of beer."

A complete set of resources includes everything that the business will need. A key point to remember when deciding to acquire those resources is that a business does not have to do all its work in-house with its own employees. It is often more effective to subcontract the work. That way it need not own or lease its own manufacturing plant and equipment. Nor does it have to worry about recruiting and training production workers. Often, it can keep overhead lower by using outside firms to do work such as payroll, accounting, advertising, mailing promotions, janitorial services, and so on.

Even startup companies can get amazingly good terms from outside suppliers. An entrepreneur should try to understand the potential suppliers' marginal costs. Marginal cost is the cost of producing one extra unit beyond what is presently produced. The marginal cost of the laborers who gutted Milstein's building while sheltering from the rain was virtually zero. They were being paid by another firm, and they didn't have to buy materials or tools.

A small electronics company was acquired by a much larger competitor. The large company took over the manufacturing of the small company's products. Production costs shot up. An analysis revealed that much of the increase was due to a rise in the cost of purchased components. In one instance, the large company was paying 50% more than the small company had been paying for the same item. It turned out that the supplier had priced the item for the small company on the basis of marginal costs and for the large company on the basis of total costs.

Smart entrepreneurs find ways of controlling critical resources without owning them. A startup business never has enough money. It should not buy what it can lease. It must be resourceful. Except when the economy is red hot, there is almost always an excess of capacity of office and industrial space. Sometimes a landlord will be willing to offer a special deal to attract even a small startup company into a building. Such deals may include reduced rent, deferral of rent payments for a period of time, and building improvements at low cost or even no cost. In some high-tech regions, there are landlords who will exchange rent for equity in a high-potential startup.

When equipment is in excess supply, it can be leased on very favorable terms. A young database company was negotiating a lease with IBM for a new minicomputer when its chief engineer discovered that a leasing company had identical secondhand units standing idle in its warehouse. It was able to lease one of the idle units for one-third of IBM's price. About 18 months later, the database company ran out of cash. Nevertheless, it was able to persuade the leasing company to defer payments, because by then there were even more minicomputers standing idle in the warehouse, and it made little economic sense to repossess one and add it to the idle stock.

Startup Capital

You have reached the point where you have developed your idea; you have carefully assessed what resources you will need to open your business and make it grow; you have pulled all your strategies together into a business plan; and now you know how much startup capital you will need to get you to the point where your business will generate a positive cash flow. How are you going to raise that startup capital?

There are two types of startup capital: debt and equity. With debt you don't have to give up any ownership of the business, but you have to pay current interest and eventually repay the principal; with equity you have to give up some of the ownership to get it, but you may never have to repay it or even pay a dividend. So you must choose between paying interest and giving up some of the ownership.

What usually happens, in practice, depends on how much of each type of capital you can raise. Most startup entrepreneurs do not have much flexibility in their choice of financing. If it is a very risky business without any assets, it will be impossible to get any bank debt without putting up some collateral other than the business's assets—most likely that collateral will be personal assets. Even if entrepreneurs are willing to guarantee the whole loan with their personal assets, the bank will expect them to put some equity into the business, probably equal to 25% of the amount of the loan.

The vast majority of entrepreneurs start their businesses by leveraging their own savings and labor. Consider how Apple, one of the most spectacular startups of all time, was funded. Steven Jobs and Stephan Wozniak had been friends since their school days in Silicon Valley. Wozniak was an authentic computer nerd. He had tinkered with computers from childhood, and he built a computer that won first prize in a science fair. His SAT math score was a perfect 800, but after stints at the University of Colorado, De Anza College, and Berkeley, he dropped out of school and went to work for Hewlett-Packard. His partner, Jobs, had an even briefer encounter with higher education: After one semester at Reed College, he left to look for a swami in India. When he and Wozniak began working on their microcomputer, Jobs was working at Atari, the leading video game company.

Apple soon outgrew its manufacturing facility in the garage of Jobs' parents' house. Their company, financed initially with $1,300 raised by selling Jobs' Volkswagen and Wozniak's calculator, needed capital for expansion. They looked to their employers for help. Wozniak proposed to his supervisor that Hewlett-Packard should produce what later became the Apple II. Perhaps not surprisingly, he was rejected. After all, he had no formal qualification in computer design; indeed, he did not even have a college degree. At Atari, Jobs tried to convince founder Nolan Bushnell to manufacture Apples. He too was rejected.

However, on the suggestion of Bushnell and Regis McKenna, a Silicon Valley marketing ace, they contacted Don Valentine, a venture capitalist in the fall of 1976. In those days, Jobs' appearance was a hangover from his swami days. It definitely did not project the image of Doriot's grade A man, even by Silicon Valley's casual standards. Valentine did not invest. But he did put them in touch with Armas Markkula Jr., who had recently retired from Intel a wealthy man. Markkula saw the potential in Apple, and he knew how to raise money. He personally invested $91,000, secured a line of credit from Bank of America, put together a business plan, and raised $600,000 of venture capital.

The Apple II was formally introduced in April 1977. Sales took off almost at once. Apple's sales grew rapidly to $2.5 million in 1977 and $15 million in 1978. In 1978, Dan Bricklin, a Harvard business student and former programmer at DEC, introduced the first electronic spreadsheet, VisiCalc, designed for the Apple II. In minutes it could do tasks that had previously taken days. The microcomputer now had the power to liberate managers from the data guardians in the computer departments. According to one source, "Armed with VisiCalc, the Apple II's sales took off, and the personal computer industry was created." Apple's sales jumped to $70 million in 1979 and $117 million in 1980.

In 1980, Apple sold some of its stock to the public with an initial public offering (IPO) and raised more than $80 million. The paper value of their Apple stock made instant millionaires out of Jobs ($165 million), Markkula ($154 million), Wozniak ($88 million), and Mike Scott ($62 million), who together owned 40% of Apple. Arthur Rock's venture capital investment of $57,000 in 1978 was suddenly worth $14 million, an astronomical compound return of more than 500% per year, or 17% per month.

By 1982, Apple IIs were selling at the rate of more than 33,000 units a month. With 1982 sales of $583 million, Apple hit the *Fortune* 500 list. It was a record. At five years of age, it was at that time the youngest company ever to join that exclusive list.

Success as spectacular as Apple's has seldom been equaled. Nonetheless, its financing is a typical example of how successful high-tech companies are funded. First, the entrepreneurs develop a prototype with sweat equity and personal savings. Sweat equity is ownership earned in lieu of wages. Then a wealthy investor—sometimes called an informal investor or business angel who knows something about the entrepreneurs, or the industry, or both, invests some personal money in return for equity. When the company is selling product, it may be able to get a bank line of credit secured by its inventory and accounts receivable. If the company is growing quickly in a large market, it may be able to raise capital from a formal venture capital firm in return for equity. Further expansion capital may come from venture capital firms or from a public stock offering.

Would-be entrepreneurs sometimes tell me that they did not start their ventures because they could not raise sufficient money to get started. More often than not, they were unrealistic about the amount of money that they could reasonably have expected to raise for their startup businesses. I tell them that many of the best companies started with very little capital. For example, 42% of the *Inc. 500* companies had initial capital of less than $10,000, 58% less than $20,000, and 68% less than $50,000. Only 21% started with more than $100,000.[6] Only a few percent of this cream of the crop of entrepreneurs started their companies with venture capital, which is by far the rarest source of seed investment. It is estimated that at most only 1 in 10,000 of all new ventures in the United States have venture capital in hand at the outset.

The vast majority of new firms will never be candidates for formal venture capital or a public stock offering. Nevertheless, they will have to find some equity capital. In most cases, after they have exhausted their personal savings, entrepreneurs will turn to family, friends, and acquaintances (see Exhibit 1.4). It can be a scary business. Entrepreneurs often find themselves with all their personal net worth tied up in the same business that provides all their income. That is double jeopardy, because if their businesses fail, they lose both their savings and their means of support. Risk of that sort can be justified only if the profit potential is high enough to yield a commensurate rate of return.

Profit Potential

The level of profit that is reasonable depends on the type of business. On average, U.S. companies make about 5% net income. Hence, on one dollar of revenue, the average company makes five cents profit after paying all expenses and taxes. A company that consistently makes 10% is doing very well, and one that makes 15% is truly exceptional. Approximately 50% of the *Inc. 500* companies make 5% or less; 13% of them make 16% or more. Profit margins in a wide variety of industries for companies both large and small are published by

EXHIBIT 1.4   Relationship of investor to entrepreneur.

	All Nations (%)	USA (%)
Close family member	40	44
Other relative	11	6
Work colleague	10	9
Friend/neighbor	28	28
Stranger	9	7
Other	2	6
	100	100

Data Source: Global Entrepreneurship Monitor 2002, www.gemsonsortium.org.

Robert Morris Associates. Hence it is possible for entrepreneurs to compare their forecasts with the actual performance of similar-sized companies in the same industry.

Any business must make enough profit to recompense its investors (in most cases that is the entrepreneur) for their investment. It must be profit after all normal business expenses have been accounted for, including a fair salary for the entrepreneur and any family members who are working in the business. A common error in assessing the profitability of a new venture is to ignore the owner's salary. Suppose someone leaves a secure job paying $50,000 per year plus fringe benefits and invests $100,000 of personal savings to start a new venture. That person should expect to take a $50,000 salary plus fringe benefits out of the new business. Perhaps in the first year or two, when the business is being built, it may not be possible to pay $50,000 in actual cash; in that case, the pay that is not actually received should be treated as deferred compensation to be paid in the future. In addition to an adequate salary, the entrepreneur must also earn a reasonable return on the $100,000 investment. A professional investor putting money into a new, risky business would expect to earn an annual rate of return of at least 40%, which would be $40,000 annually on a $100,000 investment. That return may come as a capital gain when the business is sold, or as a dividend, or a combination of the two. But remember that $100,000 compounding annually at 40% grows to almost $2.9 million in 10 years. When such large capital gains are needed to produce acceptable returns, big capital investments held for a long time do not make any sense unless very substantial value can be created, as occasionally happens in the case of high-flying companies, especially high-tech ones. In most cases, instead of a capital gain, the investor's return will be a dividend, which must be paid out of the cash flow from the business.

The cash flow that a business generates is not to be confused with profit. It is possible, indeed very likely, that a rapidly growing business will have a negative cash flow from operations in its early years even though it may be profitable. That may happen because the business may not be able to generate enough cash flow internally to sustain its ever-growing needs for working capital and the purchase of long-term assets such as plant and equipment. Hence, it will have to borrow or raise new equity capital. It is very important that a high-potential business intending to grow rapidly make careful cash-flow projections so as to predict its needs for future outside investments. Future equity investments will dilute the percentage ownership of the founders, and if the dilution becomes excessive, there may be little reward remaining for the entrepreneurs.

Biotechnology companies are examples of this; they have a seemingly insatiable need for cash infusions to sustain their R&D costs in their early years. Their negative cash flow, or *burn rate,* sometimes runs as high as $1 million per month. A biotechnology company can easily burn up $50 million before it generates a meaningful profit, let alone a positive cash flow. The expected future capital gain from a public stock offering or sale to a large pharmaceutical company has to run into hundreds of millions of dollars, maybe into the billion-dollar range, for investors to realize an annual return of 50% or higher, which is what they expect to earn on money invested in a seed-stage biotechnology company. Not surprisingly, to finance their ventures, biotechnology entrepreneurs as a group have to give up most of the ownership. A study of venture-capital-backed biotechnology companies found that after they had gone public, the entrepreneurs and management were left with less than 18% of the equity, compared with 32% for a comparable group of computer software companies.

As has already been mentioned, the vast majority of businesses will never have the potential to go public. Nor will the owners ever intend to sell their businesses and thereby realize a capital gain. In that case, how can those owners get a satisfactory return on the money they have invested in their businesses? The two ingredients that determine return on investment are (1) amount invested, and (2) annual amount earned on that investment. Hence, entrepreneurs should invest as little as possible to start their businesses and make sure that their firms will be able to pay them a "dividend" big enough to yield an appropriate annual rate of return. For income tax purposes, that dividend may be in the form of a salary bonus or fringe benefits rather than an actual dividend paid out of retained earnings. Of course, the company must be generating cash from its own operations before that dividend can be paid. For entrepreneurs, happiness is a positive cash flow. The day a company begins to generate cash is a very happy day in the life of a successful entrepreneur.

For entrepreneurs, happiness is a positive cash flow.

INGREDIENTS FOR A SUCCESSFUL NEW BUSINESS

The great day has arrived. You found an idea, wrote a business plan, and gathered your resources. Now you are opening the doors of your new business for the first time, and the really hard work is about to begin. What are the factors that distinguish winning entrepreneurial businesses from the also-rans? Rosabeth Kanter prescribed four Fs for a successful business, a list that has been expanded into the nine Fs for entrepreneurial success (see Exhibit 1.5).

First and foremost, the founding entrepreneur is the most important factor. Next comes the market. This is the "era of the other," in which, as Regis

EXHIBIT 1.5   The nine Fs.

Founders	Every startup company must have a first-class entrepreneur.
Focused	Entrepreneurial companies focus on niche markets. They specialize.
Fast	They make decisions quickly and implement them swiftly.
Flexible	They keep an open mind. They respond to change.
Forever-innovating	They are tireless innovators.
Flat	Entrepreneurial organizations have as few layers of management as possible.
Frugal	By keeping overhead low and productivity high, entrepreneurial organizations keep costs down.
Friendly	Entrepreneurial companies are friendly to their customers, suppliers, and workers.
Fun	It's fun to be associated with an entrepreneurial company.

McKenna observed, the fastest growing companies in an industry will be in a segment labeled "others" in a market share pie-chart. By and large, they will be newer entrepreneurial firms rather than large firms with household names; hence specialization is the key. A successful business should focus on niche markets.

The rate of change in business gets ever faster. The advanced industrial economies are knowledge based. Product life cycles are getting shorter. Technological innovation progresses at a relentless pace. Government rules and regulations keep changing. Communications and travel around the globe keep getting easier and cheaper. And consumers are better informed about their choices. To survive, let alone succeed, in business, a company has to be quick and nimble. It must be fast and flexible. It cannot allow inertia to build up. Look at retailing: The historical giants such as Kmart are on the ropes, while nimble competitors dance around them. Four of the biggest retailing successes are Les Wexner's The Limited, the late Sam Walton's Wal-Mart, Bernie Marcus and Arthur Blank's Home Depot, and Anita Roddick's The Body Shop. These entrepreneurs know that they can keep inertia low by keeping the layers of management as few as possible. Tom Peters, an authority on business strategy, liked to point out that Wal-Mart had three layers of management, whereas Sears had 10 a few years back when Wal-Mart displaced Sears as the nation's top chain of department stores. "A company with three layers of management can't lose against a company with 10. You could try, but you couldn't do it!" says Peters. So keep your organization flat. It will facilitate quick decisions and flexibility, and keep overhead low.

Small entrepreneurial firms are great innovators. Big firms are relying increasingly on strategic partnerships with entrepreneurial firms in order to get access to desirable R&D. It is a trend that is well under way. Hoffmann-La Roche, hurting for new blockbuster prescription drugs, purchased a majority interest in Genentech and bought the highly regarded biotechnology called PCR (polymerase chain reaction) from Cetus for $300 million. Eli Lilly purchased Hybritech. In the 1980s, IBM spent $9 billion a year on research and development, but even that astronomical amount of money could not sustain Big Blue's commercial leadership. As its market share was remorselessly eaten away by thousands of upstarts, IBM entered into strategic agreements with Apple, Borland, Go, Lotus, Intel, Metaphor, Microsoft, Novell, Stratus, Thinking Machines, and other entrepreneurial firms for the purpose of gaining computer technologies.

When it introduced the first personal computer in 1981, IBM stood astride the computer industry like a big blue giant. Two suppliers of its personal computer division were Intel and Microsoft. Compared with IBM, Intel was small and Microsoft was a midget. By 2002, Intel's revenue was $26.8 billion and Microsoft's was $28.4 billion. Between 1998 and 2002, Microsoft's revenue increased 86% while IBM's stood still. In 2002, IBM—the company that invented the PC—had only 6% of the worldwide market for PCs. Today, it is Microsoft's Windows operating system and Intel's microprocessors—the so-called WINTEL—that are shaping the future of information technology.

When it comes to productivity, the best entrepreneurial companies leave the giant corporations behind in the dust. According to 2002 computer industry statistics, Microsoft's revenue per employee was $1,001,000, Dell's was $901,000, while Hewlett-Packard's was $401,333, and IBM's was $253,700.

No wonder Carly Fiorina of Hewlett-Packard and Samuel Palmisano of IBM and have been busily downsizing their companies. Dell subcontracts more of its manufacturing, but this does not explain the difference. Whether you hope to build a big company or a small one, the message is the same: Strive tirelessly to keep productivity high.

But no matter what you do, you probably won't be able to attain much success unless you have happy customers, happy workers, and happy suppliers. That means you must have a friendly company. It means that everyone must be friendly, especially anyone who deals with customers.

"The most fun six-month period I've had since the start of Microsoft," is how Bill Gates described his astonishing accomplishment in re-inventing his

20-year-old company to meet the threat posed by Internet upstarts in the mid-1990s. In not much more than six months of Herculean effort, Microsoft has developed an impressive array of new products to match those of Netscape. Having fun is one of the keys to keeping a company entrepreneurial. If Microsoft's product developers were not having fun, they would not have put in 12-hour days and sometimes overnighters to catch up with the Netscape.

Most new companies have the nine Fs at the outset. Those that become successful and grow pay attention to keeping them and nurturing them. The key to sustaining success is to remain an entrepreneurial gazelle and never turn into a lumbering elephant and finally a dinosaur, doomed to extinction.

2 OPPORTUNITY RECOGNITION
Jeffry A. Timmons

I was seldom able to see an opportunity until it had
ceased to be one.

> —*Mark Twain*

As incomprehensible as 39 rejections may be for many, the original proposal by
founder Scott Cook to launch a new software company called Intuit, was turned
down by that many venture capital investors before it was funded. Thousands of
similar examples illustrate just how complex, subtle, and situational (at the time,
in the market space, the investor's other alternatives, etc.) is the opportunity
recognition process. If the brightest, most knowledgeable, and most sophisticated investors in the world miss opportunities like Intuit, we can conclude that
the journey from idea to high-potential opportunity is illusive, contradictory,
and perilous. Think of this journey as a sort of road trip through varied terrain
and weather conditions. At times, the journey consists of full sunshine and
straight, smooth superhighways, as well as twisting, turning, up and down narrow one-lane passages that lead to some of the most breathtaking views. Along
the way, you also will unexpectedly encounter tornadoes, dust storms, hurricanes, and volcanoes. All too often you seem to run out of gas with no service
station in sight, and flat tires come when you least expect them. This is the entrepreneur's journey.

Excerpted from Jeffry A. Timmons, *New Venture Creation: Entrepreneurship for the Twenty-
First Century* (Burr Ridge, IL: Irwin/McGraw-Hill, 1999). Used with permission.

OPPORTUNITY THROUGH A ZOOM LENS

This chapter is dedicated to making that journey friendlier by focusing a zoom lens on the opportunity. It shares the road maps and benchmarks used by successful entrepreneurs, venture capitalists, angels, and other private equity investors in their quest to transform the often-shapeless caterpillar of an idea into a spectacularly handsome butterfly of a venture. Finally, this chapter examines the role of ideas and pattern recognition in the creative process of entrepreneurship.

You will come to see the criteria used to identify higher potential ventures as jumping-off points at this rarefied end of the opportunity continuum, rather than mere endpoints. One to 10 out of 100 entrepreneurs create ventures that emerge from the pack. Examined through a zoom lens, these ventures reveal a highly dynamic, constantly changing work of art in progress, not a pat formula or items on a checklist. This highly organic and situational character of the entrepreneurial process underscores the criticality of determining *fit* and balancing *risk and reward.* As the author has argued for three decades: The business plan is obsolete as soon as it is printed. It is in this shaping process that the best entrepreneurial leaders and investors add the greatest value to the enterprise.

THE ROLE OF IDEAS

A good idea is nothing more than a tool in the hands of an entrepreneur. Finding a good idea is the first step in the task of converting an entrepreneur's creativity into an opportunity.

The importance of the idea is often over rated, usually at the expense of underemphasizing the need for products or services, or both, which can be sold in enough quantity to real customers.

Further, the new business that simply bursts from a flash of brilliance is rare. What is usually necessary is a series of trial-and-error iterations, or repetitions, before a crude and promising product or service fits with what the customer is willing to pay for. For example, Howard Head made 40 different metal skis before he finally made the model that worked consistently. With surprising frequency, major businesses are built around totally different products than those originally envisioned.

Consider these examples:

- F. Leland Strange, the founder and president of Quadram, a maker of graphics and communications boards and other boards for microcomputers, told the story of how he developed his marketing idea into a company with

$100 million in sales in three years.[1] He stated that he had developed a business plan to launch his company and the company even hit projected revenues for the first two years. He noted, however, that success was achieved with completely *different* products than those in the original plan.

- Polaroid Corporation was founded with a product based on the principle of polarized light. It was thought that polarized lamps would prevent head-on collisions between cars by preventing the blinding glare of oncoming headlights. The company grew to become an industry leader based on another application of the same technology: instant photography.

- IBM began in the wire and cable business and later expanded to time clocks. Sales in the 1920s were only a few million dollars a year. Its successful mainframe computer business and then its successful personal computer business emerged much later.

As one entrepreneur expressed it:

Perhaps the existence of business plans and the language of business give a misleading impression of business building as a rational process. But, as any entrepreneur can confirm, starting a business is very much a series of fits and starts, brainstorms and barriers. Creating a business is a round-of-chance encounters that leads to new opportunities and ideas, mistakes that turn into miracles.[2]

The Great Mousetrap Fallacy

Perhaps no one did a greater disservice to generations of would-be entrepreneurs than Ralph Waldo Emerson in his oft-quoted line: "If a man can make a better mousetrap than his neighbor, though he builds his house in the woods the world will make a beaten path to his door."

What can be called *the great mousetrap fallacy* was thus spawned. Indeed, its success is often assumed to be possible if an entrepreneur can just come up with a new idea. Moreover, in today's changing world, if the idea has anything to do with technology, success is certain—or so it would seem.

The truth of the matter is that ideas are inert and, for all practical purposes, worthless. Further, the flow of ideas is really quite phenomenal. Venture capital investors, for instance, during the investing boom of the 1990s, received as many as 100 to 200 proposals and business plans each week. Only 1% to 3% of these actually received financing, however.

Yet the fallacy persists despite the lessons of practical experience noted long ago in the insightful reply to Emerson by O. B. Winters: "The manufacturer who waits for the world to beat a path to his door is a great optimist. But the manufacturer who shows this 'mousetrap' to the world keeps the smoke coming out his chimney."

Contributors to the Fallacy

There are several reasons for the perpetuation of the fallacy. One is the portrayal in oversimplified accounts of the ease and genius with which such ventures as IBM, Microsoft, and Amazon.com made their founders wealthy. Unfortunately, these exceptions do not provide a useful rule to guide aspiring entrepreneurs.

Another is that inventors seem particularly prone to mousetrap myopia. Perhaps, like Emerson, they are substantially sheltered in viewpoint and experience from the tough, competitive realities of the business world. Consequently, they may underestimate, if not seriously downgrade, the importance of what it takes to make a business succeed. Frankly, inventing and brainstorming may be a lot more fun than the careful diligent observation, investigation, and nurturing of customers that are often required to sell a product or service.

Contributing also to the great mousetrap fallacy is the tremendous psychological ownership attached to an invention or, after, to a new product. This attachment is different from attachment to a business. While an intense level of psychological ownership and involvement is certainly a prerequisite for creating a new business, the fatal flaw in attachment to an invention or product is the narrowness of its focus. The focal point needs to be the building of the business, rather than just one aspect of the idea.

Another source of mousetrap fallacy myopia is the technical and scientific orientation, that is, a desire to do it better. A good illustration of this is the experience of a Canadian entrepreneur who founded, with this brother, a company to manufacture truck seats. The entrepreneur's brother had developed a new seat for trucks that was a definite improvement over other seats. The entrepreneur knew he could profitably sell the seat his brother had designed, and they did so. When they needed more manufacturing capacity, one brother was not as interested in manufacturing more of the first seat, but he had several ideas on how to improve the seat. The first brother stated: "If I had listened to him, we probably would be a small custom shop today, or out of business. Instead, we concentrated on making seats that would sell at a profit, rather than just making a better and better seat. Our company has several million dollars of sales today and is profitable."

Being There First

Having the best idea first by no means is a guarantee of long-lasting success. Again, just ask Bob Frankston or Dan Bricklin, who were first with the spreadsheet software VisiCalc. Today, Microsoft owns the market with Excel.

Unless having the best idea also includes the capacity to preempt other competitors by capturing a significant share of the market or by erecting insurmountable barriers to entry, being first can mean proving for the competition that the market exists to be snared.

PATTERN RECOGNITION

Since ideas are building tools, you cannot build a successful business without them, as you could not build a house without a hammer. In this regard, experience is vital in looking at new venture ideas. Those with experience have been there before.

The Experience Factor

Time after time, experienced entrepreneurs exhibit an ability to recognize quickly a pattern—and an opportunity—while it is still taking shape. The late Herbert Simon, Nobel laureate and Richard King Melon University Professor of Computer Science and Psychology at Carnegie-Mellon University, wrote extensively about pattern recognition. He described the recognition of patterns as a creative process that is not simply logical, linear, and additive but intuitive and inductive as well. It involves, he said, the creative linking, or cross-association, of two or more in-depth "chunks" of experience, know-how, and contacts.[3] Simon contended that it takes 10 years or more for people to accumulate what he called the "50,000 chunks" of experience that enable them to be highly creative and recognize patterns—familiar circumstances that can be translated from one place to another.

Thus, the process of sorting through ideas and recognizing a pattern can also be compared to the process of fitting pieces into a three-dimensional jigsaw puzzle. It is impossible to assemble such a puzzle by looking at it as a whole unit. Rather, one needs to see the relationships between the pieces, and be able to fit together some that are seemingly unrelated before the whole is visible.

Recognizing ideas that can become entrepreneurial opportunities stems from a capacity to see what others do not—that one plus one equals three, or more. Consider the following examples of the common thread of pattern recognition and creating new businesses by linking knowledge in one field or marketplace with quite different technical, business, or market expertise:

- A middle manager employed by a larger company was on a plant tour of a small machinery manufacturer, a customer, in the Midwest. A machinist was mechanically cutting metal during a demonstration of a particular fabricating operation. Shockingly, the machinist accidentally sliced his hand in the cutting machine, removing two fingers. Instantly, the manager recognized that the application of new laser technology was a significant business opportunity that would make it possible to eliminate horrible accidents such as the one he had just witnessed. He subsequently launched and built a multimillion-dollar company. Here linking the knowledge of the capabilities of laser technology to an old, injury-prone metal-cutting technology yielded an opportunity.

- During travel throughout Europe, the eventual founders of Crate & Barrel frequently saw stylish and innovative products for the kitchen and home that were not yet available in the United States. When they returned home, the founders created Crate & Barrel to offer these products for which market research had, in a sense, already been conducted in Europe. This knowledge of consumer buying habits in one geographical region, Europe, was transferred successfully to a previously untapped consumer market in another country, the United States.

- During World War II, Howard Head was an aeronautical design engineer working with new light metal alloys to build airfoils that were more efficient. Head transferred his knowledge of metal honing technology from the aircraft manufacturing business to a consumer product, metal skis, and then to another, tennis rackets. In the first case, although he had limited skiing experience, he concluded that if he could make a metal ski, there would be a significant market because of the limitations of wooden skis. His company dominated the ski industry for many years. In talking about his decision to develop the oversized Prince tennis racket after he saw a need for ball control among players learning tennis, Head said, "I saw the pattern again that had worked at Head Ski. . . . I had proven to myself before that you can take different technology and know-how and apply it to a solution in a new area."[4] He set about learning the physics of tennis rackets and surfaces and developed the Prince racket.

- In Texas, a young entrepreneur launched a modular home sales business in the late 1970s. First, he parlayed experience as a loan officer with a large New York City bank into a job with a manufacturer of mobile and modular homes in Texas. This enabled him, over a three-year period, to learn the business and to understand the market opportunity. He then opened a sales location in a growing suburb about 25 miles from booming larger cities. By studying his competitors and conducting an analysis of how customers actually went about purchasing new modular homes, he spotted a pattern that meant opportunity. Customers usually shopped at three different locations, where they could see different models and price ranges, before making a purchase decision. Since his market analysis showed there was room in the city for three or four such businesses, he opened two additional sites, each with a different name and with different but complementary lines. Within two years, despite record high interest rates, his business had nearly tripled to $17 million in annual sales, and his only competitor was planning to move.

Enhancing Creative Thinking

The creative thinking described in these examples is of great value in recognizing opportunities, as well as other aspects of entrepreneurship. The notion that creativity can be learned or enhanced holds important implications for entrepreneurs who need to be creative in their thinking. Most people can certainly spot creative flair. Children seem to have it, and many seem to lose it. Several studies suggest that creativity actually peaks around the first grade because a person's life tends to become increasingly structured and defined by others and by institutions. Further, the development in school of intellectual discipline and rigor in thinking takes on greater importance than during the formative years, and most of our education beyond grade school stresses a logical, rational mode of orderly reasoning and thinking. Finally, social pressures may tend to be a taming influence on creativity.

There is evidence that you can enhance creative thinking in later years. Take, for instance, a group called Synectics of Cambridge, Massachusetts, one of the first organizations in the early 1950s to investigate systematically the process of creative thinking and to conduct training sessions in applying creative thinking to business. The following theories underlay the Synectics approach to developing creativity:[5]

- The efficiency of a person's creative process can be markedly increased if he or she understands the psychological process by which the process operates.
- The emotional component in the creative process is more important than the intellectual, and the irrational more important that the rational.
- The emotional, irrational elements need to be understood to increase the probability of success in a problem-solving situation.

I participated in one of these training sessions, and it became evident during the sessions that the methods did unlock the thinking process and yielded very imaginative solutions.

Approaches to Unleashing Creativity

Since the 1950s, a good deal has been learned about the workings of the human brain. Today, there is general agreement that the two sides of the brain process information in quite different ways. The left side performs rational, logical functions, while the right side operates the intuitive and nonrational modes of thought. A person uses both sides, actually shifting from one mode to the other (see Exhibit 2.1). How to control modes of thought is of interest to entrepreneurs, and they can, perhaps, draw on two interesting approaches.

More recently, professors have focused on the creativity process. For instance, Michael Gordon stressed the importance of creativity and the need for brainstorming in a presentation on the elements of personal power. He suggested that using the following 10 brainstorming rules could enhance creative visualization:[6]

1. Define your purpose.
2. Choose participants.
3. Choose a facilitator.
4. Brainstorm spontaneously, copiously.

EXHIBIT 2.1   Comparison of left-mode and right-mode characteristics.

Left Mode	Right Mode
Verbal: Using words to name, describe, and define.	*Nonverbal:* Awareness of things, but minimal connection with words.
Analytic: Figuring things out step-by-step and part-by-part.	*Synthetic:* Putting things together to form wholes.
Symbolic: Using a symbol to *stand for* something. For example the + sign for the process of addition.	*Analogic:* Seeing likenesses between things; understanding metaphoric relationships.
Abstract: Taking out a small bit of information and using it to presented the whole thing.	*Concrete:* Relating to things as they are at the present moment.
Temporal: Keeping track of time, sequencing one thing after another, doing first things first, second thing second, etc.	*Nontemporal:* Without a sense of time.
Rational: Drawing conclusions based on reason and *facts.*	*Nonrational:* Not requiring a basis of reason or facts; willingness to suspend judgment.
Digital: Using numbers as in counting.	*Spatial:* Seeing where things are in relations to other things, and how parts go together to form a whole.
Logical: Drawing conclusions based on logic; one thing following another in logical order—for example, a mathematical theorem or a well-stated argument.	*Intuitive:* Making leaps of insight, often based on incomplete patterns, hunches, feelings, or visual images.
Linear: Thinking in terms of linked ideas, one thought directly following another, often leading to a convergent conclusion.	*Holistic:* Seeing whole things all at once; perceiving the overall patterns and structures, often leading to divergent conclusions.

Source: Betty Edwards, *Drawing on the Right Side of the Brain* (Boston, MA: Houghton, Mifflin, 1979), p. 40.

5. No criticisms, no negatives.
6. Record ideas in full view.
7. Invent to the "void."
8. Resist becoming committed to one idea.
9. Identify the most promising ideas.
10. Refine and prioritize.

Team Creativity

Teams of people can generate creativity that may not exist in a single individual. The creativity of a team of people is impressive, and comparable or better creative solutions to problems evolving from the collective interaction of a small group of people have been observed.

A good example of the creativity generated by using team approach is that of a company founded by a Babson College graduate with little technical training. He teamed up with a talented inventor, and the entrepreneurial and business expertise of the founder complemented the creative and technical skills of the inventor. The result has been a rapidly growing multimillion-dollar venture in the field of video-based surgical equipment.

When Is an Idea an Opportunity?

If an idea is not an opportunity, what is an opportunity?[7] *An opportunity has the qualities of being attractive, durable, and timely and is anchored in a product or service, which creates or adds value for its buyer or end user.*

For an opportunity to have these qualities, the "window of opportunity" must be open and remain open long enough (see Exhibit 2.2). Further, entry into a market with the right characteristics is feasible and the management team is able to achieve it. The venture has or is able to achieve a competitive advantage (i.e., to achieve leverage). Finally, the economics of the venture must be rewarding and forgiving and allow significant profit and growth potential.

EXHIBIT 2.2   Sources of opportunities.

Sources	Percentage of Companies
Work activity	47
Improving an existing product/service	15
Identifying an unfilled niche	11
Other sources	16

Source: Adapted from John Case, "The Origins of Entrepreneurship," *Inc.* (June 1989): 54. The survey involved 500 of the fastest growing companies.

To repeat, opportunities that have the qualities named above are anchored in a product or service that creates or adds value for its buyer or end user. The most successful entrepreneurs, venture capitalists, and private investors are opportunity-focused; that is, they start with what customers and the marketplace want and do not lose sight of this.

The Real World

Opportunities are created, or built, using ideas and entrepreneurial creativity. Yet, while the image of a carpenter or mason at work is useful, in reality the process is more like the collision of particles in the process of a nuclear reaction or like the spawning of hurricanes over the ocean. Ideas interact with real-world conditions and entrepreneurial creativity at a point in time. The product of this interaction is an opportunity around which a new venture can be created.

The business environment in which an entrepreneur launches his or her venture is usually given and cannot be altered significantly. Despite the assumptions individuals make about social and nonprofit organizations, they too are subject to market forces and economic constraints. Consider, for instance, what would happen to donations if it were perceived that a nonprofit organization was not reinvesting its surplus returns, but instead was paying management excessive salaries. Or what if a socially-oriented organization, like the Body Shop, concentrated all its efforts on the social mission, while neglecting profits? Clearly, dealing with suppliers, production costs, labor, and distribution are critical to the health of these social corporations. Thus, social and nonprofit organizations are just as concerned with positive cash flow and generating sufficient cash flows, even though they operate in a different type of market than for-profit organizations. For-profit businesses operate in a free enterprise system characterized by private ownership and profits.

Spawners and Drivers of Opportunities

In a free enterprise system, *opportunities* are spawned when there are changing circumstances, chaos, confusion, inconsistencies, lags or leads, knowledge and information gaps, and a variety of other vacuums in an industry or market.

Changes in the business environment and, therefore, anticipation of these changes are so critical in entrepreneurship that constant vigilance for changes is a valuable habit. This is how an entrepreneur with credibility, creativity, and decisiveness can seize an opportunity while others study it.

Opportunities are situational. Some conditions under which opportunities are spawned are entirely idiosyncratic, while at other times they are generalizable and can be applied to other industries, products, or services.

Cross-association can trigger in the entrepreneurial mind the crude recognition of existing or impending opportunities. It is often assumed that a marketplace dominated by large, multibillion-dollar players is impenetrable by smaller, entrepreneurial companies. After all, how can you possibly compete with entrenched, resource-rich, established companies? The opposite can be true for several reasons. A number of research projects have shown that it can take several years for a large company to change its strategy, and even longer to implement the new strategy since it can take six years or more to change the culture enough to operate differently. For a new or small company 10 or more years is forever. When Cellular One was launched in Boston, giant NYNEX was the sole competitor. From all estimates they built twice as many towers (at $500,000 each), spent two to three times as much on advertising and marketing, in addition to having a larger head-count. Yet, Cellular One grew from scratch to $100 million in sales in five years and won three customers for every one that NYNEX won. What made this substantial difference? It was an entrepreneurial management team at Cellular One.

Some of the most exciting opportunities have actually come from fields the conventional wisdom said are the domain of big business: technological innovation. The performance of smaller firms in technological innovation is remarkable—95% of the radical innovations since World War II have come from new and small firms, not the giants. In fact, another study from the National Science Foundation found that smaller firms generated 24 times as many innovations per research and development dollar versus firms with 10,000 or more employees.

There can be exciting opportunities in plain vanilla businesses that might never get the attention of venture capital investors. The revolution in microcomputers, management information systems (MIS), and computer networking had a profound impact on a number of businesses that had changed little in decades. The used auto-wreck and used auto-parts business is a good example of one that has not changed in decades. Yet, the team at Pintendre Auto, Inc. saw a new opportunity in this field by applying the latest computer and information technology to a traditional business that relied on crude, manual methods to track inventory and find parts for customers.[8] In just three years, Pintendre Auto built a business with $16 million in sales.

Other regulatory and technology changes can radically alter the way you think about the opportunities because of the economics of sales and distribution for many customer products, from fishing lures to books to cosmetics to sporting goods. Today, there are hundreds of cable television channels in America versus 40 to 50 for most markets in 1993. A number of new companies with up to $100 million in sales have already been built using "infomercials." A 30-minute program can be produced for $50,000 to $150,000, and a half hour of air time can be purchased today for about $20,000 in Los Angeles or for about

$4,000 in smaller cities. Compare that with a $25,000+ cost of a full-page advertisement in a monthly magazine. With a large increase in the number of channels, the cost and market focus will undoubtedly improve. Traditional channels of distribution through distributors, wholesales, specialty stores, and retailers will be leapfrogged. Entrepreneurs will find ways to convert those funds previously spent on the profit margin that went to the distribution channel (30% to 50+%) to their infomercial marketing budget and to an increased gross margin for their business.

Consider the following broad range of examples that illustrate the phenomenon of vacuums in which opportunities are spawned:

- Deregulation of telecommunications and the airlines led to the formation of tens of thousands of new firms, including Cellular One and Federal Express.

- Many opportunities exist in fragmented, traditional industries that may have a craft or mom-and-pop character and where there is little appreciation or expertise in marketing and finance. Such possibilities can range from fishing lodges, inns, and hotels to cleaners/laundries, hardware stores, pharmacies, waste management plants, flower shops, nurseries, tents, and auto repairs.

- In our service-dominated economy (where 70% of businesses are service businesses, versus 30% just 25 years ago), customer service, rather than the product itself, can be the critical success factor. One study by the Forum Corporation in Boston showed that 70% of customers leave because of poor service and only 15% because of price or product quality. Can you think of your last "wow" experience with exceptional customer service?

- Sometimes existing competitors cannot, or will not, increase capacity as the market is moving. For example, in the late 1970s, some steel firms had a 90-week delivery lag, with the price to be determined, and foreign competitors certainly took notice.

- The tremendous shift to offshore manufacturing of labor-intensive and transportation-intensive products in Asia, Eastern Europe, and Mexico, such as computer-related and microprocessor-drive consumer products, is an excellent example.

- In a wide variety of industries, entrepreneurs sometimes find that they are the only ones who can perform. Such fields as consulting, software design, financial services, process engineering, and technical and medical products and services abound with examples of know-how monopolies. Sometimes a management team is simply the best in an industry and irreplaceable in the near term, just as is seen with great coaches with winning records.

Exhibit 2.3 summarizes the major types of discontinuities, asymmetries, and changes that can result in high-potential opportunities. Creating such changes, by technical innovation (PCs, wireless telecommunications, Internet servers, software), influencing and creating the new rules of the game (airlines, telecommunications, financial services and banking, medical products) and anticipating the various impacts of such changes is central to the opportunity recognition process.

Big Opportunities with Little Capital

Within the dynamic free enterprise system, opportunities are apparent to a limited number of individuals—and not just to the individuals with financial

EXHIBIT 2.3   Summary of opportunity spawners and drivers.

Root of Change/ Chaos/Discontinuity	Opportunity Creation
Regulatory changes	Cellular, airlines, insurance, radio and television, telecommunications, medical, pension fund management, financial services, banking, tax, and SEC laws.
Ten-fold change in 10 years or less	Moore's Law—computer chips double productivity every 18 months; financial services; private equity, consulting, Internet, biotech, information age, publishing.
Reconstruction of value chain and channels of distribution	Superstores: Staples, Home Depot; all publishing; autos; Internet sales and distribution of all services.
Proprietary or contractual advantage	Technological innovation; patent, license, contract, franchise, copyrights, distributorship.
Existing management/ investors burned out/ under-managed	Turnaround, new capital structure, new break-even, new free cash flow, new team, new strategy; owners desires for liquidity, exit; telecom, waste management service, retail businesses.
Entrepreneurial leadership	New vision and strategy, new team = secret weapon; organization thinks, acts like owners.
Market leaders are customer obsessed or customer blind	New, small customers are low priority or ignored; hard disk drives, paper, chemicals, main frame computers, centralized data processing, desk top computers, corporate venturing, office superstores, automobiles, software, most services.
Imperfect information and markets	Intangibles, art, private equity and venture capital, antiques.
Disruptive technologies and exogenous events	Internet services, wireless telecommunications, LED lighting, hand-held personal communications devices; September 11, 2001.

resources. Ironically, successful entrepreneurs like Howard Head attribute their success to the discipline of limited capital resources. Thus, many entrepreneurs have been learning the key to success is in the art of bootstrapping, which "in a startup is like zero inventory in a just-in-time system: it reveals hidden problems and forces the company to solve them."[9] Consider the following:

- A 1991 study revealed that of the 110 startups researched, 77 had been launched with $50,000 or less; 46% were started with $10,000 or less as seed capital. Further, the primary source of capital was, overwhelmingly, personal savings (74%), rather than outside investors with deep pockets.[10]

- In the 1930s, Josephine Esther Mentzer assisted her uncle by selling skin care balm and quickly created her own products with $100 initial investment. After convincing the department stores rather than the drug stores to carry her products, Estee Lauder was on its way to a $4 billion corporation.[11]

- Putting their talents (cartooning and finance) together, Roy and Walt Disney moved to California and started their own film studio—with $290 in 1923. By mid-2001, the Walt Disney Co. had a market capitalization exceeding $40 billion.[12]

- While working for a Chicago insurance company, a 24-year-old sent out 20,000 inquiries for a black newsletter. With 3,000 positive responses and $500, John Harold Johnson published *Jet* for the first time in 1942. Today, Johnson Publishing publishes various magazines, including *Ebony*.[13]

- With $100 Nicholas Graham, age 24, went to a local fabric store, picked out some patterns, and made $100 worth of ties. Having sold the ties to specialty shops, Graham was approached by Macy's to place his patterns on men's underwear. So Joe Boxer Corporation was born and "six months into Joe Boxer's second year, sales had already topped $1 million."[14]

Real Time

Opportunities exist or are created in real time and have what we call a window of opportunity. For an entrepreneur to seize an opportunity, the window must be opening, not closing, and it must remain open long enough (Exhibit 2.4).

Markets grow at different rates over time and as a market quickly becomes larger, more and more opportunities are possible. As the market becomes larger and established, conditions are not as favorable. Thus, as the point where a market starts to become sufficiently large and structured (e.g., at 5 years), the window opens; the window begins to close as the market matures (e.g., at 15 years).

EXHIBIT 2.4   Changes in the placement of the window of opportunity.

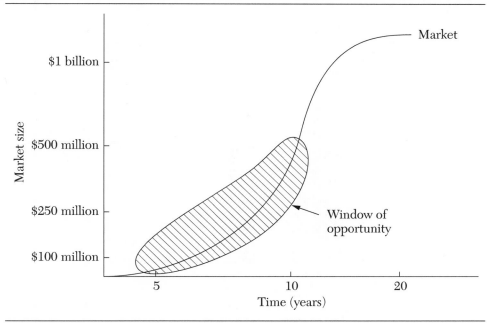

The curve shown describes the rapid growth pattern typical of such new industries as microcomputers and software, cellular car phones, quick oil changes, and biotechnology. In other industries, such as a mature industry, where growth is not so rapid, the slope of a curve would be less steep and the possibilities for opportunities fewer.

Finally, in considering the window of opportunity, the length of time the window will be open is important. It takes a considerable length of time to determine whether a new venture is a success or a failure. In addition, if it is to be a success, the benefits of that success need to be harvested.

Exhibit 2.5 shows that for venture-capital-backed firms, the lemons (i.e., the losers) ripen in about two-and-a-half years, while the pearls (i.e., the winners) take seven or eight years. An extreme example of the length of time it can take for a pearl to be harvested is the experience of a Silicon Valley venture capital firm that invested in a new firm in 1966 and was finally able to realize a capital gain in early 1984.

Another way to think of the process of creating and seizing an opportunity in real time is to think of it as a process of selecting objects (opportunities) from a conveyor belt moving through an open window, the window of opportunity. The speed of the conveyor belt changes and the window through which it

EXHIBIT 2.5   Lemons and pearls.

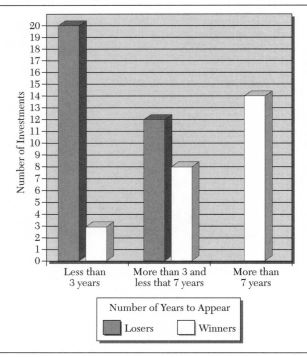

moves is constantly opening and closing. The continually opening and closing window and the constantly changing speed of the conveyor belt represent the volatile nature of the marketplace and the importance of timing. For an opportunity to be created and seized, it needs to be selected from the conveyor belt before the window closes.

The ability to recognize a potential opportunity when it appears and the sense of timing to seize that opportunity, as the window is opening, rather than slamming shut, are critical. The fact that opportunities are a function of real time is illustrated in a statement made by Ken Olsen, then president and founder of Digital Equipment Corporation, in 1977: "There is no reason for any individual to have a computer in their home." Nor is it so easy for even the world's leading experts to predict just which innovative ideas and concepts for new business will evolve into the major industries of tomorrow. This is vividly illustrated by several quotations from very famous innovators. In 1901, two years before the famous flight, Wilbur Wright said, "Man will not fly for 50 years." In 1910, Thomas Edison said, "The nickel-iron battery will put the gasoline buggy . . . out of existence in no time." Moreover, in 1932, Albert Einstein made it clear: "There is not the slightest indication that nuclear energy will ever be obtainable. It would mean that the atom would have to be shattered at will."

Relation to the Framework of Analysis

It is also important to remember that successful opportunities, once recognized, fit with the other forces of new venture creation. Of utmost importance when talking of opportunity recognition is the fit of the lead entrepreneur and the management team with an opportunity. Good opportunities are both *desirable to* and *attainable by* those on the team using the resources that are available.

To understand how the entrepreneurial vision relates to the analytical framework, it may be useful to look at an opportunity as a three-dimensional relief map with its valleys, mountains, and so on, all represented. Each opportunity has three or four critical factors (e.g., proprietary license, patented innovation, sole distribution rights, an all-star management team, breakthrough technology). These elements pop out at the observer; they indicate huge possibilities where others might see obstacles. Thus, it is easy to see why there are thousands of exceptional opportunities that will fit with a wide variety of entrepreneurs, but that might not fit neatly into the framework outlined in Exhibit 2.6 on pages 46–48.

SCREENING OPPORTUNITIES

Opportunity Focus is also the most fruitful point of departure for screening opportunities. The screening process should not begin with strategy (which derives from the nature of the opportunity), nor with financial and spreadsheet analysis (which flow from the former), nor with estimations of how much the company is worth and who will own what shares.[15]

These starting points, and others, usually place the cart before the horse. Perhaps the best evidence of this phenomenon comes from the tens of thousands of me-too dot-com companies formed in the late 1990s. In addition, as has been noted, a good number of entrepreneurs who start businesses—particularly those for whom the ventures are their first—run out of cash at a faster rate than they bring in customers and profitable sales. There are many reasons why this happens, but one thing is certain: These entrepreneurs have not focused on the right opportunity.

Over the years, those with experience in business and in specific market areas have developed rules of thumb to guide them in screening opportunities. For example, a firm used one such rule of thumb in evaluating startups in the minicomputer industry in the mid-1980s. This firm believed, based on an analysis of performance data relating to 60 computer-related startups in the United States from 1975 to 1984, that one leading indicator of the progress of new firms and a good boundary measure of positive performance and a healthy start was

EXHIBIT 2.6   Criteria for evaluating venture opportunities.

	Attractiveness	
Criteria	**Highest Potential**	**Lowest Potential**
Industry and Market	Changes way people live and work	Incremental improvement only
Market:	Market driven; identified; recurring revenue niche	Unfocused; one-time revenue
Customers	Reachable; purchase orders	Loyal to others or unreachable
User benefits	Less than one-year payback	Three years plus payback
Value added	High; advance payments	Low; minimal impact on market
Product life	Durable	Perishable
Market structure	Imperfect, fragmented competition or emerging industry	Highly concentrated or mature or declining industry
Market size	$100+ million to $1 billion sales potential	Unknown, less than $20 million or multibillion sales
Growth rate	Growth at 30% to 50% or more	Contracting or less than 10%
Market capacity	At or near full capacity	Under capacity
Market share attainable (Year 5)	20% or more; leader	Less than 5%
Cost Structure	Low-cost provider; cost advantages	Declining cost
Economics		
Time to breakeven/positive cash flow	1½ to 2 years	More than 4 years
ROI potential	25% or more per year	Less than 15% to 20%
Capital requirement	Low to moderate; fundable	Very high; unfundable
Internal rate of return potential	25% or more per year	Less than 15% per year
Free cash flow characteristics:	Favorable; sustainable; 20% to 30% or more of sales	Less than 10% of sales
Sales growth	Moderate to high +15% to +20%	Less than 10%
Asset intensity	Low/sales $	High
Spontaneous working capital	Low, incremental requirements	High requirements
R&D/capital expenditures	Low requirements	High requirements

EXHIBIT 2.6   Continued.

| Criteria | Attractiveness | |
	Potential	Lowest Potential
Gross margins	Exceeding 40% durable	Under 20%
After-tax profits	High; greater than 10%; durable	Low
Time to break-even profit and loss	Less than two years; breakeven not creeping	Greater than four years; breakeven creeping up
Harvest Issues		
Value-added potential	High strategic value	Low strategic value
Valuation multiples and comparables	20x P/E 8–10x EBIT 1.5–2x revenue 8–10x free cash flow	< 5x P/E 3–4x EBIT < 4x revenue
Exit mechanism and strategy	Present or envisioned options	Undefined; illiquid investment
Capital market content	Favorable valuations, timing, capital available; realizable liquidity	Unfavorable; credit crunch
Competitive Advantage Issues		
Fixed and variable costs	Lowest; high operating leverage	Highest
Control over costs, prices, and distribution	Moderate to strong	Weak
Barriers to entry		
Proprietary protection	Have or can gain	None
Response/lead time	Competition slow or napping	Unable to gain edge
Legal, contractual advantage	Proprietary or exclusivity	None
Contracts and networks	Well-developed; accessible	Crude; limited
Key people	Top talent; an A team	B or C team
Management Team		
Entrepreneurial team	All-star combination; free agents	Weak or solo entrepreneur
Industry and technical experience	Top of the field; super track-record	Underdeveloped
Integrity	Highest standards	Questionable
Intellectual honesty	Know what they do not know	Do not want to know what they do not know
Fatal-flaw issue	Non-existent	One or more

(continued)

EXHIBIT 2.6   Continued.

Criteria	Attractiveness	
	Potential	**Lowest Potential**
Personal Criteria		
Goals and fit	Getting what you want; but wanting what you get	Surprises, as in *The Crying Game*
Upside/downside issues	Attainable success/limited risks	Linear; on same continuum
Opportunity costs	Acceptable cuts in salary, etc.	Comfortable with status quo
Desirability	Fits with lifestyle	Simply pursuing big money
Risk/reward tolerance	Calculated risk; low risk/reward ratio	Risk averse or gambler
Stress tolerance	Thrives under pressure	Cracks under pressure
Strategic Differentiation		
Degree of fit	High	Low
Team	Best in class; excellent free agents	B team; no free agents
Service management	Superior service concept	Perceived as unimportant
Timing	Rowing with the tide	Rowing against the tide
Technology	Groundbreaking; one of a kind	Many substitutes or competitors
Flexibility	Able to adapt; commit and decommit quickly	Slow; stubborn
Opportunity orientation	Always searching for opportunities	Operating in a vacuum; napping
Pricing	At or near leader	Undercut competitor; low prices
Distribution channels	Accessible; networks in place	Unknown; inaccessible
Room for error	Forgiving strategy	Unforgiving; rigid strategy

sales per employee of $75,000 or more. To this firm, sales of less than $50,000 per employee signaled serious trouble. While there is always the risk of over-simplification in using rules of thumb, it is true also, that one can miss the fundamentals while searching for subtleties.

Screening Criteria: The Characteristics of High-Potential Ventures

Venture capitalists, savvy entrepreneurs, and investors also use this concept of boundaries in screening ventures. Exhibit 2.6 summarizes criteria used by venture capitalists to evaluate opportunities. This group uses these criteria to evaluate a select group of opportunities that tend to have a high-technology bias. As will be seen later, venture capital investors reject 60% to 70% of the new ventures presented to them very early in the review process, based on how the entrepreneurs satisfy these criteria.

However, these criteria are not the exclusive domain of venture capitalists. These criteria are based on plain good business sense that is used by successful entrepreneurs, private investors, and venture capitalists. Consider the following examples of great small companies built without a dime of professional venture capital:

- Paul Tobin, who built Cellular One in eastern Massachusetts from the ground up to $100 million in revenue in five years, started Roamer Plus with less than $300,000 of internally generated funds from other ventures. Within two years, it grew to a $15 million annual sales rate and was very profitable.

- Another entrepreneur started a small specialty publishing company with minimal capital and grew it to over $12 million in highly profitable sales by 1987. While looking for acquisitions, he discovered that valuations were at an all-time high. Instead of buying, he decided to sell. In 1988, he sold his small firm for over $70 million.

- Morris Alper & Sons was a third-generation, small, traditional food brokerage business with around 40 employees when the founder's grandson joined the firm in the early 1970s. By 1993, financed entirely by internally generated cash flow, they had grown to nearly 350 employees. The company has become an integrated marketing services firm whose clients are 70 of the largest consumer food product companies in North America.

- In 1983, Charlie Butcher, at age 66, had to decide whether to buy out an equal partner in his 100-year-old industrial polish and wax business with less than $10 million in sales. This niche business had high gross margins, very low working capital and fixed-asset requirements for increased sales, substantial steady growth of over 18% per year, and excellent products. The result was a business with very high free cash flow and potential for growth. He acquired the company with a bank loan and seller financing, and then he increased sales to over $50 million by 1993. The company continues to be highly profitable. Charlie vows never to utilize venture capital money or to take the company public.

The point of departure here is opportunity and, implicitly, the customer, the marketplace, and the industry. As Exhibit 2.6 shows, higher and lower potential opportunities can be placed along an attractiveness scale. The criteria provide some quantitative ways in which an entrepreneur can make judgments about industry and market issues, competitive advantage issues, economic and harvest issues, management team issues, and fatal flaw issues and whether these add up to a compelling opportunity. For example, *dominant* strength in any one of these criteria can readily translate into a winning entry, whereas a flaw in any one can be fatal.

Entrepreneurs contemplating opportunities that will yield attractive companies, not high-potential ventures, can also benefit from paying attention to these criteria. These entrepreneurs will then be in a better position to decide how these criteria can be compromised. As outlined in Exhibit 2.6, business opportunities with the greatest potential will possess many of the following, or they will dominate in one or a few for which the competition cannot come close.

Industry and Market Issues

Market

Higher potential businesses can identify a market niche for a product or service that meets an important customer need and provides high value-added or value-created benefits to customers. Customers are reachable and receptive to the product or service, with no brand or other loyalties. The potential payback to the user or customer of a given product or service through cost savings or other value-added or valued-created properties is one year or less and is identifiable, repeatable, and verifiable. Further, the life of the product or service exists beyond the time needed to recover the investment, plus a profit. Moreover, the company is able to expand beyond a one-product company. If benefits to customers cannot be calculated in dollar terms, then the market potential is far more difficult and risky to ascertain.

Lower potential opportunities are unfocused regarding customer need, and customers are unreachable and/or have brand or other loyalties to others. A payback to the user of more than three years and low value-added or value-created properties also makes an opportunity unattractive. Being unable to expand beyond a one-product company can make for a lower potential opportunity. The failure of one of the first portable computer companies, Osborne Computer, is a prime example of this.

Market Structure

Market structure, such as evidenced by the number of sellers, size distribution of sellers, whether products are differentiated, conditions of entry and exit, number of buyers, cost conditions, and sensitivity of demand to changes in price, is significant.

A fragmented, imperfect market or emerging industry often contains vacuums and asymmetries that create unfilled market niches—for example, markets where resource ownership, cost advantages, and the like can be achieved. In addition, those where information or knowledge gaps exist and where competition is profitable, but not so strong as to be overwhelming, are attractive. An example of a market with an information gap is that of the experience a Boston entrepreneur encountered with a large New York company that wanted to dispose of a small, old office building in downtown Boston. This office building, because its book value was about $200,000, was viewed by the financially oriented firm as a low-value asset, and the company wanted to dispose of it so the resulting cash could be put to work for a higher return. The buyer, who had done more homework than the out-of-town sellers had bought the building for $200,000 and resold it in less than six months for over $8 million.

Industries that are highly concentrated, that are perfectly competitive, or that are mature or declining industries are typically unattractive. The capital requirements and costs to achieve distribution and marketing presence can be prohibitive, and such behavior as price-cutting and other competitive strategies in highly concentrated markets can be a significant barrier to entry. (The most blatant example is organized crime and its life-threatening actions when territories are invaded.) Yet, revenge by normal competitors who are well positioned through product strategy, legal tactics, and the like, also can be punishing to the pocketbook.

The airline industry, after deregulation, is an example of a perfectly competitive market and one where many of the recent entrants will have difficulty. The unattractiveness of perfectly competitive industries is captured by the comment of prominent Boston venture capitalists William Egan, who put it this way: "I want to be in a nonauction market."[16]

Market Size

An attractive new venture sells to a market that is large and growing (i.e., one where capturing a small market share can represent significant and increasing sales volume). A minimum market size of over $100 million in sales is attractive. Such a market size means it is possible to achieve significant sales by capturing roughly 5% or less and thus not threatening competitors. For example, to achieve a sales level of $1 million in a $100 million market requires only 1% of the market. Thus, a recreational equipment manufacturer entered a $60 million market that was expected to grow at 20% per year to over $100 million by the third year. The founders were able to create a substantial smaller company without obtaining a major market share and possibly incurring the wrath of existing companies.

However, such a market can be too large. A multibillion-dollar market may be too mature and stable, and such a level of certainty can translate into competition from Fortune 500 firms and, if highly competitive, into lower margins and profitability. Further, an unknown market or one that is less than

$10 million in sales also is unattractive. To understand the disadvantages of a large, more mature market consider the entry of a firm into the microcomputer industry today versus the entry of Apple Computer into that market in 1975.

Growth Rate

An attractive market is large and growing (i.e., one where capturing a good share of the increase is less threatening to competitors and where a small market share can represent significant and increasing sales volume). An annual growth rate of 30% to 35% creates new niches for new entrants, and such a market is a thriving and expansive one, rather than a stable or contracting one, where competitors are scrambling for the same niches. Thus, for example, a $100 million market growing at 50% per year has the potential to become a $1 billion industry in a few years, and if a new venture is able to capture just 2% of sales in the first year, it can attain sales in the first year of $1 million. If it just maintains its market share over the next few years, sales will grow significantly.

Market Capacity

Another signal of the existence of an opportunity in a market is a market at full capacity in a growth situation—in other words, a demand that the existing suppliers cannot meet. Timing is of vital concern in such a situation, which means the entrepreneur should be asking himself or herself, "Can a new entrant fill that demand before the other players can decided to and then actually increase capacity?"

Market Share Attainable

The potential to be a leader in the market and capture at least a 20% share of the market is important. The potential to be a leader in the market and capture at least 20% can create a very high value for a company that might otherwise be worth not much more than book value. For example, one such firm, with less than $15 million in sales, became the dominant factor in its small market niche with a 70% market share. The company was acquired for $23 million in cash.

A firm that will be able to capture less than 5% of a market is unattractive in the eyes of most investors seeking a higher potential company.

Cost Structure

A firm that can become the low-cost provider is attractive, but a firm that continually faces declining cost conditions is less so. Attractive opportunities exist in industries where economies of scale are insignificant (or work to the advantage of the new venture). Attractive opportunities boast of low costs of learning by doing. Where costs per unit are high when small amounts of the product are sold, existing firms that have low promotion costs can face attractive market opportunities.

For instance, consider the operating leverage of Johnsonville Sausage. Their variable costs were 6% labor and 94% materials. What aggressive incentives could management put in place for the 6% to manage and to control the 94%? Imagine the disasters that would occur if the scenario were reversed!

A word of caution from Scott W. Kunkel and Charles W. Hofer, who observed that:

> Overall, industry structure . . . had a much small impact on new venture performance than has previously been suggested in the literature. This finding could be the result of one of several possibilities:
>
> 1. Industry structure impacts the performance of established firms, but does NOT have a significant impact on new venture performance.
> 2. The most important industry structural variables influencing new ventures are different from those which impact established firms and thus research has yet to identify the industry structural variables that are most important in the new venture environment.
> 3. Industry structure does NOT have a significant DIRECT impact on firm performance, as hypothesized by scholars in the three fields of study. Instead, the impact of industry structure is strongly mitigated by other factors, including the strategy selected for entry.[17]

Economics

Profits after Tax

High and durable growth margins usually translate into strong and durable after-tax profits. Attractive opportunities have potential for durable profits of at least 10% to 15%, and often 1% to 20% or more. Those generating after-tax profits of less than 5% are quite fragile.

Time to Breakeven and Positive Cash Flow

As mentioned, breakeven and positive cash flow for attractive companies are possible within two years. Once the time to breakeven and positive cash flow is greater than three years, the attractiveness of the opportunity diminishes accordingly.

ROI Potential

An important corollary to forgiving economics is reward. Very attractive opportunities have the potential to yield a return on investment of 25% or more per year. After all, since the dot-com bust, many venture capital funds have struggled to generate even single-digit returns on investment. High and durable gross margins and high and durable after-tax profits usually yield high earnings per share and high return on stockholders' equity, thus generating a satisfactory "harvest" price for a company. This is most likely true whether the company is sold through an initial public offering or privately, or whether it is acquired. Given the risk typically involved, a return on investment potential of less than 15% to 20% per year is unattractive.

Capital Requirements

Ventures that can be funded and have capital requirements that are low to moderate are attractive. Realistically, most higher potential businesses need significant amounts of cash—several hundred thousand dollars and up—to get started. However, a business that can be started with little or no capital is rare, but they do exist. In today's venture capital market the first round of financing is typically $2 million to $4 million or more for a startup.[18] Some higher potential ventures, such as those in the service sector or "cash sales" businesses, have lower capital requirements than do high-technology manufacturing firms with continual large research and development expenditures.

If the venture needs too much money or cannot be funded, it is unattractive. An extreme example is a venture that a team of students recently proposed to repair satellites. The students believed that the required startup capital was in the $50 million to $200 million range. Projects of this magnitude are in the domain of the government and the very large corporations, rather than that of the entrepreneur and the venture capitalist.

Internal Rate of Return Potential

Is the risk reward relationship attractive enough? The response to this question can be quite personal, but the most attractive opportunities often have the promise of—and deliver on—a very substantial upside of 5 to 10 times the original investment in 5 to 10 years. Of course, the extraordinary successes can yield 50 to 100 times or more, but these truly are exceptions. A 25% or more annual compound rate of return is considered very healthy. In 2003, investments considered risk-free have yields of approximately 4%.

Free Cash Flow Characteristics

Free cash flow is a way of understanding a number of crucial financial dimensions of any business: the robustness of its economics; its capital requirements, both working and fixed assets; its capacity to service external debt and equity claims; and its capacity to sustain growth.[19] We define unleveraged free cash flow (FCF) as earnings before interest but after taxes (EBIAT) *plus* amortization (A) and depreciation (D) *less* spontaneous working capital requirements

(WC) *less* capital expenditures (CAPex), or FCF = EBIAT + (A + D) − (±WC) − CAPex. EBIAT is driven by sales, profitability, and asset intensity. Low-asset-intensive, high-margin businesses generate the highest profits and sustainable growth.[20]

Gross Margins

The potential for high and durable gross margins (i.e., the unit selling price less all direct and variable costs) is important. Gross margins exceeding 40% to 50% provide a tremendous built-in cushion that allows for more error and more flexibility to learn from mistakes than do gross margins of 20% or less. High and durable gross margins, in turn, mean that a venture can reach breakeven earlier, an event that preferably occurs within the first two years. Thus, for example, if gross margins are just 20%, for every $1 increase in fixed costs (e.g., insurance, salaries, rent, and utilities), sales need to increase $5 just to stay even. If gross margins are 75%, however, a $1 increase in fixed costs requires a sales increase of just $1.33. One entrepreneur who built the international division of an emerging software company to $17 million in highly profitable sales in just five years (when he was 25 years of age), offers an example of the cushion provided by high and durable gross margins. He stresses there is simply no substitute for outrageous gross margins by saying, "It allows you to make all kinds of mistakes that would kill a normal company. And we made them all. But our high gross margins covered all the learning tuition and still left a good profit."[21] Gross margins of less than 20%, particularly when they are fragile, are unattractive.

Time to Breakeven—Cash Flow and Profit and Loss (P&L)

New businesses that can quickly achieve a positive cash flow and become self-sustaining are highly desirable. It is often the second year before this is possible, but the sooner the better. Obviously, simply having a longer window does not mean that the business will be lousy. Two great companies illustrate that a higher potential business can have a longer window. Pilkington Brothers, an English firm that developed plate glass technology, ran huge losses for over two and a half years before it was regarded as a great company. Similarly, Federal Express went through an early period of enormous negative cash flows of $1 million a month.

Harvest Issues

Value-Added Potential

New ventures that are based on strategic value in an industry, such as valuable technology, are attractive, while those with low or no strategic value are less attractive. For example, most observers contend that a product technology of compelling strategic value to Xerox was owned, in the mid-1980s, by a small company with about $10 million in sales and showing a prior-year loss of $1.5 million. Xerox purchased the company for $56 million. Opportunities with extremely large capital commitments, whose value on exit can be severely eroded by unanticipated circumstances, are less attractive. Nuclear power is a good example.

Thus, one characteristic of businesses that command a premium price is that they have high value-added strategic importance to their acquirer: distribution, customer base, geographic coverage, proprietary technology, contractual rights, and the like. Such companies might be valued at four, five, or even six times (or more) last year's *sales*, whereas perhaps 60% to 80% of companies might be purchased at .75 to 1.25 times sales.

Valuation Multiples and Comparables
Consistent with the above point, there is a large spread in the value the capital markets place on private and public companies. Part of your analysis is to identify some of the historical boundaries for valuations placed on companies in the market/industry/technology area you intend to pursue. The rules of thumb outlined in Exhibit 2.6 (Criteria for Evaluating Venture Opportunities) are variable and should be thought of as a boundary and a point of departure.

Exit Mechanism and Strategy
Businesses that are eventually sold—privately or to the public—or acquired usually are started and grown with a harvest objective in mind. Attractive companies that realize capital gains from the sale of their businesses have, or envision, a harvest or exit mechanism. Unattractive opportunities do not have an exit mechanism in mind. Planning is critical because, as is often said, it is much harder to get out of a business than to get into it. Giving some serious thought to the options and likelihood that the company can eventually be harvested is an important initial and ongoing aspect of the entrepreneurial process.

Capital Market Context
The context in which the sale or acquisition of the company takes place is largely driven by the capital market context at that particular point in time. Timing can be a critical component of the exit mechanism because, as one study indicated, since World War II, the average bull market on Wall Street has lasted just six months. For a keener appreciation of the critical difference the capital markets can make, one only has to recall the stock market crash of October 19, 1987, or the bank credit crunch of 1990 to 1992, or the dot-com collapse in 2000. By the end of 1987, for example, the valuation of the Venture Capital 100 index dropped 43% and private company valuations followed. Initial public offerings

are especially vulnerable to the vicissitudes of the capital markets; here the timing is vital. Some of the most successful companies seem to have been launched when debt and equity capital were most available and relatively cheap.

Competitive Advantages Issues

Variable and Fixed Costs
An attractive opportunity has the potential for being the lowest-cost producer and for having the lowest costs of marketing and distribution. Being unable to achieve and sustain a position as a low-cost producer shortens the life expectancy of a new venture.

Degree of Control
Attractive opportunities have potential for moderate-to-strong degree of control over prices, costs, and channels of distribution. Fragmented markets where there is no dominant competitor—no IBM—have this potential. These markets usually have a market leader with a 20% market share *or less.* For example, sole control of the source of supply of a critical component for a product or of channels of distribution can give a new venture market dominance even if other areas are weak. Lack of control over such factors as product development and component prices can make an opportunity unattractive.

A market where a major competitor has a market share of 40%, 50%, or especially 60% usually implies a market where power and influence over suppliers, customers, and pricing create a serious barrier and risk for a new firm. Such a firm will have few degrees of freedom. However, if a dominant competitor is at full capacity, is slow to innovate or to add capacity in a large and growing market, or routinely ignores or abuses the customer (remember "Ma Bell"), there may be an entry opportunity. However, entrepreneurs usually do not find such sleepy competition in dynamic, emerging industries dense with opportunity.

Entry Barriers
Having a favorable window of opportunity is important. Having or being able to gain proprietary protection, regulatory advantage, or other legal or contractual advantage, such as exclusive rights to a market or with a distributor, is attractive. Having or being able to gain an advantage in response/lead times is important since these can create barriers to entry or expansion by others. For example, advantages in response/lead times in technology, product innovation, market innovation, people, location, resources, or capacity make an opportunity attractive. Possession of well-developed, high-quality, and accessible contacts that are the product of years of building a top-notch reputation and that cannot be acquired quickly is also advantageous. In fact, there are times when

this competitive advantage may be so strong as to provide dominance in the marketplace, even though many of the other factors are weak or average.

If a firm cannot keep others out or if it faces already existing entry barriers, it is unattractive. An easily overlooked issue is a firm's capacity to gain distribution of its product. As simple as it may sound, even venture-capital-backed companies fall victim to this market issue. Air Florida apparently assembled all the right ingredients, including substantial financing, yet was unable to secure sufficient gate space for its airplanes. Even though it sold passenger seats, it had no place to pick the passengers up or drop them off.

Management Team Issues

Entrepreneurial Team
Attractive opportunities have existing teams that are strong and contain industry superstars. The team has proven profit and loss experience in the same technology, market, and service area, and members have complementary and compatible skills. An unattractive opportunity does not have such a team in place, or has no team.

Industry and Technical Experience
A management track record of significant accomplishment in the industry (with the technology) and in the market area (with a proven profit), and many achievements where the venture will compete, is highly desirable. A top-notch management team can become the most important strategic competitive advantage in an industry. Imagine relocating the L.A. Lakers or the San Antonio Spurs to Halifax, Nova Scotia: Do you think you would have a winning competitor in the National Basketball Association?

Integrity
Trust and integrity are the oil and glue that make economic interdependence possible. Having an unquestioned reputation in this regard is a major long-term advantage for entrepreneurs and should be sought in all personnel and backers. A shady past or record of questionable integrity is for B team players only.

Intellectual Honesty
There is a fundamental issue of whether the founders know what they do and do not know, as well as whether they know what to do about shortcomings or gaps in the team and the enterprise.

Fatal-Flaw Issues
Basically, attractive ventures have no fatal flaws; an opportunity is rendered unattractive if it suffers from one or more fatal flaws. Usually, these relate to

one of the above criteria, and examples abound of markets that are too small, which have overpowering competition, where the cost of entry is too high, where an entrant is unable to produce at a competitive price, and so on. An example of an entry barrier's being a fatal flaw, was again Air Florida and their inability to get flights listed on reservation computers.

Personal Criteria

Goals and Fit
Is there a good match between the requirements of business and what the founders want out of it? A very wise woman, Dorothy Stevenson, pinpointed the crux of it with this powerful insight: "Success is *getting* what you want. Happiness is *wanting* what you get."

Upside/Downside Issues
An attractive opportunity does not have excessive downside risk. The upside and the downside of pursuing an opportunity are not linear, nor are they on the same continuum. The upside is easy, and it has been said that success has a thousand sires. The downside is another matter, since it has also been said that failure is an orphan. An entrepreneur needs to be able to absorb the financial downside in such a way that he or she can rebound, without becoming indentured to debt obligations. If an entrepreneur's financial exposure in launching the venture is greater than his or her net worth—the resources he or she can reasonably draw upon, and his or her alternative disposable earnings stream if it does not work out—the deal may be too big. While today's bankruptcy laws are generous, the psychological burdens of living through such an ordeal are infinitely more painful than the financial consequences. An existing business needs to consider if a failure will be too demeaning to the firm's reputation and future credibility, aside from the obvious financial consequences.[22]

Opportunity Cost
In pursuing any venture opportunity, there are also opportunity costs. An entrepreneur who is skilled enough to grow a successful, multimillion-dollar venture has talents that are highly valued by medium- to large-sized firms as well. While assessing benefits that may accrue in pursuing an opportunity, an entrepreneur needs to take a serious look at other alternatives, including potential "golden handcuffs" and account honestly for any cut in salary that may be involved in pursuing a certain opportunity.

Further, pursuing an opportunity can shape an entrepreneur in ways that are hard to imagine. An entrepreneur will probably have time to execute between two to four multimillion-dollar ventures between the ages of 25 and 50. Each of these experiences will position him or her, *for better or for worse*, for the next opportunity. Since it is important for an entrepreneur, in the early years, to gain relevant management experience and since building a venture (either one that works out or one that does not) takes a lot more time than is commonly believed, it is important to consider alternatives while assessing an opportunity.

Desirability

A good opportunity is not only attractive but also desirable (i.e., good opportunity fits). An intensely personal criterion would be the desire for a certain lifestyle. This desire may preclude pursuing certain opportunities (i.e., certain opportunities may be opportunities for someone else). The founder of a major high-technology venture in the Boston area was asked why the headquarter of his firm was located in downtown Boston, while those of other such firms were located on the famous Route 128 outside of the city. His reply was that he wanted to live in Boston because he loved the city and wanted to be able to walk to work. He said, "The rest did not matter."

Risk/Reward Tolerance

Successful entrepreneurs take calculated risks or avoid risks they do not need to take; as a country western song puts it: "You have to know when to hold 'em, know when to fold 'em, know when to walk away, and know when to run." This is not to suggest that all entrepreneurs are gamblers or have the same risk tolerance; some are quite conservative while others actually seem to get a kick out of the inherent danger and thrill in higher risk and higher stake games. The real issue is fit—recognizing that gamblers and overly risk-averse entrepreneurs are unlikely to sustain any long-term successes.

Stress Tolerance

Another important dimension of the fit concept is the stressful requirements of a fast-growth high-stakes venture. Or as President Harry Truman said so well: "If you can't stand the heat, then stay out of the kitchen."

Strategic Differentiation

Degree of Fit

To what extent is there a good fit among the driving forces (founders and team, opportunity, and resource requirements) and the timing given the external environment?

Team

There is no substitute for an absolute top quality team, since the execution, the ability to adapt, and to devise new strategies is so vital to survival and success.

A team is nearly unstoppable if it can inculcate into the venture a philosophy and culture of superior learning, as well as teaching skills, an ethic of high standards, delivery of results, and constant improvement. Are they free agents—clear of employment, noncompete, proprietary rights, and trade secret agreements—who are able to pursue the opportunity?

Service Management
Having a "turbo-service" concept that can be delivered consistently can be a major competitive weapon against small and large competitors alike. Home Depot, in the home supply business, and Lexus, in the auto industry, have set an entirely new standard of service for their respective industries.

Timing
From business to historic military battles to political campaigns, timing is often the one element that can make a significant difference. Time can be an enemy or a friend; being too early or too late can be fatal. The key is to row with the tide, not against it. Strategically, ignoring this principle is perilous.

Technology
A breakthrough, proprietary product is no guarantee of success, but it certainly creates a formidable competitive advantage.

Flexibility
Maintaining the capacity to commit and decommit quickly, to adapt, and to abandon if necessary is a major strategic weapon, particularly when competing with larger organizations. Larger firms can typically take 6 years or more to change basic strategy and 10 years or more to change the culture.

Opportunity Orientation
To what extent is there a constant alertness to the marketplace? A continual search for opportunities? As one insightful entrepreneur put it, "Any opportunity that just comes in the door to us, we do not consider an opportunity. And we do not have a strategy until we are saying no to lots of opportunities."

Pricing
One of the most common mistakes of new companies, with high-value-added products or services in a growing market, is to underprice. A price slightly below to as much as 20% below competitors is rationalized as necessary to gain market entry. In a 30% gross margin business, a 10% price increase results in a 20% to 36% increase in gross margin and will lower the breakeven sales level of a company with $900,000 in fixed costs to $2.5 million from $3 million. At the $3 million sales level, the company would realize an extra $180,000 in pretax profits.

Distribution Channels

Having access to the distribution channels is sometimes overlooked or taken for granted. New channels of distribution can leapfrog and demolish traditional channels; take for instance, direct mail, home shopping networks, infomercials, and the Web.

Room for Error

How forgiving is the business and the financial strategy? How wrong can the team be in estimates of revenue costs, cash flow, timing, and capital requirements? How bad can things get, yet be able to survive? If some single engine planes are more prone to accidents, by 10 or more times, which plane do you want to fly in? High leverage, lower gross margins, and lower operating margins are the signals in a small company of these flights destined for fatality.

GATHERING INFORMATION

Factors suggest that finding the right idea that is a potential opportunity is most often a matter of being the right person, in the right place, at the right time. So how can you increase your chances of being the next Anita Roddick of The Body Shop? There are numerous sources of information that can help generate ideas:

- *Existing businesses.* Purchasing an ongoing business is an excellent way to find a new business idea. Such a route to a new venture can save time and money and can reduce risk as well. Investment bankers and business brokers are knowledgeable about businesses for sale, as are trust officers. It is worth noting, however, that brokers do not advertise the very best private businesses for sale, and the real gems are usually bought by the individuals or firms closest to them, such as management, directors, customers, suppliers, or financial backers. Bankruptcy judges have a continual flow of ventures in serious trouble. There can be some excellent opportunities buried beneath all the financial debris of a bankrupt firm.
- *Franchises.* Franchising is another way to enter an industry, by either starting a franchise operation or becoming a franchisee. This is a fertile area. The number of franchisors nationally now stands at over 2,000, according to the International Franchise Association and the Department of Commerce, and franchisors account for nearly $1 trillion in sales annually and one-third of all retail sales.[23]
- *Patents.* Patent brokers specialize in marketing patents that are owned by individual inventors, corporations, universities, or other research

organizations to those seeking new commercially viable products. Some brokers specialize in international product licensing and occasionally a patent broker will purchase an invention and then resell it. Although, over the years, a few unscrupulous brokers have tarnished the patent broker's image, acquisitions effected by reputable brokers have resulted in significant new products. Notable among these was Bausch & Lomb's acquisition, through National Patent Development Corporation, of the U.S. right to hydron, a material used in contact lenses. Some patent brokers are:

— MGA Technology, Inc., Chicago, IL

— New Product Development Services, Inc., Kansas City, MO

— University Patents, Chicago, IL

— Research Corporation, New York, NY

— Pegasus Corporation, New York, NY

— National Patent Development Corporation, New York, NY

- *Product licensing.* A good way to obtain exposure to a large number of product ideas available from universities, corporations, and independent investors is to subscribe to information services such as the *American Bulletin of International Technology, Selected Business Ventures* (published by General Electric Company), *Technology Mart, Patent Licensing Gazette,* and the National Technical Information Service. In addition, corporations, not-for-profit research institutions, and universities are sources of ideals:

  — *Corporations* engaged in R&D develop inventions or services that they do not exploit commercially. These inventions either do not fit existing product lines or marketing programs or do not represent sufficiently large markets to be interesting to big corporations. Many corporations license these kinds of inventions, through either patent brokers, product-licensing information services, or their own patent-marketing efforts. Directly contacting a corporation with a licensing program may prove fruitful. Among the major corporations known to have active internal patent-marketing efforts are the following:

    Gulf and Western Invention Development Corporation

    Kraft Corporation, Research and Development

    Pillsbury Company, Research and Development Laboratories

    Union Carbide Corporation, Nuclear Division

    RCA Corporation, Domestic Licensing

    TRW Corporation, System Group

    Lockheed Corporation, Patent Licensing

    IBM, Intellectual Property and Licensing

— *Not-for-Profit Research Institutions.* These nonprofit organizations do research and development under contract to the government and private industry as well as some internally sponsored research and development of new products and processes that can be licensed to private corporations for further development, manufacturing, and marketing. Perhaps the best example of how this works is Battelle Memorial Institute's participation in the development of xerography and the subsequent license of the technology to the Haloid Corporation, now Xerox Corporation. Some nonprofit research institutes with active licensing programs are:

> Battelle Memorial Institute
> ITT Research Institute
> Stanford Research Institute
> Southwest Research Institute

— *Universities.* A number of universities are active in research in the physical sciences and seek to license inventions that result from this research either directly or through an associated research foundation that administers its patent program. Massachusetts Institute of Technology and the California Institute of Technology publish periodic reports containing abstracts of inventions they own that are available for licensing. In addition, since a number of very good ideas developed in universities never reach formal licensing outlets, another way to find these ideas is to become familiar with the work of a researcher in your area of interest. As mentioned in Chapter 1, Genentech came into being because Robert Swanson deliberately searched for a leading scientist in biotechnology and found Herb Boyer at the University of California, San Francisco. Universities that have active licensing programs include:

> Massachusetts Institute of Technology
> California Institute of Technology
> University of Wisconsin
> Iowa State University
> Purdue University
> University of California
> University of Oregon

Industry and Trade Contacts

- *Trade Shows and Association Meetings* in a number of industries can be an excellent way to examine the products of many potential competitors, meet distributors and sales representatives, learn of product and market trends, and identify potential products. The American Electronics Association is a good example of an association, that holds such seminars and meetings.

- *Customers.* Contacting potential customers of a certain type of product can identify a need and where existing products might be deficient or inadequate. Discussions with doctors who head medical services at leading hospitals might lead to product ideas in the biomedical equipment business.

- *Distributors and Wholesalers.* Contacting people who distribute a certain type of product can yield extensive information about the strengths and weaknesses of existing products and the kinds of product improvements and new products that are needed by customers.

- *Competitors.* Examining products offered by companies competing in an industry can show whether an existing design is protected by patent and whether it can be improved or imitated.

- *Former Employers.* Many businesses are started with products or services, or both, based on technology and ideas developed by entrepreneurs while others employed them. In some cases, research laboratories were not interested in commercial exploitation of technology, or the previous employer was not interested in the ideas for new products, and the rights were given up or sold. In others, the ideas were developed under government contract and were in the public domain. In addition, some companies will help entrepreneurs set up companies in return for equity.

- *Professional Contact.* Ideas can also be found by contacting such professionals as patent attorneys, accountants, commercial bankers, and venture capitalists who come into contact with those seeking to license patents or to start a business using patented products or processes.

- *Consulting.* A method for obtaining ideas that has been successful for technically trained entrepreneurs is to provide consulting and one-of-a-kind engineering designs for people in fields of interest. For example, an entrepreneur wanting to establish a medical equipment company can do consulting or can design experimental equipment for medical researchers. These kinds of activities often lead to prototypes that can be turned into products needed by a number of researchers. For example, this approach was used in establishing a company to produce psychological testing equipment that evolved from consulting done at the Massachusetts General Hospital and, again, in a company to design and manufacture oceanographic instruments that were developed from consulting done for an oceanographic institute.

- *Networking* can be stimulating and a source of new ideas, as well as a source of valuable contacts with people. Much of this requires personal initiative on an informal basis; but around the country, organized networks can facilitate and accelerate the process of making contacts and finding new business ideas. In the Boston area, a high-density area of exceptional entrepreneurial activity, several networks have emerged in recent years, including the Babson Entrepreneurial Exchange, the Smaller Business Association of New England (SBANE), the MIT Enterprise Forum, the 128 Venture Group, and the Boston Computer Society, to name a few. Similar organizations can be found across the United States. A sampling includes the American Women's Economic Development Corporation in New York City, the Association of Women Entrepreneurs; the Entrepreneur's Roundtable of the UCLA Graduate Student Association; and the Association of Collegiate Entrepreneurs.

SHAPING YOUR OPPORTUNITY

You will need to invest in some thorough research to shape your idea into an opportunity. Data available about market characteristics, competitors, and so on, is frequently inversely related to the real potential; an opportunity. That is, if market data are readily available and if the data clearly show significant potential, then a large number of competitors will enter the market and the opportunity will diminish.

The good news: Most data will be incomplete, inaccurate, and contradictory, and their meaning will be ambiguous. For entrepreneurs, gathering the necessary information, seeing possibilities, and making linkages where others see only chaos are essential.

Leonard Fuld defined competitor intelligence as "high specific and timely information about a corporation."[24] Finding out about competitors' sales plans, key elements of their corporate strategies, the capacity of their plants and the technology used in them, who their principal suppliers and customers are, and a good bit about the new products that rivals have under development, is difficult, but not impossible, even in emerging industries, when you talk to intelligence sources.[25]

Using published resources is one source of such information. Interviewing people and analyzing data is also critical. Fuld believes that since business transactions generate information, which flows into the pubic domain, one can locate intelligence sources by understanding the transaction and how intelligence behaves and flows.[26]

This can be done legally and ethically. There are, of course, less-than-ethical (not to mention illegal) tactics, which include conducting phony job interviews, getting customers to put out phony bid requests, and lying, cheating, and stealing. Entrepreneurs need to be very careful to avoid such practices and are advised to consult legal counsel when in doubt.

Note that the sources of information given below are just a small start. Much creativity, work, and analysis will be involved to find intelligence and to extend the information obtained into useful form. For example, a competitor's income statement and balance sheet will rarely be handed out. Rather, this information must be derived from information in public filings, news articles, or from reports, financial ratios, and interviews.[27]

PUBLISHED SOURCES

The first step is a complete search of materials in libraries and on the Internet. You can find a huge amount of published information, databases, and other sources about industry, market, competitor, and personnel information. Some of this information will have been uncovered when you search for ideas. Listed are additional sources that should help get you started.

Valuable information is available in special issues of *Forbes, Inc., The Economist, Fast Company,* and *Fortune,* and in the following:

Guides and Company Information

- Compact D/SEC
- Compustat
- Thomas Register
- Directory of Corporate Affiliations
- Standard & Poor's Register of Corporations, Directors, and Executive
- Standard & Poor's Corporation Records
- Dun & Bradstreet Million Dollar Directory
- Dunn's Million Dollar Disc Plus
- Moody's Manuals
- World Almanac
- Worldscope

Valuable Sites on the Internet

- Entreworld (http://www.entreworld.org)—the Web site of the Kauffman Center for Entrepreneurial Leadership, Ewing Marion Kauffman Foundation
- *Fast Company* (http://www.fastcompany.com)
- Securities Data (http://www.securitiesdata.com)

- Ernst & Young (http://www.ey.com)
- Global Access—SEC documents through a subscription-based Web site (http://www.disclosure.com)
- *INC.* magazine (http://www.inc.com)

Journal Articles via Computerized Indexes

- Dow Jones News
- FirstSearch
- Ethnic News Watch
- LEXIS/NEXIS
- *New York Times* Index
- Reuters Business Briefings
- Searchbank
- Uncover (http://uncweb.carl.org)
- ABI/Inform
- *Wall Street Journal* Index

Statistics

- Profiles in Business and Management
- United States Countries
- Zip Code Business Patterns
- Stat-United States (http://www.stat-usa.gov)
- http://www.census.gov (This is the URL for the U.S. Census Bureau that is listed in statistics and financial and operating issues.)
- http://www.census.gov/stat-abstract (This is the URL for the Statistical Abstract of the United States that is listed in statistics and financial and operating issues section.)
- Knight Ridder . . . CRB Commodity Year Book
- Manufacturing United States
- Economic Census
- Economic Statistics Briefing Room (http://www.whitehouse.gov/fsbr/esbr.html)
- Federal Reserve Bulletin
- Survey of Current Business
- Labstat (http://stats.bls.gov/labstat.htm)
- DRI (aka Citibase)
- International Financial Statistics

- Reuterlink PC
- Bloomberg Database
- USA Countries

Projections and Forecasts

- Proquest Direct
- Computer Industry Forecasts
- Guide to Special Issues and Indexes to Periodicals
- Value Line Investment Survey

Market Studies

- LifeStyle Market Analyst

Consumer Expenditures

- The Official Guide to American Incomes
- Consumer Expenditure Survey

Other Sources

- Wall Street Transcript
- CIRR: Company & Industry Research Reports
- Brokerage house reports
- Company annual reports

Other Intelligence

Everything entrepreneurs need to know will not be found in libraries, since this information needs to be highly specific and current. This information is most likely available from people—industry experts, suppliers, and the like. Summarized below are some useful sources of intelligence:

- Trade associations, especially the editors of their publications and information officers are good sources of information.[28] Trade shows and conferences are prime places to discover the latest activities of competitors.
- Employees who have left a competitor's company often can provide information about the competitor, especially if the employee departed on bad terms. Also, a firm can hire people away from a competitor. While consideration of ethics in this situation is very important, certainly the number of experienced people in any industry is limited, and competitors must prove that a company hired a person intentionally to get specific trade secrets in

order to legally challenge any hiring. Students who have worked for competitors are another source of information.

- Consulting firms frequently conduct industry studies and then make this information available. Frequently, in such fields as computers or software, competitors use the same design consultants, and these consultants can be sources of information.

- Market research firms doing the market studies, such as those listed under published sources above, can be sources of intelligence.

- Key customers, manufacturers, suppliers, distributors, and buyers: these groups are often a prime source of information.

- Public filings: Federal, State, and local filings, such as filings with the Securities and Exchange Commission (SEC) or Freedom-of-Information Act filings can reveal a surprising amount of information. There are companies that process inquiries of this type.

- Reverse engineering can be used to determine costs of production and sometimes even manufacturing methods. An example of this practice is the experience of Advanced Energy Technology, Inc., of Boulder, Colorado, which learned first-hand about such tactics. No sooner had it announced a new product that was patented, it received 50 orders, half of which were from competitors asking for only one or two of the items.

- Networks that are sources of new venture ideas also can be sources of competitor intelligence.

- Other: Classified ads, buyers guides, labor unions, real estate agents, courts, local reporters, and so on, can all provide clues.[29]

3 ENTREPRENEURIAL MARKETING

Abdul Ali and Kathleen Seiders

Marketing's task is to identify and serve customers' needs. In essence, marketing spans the boundaries between a company and its customers. It is marketing that delivers a company's products and services to customers, and marketing that takes information about those products and services, as well as about the company itself, to the market. In addition, it is marketing's role to bring information about the customers back to the company.

Although many people relate the term *marketing* to advertising and promotion, the scope of marketing is actually much broader. The American Marketing Association defines marketing as:

> The process of planning and executing the conception, pricing, promotion, and distribution of ideas, goods, and services to create exchanges that satisfy individual and organizational goals.

Marketing practices vary depending on the type of company and the products and services it sells. Marketers of consumer products, such as carbonated soft drinks, use different tools than marketers of business-to-business products, such as network software. Companies in the services sector, such as banks, market differently from companies that sell durable goods, such as automobile manufacturers. Successful entrepreneurs select and optimize the marketing tools that best fit their unique challenges.

71

MARKETING IS CRITICAL FOR ENTREPRENEURS

No venture can become established and grow without a customer market. Quite simply, without customers, there is no venture, and the process of acquiring and maintaining customers is at the core of marketing. Entrepreneurs must create the offer (design the product and set the price), take the offer to the market (through distribution), and, at the same time, tell the market about the offer (communications). These activities define the 4 Ps of marketing: product, price, place, and promotion.

Entrepreneurs often are faced with designing the entire marketing system—from the product and price to distribution and advertising. Because it is difficult and expensive to bring new products and services to market—even more difficult for new companies—entrepreneurs need to be creative and resourceful in their marketing. Many entrepreneurs must rely on creativity, rather than cash, to create a compelling image in a busy marketplace.

Any startup or early stage venture must gain the market's acceptance of its products or services. An important part of this process is building brand awareness, which, depending on the stage of the venture, may be small or even nonexistent. Another key part of gaining market acceptance is differentiating the product or service so the distinctiveness and value of what is being sold is clear to the customer. Beyond gaining initial acceptance, marketing plays a central role in a venture's early growth stages when changes to the original business model may be necessary. Companies focused on market growth must be able to switch gears quickly and attract new and different customer segments.

ENTREPRENEURS FACE UNIQUE MARKETING CHALLENGES

Entrepreneurial marketing is different from marketing done by established companies for a number of reasons. First, entrepreneurial companies typically have limited resources—financial as well as managerial. Just as they rarely have enough money to support marketing activities, they also rarely have proven marketing expertise within the company. Most entrepreneurs do not have the option of hiring experienced marketing managers. Time—as well as money and marketing talent—is also often in short supply. Many entrepreneurs don't have the luxury of conducting marketing research, testing strategies, or carefully designing marketing campaigns.

Most entrepreneurial companies have little or no market share and have a confined geographic market presence. As a result, they enjoy few economies of scale; for example, it is difficult for small companies to make good media buys because their range of advertising is so limited. Entrepreneurs usually are limited in their access to distributors—both wholesalers and retailers. On the customer side, entrepreneurs struggle with low brand awareness and customer loyalty, both of which must be slowly cultivated.

Entrepreneurs face daunting marketing challenges. Not only is information limited, but decision-making can be muddled by strong, personal biases and beliefs. Early-stage companies often stumble in their marketing because of a product focus that is excessively narrow. Companies may assume that their products will be embraced by enthusiastic consumers when, in reality, consumer inertia prevents most new products from being accepted at all. Common marketing-related dangers for entrepreneurs include: overestimating demand, underestimating competitor response, and making uninformed distribution decisions.

Entrepreneurs market to multiple audiences: investors, customers, employees, and business partners. Because none of these bonds is well established for early-stage companies, it is imperative that entrepreneurs be both customer-oriented and relationship-oriented. A customer orientation involves understanding the market and where it is going. A relationship orientation is needed to create structural and emotional ties with all stakeholders.

In this chapter, we consider entrepreneurial marketing in depth. First, we address identifying and assessing opportunities. Next, we focus on implementing marketing strategies that best optimize these opportunities. We also look at how certain marketing skills support a new company's growth.

IDENTIFYING AND EXPLORING OPPORTUNITY

Behind every successful new venture is the story of a business opportunity that was recognized for its potential worth and profitably developed before others realized that potential. Identifying and assessing opportunity are two critical steps that an entrepreneur must take before starting a new venture.

Sometimes, an entrepreneur stumbles on an opportunity in her daily life. While serendipity may occasionally play a role in identifying an opportunity, more often it is a systematic analysis of the business environment that is required. How do you identify an opportunity that is worth exploiting?

The sources of marketing opportunity may be thought of in terms of the five Cs framework (Exhibit 3.1):[1]

1. Context: Changes in macro environment
2. Customers: Dissatisfaction and/or unmet needs

EXHIBIT 3.1 A framework for analyzing market opportunity.

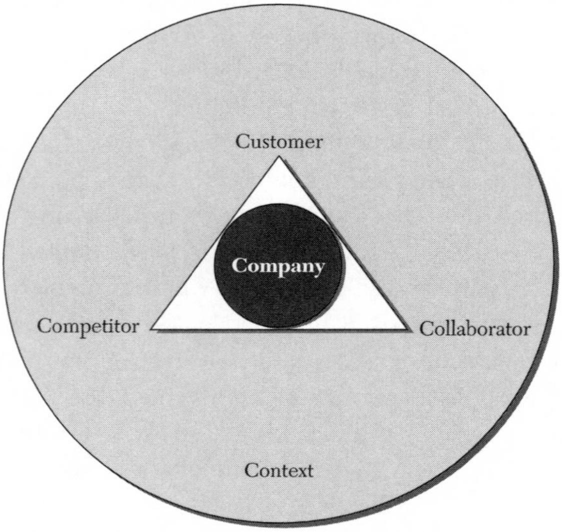

Customer

Company

Competitor   Collaborator

Context

Source: Robert J. Dolan. *Note on Marketing Strategy* (Harvard Business School Publications, 2000).

3. Competitors: Weaknesses
4. Collaborators: Control conflict and/or coordination
5. Company: Competitive advantages

Context

Changes in the political, economic, social, and technological environment disrupt the equilibrium in the marketplace and consequently create new business opportunities. For example, deregulation in the telecommunications industry helped MCI and Sprint enter into the long-distance telephone market. The advent of the World Wide Web saw the emergence of the dot-com boom. The increase in consumer affluence and willingness to indulge in affordable luxury allowed Starbucks to successfully charge a premium price for coffee.

Customers

Customers' dissatisfaction with the ability of existing products and services to meet their needs indicates an opportunity that begs for exploitation. Federal Express (FedEx) successfully exploited customers' frustration with slow and unreliable postal service to launch its guaranteed delivery business.

Competitors

Competitors' inability to adequately serve their customers sometimes opens the door for other firms to enter the market. The entry of Jet Blue into the airline industry shows that an entrepreneur can find an opportunity in a mature industry by serving a segment that was neglected by the larger airlines.

Collaborators

The availability of a new distribution channel or supplier makes it easier for a new player to enter a market, as incumbent companies may face too much potential conflict with existing channel members. The emergence of the Internet as a new distribution intermediary helped E-Trade enter the discount brokerage market while established financial institutions such as Merrill Lynch could not risk alienating their full-service brokers by introducing online service.

Company

A company should look for an opportunity that meshes well with its core competency. For an entrepreneur, personal expertise is an excellent source for a new opportunity. For example, Jim Gentes, a champion cyclocross rider, used his personal experience with bicycle racing to design a safe, lightweight, high performance bicycle helmet, called *Giro* that revolutionized the helmet industry.

ASSESSING MARKET OPPORTUNITY

While an entrepreneur may have no shortage of ideas, and may think passionately about those ideas, it pays to assess an opportunity before spending the time and effort to start a business only to see the idea fall flat with target customers. Assessing market opportunity may be thought of in terms of: *fit*, external and internal; *time frame*, including the speed of development; and *decision outcome*.

Fit

In assessing an opportunity, an entrepreneur must ask: Is there a demand for this product or service (product-market fit) and are we the right company to sell such a product (product-company fit)? Apple's launch of Newton, a precursor to current PDAs, was considered to be too little, too early and did not succeed in the marketplace. Clearly, Apple had the product-company fit but there was no

EXHIBIT 3.2   Company's position on newness map.

		Newness to Market	
		Low	High
Newness to Firm	**High**	Product-company fit issue	Maximum uncertainty and risk
	Low	Cannibalization: Size of incremental impact	Product-market fit issue

Source: Robert J. Dolan, *Managing the New Product Development Process* (Harvard Business School Press, 1993), 10.

product-market fit at that time. On the other hand, IBM's ill-fated decision to open retail stores selling its computers was an example of poor product-company fit, though there was a product-market fit, that is, customers were willing to buy computers from other retailers.

Assessing product-market fit requires knowledge of the marketplace as well as an understanding of customers' willingness to purchase the product or service from an entrepreneur. Likewise, assessing product-company fit involves considering one's own company's resources, skills, and capabilities that are needed to exploit the opportunity. Exhibit 3.2 can be used to assess the fit based on the company's position on the newness map.

Time Frame

In assessing an opportunity, an entrepreneur must ask: How much time do we have to develop this opportunity? Speed of development is a critical factor in gaining a competitive advantage in the marketplace. Obviously, the decision to speed up depends on the development risk and the opportunity cost. While an entrepreneur may have some latitude in developing a *radical innovation,* she has very little leeway in developing an *incremental innovation.* The window of opportunity for such an incremental product is short, and customers will not accept a product/service that is perceived to be "too little, too late." Exhibit 3.3

EXHIBIT 3.3   Company's position on risk map.

		Development Risk	
		Low	High
Opportunity Cost	**High**	Crash program	Challenging
	Low	No problem	100% right

Source: E. G. Krubasik, "Customize Your Product Development" (*Harvard Business Review,* November–December, 1988), 46–53.

can be used to evaluate the time frame based on the company's position on the risk/cost map.

Decision Outcome

An entrepreneur must make a commitment to pursuing a business opportunity long before the outcome of that decision is known. Naturally, opportunity assessment should consider the potential pitfall of making the wrong decision. An entrepreneur should ask whether she is making a mistake by pursuing an opportunity with poor potential ("sinking-the-boat" error). On the other extreme, if an entrepreneur decides *not* to pursue an opportunity, is she making the mistake of forsaking a good chance ("missing-the-boat" error)? For example, Xerox's Palo Alto Research Center developed a technology that it put on hold for years; later, the technology was successfully introduced by Apple. Exhibit 3.4 can be used to evaluate the outcome related to an entrepreneur's decision to pursue an opportunity.

How can entrepreneurs know whether the opportunities they are pursuing have a perfect fit with the marketplace, need to be expedited on a rush basis, and are the right decisions to go ahead with? Our advice to entrepreneurs is: *Start on intuition, build on research!*

ACQUIRING MARKET INFORMATION

An entrepreneur needs to do research to identify and assess an opportunity. Intuition, personal expertise, and passion can take you only so far. Some studies show that good "preventure" market analysis could reduce venture failure rates by as much as 60%. But many entrepreneurs tend to ignore negative market information because of their strong commitment to their idea.

We define marketing research as the collection and analysis of any reliable information that improves managerial decisions. Questions that marketing

EXHIBIT 3.4   Decision-outcome analysis.

		Outcome/Performance	
		Bad	**Good**
Strategic Decision	**Go**	Type I error°	Right decision
	No-Go	Right decision	Type II error°

° In statistics, "sinking-the-boat" error is referred to as "error of commission" or Type I error, and "missing-the-boat" error is defined as "error of omission" or Type II error.

research can be used to answer include: What product attributes are important to customers? How is customers' willingness to buy influenced by product design, pricing, and communications? Where do customers buy this kind of product? How is the market likely to change in the future?

Both traditional and nontraditional marketing research can be used to assess opportunity. Often entrepreneurs do not conduct extensive marketing research because of time and resource constraints. However, entrepreneurs can overcome some of these constraints by being creative in collecting information.

There are two basic types of market data: *secondary data,* which is gathered from already published sources, like an industry association study or census reports, and *primary data,* which is collected specifically for a particular purpose through surveys, focus groups, or experiments.

A great deal of market information can be acquired from secondary resources. Since secondary research requires less time and money than primary research, we recommend that entrepreneurs first try to find the information with secondary sources. Some successful entrepreneurs use databases at college libraries to collect baseline information about product and geographic markets.

For primary research, entrepreneurs may have faculty members from business schools assign the company's project to a student team. For example, most marketing research classes are structured so that the students do a real-world project as part of the course requirement. However, quality and time considerations may be such that entrepreneurs will choose marketing research firms for primary research. Some types of primary data can be collected easily, as with personal interviews or focus groups, but the limitations of such data, such as lack of statistical significance, must be recognized.

EXHIBIT 3.5   Focus group overview.

Stage	Examples of Effective Questions
Introduction	• Think of last time you purchased Product X, what prompted to triggered this activity?
	• How often do you use X?
Rapport building	• What are some of the reasons for so many products in this industry?
In-depth investigation	• Here is a new idea about this market. In what ways is this idea different from what you see in the marketplace?
	• What features are missing from this new product?
	• What would you need to know about this idea in order to accept it?
Closure	• Is this focus group discussion what you expected?

EXHIBIT 3.6   Understanding the customer choice process.

Provider	Customer
Create and capture value	Awareness
—Product /service features	↓
—Price	Perceptions
Deliver and communicate value	↓
—Availability	Preferences
—Advertising	↓
—Sales force	Choice
—Public relation	↓
—Guerrilla marketing	Satisfaction/loyalty

The Appendix at the end of this chapter provides a checklist of possible questions that an entrepreneur can address in a customer interview format. Such an interview can be structured as one-on-one or as a focus group. In focus groups, 5 to 10 people, moderated by a discussion leader, are encouraged to express views related to the company's products or services. The focus group has distinct stages and you need to ask specific questions to get quality information from the group participants. Exhibit 3.5 displays these stages and the techniques used to ask effective questions.

The proof that an opportunity is worth pursuing is in customers' acceptance of the idea that an entrepreneur wants to sell. Entrepreneurs must understand the customer decision-making process and how they can influence a customer's choice. Exhibit 3.6 provides an illustration of the role marketing tools play in affecting the customer choice process.

DEVELOPING AND IMPLEMENTING MARKETING STRATEGY

Any company's marketing strategy must be closely aligned with its resources and capabilities. For an entrepreneurial company, this is particularly important because, with limited resources, there is little room for strategic mistakes or failure. Segmentation, targeting, and positioning are key marketing dimensions that set the strategic framework. We begin this section by discussing these three activities and their role in marketing strategy. Then we examine the widely studied marketing elements known as the marketing mix: product, price, distribution (place), and communications (promotion).

Segmentation, Targeting, and Positioning

Segmentation and *targeting* are the processes used to identify the "right" customers for a company's products and services. A segment is a group of customers, defined by certain common characteristics that may be demographic or *psychographic* (commonly called *lifestyle*) in nature. Demographic characteristics include age, education, gender, and income; lifestyle characteristics include descriptors like active, individualistic, risk-taking, and time-pressured. The segmentation process involves identifying the most relevant *bases* (characteristics) for segmentation and then developing segment profiles. It is common to define a segment using a combination of demographic and lifestyle characteristics, for example high-income, sophisticated, baby boomers. Marketers also segment customers based on where they live (geography), how often they use a product (usage rates), and what they value in a product (product attribute preferences).

Targeting involves comparing the attractiveness of various segments and then selecting the most attractive, which becomes the target segment, also called the target market. Target market definition is essential because it is the means by which companies engage in *customer selection.* The attractiveness of a segment is related to its size, growth rate, and profit potential. Targeting decisions should also be influenced by a company's specific capabilities and long-term goals. Accurate targeting is important for entrepreneurs: it is not always apparent which customer segment(s) represents the best target market, but because of resource constraints, identifying the appropriate target market early on is critical. Pursuing multiple targets or waiting for one to emerge is an expensive strategy.

To illustrate segmentation and targeting, we offer the example of Nantucket Nectars, the new-age beverage company founded by marketing-savvy entrepreneurs, Tom Scott and Tom First. Relevant segment characteristics for this company are age, individualism, and health-consciousness. In Nantucket Nectars' early days, its primary target market was young, active, health-oriented consumers who enjoyed breaking with conformity by choosing a noncarbonated soft drink alternative.

While segmentation and targeting are performed in relation to a company's customers, *positioning* is performed in relation to competitors. Positioning relates to customers' *perceptions* about the entrepreneur's product rather than what the entrepreneur believes or claims about the product. Positioning usually refers to a company's offering relative to certain product attributes—the ones customers care about most. Such attributes often include price, quality, and variety, all of which can be scaled from high to low. For example, if brands of single-serve beverages were shown on a positioning map with the two dimensions of *price* and *quality,* Nantucket Nectars would be positioned in the high price, high quality (upper right) quadrant whereas a store-brand, canned cola would likely be positioned in a lower price, lower quality (lower left) quadrant.

The Marketing Mix

The marketing mix—the 4 Ps—is a set of tools used by a company to achieve marketing-related goals. In fact, the marketing mix is so basic to a company's business model that *marketing* strategy often defines company or corporate strategy. In this section, we discuss the individual elements of the marketing mix, shown in Exhibit 3.7. Our focus is on the particular challenges of entrepreneurial marketers.

Product Strategy

This element of the marketing mix is often divided into the *core product* and the *augmented product.* The core product is the essential good or service,

EXHIBIT 3.7   Marketing mix strategy for an entrepreneur.

while the augmented product is the set of attributes peripherally related to the product. For example, Dell is a major marketer of personal computers (core product), but it also provides online and telephone service for troubleshooting, repair, and parts replacement (augmented service).

Another way to look at the product variable is in terms of goods and services. Whereas beverages and computers are obviously tangible goods, supermarkets, Internet service providers, and banks are services, and offer service products, such as food shopping, Internet connection, and checking accounts. The line between products and services is eroding. Moreover, we live in a services economy, where the majority of the gross national product and new job creation is tied to services. Remember that the word *product* may refer to either a service or a good.

In using product strategy, entrepreneurs must pay attention to the strength of the *value proposition* they are offering customers, and ensure that *product differentiation* is maximized and clear to customers. They also should be guided by the *product life cycle* in crafting their strategy, and by *product diffusion theory* in assessing how fast consumers will adopt their products. Finally, from the beginning, entrepreneurs should be obsessively focused on *quality*.

Many entrepreneurs establish companies based on a new product or product line. When a new product is being developed, the company must ensure that an unmet consumer need truly is being addressed—that there is a real *customer value proposition* (CVP). Customer value is defined as the difference between total customer benefits and total customer costs. A product attribute is not a benefit until consumers buy-in to the advantage. Entrepreneurs need to know which attributes customers consider important and how customers rate the company's products—and competing products—on each attribute. Exhibit 3.8 can be used to identify the product/service attributes entrepreneurs should consider when designing their offerings.

Product differentiation is important for initial product success as well as for longer term brand building. In its early days, Maker's Mark, a sixth-generation, family-run Kentucky bourbon producer, leveraged the product attributes that make Maker's Mark unique (wheat instead of rye, 6-year fermentation,

EXHIBIT 3.8   Importance-performance analysis.

		Perceived Performance	
		Poor	**Good**
Attribute Importance	**High**	Improve	Maintain
	Low	Monitor	De-emphasize

Source: Adapted from John A. Martilla and John C. James, "Importance-Performance Analysis" (*Journal of Marketing*, January 1977), 77–79.

rollermill, open cooker, and small batch production) to build a distinctive image for the brand. For decades, the company has been able to rely on these product differences to reinforce its quality position.

A framework that has long been used to understand product strategy is the *product life cycle.* The stages of the product life cycle are introduction, growth, maturity, and decline, and marketing during each stage will be different. During the introduction stage, marketers must educate the customer and secure distribution. During the growth stage, customer loyalty must be cultivated and the brand must be built. Differentiation is important during maturity, and marketing efficiency is critical during the decline stage. Product life cycle analysis recognize how marketing requirements differ at each stage of a company's growth.

The marketing challenges that face entrepreneurs are formidable, in part, because their companies are operating in the introduction and/or growth stages of both the product and the company life cycle. Consider the example of Stacy's Pita Chip Company, a fast-growing gourmet snack food manufacturer. The company began its marketing efforts in the introduction stage of both the company life cycle, as *Stacy's,* and the product life cycle, as a producer of pita chips, a product the founders accidentally created by baking pita bread left over from their sandwich shop in downtown Boston. Stacy's faced great obstacles in entering an industry dominated by giants such as Frito-Lay. But by creating a high-energy presence at every major food trade show, where thousands of buyers would taste their distinctive products, Stacy's was able to steadily gain retail customers and shelf space.

An entrepreneur often builds a new venture around an innovative product. In our current business environment, with intense global competition and fast-paced technology development, entrepreneurs face increasing pressure. Even after creating a winning new venture, they must continue to develop new products in order to maintain a profitable market position. New product development is critical for market success. Entrepreneurship combined with innovation equals success. Naturally, entrepreneurs need to understand new product opportunities and the new product development process if they are to ensure their venture's survival.

Because new products have varying levels of *newness* to both the company and the marketplace, entrepreneurs must make different *risk-return* trade-offs. At one extreme, pioneering or radical innovation represents a technological breakthrough or new-to-the-world product. Although pioneering products may be risky investments, they may produce handsome returns. At the other extreme, entrepreneurs may develop *incremental* products that are modifications of existing products, or *product line extensions.* Incremental products are less risky to develop but typically produce a more modest return.

Regardless of the type of new products entrepreneurs develop, bringing products to market quickly—by mastering the new product development process—is critical for gaining a competitive advantage. Key stages of the new product development process are shown in Exhibit 3.9. Developing new products consumes considerable time and financial resources, both of which are in short supply for entrepreneurs. Therefore, entrepreneurs must be flexible and choose the steps that are most instrumental to their specific product development process.

Entrepreneurs that introduce products that are very innovative must be particularly attentive to consumer adoption behavior. Consumer willingness to adopt a new product also is a major factor in the realm of technology products. One way to consider this is to use the *product diffusion curve* (see Exhibit 3.10, which shows customer segments comprised of innovators, early adopters, early majority, late majority, and laggards). A number of factors affect the rate of diffusion, or how fast customers adopt a new product. If a product represents risk

EXHIBIT 3.9   New product development process.

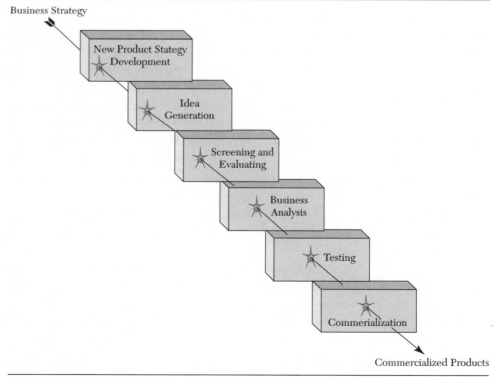

Source: Booz, Allen, and Hamilton, "New Products Management for the 1980s" (Booz, Allen, & Hamilton, Inc., 1982), 11.

EXHIBIT 3.10 Product diffusion curve.

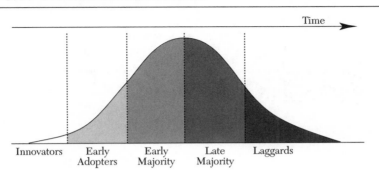

or is complex, or not completely compatible with existing products, then the market usually will adopt it at a fairly slow rate.

Entrepreneurs sometimes err in being overly product focused, concentrating on the product as they conceive it rather than as customers may want it. One way to offset the danger of this mind-set is to involve the customer in the design process. Custom Research, a Baldrige National Quality Award-winning marketing research firm, surveys each of its clients prior to beginning a project. This allows the company to learn exactly what the client hopes to gain from its investment. The practice of studying the customer upfront not only results in better service quality, but also enables the company to deliver a highly customized product.

Perhaps the most important product attribute for entrepreneurs is quality. Quality of product or service is an imperative, not only because it serves as a powerful differentiator, but because it is needed to gain the recommendation of customers and generate positive word-of-mouth. Companies with a quality orientation also find it easier to engage in internal marketing. Employees are more enthusiastic and proud about selling high-quality products than products of mediocre quality.

Pricing Strategy

Developing an optimal pricing strategy is a daunting challenge for even the most sophisticated entrepreneurial company. Exhibit 3.11 outlines various price-setting options.

An entrepreneur incurs many costs in starting a venture. Some are fixed costs, which do not change with volume of production (i.e., facility, equipment, and salaries), and some are variable costs, which do change with the volume of production (i.e., raw materials, hourly labor, and sales commissions). The price

EXHIBIT 3.11 Pricing decision for an entrepreneur.

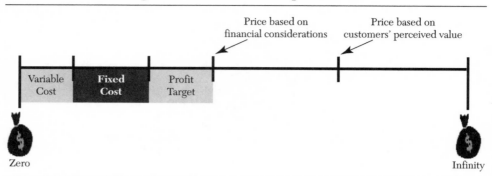

of a product/service must be higher than its variable cost or an entrepreneur will sustain losses with the sale of each additional unit. To operate successfully, an entrepreneurial venture must not only recover both fixed and variable costs but also must make a reasonable profit. The crash of many dot-com businesses bears testimony to this simple financial logic: Many of these companies followed a get-big-fast strategy by aggressively selling their products below cost.

An entrepreneur can set the price of a product/service based on financial considerations. In fact, most entrepreneurs, in setting prices, use a *cost-based method,* marking up a product based on its cost and a desired profit margin. Another method, often used in conjunction with a cost-based approach, involves matching competitors' prices. A common problem with these methods is that entrepreneurs often price too low. Pricing too low can have an unanticipated effect on the longer term profitability of the venture. Pricing too high also has a serous downside, because it can create a purchase barrier and limit sales.

What choices does an entrepreneur have relative to identifying the most appropriate price? An alternative to cost-based and competitive pricing is *perceived value pricing,* that is especially viable for pricing a new or innovative product or service. Entrepreneurs also can pursue strategies that trade off high profit margins for high sales, or vice versa. Determining the full value of a product/service and then using effective communications to convince target customers to pay for that value are challenging tasks even for an established company.

If possible, entrepreneurs should approach perceived value pricing with premarket price testing, estimating the number of units that will be purchased at different price points. Two well-known pricing strategies, which represent opposite ends of the pricing spectrum, are price skimming and penetration pricing. *Price skimming* involves high margins with the expectation of gaining limited market share because prices are relatively high. *Penetration pricing* aims to gain high market share with lower margins and relatively lower prices. For entrepreneurs with a product that brings something new to the marketplace, a skimming (or modified-skimming) strategy usually is preferred. Unless channels of distribution are very well established, a penetration strategy, which generally is reserved for mature products, is hard to implement.

Price can be represented in a variety of ways. There are basic price points or price levels that are standardized or fixed, and there is *price promotion*—a valuable tool that allows marketers to achieve specific goals, such as introducing a product to a new customer market. Price promotions are short-term and use regular prices as a base to discount from; they provide a way to offer customers good deals. The use of price promotions allows a company to increase sales, reward distributors, gain awareness for a new product, and clear excess inventory. Nantucket Nectars' 16 oz. Peach Nectar sells for $1.29 in most retail channels. Periodically, the company coordinates a price promotion with its retailers, and when the Peach Nectar price drops to $0.99 and the special is supported with advertising, its sales will come close to doubling, benefiting both manufacturer and retailer.

Price promotions often are necessary to maintain good relationships with distributors: both wholesalers and retailers must offer price promotions in order to stay competitive. Price promotions also are widely used in business-to-business markets; for example, companies often reward their business customers with volume discounts applied to the ongoing purchase of particular goods and services. Promotions are an important tool for entrepreneurs, who often use them to gain an initial position in the marketplace. Nantucket Nectars used promotions to motivate retailers to make the initial purchase of their products (trade promotion) and offered promotions to the retailers' customers to motivate them to try the product (consumer promotion).

A common pricing strategy is *price discrimination,* where different prices are charged to different customer segments. Examples of this practice include the lower prices received by shoppers using store loyalty cards and the differing price structures used to charge airline passengers. *Couponing* is a widely used form of price discrimination that rewards customers who care about receiving a discount but does not reward those who don't care enough to put forth the extra effort to redeem the coupon. Couponing is used by product manufacturers as well as service companies. Coupons for discounts from retailers, rental car companies, and dry cleaners all reflect price discounting in the services sector.

Pricing is important to entrepreneurs not just because it impacts revenue and profit, but also because price plays a role in how consumers perceive a product's position in the market. Price serves as a quality cue to consumers, who often base their quality perceptions on a product's price. This is especially true when a consumer has had limited experience with the product. The *economic perspective* views consumers as rational actors who buy when the perceived benefits of a product exceeds its price. Those who study consumer behavior, however, understand that consumers' *willingness to pay* is affected by a variety of psychological factors. If a price is out of line with a consumer's price expectations, that price might be perceived as unfair.

In summary, entrepreneurs can use some marketplace wisdom relative to pricing. First, the selling effort of a product must match its price. It is easier to lower than raise prices because customers are resistant to price increases. The more established the differentiation and/or quality of a product or service, the more price insensitive the consumer—if the perceived benefits are valued. Customers also are less price sensitive when products and services are bundled into a single offer because this makes prices more difficult to compare. A good entrepreneur will be aware of both the pricing practices of competing companies and the pricing related purchase behavior of consumers.

Distribution Strategy

Distribution presents special challenges for entrepreneurs because channels of distribution often are difficult to set up initially. Exhibit 3.12 shows the structure of traditional distribution channels for consumer and business-to-business marketing. While established businesses may introduce new products, price points, and communications strategies, they usually rely on existing channels of distribution. For example, Colgate-Palmolive may introduce a new sunscreen product, with a distinctive price position and an innovative advertising campaign, but they most likely will use their existing network of wholesalers and retailers to actually distribute the product. Entrepreneurs don't have this luxury.

Finding the right channel can be far less difficult than breaking into the right channel. Entrepreneurs who want to market food products, for instance, face enormous barriers when they try to get their products on supermarket shelves. Most supermarkets are national chains that charge large slotting allowances—fees manufacturers must pay to, in effect, lease shelfspace. Even when brokers and distributors accept new products into their lines, they may be unwilling to dedicate much effort to selling them when the products are unknown.

Distribution can be problematic for entrepreneurial service companies as well as for those that manufacture goods. Distribution decisions for a service

EXHIBIT 3.12 Traditional distribution channels.

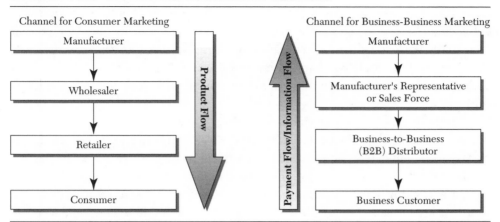

company often are location decisions; because many services require that service providers interact directly with customers, services tend to be local in nature. Effective distribution is the availability and accessibility of a service to its target customers. As early-stage service companies grow, new locations often are the most important means of attracting new customers and increasing sales.

Starbucks is an international services-sector company with thousands of stores; nevertheless, the service is sold locally, and one location may be more or less successful than another. If a Starbucks location is unsuccessful, the company can cancel its lease and open an alternative location in that neighborhood, or focus on locations in other neighborhoods. But if an entrepreneur makes a bad location decision for his or her first or second or third location, the financial loss can paralyze the company.

Finding the Right Channel Design

Poor distribution decisions have haunted many entrepreneurial companies. Dell Computer, in its early years, became worried about the limitations of its direct model and decided to go into the retail marketplace with its computers. The low product margins and high promotional costs of the new channel took Dell by surprise, and the company lost millions of dollars before it quickly pulled out of the retail channel. Were it not for Michael Dell's decision to admit his mistake and execute a fast about-face, Dell might have stumbled fatally trying to make the strategy succeed.

There is a great deal of *interdependency* in a distribution channel: Each channel has a particular function to perform, and each relies on the others. Entrepreneurs especially are inclined to rely on other companies to fulfill certain distribution tasks. Many companies were able to enter the Internet retailing sector quickly because they could outsource *fulfillment*—warehousing, picking, and delivering the order—to another company, allowing them to maintain *virtual* companies with low fixed costs. There are disadvantages to this kind of outsourcing though: quality is hard to control, the information flow between you and your customer is interrupted, and longer term cost economies are harder to achieve.

Sometimes channel partners don't do what you want or expect them to do. When Nantucket Nectars' "Tom and Tom," as they are known in their advertising, became frustrated with their distributor's slow progress in getting the brand established, they took over distribution themselves. Like Dell, the company lost millions of dollars trying to change its distribution model, and went back to contracting with distributors after it found more capable partners. Although distribution mistakes such as those made by Dell and Nantucket Nectars extract a price, they also teach early-stage companies what their capabilities are and what they are not.

Channel Dynamics

Distribution channel strategy includes three types of *channel coverage: intensive, selective,* and *exclusive.* The appropriate strategy depends on the type of product or service that is being sold. Intensive coverage is used for consumer goods and other fast-moving products. The carbonated soft drink category is one of the most intensively distributed: It is sold in supermarkets, drugstores, convenience stores, restaurants, vending machines, sporting event concessions, and fast-food outlets. *Selective* distribution involves selecting specific distributors, often limiting selection geographically by establishing a dealer network. J-Boats, a sailboat company based in Newport, Rhode Island, established a dealer network in its early stage, selecting preferred boat dealers in various regions across the country. Selective distribution can protect dealers and retailers from competition, while helping manufacturers maintain prices by thwarting price competition. The third coverage strategy, *exclusive* distribution, is often used for luxury products. For example, Neiman-Marcus had exclusive rights to distribute the Hermes line of very high-end leather goods and fashion accessories, for some time.

Channel partnerships or relationships have important implications for entrepreneurs. J-Boats grew to be dissatisfied with some of its dealers but had no clear remedy because it had never established specific dealer requirements in its original contracts. Dunkin' Donuts, a large quick-serve franchisor, became frustrated with some of its franchisees that were not motivated to maintain high levels of service quality. The nature of channel dynamics is that different channel partners have different goals. Often the channel member with the most power will prevail; for this reason, *channel power* is an important concept in distribution strategy. While channel partnerships can speed a young company's growth, preserve resources, and transfer risk, entrepreneurs must be careful to not sacrifice its direct relationship with its customers. Most important, relationships with channel partners must be carefully managed and monitored.

Another widely applied concept, *channel conflict,* refers to situations where differing objectives and turf overlap lead to true disharmony in the channel. Channel conflict was a high-profile phenomenon in the early days of the Internet, when many startup companies were using the strategy of *disintermediation*—cutting intermediaries out of traditional distribution channels by selling direct. Amazon, the large online bookseller, created conflict between book publishers and distributors and traditional book retailers. Because Amazon could buy in volume and avoid the high occupancy costs retailers pay, it could offer an enormous assortment at deeply discounted prices. Independent book retailers felt deserted by book publishers and wholesalers, who did not give these traditional stores the discounts they gave Amazon or the big bookstore chains.

Entrepreneurs succeed with their distribution strategies when they have a strong understanding of channel economics. Giro, the bicycle helmet company that has helmeted both Greg LeMonde and Lance Armstrong—American winners of the Tour de France—gained initial access to the retail channel by offering high margins and selective distribution to selected bike shops. This allowed the company to maintain its premium prices and establish loyalty among experts and cycling enthusiasts. Giro's founder understood the need to make his product attractive to the channel as well as to the customer.

Current practice reflects a focus on multichannel distribution, which gives a company the ability to reach multiple segments, gain marketing synergies, provide flexibility for customers, save on customer acquisition costs, and build a robust database of purchase information. J. Crew, for instance, has been successful diversifying its store-based business to include strong catalog and online channels. But a multichannel strategy adds operating complexity and demands more resources, so entrepreneurs are wise to approach these opportunities cautiously and be careful that their timing is in line with their capabilities and resources. For example, many experts have debated the relative advantages of *brick-and-mortar* (store-based) retailing versus *bricks-and-clicks* (Internet or Web-based) retailing. As Exhibit 3.13 suggests, the companies with the strongest competitive advantage in Internet retailing, with a few exceptions, are those with already established store- and catalog-based channels. This helps to explain why so many

EXHIBIT 3.13 Capabilities needed to compete in electronic channels.

Required Capability	Level of Capability for Each Type of Company			
	Internet-Only Channel	Store-Based Channel	Catalog Channel	Manufacturer
Strong brand name and image to build traffic and reduce customers' perceived risk	Low	Medium to high	High	Medium to high
Availability of customer information to tailor communications	Medium to high	High	Medium to high	Low
Providing complementary products and services	High	High	High	Medium
Offering unique merchandise	Low	Medium to high	Medium to high	High
Ability to present products and information in an electronic format	High	High	Medium to high	Medium
Efficient distribution system to deliver products and accept returns	Low	Medium to high	High	Low

Source: Adapted from Michael Levy and Barton A. Weitz, *Retailing Management,* 5th ed. (New York, NY: McGraw-Hill/Irwin, 2004), 92.

pure Internet—*pure play*—retailers, who proliferated in the early 2000s, ultimately failed.

Many of the most serious obstacles to entrepreneurial success are related to distribution. Entrepreneurs tend to be over dependent on channel partners and short on understanding of channel behavior in their industry. It is critical that entrepreneurs take the time to learn about distribution and make fact-based decisions about channel design and channel partnerships to overcome these threats to good distribution strategy.

Marketing Communications Strategy

Marketing communications involves conveying messages to the market—messages about the company's products and services as well as about the company itself.

The marketing communications element of the marketing mix is a mix within a mix: the *communications mix* is defined as *advertising, sales promotion, public relations, personal selling,* and *direct marketing* (sometimes included with advertising). The marketing communications mix and some of its key elements are shown in Exhibit 3.14.

EXHIBIT 3.14 Marketing communications.

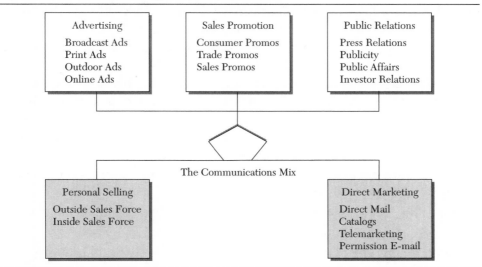

The components of the communications mix, like the marketing mix, are often referred to as *tools*. The use of these tools by marketers differs substantially across business and industry contexts. Consumer product companies' communications often involve mass market approaches, such as advertising and sales promotion, whereas business-to-business companies use more customized, interactive tools, such as personal selling performed by a salesforce. The communications a marketer uses are closely aligned with the specific type of product the company is attempting to sell as well as the company's marketing objectives.

It is common marketing wisdom that a variety of tools should be used in marketing any product or service. Because of this focus on multiple methods, and the need to integrate and coordinate these methods, the term "integrated marketing communications" is often used. A range of factors—including cost, timing, and target market—determines the selection of a company's key communications tools. The question a company must answer is: What is the most effective way to communicate with my customers and influence their actions? The sooner an entrepreneur can answer this question, the better.

Two commonly used terms to describe communications strategies are *push* and *pull*. A *push strategy* is one that aims to push a product through the channel using tools such as trade promotions, trade shows, and personal selling to distributors or other channel members. A *pull strategy's* goal is to create end-user demand, and rely on that demand to pull the product through the channel. Pull strategies, which are directly targeted to end users, often employ advertising and consumer sales promotions, such as sampling or couponing.

These strategies also are relevant for service companies. American Express, for example, can push its mutual funds through brokers or advertise them directly to investors, who then, hopefully, will request them.

Marketing communications is a broad and sophisticated field. Many of the tools that are the most visible are primarily accessible to large companies with deep marketing budgets and in-house marketing talent. This is usually the case for large, national television and print advertising and high-penetration direct mail campaigns. Probably the greatest breadth of tools exists within the domain of advertising, which includes everything from billboards to the Yellow Pages to local newspapers to Super Bowl commercials. There also are a variety of direct marketing tools, including catalogs, direct mail pieces, telemarketing, and infomercials (vehicles for direct selling). The newest communications medium, the Internet, includes banner ads, pop-up ads, and direct e-mail marketing.

Advertising

What advertising choices are available to an entrepreneur? Anything that is appropriate, affordable, and measurable or at least possible to evaluate. Entrepreneurs can use traditional major media by focusing on scaled-back options, such as regional editions of national magazines, locally broadcast commercials on cable television stations, and local newspapers and radio stations. The disadvantage for entrepreneurs is that advertising economies of scale are almost impossible to achieve. But tightly targeted campaigns can be conducted efficiently with a focus on cost control.

In addition to regionalized or localized major media, there are a number of minor media options for entrepreneurs. These include classified ads, the Yellow Pages and online information services, brochures, flyers, online bulletin boards, local canvassing (for business-to-business), and educational seminars or demonstrations. As mentioned, most marketing experts support using multiple methods in combination, in part because different methods have particular strengths and weaknesses. But even though the media are varied, the message and the brand image that an entrepreneur wishes to communicate should be strictly consistent. Two terms that are frequently mentioned in relation to advertising objectives are *reach* and *frequency.* Reach is the percentage of a company's target market that is exposed to an ad campaign within a specific period of time. Frequency is the number of times a target market member is exposed during that time period.

When selecting media, entrepreneurs match their communications goals to media capabilities. Radio is more targeted and intimate than other advertising media; it allows flexibility for the advertiser, but requires repetition for the message to get through. Television has large reach and is good for demonstrating product benefits, but is usually expensive and involves substantial production costs. Many magazines are well targeted, involving, and have a long shelf life (consider how many times a magazine may be read in a doctor's waiting room). Newspapers are good for geographical targeting and promotional advertising, but have a very short shelf life. Infomercials, which may also be considered a direct marketing tool, have production costs and a short life span, but are persuasive and good for telling the product story. Online advertising, which continues to grow in importance, allows companies to reach a specific and often desirable (relatively young and well-educated) customer market. Brief guidelines for strategic use of advertising media are presented in Exhibit 3.15.

Even entrepreneurs often go to marketing experts for advice about how to execute campaigns and how to frame an effective message. While some early-stage companies use established advertising agencies, others contract with freelance marketing professionals, many of whom have experience in the entrepreneurial domain. It is advisable for any entrepreneur to learn the basics of advertising, public relations, and marketing research to be able to select and evaluate agencies or individuals brought in to assist a company with its early-stage marketing.

Sales Promotion

The three primary types of sales promotion are consumer promotions, trade promotions, and salesforce promotions. Consumer promotions are deals that are offered directly to consumers and are used to support a pull strategy. Trade promotions are deals offered to a company's trade or channel partners—such as distributors or retailers—and are used to support a traditional push strategy. Salesforce promotions are used by companies to motivate and reward their own salesforce or their distributors' salesforces.

There are two basic types of sales promotions: price and nonprice. We discussed price promotions earlier in the section on pricing strategy. Consumer *price* promotions include coupons, rebates, and loyalty rewards; trade price promotions include discounts, allowances, buy-back guarantees, and slotting fees. Types of consumer *nonprice* promotions include product sampling, advertising specialties (i.e., t-shirts with a brand logo), contests, and sweepstakes. Trade nonprice promotions include trade shows and sales contests.

The effects of sales promotions differ from the effects of advertising. In general, sales promotions produce more immediate, sales-driven results whereas advertising produces a more long-term, brand-building result. Sales promotions have become increasingly popular with companies in the past couple of decades.

EXHIBIT 3.15 Strategic use of advertising media.

Advertising Medium	Key Factors for Entrepreneurs to Consider
Brochures and Flyers	• Allows creative flexibility and focused message • Production quantity and distribution must be well planned
Direct Mail	• Permits precise targeting and encourages direct response • Results are measurable and can guide future campaigns
Infomercials	• Effective for telling a story and communication or endorsing produce benefits • Costly to produce but measurable and good for collecting data
Internet Communications	• A variety of options, such as banner ads and permission e-mail marketing • Superior for collecting data and measuring responses
Magazines	• Can easily be targeted, and involving for readers, and have a long shelf life • Offer budget flexibility but involves a long lead time
Newsletters	• Good creative opportunities and maximum control • Cost factors (time and money) should be carefully considered
Newspapers	• Best medium for advertising promotions and reaching a geographically-based or local market • Shelf life is fairly short and ads are usually not carefully read
Outdoor	• Can have strong visual impact and repeat exposure; this medium is believed to offer a high return on investment • Targeting is difficult because ads are location-bound
Radio	• Good potential for creativity and connecting with the audience; message can be easily varied • Excellent for targeting but ads must be repeated to be effective
Telemarketing	• Interactive communication with one-on-on selling capabilities • A direct response method that has faced increased regulation because it is seen by many to be intrusive
Television	• High media and production costs but superior reach; most effective way to present and demonstrate a product • Commonly used for brand building
Yellow Pages	• An important local medium used as a basic reference by consumers; necessary for credibility • Low cost but standardized format limits creativity

Source: Philip Kotler, *Marketing Management,* 11th ed. (Upper Saddle River, NJ: Prentice Hall, 2003), 601.

Public Relations

Many entrepreneurs derive great value from using public relations as a strategic communications tool. Public relations has two major dimensions: one is publicity and one is corporate communications. When Merrill Lynch published a full-page tribute to the victims of the September 11 World Trade

Center attack, that was a corporate communication designed to convey sympathy for the families and colleagues of those killed. When Merrill Lynch presents itself as the sponsor of a public television fund-raiser or a golf tournament, or issues a press release announcing the promotion of an executive, it does so to gain positive publicity. Bill Samuels Jr., the CEO of Maker's Mark Bourbon, used a personal connection and an elaborate plan to gain major-league publicity:

> Dave Garino covered the Kentucky area for the *Wall Street Journal*. Bill Jr. discovered that he and Dave had a mutual friend, Sam Walker, with whom Dave had gone to journalism school. Bill Jr. knew Dave was going to be in town covering an unrelated story and decided to try a unique approach to persuade him to do a story on Maker's Mark. Bill Jr. staged an event at the distillery and awarded exclusive rights to cover the show to a local news station. He found out which hotel Dave Garino was staying in and had Sam Walker arrange to meet Dave for cocktails in the hotel's bar. Next, Bill Jr. convinced the bartender to turn all the televisions above the bar to the local station that was covering the distillery show. When Dave saw the news footage he asked Sam what Maker's Mark was and why, if there was so much interest in this distillery, had he never heard of it. When Sam replied that it was the local favorite and offered to introduce him to Bill Jr., he accepted. Subsequently, Dave and Bill Jr. spent three days developing a story that was published on the front page of the *Wall Street Journal* in August of 1980.

Bill Jr. recalled: "From that one story we received about 50,000 letters inquiring about our product. The phone lines didn't stop ringing for weeks. We had one salesman at the time and we were trying to figure out how to best capitalize from all this publicity."

And the rest, as they say, is history.

It is often argued that publicity is an entrepreneur's best friend, more valuable than millions of dollars of advertising. This is because public relations is perceived as more credible and more objective; a reporter's words are more believable than those of an advertising agency. Also, the argument goes, public relations is free. This, of course, is not true—it takes a significant amount of time and effort, sometimes money, and always the ability to leverage connections to generate good public relations. If this were not the case, there would not be so many public relations firms charging high fees and battling for the media's attention.

Personal Selling

For companies operating in a business-to-business environment, or those that need to sell into an established distribution channel, personal selling is a core component of the communications mix. Although some companies separate sales and marketing, a company's salesforce is often its primary marketing tool. Establishing and managing a salesforce requires decisions related to salesforce size, training, organization, compensation, and selling approaches.

A salesforce is often considered to be a company's most valuable asset. Maintaining a strong salesforce is an expensive proposition, though, and startup companies often face a difficult decision: whether to absorb the expense and sell directly or hire manufacturers' representatives (reps, sometimes called brokers) to sell the company's products (along with those of other companies) on commission. Reps are advantageous in that they have existing relationships with customers, but a company has more control—and a closer relationship with its customers—if it invests in its own salesforce. A salesforce may be organized geographically, by product line, by customer size, or by customer segment or industry. Compensation is usually some mix of base salary and commission, and incentives may be linked to gaining new customers, exceeding sales quotas, or increasing profitability. Current marketing practice places a high value on selecting and retaining customers based on their profit potential to the company. The salesforce typically should have access to effective selling materials, credible technical data, and sales automation software that will ensure an effective and efficient selling process.

Personal selling is an important activity for entrepreneurs on an informal, personal level—through professional networking. Leveraging personal and industry connections is a key success factor, especially in the startup or early growth stage of the venture. But this is a time-consuming and often laborious process, which is often neglected and rarely fully optimized. Giro's founder, Jim Gentes, personally attended top triathlons and other high-profile races across the country, demonstrating his helmets and giving them to the best cyclists. Jim was ahead of his time in understanding the value of endorsements from world-class athletes.

Direct Marketing

Entrepreneurs can implement direct marketing campaigns to be broad-based or to be local or limited in scope. Direct marketing methods include direct mail, catalogs, telemarketing, infomercials, and permission (where consumers "opt-in") e-mail. The effectiveness of direct media is easy to measure, and these media are ideal for building a database that can be used for future marketing and analysis. Direct marketing is an important tool for communicating with new or existing customers, who can be targeted for mailings that range from thank-you notes to announcements of future promotions.

With the increased use of technology and databases in marketing, and the growth of the Internet channel, the practice of *one-to-one* marketing has become pervasive. This type of marketing is interactive and has qualities similar to personal selling: A company can address a customer on an individual-level, factoring in that customer's previous purchasing behavior and other kinds of information, and then respond accordingly. It is the use of databases that allow marketers to personalize communications and design customer-specific messages.

Customer Relationship Management (CRM) systems are designed to help companies compile and manage data about their customers. While CRM systems are usually large-scale and expensive, an astute entrepreneur can set up a more fundamental system to capture and use customer data to facilitate relationship building. Part of this process involves capturing the right metrics—for example, the *cost of customer acquisition* or the *average lifetime value of a customer*—and knowing how to act on them.

GUERRILLA MARKETING

Guerrilla marketing is used to define marketing activities that are nontraditional, grassroots, and captivating—that gain consumers' attention and build awareness of the company. The practice of guerrilla marketing often is linked to "creating a buzz," or generating a lot of word-of-mouth in the marketplace. Some experts suggest that traditional marketers underused public relations or used it only as an afterthought, thus opening the door for creative guerrilla marketers.

It is easier to define what guerrilla marketing *does* than what it *is*. Guerrilla marketing is heard above the noise in the marketplace and makes a unique impact: it makes people talk about the product and the company, effectively becoming "missionaries" for the brand. It creates drama and interest and positive *affect,* or emotion: all pretty amazing results. But in fact, truly good guerrilla marketing is as difficult—maybe more—than good traditional marketing because many companies are trying to do it, and it is hard to break free of the pack.

Guerrilla marketing may be best understood as *tactics* that can be applied to various media or elements of the communications mix rather than as entirely different communications tools. Guerrilla tactics can be used in advertising (eye-catching posters in subways) and in personal selling (creative canvassing at a trade show), but they most often are used as a form of public relations—as tactics that garner visibility and positive publicity. The president of Maker's Mark practiced guerrilla marketing when he inspired the *Wall Street Journal*'s reporter to write the story of his bourbon. Nantucket Nectars' Tom and Tom were relentless guerrilla marketers, dressing up like grapes and making a stir on the

Cape Cod Highway on Memorial Day weekend as thousands of motorists were stuck in traffic, and sending purple vans to outdoor concerts to distribute free juice before it became common practice.

Much of what is now called *event marketing* is in the realm of guerrilla marketing because it is experiential, interactive, and light-hearted. But as noted, guerrilla tactics are becoming more and more difficult to execute because every corporate marketing executive is trying to succeed at guerrilla marketing and has a much larger budget to do so.

Sony Ericsson Mobile executed a guerrilla marketing campaign in New York City that involved trained actors and actresses pretending to be tourists and asking people passing by to snap a picture with the company's new mobile phone/digital camera product. Deceptive? Yes, but too commonplace a tactic to be truly controversial.

An elaborate guerrilla marketing campaign in Toronto, Canada, designed to promote an HBO comedy series, featured street teams with TV-equipped backpacks to show pedestrians 30-second promotional clips, chalk drawings promoting the series at major intersections, and ads in the bathrooms of major media agencies, showcasing giant quotes from reviews of the show.

The attempt by large corporations and advertising agencies to set the standard for guerrilla marketing makes these tactics less accessible to small companies. Still, as long as entrepreneurs are sparked with creativity, guerrilla successes will be possible, even though they require a continuous stream of ideas and energy.

In conclusion, entrepreneurs who create successful marketing strategies must have a clear vision of their goal. They also must understand how one strategic element affects another, because if the marketing mix elements of product, price, distribution, and communications are not perfectly compatible—if the mix is not internally logical—the strategy will not work. Even a good beginning strategy is not enough, however, because the marketplace is dynamic and entrepreneurial companies, more than more mature business, are compelled to constantly reevaluate strategy and how it is affecting growth.

MARKETING SKILLS FOR MANAGING GROWTH

It is beyond the scope of this chapter to offer a comprehensive discussion of the next step: the marketing processes and capabilities a young company needs to pursue strong growth. However, we suggest that two key areas of focus are *understanding and listening to customers* and *building a visible and enduring brand.*

Understanding and Listening to the Customer

Although intuition-based decision making can work well initially for some entrepreneurs, intuition has its limitations. Entrepreneurs must be in constant touch with their customers as they grow their companies. When a company decides to introduce its second product or open a new location, for example, it needs to be able to determine whether that product or location will be welcomed in the marketplace. Entrepreneurs with a successful first product or location often overestimate demand for the second, sometimes because their confidence encourages them to over-rely on their own intuition.

Entrepreneurs must obtain information that will allow them to understand consumer buying behavior and customer expectations related to product design, pricing, and distribution. They also need information about the best way to communicate with customers and influence their actions. Finally, they need information about the *effectiveness* of their own marketing activities, so they can continue to refine them. Marketers build relationships, in part, by using information to customize the marketing mix. Good entrepreneurial marketers do whatever it takes to build relationships with customers.

Entrepreneurs involved in a high-growth strategy often need to continuously find new customer segments to support that growth. Bill Samuels Jr. recognized that for Maker's Mark to grow significantly, a new segment would need to be reached: drinkers of other types of alcohol would need to be switched to bourbon (and to Maker's Mark) because the bourbon connoisseur market was near saturation. Rather than relying on his own intuition, Samuels studied the consumer market to understand where he would find his new customers and how he would attract them.

There are a number of ways to listen to customers; some involve formal research, and others involve informal systems for soliciting information and scanning the market environment. Leonard Berry cites a portfolio of methods that entrepreneurs can use to build a *listening system.*[2] These include:

- *Transactional surveys*: To measure customer satisfaction with the company
- *New and lost customer surveys:* To see why customers choose or leave the firm
- *Focus group interviews:* To gain information on specific topics
- *Customer advisory panels:* To get periodic feedback and advice from customers
- *Customer service reviews:* To have periodic, one-on-one assessments
- *Customer complaint/comment capture:* To track and address customer complaints

- *Total market surveys:* To assess the total market—customers and non-customers

Building the Brand

All entrepreneurs face the need for brand building, which involves the dual task of building brand awareness and brand equity. *Brand awareness* is the customer's ability to recognize and recall the brand when provided a cue. Marketing practices that create brand awareness also help shape *brand image,* that relates to how customers perceive the brand. *Brand equity* is the effect of brand awareness and brand image on customer response to the brand. It is brand equity, for example, that spurs consumers to pay a premium price for a brand—a price that exceeds the value of the product's tangible attributes.

Brand equity can be positive or negative. Positive brand equity is the degree of marketing advantage a brand would hold over an unnamed competitor. Negative brand equity is the disadvantage linked to a specific brand. Brand building is closely linked to a company's communications strategy. While brand awareness is created through sheer exposure to a brand—through advertising or publicity—brand image is shaped by how a company projects its identity, through its products, communications, and employees. The customer's actual experience with the brand also has a strong effect on brand image.

Maker's Mark used its communications strategy, implemented through humorous, distinctive print advertising in sophisticated national magazines, like *Forbes* and *BusinessWeek,* to create a brand image that would help establish a high-end market for bourbon where none had existed in the past. The company created a likeable, genuine brand personality for its bourbon. Because many of the advertisements were in the form of an open letter from Bill Samuels Jr. to his customers, Samuels was able to represent and personalize the brand.

CONCLUSION

Marketing is often described as a delicate balance of art and science. Certainly, developing the expertise to be a master marketer is difficult, especially for entrepreneurs who are constantly pulled in a thousand directions. Nevertheless, the task remains: to have customer knowledge and PR mastery; to recognize effective advertising as well as effective experiential promotion. Entrepreneurial marketers must, first and foremost, be able to sell: sell their ideas, their products, their passion, and their company's long-term potential.

They must learn the skill of knowing where the market is going, now and into the future.

Early-stage companies often find it necessary to scale up or change focus. In these scenarios, competition can be a potent driver of marketing decisions, whether it involves staying under the radar screen of giant companies or buying time against a clone invasion. But successful entrepreneurs will have a strong, focused marketing strategy—a consistent strategy—and therefore will not easily be thrown off course.

APPENDIX:
CUSTOMER INTERVIEW

To whom should we ask the questions?
What possible information would be asked?
Should the questions be open-ended or structured?
How should the questions be sequenced?

General outline: (Should be tailored to meet your research needs.)

1. Opening Discussion (Introduction and warm up):

    Briefly, describe research purpose, introduce self, ensure confidentiality of response, and state expected duration of the interview session.

    Opening Statement: Think of the last time you purchased or used such a product.

    What prompted or triggered this activity? What specific activities did you perform to get the product or service? What was the outcome or your shopping experience?

2. Current Practice:

    How do you currently purchase or use a product/service of interest? How did you go about deciding on what to buy? How frequently do you buy/use this product/service? How much do you buy/use each time? Where do you buy?

3. Familiarity/Awareness about product/service:

    What other products/services/stores have you considered before deciding on the final product/service you bought?

4. Important attributes:

    If you were shopping for such a product, what would you look for? What is important? What characteristic(s) are important to you?

5. Perception of respondents:

    How would you compare different products/services? How well do you think of the product/service you bought compared with those of its competitors with respect to these attributes?

6. Overall satisfaction or liking toward the product/service:

    Ask satisfaction level and preference ranking among competitive products.

This appendix was prepared by Abdul Ali, Associate Professor of Marketing, as a basis for class discussion. Copyright © by Abdul Ali, Babson College, 2002.

7. Product Demo/Introduction/Description:

   Purpose: Get reactions to the product concept and elicit a response that may identify additional decision drivers.

   What do you like about this idea? What do you dislike? Does listening to this idea suggest some factors that you would consider important and which we have not discussed so far? Does it change the importance you attach to different factors before choosing a product or service?

   Purchase Intent of New Product or Service: What will be the level of interest or willingness of respondents to buy or use this new product/service? At what price?

   We would like to know how likely it is that you would buy such a product or service.

   ❑ Would definitely buy

   ❑ Would probably buy

   ❑ Might or might not buy

   ❑ Would probably not buy

   ❑ Would definitely not buy

   We would like to know now how much you would be willing to pay for such a product or service:

   ❑ Would definitely pay $_____.

   Please note that comparable products are priced at $_____. Now how much will you be willing to pay for such a product or service?

   ❑ Would definitely pay $_____.

8. Media Habit:

   How do you find out about a product or service?

   What (*media*) do you read, listen or watch?

9. Demographic Information:

   Personal information should be asked at the end of the interview.

   Age, income, occupation, gender, education, etc.

   Size of the firm (revenue, total full-time staff, R&D staff), resources, experience, skills, and so on.

10. Wrap-Up:

   Any final comments or ideas?

   Thank you for your time.

4 WRITING A BUSINESS PLAN[1]
Andrew Zacharakis

The purpose of a business plan is to tell a story; the story of your business. The plan must establish that there is an opportunity worth exploiting and must then describe the details of how this will be accomplished. During the dot-com boom of the late 1990s, many entrepreneurs and venture capitalists questioned the importance of the business plan. Typical of this hyper-startup phase are stories like that of James Walker who generated financing on a 10-day-old company based on "a bunch of bullet points on a piece of paper." He stated, "It has to happen quick in the hyper-competitive wireless-Internet-technology world. There's a revolution every year and a half now."[2] The implication was simple. Business plans took time; time that entrepreneurs didn't have.

Media stories abounded of the whiz kid college dropout who received venture capital, zoomed to an IPO, and cashed out a multimillionaire in 18 months or less. The folklore of the dot-com entrepreneur was that he or she didn't have a business plan, only a couple of PowerPoint slides. That was all it took to identify the opportunity, secure venture backing, and go public. Why spend the weeks of effort that a solid business plan often takes? The Nasdaq crash of April 2000 and the subsequent demise of many high-flying dot-coms revealed that the majority of these businesses never had the potential to derive profits—not then, not now, and not anytime in the future. The easy money and quick returns of the late 1990s have disappeared. Today, entrepreneurial gold is found by executing on solid business plans targeted at significant, well-researched market opportunities.

There is a common misperception that a business plan is primarily used for raising capital. Although a good business plan assists in raising capital, the primary purpose of the process is to help entrepreneurs gain a deeper understanding of the opportunity they are envisioning. Many would-be entrepreneurs doggedly pursue ideas that will never be profitable because they lack a deep understanding of the business model. A relatively little time spent developing a sound business plan can save thousands or even millions of dollars that might be wasted on a wild goose chase. For example, if a person makes $100,000 per year, spending 200 hours on a business plan equates to a $10,000 investment in time spent ($50/hour times 200 hours). However, launching a flawed business concept can quickly accelerate into millions in spent capital. Most entrepreneurial ventures raise enough money to survive two years even if the business will ultimately fail. Assuming the only expense is the time value of the lead entrepreneur, a two-year investment equates to $200,000, not to mention the lost opportunity cost and the likelihood that other employees were hired and paid and that other expenses were incurred. Do yourself and your company a favor and spend the time and money up front.

The business plan *process* helps the entrepreneur shape her original vision into a better opportunity by raising critical questions, researching answers for those questions, and then answering them. For example, one question that every entrepreneur needs to answer is: What is the customer's need? Conversations with customers and other trusted advisors assist in better targeting product offerings to what customers need and want. This prestartup work saves untold effort and money that an entrepreneur might spend trying to reshape the product after the business has been launched. While all businesses adjust their offerings based on customer feedback, the business plan process helps the entrepreneur to anticipate some of these adjustments in advance of the initial launch.

Perhaps the greatest benefit of the business plan process is that it allows the entrepreneur to articulate the business opportunity to various stakeholders in the most effective manner. The plan provides the background so the entrepreneur can communicate the upside potential and attract equity investment. The business plan provides the validation needed to convince potential employees to leave their current jobs for the uncertain future of a new venture. It is also the instrument that can secure a strategic partner, key customer, or supplier. In short, the business plan provides the entrepreneur with the deep understanding she needs to answer the critical questions that various stakeholders will ask. Completing a well-founded business plan gives the entrepreneur credibility in the eyes of various stakeholders.

TYPES OF PLANS

A business plan can take a number of forms depending on its purpose. Each form requires the same level of effort and leads to the same conclusions, but the final document is crafted differently depending on who uses it and when they use it. For instance, when you are introducing your concept to a potential investor, you might send her a short, concise summary plan. As the investor's interest grows and she wants to more fully investigate the concept, the investor may ask for a more detailed plan. Even though the equity boom of the late 1990s essentially equated entrepreneurship with venture capital, a business plan serves so much more than the needs of potential investors. Employees, strategic partners, financiers, and board members all may find use for a well-developed business plan. Most importantly, the entrepreneur herself gains immeasurably from the business planning process because it allows her to not only run the company better, but also to clearly articulate her story to stakeholders who may never read the plan. In sum, different consumers of the business plan require different presentation of the work.

If outside capital is needed, a business plan geared toward equity investors or debt providers typically is 25 to 40 pages long. Entrepreneurs need to recognize that professional equity investors, such as venture capitalists, and professional debt providers, such as bankers, will not read the entire plan from front to back. That being the case, the entrepreneur needs to produce the plan in a format that facilitates spot reading. We investigate the major sections of the business plan in this chapter. Generally, "less is more." For instance, I've seen more plans receive venture funding that were closer to 25 pages than 40 pages.

A second type of business plan, the *operational plan,* is primarily for the entrepreneur and her team to guide the development, launch, and initial growth of the venture. There is no length specification for this type of plan; however, it is common for these plans to exceed 80 pages. The basic organization format between the two types of plans is the same; however, the level of detail tends to be much greater in an operational plan. The creation of this document helps the entrepreneur gain the deep understanding so important in deciding how to build and run the business.

Dehydrated business plans are considerably shorter than the previous two; typically no more than 10 pages. The purpose of this type of plan is to provide an initial conception of the business to test initial reaction to the entrepreneur's idea. It is a document that the entrepreneur can share with her confidantes and receive feedback before investing significant time and effort on a longer business plan.

After entrepreneurs complete the business planning process, they should rewrite the dehydrated plan (or what I call an *expanded executive summary*). This expanded executive summary can be used to attract attention. For instance, entrepreneurs may send it to potential investors to spur interest and a meeting. It is usually better to send an expanded executive summary than a full business plan because the investors will be more apt to read it. If an investor is interested, she will call the entrepreneur to arrange a meeting. If the meeting goes well, the investor will ask for the full business plan.

FROM GLIMMER TO ACTION: THE PROCESS

Perhaps the hardest part of writing any business plan is getting started. Compiling the data, shaping it into an articulate story, and producing the finished product can be a daunting task. That being the case, the best way to attack a business plan is in steps. First, write a short (less than five pages) summary of your vision. This provides a road map for you and others to follow as you complete the rest of the plan. Second, start preparing major sections of the plan. Although each section interacts and influences every other section, it is often easiest for entrepreneurs to write the product/service description first. This is usually the most concrete component of the entrepreneur's vision. Keep in mind however, that writing a business plan isn't purely a sequential process. You will be filling in different parts of the plan simultaneously or in whatever order makes the most sense in your mind. Finally, after completing a first draft of all the major sections, it is time to come back and rewrite a shorter, more concise executive summary. Not too surprisingly, the executive summary will be quite different then the original summary because of all the learning and reshaping that the business plan process facilitates.

The business plan is a *living document*. Although your first draft will be polished, most business plans are obsolete the day they come off the presses. It means that entrepreneurs are continually updating and revising their business plans. Each major revision should be kept and filed, and occasionally looked back at for the lessons you have learned. Remember, the importance of the business plan isn't the final product, but the learning that is gained from writing the plan for your vision. The plan articulates what you see in your mind, as well as crystallizes that vision for you and your team. It also provides a history of the birth, growth, and maturity of your business. Writing a business plan can be exciting and creative, especially if you are working on it with a founding team. Next we examine how to write an effective business plan.

THE STORY MODEL

One of the major goals for business plans is to attract various stakeholders and convince them of the potential of your business. Therefore, you have to keep in mind how these stakeholders will interpret your plan. The guiding principle is that you are writing a story. All good stories have a theme, a unifying thread that ties the setting, characters, and plot together. If you think about the most successful businesses in America, they all have well-publicized themes. When you hear these taglines, you instantly gain insight into the business. For example, when you hear "absolutely, positively has to be there overnight," most people connect that tagline with Federal Express (FedEx) and package delivery. They think of reliability—the quality that FedEx identifies itself with. Similarly, "just do it" is intricately linked to Nike and the image of athletic proficiency (see Exhibit 4.1). A tagline is a sentence, or even a fragment of a sentence, that summarizes the pure essence of your business. It is the theme that every sentence, paragraph, page, diagram, and so on within your business plan should adhere to, the unifying idea of your story. One useful tip is to put that tagline in a footer that runs on the bottom of every page. Most word processing packages, such as Microsoft Word, enable you to insert a footer that you can see as you type. As you are writing, if the section doesn't build on, explain, or otherwise directly relate to the tagline, it most likely isn't a necessary component to the business plan. Rigorous adherence to the tagline facilitates writing a concise and coherent business plan.

The key to the story model is capturing the reader's attention. The tagline is the foundation, but in writing the plan you want to create a number of visual key points. Too many business plans are text-laden, dense manifestos. Only the most diligent reader will wade through all that text. Help the reader by highlighting different key points (sometimes called catch points) throughout the plan. How do you create these catch points? Some effective techniques include extensive use of headings and subheadings, strategically placed bullet point

EXHIBIT 4.1   Taglines.

Nike	*Just Do It!*
Federal Express	*Absolutely, Positively Has to Be There Overnight*
McDonalds	*We Love to See You Smile*
Cisco Systems	*Discover All That's Possible on the Internet*
Microsoft	*Where Do You Want to Go Today*

lists, diagrams, charts, and the use of sidebars.[3] The idea is to make the document not only content rich, but visually attractive.

Let's take a look at the major sections of the plan (see Exhibit 4.2). Keep in mind that although there are variations, most plans have these components. It is important to keep your plan as close to this format as possible because many stakeholders are accustomed to the format and it facilitates spot reading. If you are seeking venture capital, for instance, you want to facilitate quick perusal because venture capitalists often spend as little as five minutes on a plan before rejecting it or putting it aside for further attention. If a venture capitalist becomes frustrated with an unfamiliar format, it is more likely that he will reject it rather than try to pull out the pertinent information. Even if you aren't seeking venture capital, the structure in Exhibit 4.2 is easy for other investors to follow and understand.

THE BUSINESS PLAN

We will progress through the sections in the order that they typically appear, but keep in mind that you can work on the sections in any order that you wish.

The Cover

The cover of the plan should include the following information: Company Name, Tagline, Contact Person and Address, Phone, Fax, E-mail address, Date,

EXHIBIT 4.2   Business plan outline.

I.	Cover
II.	Title Page
III.	Executive Summary
IV.	Industry, Customer, and Competitor Analysis
V.	Company and Product Description
VI.	Marketing Plan
VII.	Operations Plan
VIII.	Development Plan
IX.	Team
X.	Critical Risks
XI.	Offering
XII.	Financial Plan
XIII.	Appendices

EXHIBIT 4.3 Cover.

THE HISTORY SHOPPE™

Making history come to life.

Matthew J. Feczko
13333 Washington Street Suite 33
Wellesley, MA 02481
mfellows@historyshoppe.com

Dated: December 4, 2002

The components of this business plan have been submitted on a confidential basis. It may not be reproduced, stored or copied in any form. By accepting delivery of this plan, the recipient agrees to maintain its confidentiality and return it upon request. Do not copy, fax, reproduce or distribute without permission.

Copy #: **3 of 5** Distributed to: Zacharakis

Disclaimer, and Copy Number (Exhibit 4.3). Most of the information is self-explanatory, but a few things should be pointed out. First, the contact person for a new venture should be the president or some other founding team member. I have seen some business plans that failed to have the contact person's name and phone number on the cover. Imagine the frustration of an excited potential investor who can't find out how to contact the entrepreneur to gain more information. More often than not, that plan will end up in the rejected pile. Second, business plans should have a disclaimer along these lines:

> This business plan has been submitted on a confidential basis solely to selected, highly qualified investors. The recipient should not reproduce this plan, nor distribute it to others without permission. Please return this copy if you do not wish to invest in the company.

Controlling distribution is particularly important when seeking investment, especially if you do not want to violate Regulation A of the Securities Exchange Commission (SEC) that specifies that you may only solicit qualified investors (high net worth and income individuals).

The cover should also have a line stating which number copy it is, for example, "Copy 3 of 5 copies." Entrepreneurs should keep a log of who has copies so that they can control distribution. Finally, the cover should be eye-catching. If you have a product or prototype, a picture of it can draw the reader in. Likewise, a catchy tagline draws attention and encourages the reader to look further.

Table of Contents

Continuing the theme of making the document easy to read, a detailed table of contents is critical. It should include major sections, subsections, exhibits, and appendices. The contents provide the reader with a road map to your plan (see Exhibit 4.4). Note that the table of contents is customized to the specific business so that it doesn't perfectly match the business plan outline (see Exhibit 4.2) presented later. Nonetheless, a look at Exhibit 4.4 shows that the company's business plan includes most of the elements highlighted in the business outline and that the order of information is basically the same as well.

Executive Summary

This section is the most important part of the business plan. If you don't capture the reader's attention in the executive summary, it is unlikely that they will read any other parts of the plan. Therefore, you want to hit them with the most compelling aspects of your business opportunity right up front. *Hook your reader.* That means having the first sentence or paragraph highlight the potential of the opportunity. "The current market for widgets is $50 million, growing at an annual rate of 20%. Moreover, the emergence of the Internet is likely to accelerate this market's growth. Company XYZ is positioned to capture this wave with its proprietary technology; the secret formula VOOM." This creates the right tone. The first sentence tells me that the potential opportunity is huge

EXHIBIT 4.4   Table of contents.

and that company XYZ has some competitive advantage that enables it to become a big player in this market. Too many plans start with "Company XYZ, incorporated in the state of Delaware, will develop and sell widgets." Ho-hum. That does not excite me. I don't really care, at this point, that the business is incorporated or that it is a Delaware corporation (aren't they all?). Capture my attention immediately or risk losing me altogether.

Common subsections within the executive summary include:

- Description of Opportunity
- Business Concept
- Industry Overview
- Target Market
- Competitive Advantage
- Business Model and Economics
- Team and Offering

Remember that these components are covered in the body of the plan. We explore them in greater detail as we progress through the sections. Keep your discussion brief in the executive summary.

Since the executive summary is the most important part of the finished plan, it should be written after you have gained your deep learning by going through all the other sections. Don't confuse the executive summary included in the plan with the expanded executive summary that I suggested you write as the very first step of the business plan process. The later executive summary is likely to be significantly different from the initial executive summary because it incorporates all the deep learning that you have gained throughout the process. Don't recycle your initial summary. Rewrite it entirely based on the hard work you have done going through the business planning process.

Industry, Customer, and Competitor Analysis

Industry

The goal of this section is to illustrate the opportunity and how you are going to capture that opportunity. Before you can develop your plot and illustrate a theme, you need to provide a setting or context for your story. A useful framework for visualizing the opportunity is Timmon's Model of Opportunity Recognition.[4] Using the 3Ms—market demand, market size, and margin analysis—helps quantify an idea and assess how strong an opportunity the idea is. First, examine market demand: If the market is growing at 20% or better, the opportunity is more exciting. Second, we look at market size and structure: A market that is currently $50 million with $1 billion potential is attractive. This often is the case in emerging markets, those that appear poised for rapid growth and have the potential to change how we live and work. For example, the personal computer, disk drive, and computer hardware markets of the 1980s were very hot. Many new companies were born and rode the wave of the emerging technology, including Apple, Microsoft, and Intel. In the 1990s, it was anything dealing with the Internet. As we enter the twenty-first century, biotechnology has been strong. Another market structure that tends to have promise is a fragmented market where small, dispersed competitors compete on a regional basis. Many of the big names in retail revolutionized fragmented markets. For instance, category killers such as Wal-Mart, Staples, and Home Depot consolidated fragmented markets by providing quality products at lower prices. These firms replaced the dispersed regional and local discount, office supply and hardware stores. The final M is margin analysis: Do firms in the industry enjoy high gross margins (revenues minus cost of goods sold) of 40% or greater? Higher margins allow for higher returns, which again leads to greater business potential.

The 3Ms help distinguish opportunities and as such should be highlighted as early as possible in your plan. Describe your overall industry in terms of revenues, growth, and future trends that are pertinent. Within this section, avoid discussing your concept; the proposed product or service you will offer. Instead, use dispassionate, arm's-length analysis of the industry with the goal of highlighting a space or gap that is underserved. How is the industry segmented currently and how will it be segmented into the future? After identifying the relevant industry segments, identify the segment that your product will target. Again, what are the important trends that will shape the segment into the future?

Customer

Once the plan has defined the market space it plans to enter, the target customer needs to be examined in detail. The entrepreneur needs to define who the customer is by using demographic and psychographic information. The better the entrepreneur can define her specific customers, the more apt she is to deliver a product that the customer truly wants. Although you may argue that everyone who is hungry is a restaurant's customer, such a vague definition makes it hard to market to the core customer. As a man approaching middle age with a young family, I have different eating habits than I did in my twenties. I frequent different types of establishments and expect certain kinds of foods within a certain price range. The entrepreneur needs to understand who her core customer is so that she can create a product that the core customer wants and then market a message to which the core customer responds.

A venture capitalist recently told me that the most impressive entrepreneur is the one who comes into his office and not only identifies who the customer is in terms of demographics and psychographics, but who can also describe who that customer is by address, phone number, and e-mail address. When you understand who your customer is, you can assess what compels them to buy, how your company can sell to them (direct sales, retail, Internet, direct mail, etc.), how much it is going to cost to acquire and retain that customer and so forth. A schedule inserted into the text describing customers on these basic parameters can be very powerful. It communicates a great deal of data quickly.

Competitor Analysis

The competition analysis evolves directly out of the customer analysis. Specifically, you have previously identified your market segment, described what the customer looks like, and what the customer wants. The key factor leading to competitive analysis is what the customer wants in a particular product. These product attributes form a basis of comparison against your direct and indirect competitors. A competitive profile matrix not only creates a powerful visual catch-point, it conveys information regarding your competitive advantage and also the basis for your company's strategy (see Exhibit 4.5). The competitive profile matrix should lead the section and be followed by text describing the analysis and its implications. In Exhibit 4.5, the entrepreneur rates each competitor (or competitor type) on various key success factors using a five-point scale (with one being strong on the attribute and five being weak). The entrepreneur has also listed his concept, The History Shoppe (THS) in the matrix. We can see that THS expects to do well on most attributes, except for price. The rational is that customers are willing to pay a bit more for the added benefit of THS concept. To this point in his business plan, the entrepreneur has been setting the platform to introduce his concept by using dispassionate analysis of the industry, customer, and competition. By including THS in the matrix, he is foreshadowing the company section.

Finding information about your competition can be easy if the company is public, harder if it is private, and very difficult if the company is operating in "stealth" mode (it hasn't yet announced itself to the world). Most libraries have access to databases that contain a mother lode of information about publicly

EXHIBIT 4.5   Competitive profile matrix for The History Shoppe.

	THS	Big Box	Amazon	THC Web Site	Museum Stores	Specialty Web Sites
History book selection	2	3	1	3	4	3
Display of artifacts	1	5	5	5	3	5
History-related gift items	1	5	4	2	1	2
Videos/DVDs	1	4	3	3	5	2
Price	3	2	1	2	3	3
Atmosphere	1	2	5	5	4	5
Employee knowledge	1	4	5	5	2	5
Ease to shop specific item	2	2	1	1	3	4
Ease to browse	1	2	3	3	2	4

traded companies (see Exhibit 4.6 for some sample sources), but privately held companies or those stealth ventures represent a greater challenge.

The best way for savvy entrepreneurs to gather competitive information is through their network and via trade shows. Who should be in the entrepreneur's network? First and foremost are the customers the entrepreneur hopes to sell to in the near future. Just as you are (or should be) talking to your potential customers, your existing competition is interacting with the customers every day and your customers are likely aware of the stealth competition that is on the horizon. Although many entrepreneurs are fearful (verging on the brink of paranoia) that valuable information will fall in the wrong hands and lead to new competition that invalidates the current venture, the reality is that entrepreneurs who operate in a vacuum (meaning they don't talk to customers or show up at tradeshows, etc.) fail far more often than those who are talking to everybody they can. Take the risk. Talking allows entrepreneurs to get valuable feedback that enables them to reshape their offering prior to launching a product that may or may not be accepted by the marketplace. So, network not only to find out about your competition, but also to improve your own venture concept.

Company and Product Description

Completing the dispassionate analysis described in the previous section lays the foundation for describing your company and concept. In one paragraph, identify the company name, where it is incorporated, and a brief overview of the concept

---

EXHIBIT 4.6   Sample source for information on public/private companies.

Infotrac   Index/abstracts of journals, general business and finance magazines, market overviews, and profiles of public and private firms.

Dow Jones Interactive   Searchable index of articles from over 3,000 newspapers.

Lexis/Nexis   Searchable index of articles.

Dun's Principal International Business   International Business directory.

Dun's One Million Dollar Premium   Database of public and private firms with revenues greater than $1M or more than eight employees.

Hoover's Online   Profiles of private and public firms with links to Websites, and so on.

Corp Tech   Profiles of high technology firms.

Bridge Information Services   Detailed financial information on 1.4 million international securities that can be manipulated in tables and graphs.

RDS Bizsuite   Linked databases providing data and full-text searching on firms.

Bloomberg   Detailed financial data and analyst reports.

for the company. This section should also highlight what the company has achieved to date; what milestones you have accomplished that show progress.

More space should be used to describe the product. Graphic representations are visually powerful (see Exhibit 4.7). Highlight how your product fits into the customer value proposition. What is incorporated into your product and what value add-ons do you deliver to the customer? Which of the customer's unmet wants and needs are fulfilled by your offering? The History Shoppe uses retailing research by Pine and Gilmore[5] that identifies the attributes customers' desire in experiential shopping. As shown in Exhibit 4.7, The History Shoppe then illustrates how it meets the needs of the customer in each quadrant (they will have guest speakers, display historical artifacts, sell books and historical merchandize, in a pleasing atmosphere). The diagram captures The History Shoppe's value customer proposition and explains why THS believes its customers will pay a bit more for its books than they would its major competitors.

This section should clearly and forcefully identify your venture's competitive advantage. Based on your competitive analysis, why is your product better, cheaper, faster than what customers currently have access to? Your advantage may be a function of proprietary technology, patents, distribution, and so on. In fact, the most powerful competitive advantages are derived from a bundle of factors, because this makes them more difficult to copy. The History Shoppe, for example, plans on bundling product, museum-like atmosphere, educated

EXHIBIT 4.7   Customers' desires for The History Shoppe.

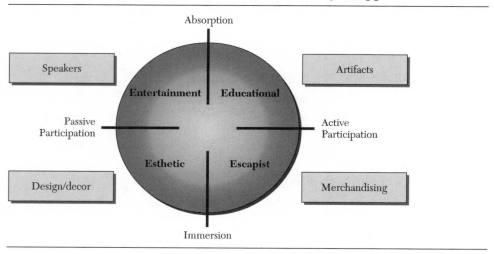

sales personnel (history buffs) with locations near historical sites. Achieving a good fit among all the items in this bundle is what will set you apart.

Entrepreneurs also need to identify their market entry and growth strategies. Since most new ventures are resource constrained, especially in terms of available capital, it is crucial that the lead entrepreneur establish the most effective way to enter the market. Based on analysis in the market and customer sections, entrepreneurs need to identify their primary target audience (PTA). Focusing on a particular niche or subset of the overall market allows new ventures to effectively utilize scarce resources to reach those customers and prove the viability of their concept.

The business plan should also sell the entrepreneur's vision for growth because that indicates the true potential for the business. Thus, a paragraph or two should be devoted to the firm's growth strategy. If the venture achieves success in its entry strategy, it will either generate internal cash flow that can be used to fuel the growth strategy, or be attractive enough to get further equity financing at improved valuations. The growth strategy should talk about the secondary target audiences and tertiary target audiences that the firm will pursue. For example, The History Shoppe plans on building a flagship store in Lexington, Massachusetts (birthplace of the Revolutionary War), and then expand to other states with strong customer demographics and important historical sites. Other industries might show grow strategies along other dimensions. For instance, technology companies might go from selling to users who want the best performance (early adopters) to users who want ease of use (mainstream market).

Marketing Plan

To this point, we have described your company's potential to successfully enter and grow in a marketplace. Now we need to devise the strategy that will allow the company to reach its potential. The primary components of this section include a description of the target market strategy, the product/service strategy, pricing strategy, distribution strategy, advertising and promotion, sales strategy, and sales and marketing forecasts. Let's take a look at each of these subsections in turn.

Target Market Strategy

Every marketing plan needs some guiding principles. Based on the knowledge gleaned from the customer analysis, entrepreneurs need to target and position their product accordingly. For instance, product strategies often fall on a continuum with the endpoints being rational purchase to emotional purchase. As an example, when I buy a new car, the rational purchase might be a low-cost reliable car such as the Ford Aspire. However, there is an emotional element as well. I want the car to be an extension of my personality so, based on my economic means and self-perception, I will buy a BMW or Audi because of the emotional benefits I derive. Within every product space, there is room for products measured at different points along this continuum. You may also find other dimensions that define continuums on which you can classify your marketplace. These tools help entrepreneurs decide where their product fits (or where they would like to position it). Your target market strategy determines the other aspects of the marketing plan.

Product/Service Strategy

Building from the target market strategy, this section of the plan describes how your product is differentiated from the competition. Discuss why the customer will switch to your product and how you will retain customers so that they don't switch to your competition in the future. Using the attributes defined in your customer profile matrix, a powerful visual is to create a product attribute map showing how your firm compares to the competition. It is best to focus on the two most important attributes, putting one on the X-axis and the other on the Y-axis. The map should show that you are clearly distinguishable from your competition on desirable attributes. Exhibit 4.8 shows the competitive map for The History Shoppe. The two attributes on which it evaluates competitors are atmosphere (is this a place that people will linger) and focus (broad topic focus or specialized). As you can see from Exhibit 4.8, The History Shoppe plans on having a high level of history specialization and atmosphere, placing it in the upper right quadrant. The competitor map identifies how The History Shoppe plans on

EXHIBIT 4.8   The competitive map for The History Shoppe.

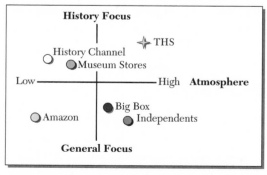

distinguishing itself from the competition. THS believes that history specialization and atmosphere will attract history buffs and entice them to return time and again.

This section should also address how you will service the customer. What type of technical support will you provide? Will you offer warranties? What kind of product upgrades will be available and when? It is important to detail all these efforts because they must all be accounted for in the pricing of the product. Many times, entrepreneurs underestimate the costs of these services, which leads to a drain on cash and ultimately to insolvency.

Pricing Strategy

Determining how to price your product is always difficult. The two primary approaches can be defined as a *cost-plus* approach and a *market-demand* approach. Entrepreneurs should avoid cost-plus pricing for a number of reasons. First, it is difficult to accurately determine your actual cost, especially if this is a new venture with a limited history. New ventures consistently underestimate the true cost of developing their products. For example, how much did it really cost to write that software? The cost would include salaries, computers and other assets, overhead contribution, and so on. Since most entrepreneurs underestimate these costs, there is a tendency to under-price the product. Often, I hear entrepreneurs claim that they are offering a low price so that they can penetrate and gain market share rapidly. The problems with a low price are that it may be difficult to raise the price later, demand at that price may overwhelm your ability to produce the product in sufficient volume, and it may unnecessarily strain cash flow.

Therefore, the better method is to canvass the market and determine an appropriate price based on what the competition is currently offering and how your product is positioned. If you are offering a low-cost value product, price below market rates. Price above market rates if your product is of better quality and has many more features (the more common case).

Distribution Strategy

This section identifies how you will reach the customer. Your distribution strategy is more than an operational detail. It can define a company's fortune as much as or more than the company's product. Much of the cost of delivering a product is tied up in its distribution. For example, the e-commerce boom of the late 1990s assumed that the growth in Internet usage and purchases would create new demand for pure Internet companies. Yet, the distribution strategy for many of these firms did not make sense. Pets.com and other online pet supply firms had a strategy where the pet owner would log-on, order the product from the site, and then receive delivery via UPS or the U.S. Postal Service. In theory this works, except that the price the market would bear for this product didn't cover the exorbitant shipping costs of a 40-pound bag of dog food.

It is wise to examine how the customer currently acquires the product. If I buy my dog food at Wal-Mart, then you should probably use primarily traditional retail outlets to sell me a new brand of dog food. This is not to say that entrepreneurs might not develop a multichannel distribution strategy, but if they want to achieve maximum growth, at some point they will have to use common distribution techniques, or re-educate the customer buying process (which can be very expensive). If you determine that Wal-Mart is the best distribution channel, the next question is: Can you access it? As a new startup in dog food, it will be difficult to get shelf space at Wal-Mart. That may suggest an entry strategy of boutique pet stores to build brand recognition. The key here is to identify appropriate channels and then assess how costly it is to access them.

Advertising and Promotion

Communicating effectively to your customer requires advertising and promotion. Resource-constrained entrepreneurs need to carefully select the appropriate strategies. What avenues most effectively reach your primary target audience (PTA)? If you can identify your PTA by names, then direct mail may be more effective than mass media blitzes. Try to utilize grass roots techniques such as public relations efforts geared toward mainstream media. Sheri Poe, founder of Ryka shoes geared toward women, appeared on the Oprah Winfrey show, touting shoes for women, designed by women. The response was overwhelming. In fact, she was so besieged by demand, that she couldn't supply enough shoes. Referring again to the dot-com boom of the late 1990s, Computer.com made a classic mistake in its attempt to build brand recognition. It blew over half of the venture capital it raised on a series of expensive Super Bowl ads for the January 2000 event ($3 million of $5.8 million raised on three Super Bowl ads).[6]

As you develop a multipronged advertising and promotion strategy, create detailed schedules that show which avenues you will pursue and the associated costs (see Exhibits 4.9 and 4.10). These types of schedules serve many purposes including providing accurate costs estimates, which will help in assessing how much capital you need to raise. These schedules also build credibility in the eyes of potential investors as it shows that you understand the nuances of your industry.

EXHIBIT 4.9   Advertising schedule.

Promotional Tools	Budget over 1 Year
Print advertising	$ 5,000
Direct mail	3,000
In-store promotions	2,000
Tour group outreach	1,000
Public relations	1,000
Total	$12,000

Sales Strategy

This section provides the backbone that supports all of the sections just discussed. Specifically, it illustrates what kind and level of human capital you will devote to the effort. How many salespeople, customer support, and so on do you need? Will these people be internal to the organization or outsourced? If they are internal, will there be a designated salesforce or will different members of the company serve in a sales capacity at different times? This section builds credibility if the entrepreneur demonstrates an understanding of how the business should operate.

Sales and Marketing Forecasts

Gauging the impact of the above efforts is difficult. Nonetheless, to build a compelling story, entrepreneurs need to show projections of revenues well into the future. How do you derive these numbers? There are two methods: the comparable method and the build-up method. After detailed investigation of the industry and market, entrepreneurs know the competitive players and have a good understanding of their history. The comparable method models sales forecasts after what other companies have achieved, adjusting for the age of the company, variances in product attributes, support services such as advertising and promotion, and so on. In essence, the entrepreneur monitors a number of comparable competitors and then explains why her business varies from those models.

EXHIBIT 4.10 Magazine advertisements.

Publication	Circulation	Ad Price for Quarter Page	Total Budget for Year 1
Lexington Minuteman Newspaper	7,886	$500	$4,000
Boston Magazine	1,400,000	$1,000	$1,000

In the build-up method, the entrepreneur identifies all the revenue sources and then estimates how much of that revenue type they can generate per day, or some other small time period. For example, The History Shoppe generates revenues from books and artifacts. The entrepreneur would then estimate the average sales price for each category. Then he might estimate the number of people to come through the store on a daily basis and what percentage would purchase each revenue source. Those estimates can then be aggregated into larger blocks of time (say months, or quarters, or years) to generate rough estimates, which might be further adjusted based on seasonality in the restaurant industry.

The build-up technique is an imprecise method for the new startup with limited operating history, but it is critically important to assess the viability of the opportunity. So important in fact, that entrepreneurs should use both the comparable and build-up techniques to assess how well they converge. If the two methods are widely divergent, go back through and try to determine why. The deep knowledge you gain of your business model will greatly help you articulate the opportunity to stakeholders, as well as manage the business when it is launched. Chapter 5 provides more detail on how to derive these estimates.

The one thing we know for certain is that these forecasts will never be 100% accurate, but the question is the degree of error. Detailed investigation of comparable companies reduces that error. Triangulating the comparable results with the build-up method reduces that error further. The smaller the error, the less likely the company will run out of cash. Also, rigorous estimates build credibility with your investors.

Operations Plan

The key in the this section is to address how operations will add value to your customers. The section details the production cycle allowing the entrepreneur to gauge the impact on working capital. For instance, when does the company pay for inputs? How long does it take to produce the product? When does the customer buy the product and, more importantly, when does the customer pay for the product? The time from the beginning of this process until the product is paid for will drain cash flow and has implications for financing. Counter intuitively, many rapidly growing new companies run out of cash even though they have increasing sales and substantial operating profit, because they fail to properly finance the time cash is tied up in the procurement, production, sales, and receivables cycle.

Operations Strategy

The first subsection provides a strategy overview. How does your business win/compare on the dimensions of cost, quality, timeliness, and flexibility? The emphasis should be on those aspects that provide your venture with a comparative advantage.

It is also appropriate to discuss geographic location of production facilities and how this enhances the firm's competitive advantage. Discuss available labor, local regulations, transportation, infrastructure, proximity to suppliers, and so on. The section should also provide a description of the facilities, how the facilities will be acquired (bought or leased), and how future growth will be handled (e.g., renting adjoining building). As with all sections detailing strategy, it is imperative that you support your plans with actual data.

Scope of Operations

What is the production process for your product or service? A diagram facilitates the decision of which production aspects to keep in-house and which to outsource (see Exhibit 4.11). Considering that cash flow is king and that resource constrained new ventures typically should minimize fixed expenses on production facilities, the general rule is to outsource as much production as possible. However, there is a major caveat to that rule. Your venture should control aspects of production that are central to your competitive advantage. Thus, if you are producing a new component with hardwired proprietary technology—let's say a voice recognition security door entry—it is wise to internally produce that hard-wired component. The locking mechanism, on the other hand, can be outsourced to your specifications. Outsourcing the aspects that aren't proprietary reduces fixed cost for production equipment and facility expenditures, which means that you have to raise less money and give up less equity.

EXHIBIT 4.11 Operations flow.

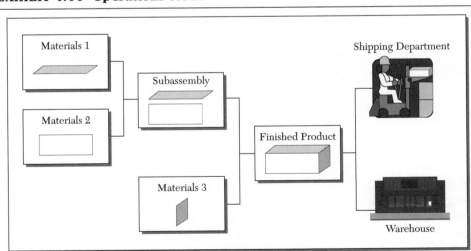

The scope of operations section should also discuss partnerships with vendors, suppliers, partners, and so on. Again, the diagram should illustrate the supplier and vendor relationships by category (or by name if the list isn't too long and you have already identified your suppliers). The diagram helps you visualize the various relationships and ways to better manage or eliminate them. The operations diagram also helps entrepreneurs to identify personnel needs. For example, the diagram provides an indication of how many production workers might be needed dependent upon the hours of operations, number of shifts, and so on.

Ongoing Operations

This section builds on the scope of operations by providing details on day-to-day activities. For example, how many units will be produced in a day and what kinds of inputs are necessary? An operating cycle overview diagram graphically illustrates the impact of production on cash flow (see Exhibit 4.12). As entrepreneurs complete this section, they can start to establish performance parameters, which will help monitor and modify the production process into the future. If this is an operational business plan, the level of detail may include specific job descriptions, but for the typical business plan, this level of detail would be much more than an investor, for example, would need or want to see in the initial evaluation phase.

Development Plan

The development plan highlights the development strategy and also provides a detailed development time line. Many new ventures require a significant level of effort and time to launch the product or service. This is the prologue of your story. For example, new software or hardware products often require months of development. Discuss what types of features you will develop and tie them to the firm's competitive advantage. This section should also talk about patent, trademark, or copyright efforts if applicable.

Development Strategy

What work remains to be completed? What factors need to come together for development to be successful? What risks to development does the firm face? For example, software development is notorious for taking longer and costing more than most companies originally imagined. Detailing the necessary work and what is required for the work to be considered successful helps entrepreneurs to understand and manage the risks involved. After you have laid out these details, a development time line is assembled.

EXHIBIT 4.12 Operating cycle overview.

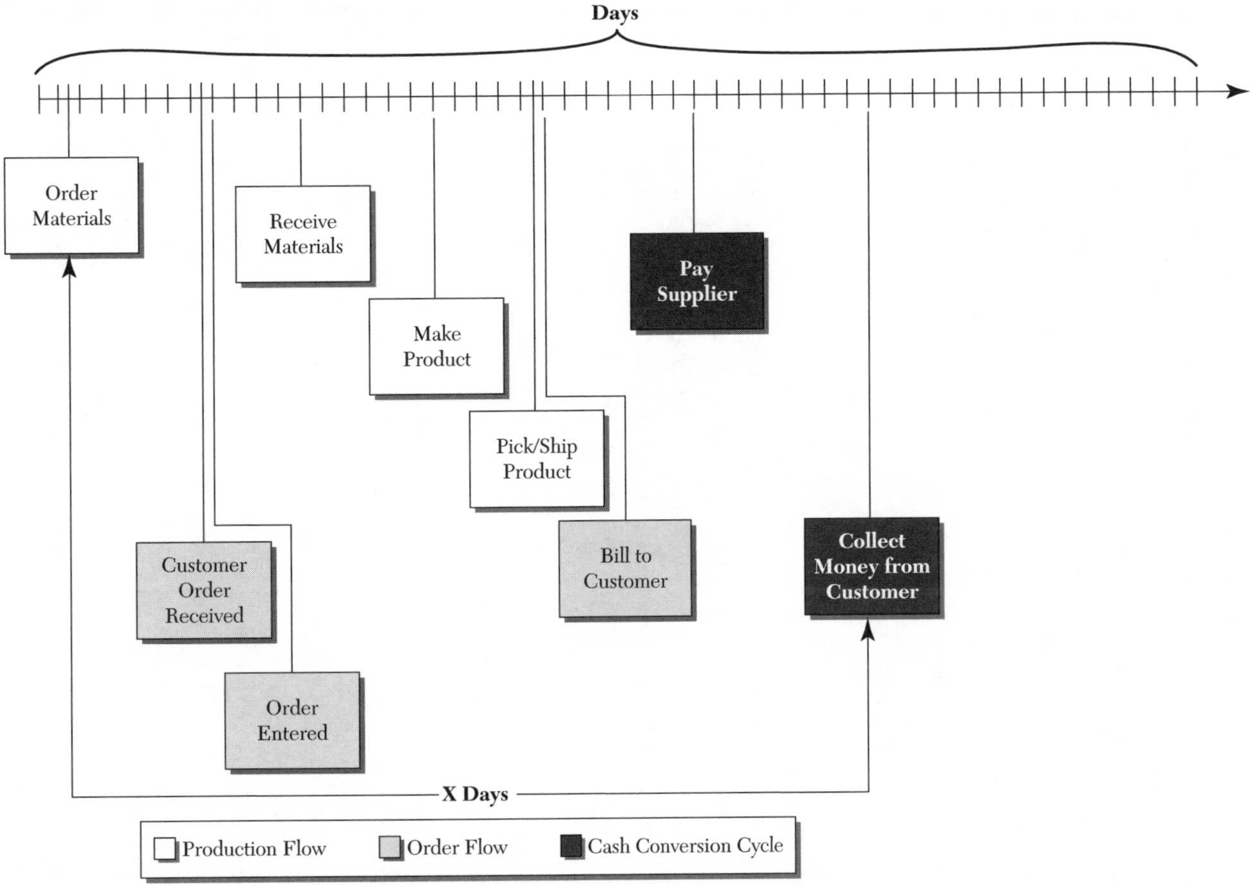

Days

Order Materials

Receive Materials

Make Product

Pick/Ship Product

Customer Order Received

Order Entered

Bill to Customer

Pay Supplier

Collect Money from Customer

X Days

Production Flow   Order Flow   Cash Conversion Cycle

Source: Adapted from Professor Bob Eng, Babson College.

Development Time Line

A development time line is a schedule that highlights major milestones and can be used to monitor progress and make changes. (Exhibit 4.13 details the steps The History Shoppe needs to take prior to opening its doors.) The time line helps entrepreneurs track major events and to schedule activities to best execute on those events. It is also a good idea to show what has already transpired as of the writing of the business plan. Illustrate which development milestones you have already achieved. It is also helpful to integrate names to the tasks. Who is responsible for ensuring that the milestone is met? For every day your product is in development and not on the market, you lose a day's worth of sales. So work hard to meet those deadlines, especially in those industries where speed to market is critical.

Team

The team section of the business plan is often the section that professional investors read after the executive summary. This section is also critically important to the lead entrepreneur. It depicts the members responsible for key activities and conveys why they are exceptionally skilled to execute on those responsibilities. The section also helps the entrepreneur consider how well this group of individuals will work together. Ventures started by strong teams tend to succeed at a greater rate.

Team Bios and Roles

Every story needs a cast of characters. The best place to start is by identifying the key team members and their titles. Often, the lead entrepreneur assumes a CEO role. However, if you are young and have limited business experience, it is usually more productive to state that the company will seek a qualified CEO as it grows. In these cases, the lead entrepreneur may assume a chief technology officer role (if he or she develops the technology) or vice president of business development. However, don't let these options confine you. The key is to convince investors that you have assembled the best team possible and that your team can execute on the brilliant concept you are proposing.

A simple, relatively flat organization chart is often useful to visualize what roles you have filled and what gaps remain. It also provides a road map for reading the bios that follow. The bios should demonstrate records of success; if you have previously started a business (even if it failed), highlight the company's accomplishments. If you have no previous entrepreneurial experience, discuss your achievements within your last job. For example, bios often contain a description

EXHIBIT 4.13 Development time line for The History Shoppe.

Activity	12	11	10	9	8	7	6	5	4	3	2	1	Open Month
10–12 Months Prior to Opening	█												
1) Finalize business plan and financials	█												
2) Review plans with local bookstores/ specialty shop owners		█	█										
3) Fill in skill gaps with advisory board		█											
4) Determine exact location possibilities		█	█										
7–9 Months Prior to Opening			█										
5) Register rights to business name			█										
6) Seek funding from appropriate sources				█									
7) Update business plan per feedback from potential financiers				█									
8) Initial contact with product vendors				█	█								
9) Contact for POS/inventory vendors and store designers					█								
4–6 Months Prior to Opening							█						
10) Determine exact store design							█						
11) Finalize product vendors								█					
12) Confirm funding								█					
3 Months Prior to Opening								█					
13) Finalize store design plans								█					
14) Open vendor/bank accounts									█				
15) Place fixture orders										█			
16) Finalize marketing plan and implement to announce store opening events										█			
17) Submit merchandise orders with all vendors										█			
One Month Prior to Opening										█			
18) Contact local media regarding placement in local newspapers and magazines										█			
19) Code merchandise category data in inventory management system										█	█		
20) Recruit and train staff										█			
21) Receive merchandise, fixtures, and complete setup of store										█			
Opening Month												█	
22) "Soft opening" of store to assess customer response, training, and system functioning												█	
Grand Opening of Store												█	

of the number of people the entrepreneur previously managed and more importantly, a measure of economic success, such as growing division sales by greater than 20%. The bio should demonstrate your leadership capabilities. To complement this description, resumes are often included as an appendix.

Advisory Boards, Board of Directors, Strategic Partners, and External Members

To enhance the team's credentials, many entrepreneurs find that they are more attractive to investors if they have strong advisory boards. In building an advisory board, identify individuals with relevant experience within your industry. Industry experts provide legitimacy to your new business as well as strong technical advice. Other advisory board members may bring other skills, such as financial, legal, or management expertise. Thus, it is common to see lawyers, professors, accountants, and so on who can assist the venture's growth on advisory boards. Moreover, if your firm has a strategic supplier or key customer, it may make sense to invite them to join your advisory board. Typically, these individuals are remunerated with a small equity stake and compensation for any organized meetings.

By law, most organization types require a board of directors. This is different than an advisory board (although these members can also provide needed expertise). The board's primary role is to oversee the company on behalf of the investors. Therefore, the business plan needs to briefly describe the size of the board, its role within the organization, and any current board members. Most major investors, such as venture capitalists, will require one or more board seats. Usually, the lead entrepreneur and one or more inside company members (e.g., chief financial officers, vice presidents) will also have board seats. The average numbers of directors for a startup is five.

Strategic partners may not necessarily be on your advisory board or your board of directors, but still provide credibility to your venture. In such cases, it makes sense to highlight their involvement in your company's success. It is also common to list external team members, such as the law firm and accounting firm that your venture uses. The key in this section is to demonstrate that your firm can successfully execute the concept. A strong team provides the foundation that conveys your venture will implement the opportunity successfully.

Compensation and Ownership

A capstone to the team section should be a table containing key team members by role, compensation, and ownership equity. A brief description should explain why the compensation is appropriate. Many entrepreneurs choose not to pay themselves in the early months. Although this strategy conserves cash flow, it would misrepresent the individual's worth to the organization. Therefore, the table should contain what salary the employee is due, and then if deemed necessary that salary can be deferred until a time when cash flow is strong. Another column, that can be powerful, shows what the person's current or most recent compensation was and what she will be paid in the new company. It is impressive to see highly qualified entrepreneurs taking a smaller salary then at their previous job. It suggests that the entrepreneur really believes in the upside payoff the company's growth will generate. Of course, the entrepreneur plans on increasing this salary as the venture grows and starts to thrive. As such, the description of the schedule should underscore the plan to increase salaries in the future. It is also a good idea to hold stock aside for future key hires and also establish a stock option pool for lower level, but critical employees, such as software engineers. Again, the plan should discuss such provisions.

Critical Risks

Every new venture faces a number of risks that may threaten its survival. Although the business plan, to this point, is creating a story of success, there are a number of threats that should be acknowledged, otherwise investors will believe that the entrepreneur is naïve or untrustworthy and may possibly withhold investment. How should you present these critical risks without scaring your investor? Identify the risk and then state your contingency plan (see Exhibit 4.14). Critical risks are critical assumptions; factors that need to happen if your venture is to succeed as currently planned. The critical assumptions vary from one

EXHIBIT 4.14 Sample critical risk for The History Shoppe.

Highly Competitive Industry

The book and video industries are highly competitive across many different channels, including superstores, independent bookstores, Internet retailers, book clubs, and specialty stores. Many of these competitors have been in business for many years, have developed significant brand recognition and loyal customers, and have substantial resources to promote their products. We believe the THS concept is in a unique position with its offering of a complete selection of historical merchandise across several product categories and its superior shopping environment. However, unexpected increases in local competition, including Internet competition, alternative delivery methods for books and video, or unanticipated margin pressures caused by irrational pricing by competitors, could have a materially adverse effect on the Company's financial results and growth plans. THS can modify its product offerings, initiate additional marketing activities, and add an Internet site if the retail store isn't generating enough sales.

company to another, but some common categories are: Market Interest and Growth Potential, Competitor Actions and Retaliation, Time and Cost of Development, Operating Expenses, Availability and Timing of Financing.

Market Interest and Growth Potential

The biggest risk any new venture faces is that once the product is developed, no one will buy it. Although there are a number of things that can be done to minimize this risk, such as market research, focus groups, beta sites, and so on, it is difficult to gauge overall demand and growth of that demand until your product hits the market. This risk must be stated, but countered with the tactics and contingencies the company will undertake. For example, sales risk can be reduced by an effective advertising and marketing plan or identifying not only a primary target customer but secondary and tertiary target customers that the company will seek if the primary customer proves less interested.

Competitor Actions and Retaliation

Having the opportunity to work with entrepreneurs and student entrepreneurs over the years, I have always been struck by the firmly held belief that direct competition either didn't exist, or that it was sleepy and slow to react. I caution against using it as a key assumption of your venture's success. Most entrepreneurs passionately believe that they are offering something new and wonderful that is clearly different from what is currently being offered. They go on to state that existing competition won't attack their niche in the near future. The risk that this assessment is wrong should be acknowledged. One counter to this threat is that the venture has room in their gross margins, and cash available to withstand and fight back against such attacks. You should also identify some strategies to protect and reposition yourself should an attack occur.

Time and Cost to Development

As mentioned in the development plan section, many factors can delay and add to the expense of developing your product. The business plan should identify the factors that may hinder development. For instance, during the extended high-tech boom of the late 1990s and into the new century, there has been an acute shortage of skilled software engineers. That leads to the risk of hiring and retaining the most qualified professionals. One way to counter the problem might be to outsource some development to the underemployed engineers in India. Compensation, equity participation, flexible hours, and other benefits that the firm could offer might also minimize the risk.

Operating Expenses

Operating expenses have a way of growing beyond expectations. Sales and administration, marketing, and interest expenses are some of the areas that the entrepreneur needs to monitor and manage. The business plan should highlight how these expenses were forecasted (comparable companies and detailed analysis), but also talk about contingencies such as slowing the hiring of support personnel, especially if development or other key tasks take longer than expected.

Availability and Timing of Financing

Cash flow is critical to the survival and flourishing of a new venture. One major risk that most new ventures face is that they will have difficulty obtaining needed financing, both equity and debt. If the current business plan is meant to attract investors and is successful, that isn't a near-term risk, but most ventures will need multiple rounds of financing. If the firm fails to make progress (or meet key milestones), it may not be able to secure additional rounds of financing on favorable terms. A contingency to this risk is to identify alternative sources that are viable or strategies to slow the "burn rate."[7]

There are a number of other risks that might apply to your business. Acknowledge them and discuss how you can overcome them. Doing so generates confidence in your investors and helps you anticipate corrective actions that you may need to take.

Offering

Based on the entrepreneur's vision and estimates of the capital required to get there, the entrepreneur can develop a sources and uses schedule (see Exhibit 4.15). The sources section details how much capital the entrepreneur needs and the types of financing such as equity investment and debt infusions. The uses section details how the money will be spent. Typically, the entrepreneur should secure enough financing to last 12 to 18 months. If the entrepreneur takes more capital than needed, she has to give up more equity. If she takes less capital than needed, it may mean that the entrepreneur runs out of cash before reaching milestones that equate to higher valuations.

Financial Plan

If the proceeding plan is your verbal description of the opportunity and how you will execute it, the financial plan is the mathematical equivalent. The growth in revenues speaks to the upside of your opportunity. The expenses illustrate what

EXHIBIT 4.15 Sources and uses schedule.

Sources of Funds			Uses of Funds		
Founder	$ 50,000		Inventory	$94,541	
Friends/family	200,000		Computers, software, &		
		$250,000	office equipment	20,000	
			Leasehold improvements	30,000	
			Furniture and fixtures	51,000	
			Opening costs	17,000	
					$212,541
			Working capital/		
			contingencies	$37,459	
					37,459
Total sources		$250,000	Total uses		$250,000

you need to execute on that opportunity. Cash flow statements serve as an early warning system to potential problems (or critical risks) and the balance sheet enables monitoring and adjustment of the venture's progress. That being said, generating realistic financial documents is one of the most intimidating hurdles that many entrepreneurs face. Chapter 5, Building Your Financial Plan, will go into detail on how to construct your pro forma financials.

This section of the plan should include a description of the key drivers that impact your revenues and costs so that the reader can follow your pro forma financials. Break the description down into four subsections. First, the Overview paragraph briefly introduces the business model. For example, The History Shoppe might highlight that the projections are based on one store in year one, growing to three stores by year five. This helps the reader understand the growth in revenues. They might then reiterate the main sources of revenues and any other information that gives a sense of the numbers behind the concept.

The next subsection should discuss the income statement. Talk about the factors that drive revenue, such as store traffic, percentage of store visitors that buy, average ticket price, and so forth. It is also important to talk about seasonality and other factors that might cause uneven sales growth. Then discuss the expense categories, paying attention to cost of goods sold and major operating expense categories, such as rent, interest expense, and so forth. Based on your description, the reader should be able to look at the actual financials and understand what is going on. The key focus here is to help the reader follow your financials; you don't need to provide the level of detail that accountants might if they were auditing your company.

The next subsection should discuss the cash flow statement. Here you focus on major infusions of cash, such as equity investments and loan disbursements. It is also good to describe the nature of your accounts receivables and payables. How long, for instance, before your receivables convert to cash? If you are spending money on leasehold improvements, plant and equipment, and other items that can be depreciated, you should mention them here. Typically, the discussion of the cash flow statement is quite a bit shorter than the discussion of the income statement. The final subsection discusses the balance sheet. Here you would talk about major asset categories, such as amount of inventory on hand, and any liabilities that aren't clear from the previous discussion.

Appendices

The appendices can include anything and everything that you think adds further validation to your concept, but doesn't fit or is too large to insert in the main parts of the plan. Common inclusions would be one-page resumes of key team members, articles that feature your venture, technical specifications, and so on. As a general rule, try to put all exhibits discussed within the written part of the plan or even on the same page where the exhibit is discussed to facilitate reading. However, some exhibits are very large (i.e., the store layout of The History Shoppe). In such cases, it is acceptable to put large exhibits into the appendix.

CONCLUSION

The business plan is more than just a document; it is a process, a story. Although the finished product is often a written plan, the deep thinking and fact-based analysis that goes into that document provides the entrepreneur keen insight needed to marshal resources and direct growth. The whole process can induce pain, but it almost always maximizes revenue and minimizes costs. The process allows the entrepreneur to anticipate better instead of react. The business plan also provides a talking point so entrepreneurs can get feedback from a number of experts, including investors, vendors, and customers. Think of the business plan as one of your first steps on the journey to entrepreneurial success.

OTHER RESOURCES

A number of resources exist for those seeking help to write business plans. There are numerous software packages, but generally the templates are too confining. The text boxes asking for information forces writers into a dull, dispassionate tone. The best way to learn about business plans is digging out the supporting data, writing sections as you feel compelled, and circulating drafts among your mentors and advisors. Nonetheless, links to some business planning software sites are provided here. The entrepreneur should read as many other articles, chapters, and books about writing business plans as possible. You will want to assimilate different perspectives so that you can find your personal voice. A number of sources that are worth your time are listed next.

For Further Reading

A. Bhide, "The Questions Every Entrepreneur Should Ask," *Harvard Business Review* (November–December 1996): 120–130.

C. Kim and R. Mauborgne, "Creating New Market Space," *Harvard Business Review* (January–February 1999): 83–93.

W. Sahlman, "How to Write a Great Business Plan," *Harvard Business Review* (July–August 1997): 98–108.

J. Timmons and S. Spinelli, *New Venture Creation,* 6th ed. (New York: Irwin McGraw-Hill, 2003). Classic text on the venture creation process.

Internet Links

Business plan preparation sites:

http://www.bplans.com
http://www.pasware.com
http://www.brs-inc.com
http://www.jian.com

Other Great Sites

http://www.entreworld.org
Kauffman Center for Entrepreneurial Leadership offers a comprehensive site providing a variety of information for entrepreneurs and links to other helpful sites.

http://www.bizmove.com
The Small Business Knowledge Base is a comprehensive, free resource of small business information packed with dozens of guides and worksheets.

http://www.babson.edu/entrep
The Babson College entrepreneurship site links to different resources of interest to those studying and practicing entrepreneurship.

http://www.nbia.org
National Business Incubation Association. Business incubators nurture young firms, helping them to survive and grow during the startup period when they are most vulnerable.

http://www.nfibonline.com

The National Federation of Independent Business (NFIB) is the largest advocacy organization representing small and independent businesses in Washington, DC, and all 50 state capitals—a great resource.

http://www.score.org/online

The SCORE Association is a national nonprofit association and a resource partner with the U.S. Small Business Administration, with 11,500 volunteer members and 389 chapters throughout the United States.

http://www.morebusiness.com

Comprehensive business resource center providing entrepreneurs with information on startup, running the business, templates, and so on. This site is updated daily.

BUILDING YOUR PRO FORMA FINANCIAL STATEMENTS[1]

5

Andrew Zacharakis

Most of the entrepreneurs I have worked with are intimidated by numbers, even after they have gone through the business planning process. Entrepreneurs understand their concept, they even have a good sense of the business model, but ask them to put together pro forma financials or read an income statement and they have panic attacks. A common refrain is that building your financials or understanding them isn't that important because an accountant can always be hired. Although an accountant is a useful advisor, in the prelaunch stage, the lead entrepreneur needs to understand the numbers inside and out. After all, the lead entrepreneur is the person who will be articulating his or her vision to potential employees, vendors, customers, and investors. If the entrepreneur is easily stumped by simple questions about profitability or costs, potential employees, customers, and other important parties to the new venture's success will lose confidence in the lead entrepreneur's ability to execute on the concept. The business plan financial statements bridge the entrepreneur's great idea and what that idea really means in terms of dollars and cents. So, although it can be painful, the entrepreneur needs to learn the numbers behind her business. The rewards of gaining this deep insight are often the difference between success and failure.

If for no other reason, the entrepreneur needs to understand the numbers so she can decide whether this business has the potential to provide her with a good living. It is too easy to get caught in a trap where a new venture is slowly draining away your investment or supports your working, in real terms, for less than the minimum wage.[2] The goal of this chapter is to give you an introduction to entrepreneurial financial planning. Unlike existing businesses who have an operating history, entrepreneurs must develop their financials from scratch. There are no previous trends in revenue and costs that you can use as a basis to project future revenues and costs. Yet, the failure to come up with solid projections may cost you your initial investment, as well as that of your investors. This chapter helps you generate sound projections.

COMMON MISTAKES

When writing this chapter, I sent an e-mail to several acquaintances who are professional equity investors (either angels or venture capitalists), asking, "What are the most common mistakes that you see when you review an entrepreneur's business proposal?" In other words, what makes you hesitant to believe that the business can survive and succeed? The following six mistakes were consistently:

1. *Not understanding the revenue drivers:* Entrepreneurs need to know what the leverage points are that drive revenues. They need to understand how many customers are likely to see the product, how many of those that see will buy, and how much, on average, they will buy each time. Although every entrepreneur claims that her estimates are "conservative," 99% of the time, entrepreneurs are overly optimistic in their projections.

2. *Underestimating costs:* If you were to graph the revenue and cost projections of entrepreneurs over time, you often see revenues growing in a "hockey stick" fashion while costs slowly progress upward (see Exhibit 5.1). You often see revenue projections of $15 million after five years on costs of only $5 million. That is unbelievable. When you dig into those numbers, you often see that the firm only has five employees in year five. That equates to revenues per employee of $3 million—that is nearly impossible. Often, entrepreneurs underestimate how much infrastructure (i.e., employees, physical assets) they need to achieve that level of sales. Entrepreneurs also underestimate the cost of acquiring and retaining customers (marketing expenditures). Poor projections lead to cash crunches and ultimately failure.

3. *Underestimating time to generate revenues:* Pro forma financials often show sales occurring immediately. Typically, a business will incur costs for many months before revenue can be generated. For instance, if you are opening a restaurant, you will incur rent, inventory, and labor costs before you generate a dime in revenue. Often, projections show the business at full capacity within the first year. That is rarely realistic.

EXHIBIT 5.1   Revenue and cost projections.

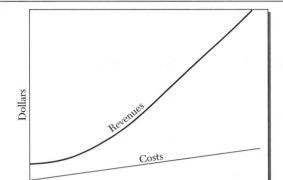

4. *Lack of comparables:* Investors typically think about the entrepreneur's concept from their knowledge of similar businesses. They compare your gross margins, net income margins, and other metrics to industry standards and selected benchmark companies. Yet, many entrepreneur projections have ratios that far exceed industry standards, and when questioned about this above-average performance, entrepreneurs often have no explanation. You need to understand your business model in relation to the industry and be able to explain any differences.

5. *Top-down versus bottom-up forecasting:* Entrepreneurs often claim that their revenues represent 3% of the market after year 3. The implied assumption is that it is easy to get that 3%. Investors know that, although it doesn't sound like much, the trick is how you get to that 3%. They want to see the process (cost of acquiring, serving, and retaining the customer). Investors won't believe that you can get 3% without causing competitors to take notice and action.

6. *Time to secure financing:* Entrepreneurs frequently assume that financing will close quickly. Whether entrepreneurs want to raise $25,000 or $1 million, they project that it will happen in the next month. In reality, it often takes as long as six months to close a round of financing. If entrepreneurs are too optimistic in how quickly they can close a round of financing, they will quickly have negative cash flow, which often means they are out of business. Remember what Fred Adler, the famous venture capitalist said, "Happiness is a positive cash flow. Everything else will come later."

Understanding these pitfalls will help you generate realistic financials, and more important, enable you to convincingly articulate your business model so that you can sell your vision to employees, customers, vendors, and investors. The next section gives a quick overview of financial statements.

FINANCIAL STATEMENT OVERVIEW

There are three standard financial statements that you will need to include in your business plan: the income statement, the statement of cash flows, and the balance sheet. Most people want to know why three statements are required. The reason is simple. Each one provides a slightly different view of the company. Any one alone is only part of the picture. Together, they provide a detailed description of the economics of your company.

The first of these statements, the income statement, describes how well a company conducted its business over a recent period of time, typically a quarter (three months) or a year. This indicator of overall performance begins with the company's revenues on the top line. From this accounting of sales, the company's expenses are subtracted. These include:

- Cost of the products that the company actually sold.
- Selling, marketing, and administrative costs.
- Depreciation, the estimated cost of using your property, plant, and equipment.
- Interest on debts.
- Taxes on profits.

The bottom line of the statement (literally) is the company's profits that are called *net income*. The income statement represents a measurement of business performance. It is *not* a description of actual flows of money.

A company needs cash to conduct business. Without it, there is no business. The third financial statement, the statement of cash flows, monitors this crucial account. As the name implies, the statement of cash flows concerns itself exclusively with transactions that involve cash. It is not uncommon to have strong positive earnings on the income statement and a negative statement of cash flows—less cash at the end of the period than at the beginning. Just because you shipped a product does not necessarily mean that you have received the cash for it yet. Likewise, you might have purchased something like inventory or a piece of equipment that will not show up on your income statement until it is consumed or depreciated. There are many noncash transactions that are represented in the income statement.

What is curious (and sometimes confusing to those who have never worked with financial statements) is the way the statement of cash flows is constructed. It starts with the bottom line (profits) of the income statement and works backward, removing all of the noncash transactions. For example, since the income statement subtracted out depreciation (the value of using your plant and equipment), the statement of cash flows adds it back in because you don't actually pay any depreciation expense to anybody. Similarly, the cash flow statement needs to include things that you paid for but that were not used that period. For example, you might have paid for a product that has not yet sold or you might have bought a piece of equipment that you will depreciate over time so you would need to put those items on the cash flow statement. After all of these adjustments, you are left with a representation of transactions that are exclusively cash.

The balance sheet enumerates all of the company's assets, liabilities, and shareholder equity. Assets are all the things that the company has that are expected to generate value over time—things like inventory, buildings, equipment, accounts receivable (money that your customers still owe you), and cash. Liabilities represent all the money the company expects to pay eventually. These include accounts payable (money the company owes its suppliers), debt, and unpaid taxes. Shareholder equity is the money that shareholders have paid into the company as well as the company's earnings so far. The income statement describes a process or flow, while the balance sheet is a snapshot of accounts at a specific point in time.

All of your assets come from a liability or shareholder equity. Therefore, the sum of the asset accounts must equal the sum of the liabilities and shareholder equity account.

$$\text{Assets} = \text{Liabilities} + \text{Shareholder equity}$$

The assets are shown on the left side of the sheet with the liabilities and shareholder equity on the right. The balance sheet *always* balances. If your balance sheet does not balance, you have made a mistake. This is only a partial treatment of financial statements but should be enough to help you understand this chapter. I strongly recommend reading John Tracy's excellent book, *How to Read a Financial Report*.[3] It is simple, short, and easy. The remainder of this chapter walks you through the process of generating your financials.

BUILDING YOUR PRO FORMA FINANCIAL STATEMENTS

Exhibit 5.2 previews the points we cover. Think of Exhibit 5.2 as a checklist in developing your financials. Rigorously completing each step will lead to better financial projections and decisions. Underlying these steps are two methods: the *build-up method* and the *comparable method*. Go through all the steps in

EXHIBIT 5.2   Financial construction checklist.

Build-Up Method

1. Identify all your sources of revenues.
2. Determine your revenues for a "typical day."
3. Understand your revenue drivers:
    a. How many customers you will serve?
    b. How much product they will buy?
    c. How much they will pay for each product?
4. Validate driver assumptions:
    a. Primary research (talk to customers, attend tradeshows, etc.)
    b. Secondary research (industry reports, company reports, etc.)
5. Recombine. Multiply the typical day by the number of days in a year.
6. Determine Cost of Goods Sold (GOGS) for typical day.
7. Recombine. Multiply COGS by number of days in a year.
8. Determine operating expenses by most appropriate time frame.
9. Refine operating costs.
10. Create preliminary income statement.

Comparable Method

11. Compare revenue projections to industry metrics.
12. Run scenario analysis.
13. Compare common sized cost percentages to industry averages.

Building Integrated Financial Statements

14. Derive monthly income statements for first 2 years.
15. Create balance sheet.
16. Create cash flow statement.

Final Steps

17. Write 2 to 3 page description of financial statements.

an iterative fashion so that you not only know the numbers, but you "own the numbers."

Build-Up Method

People make better decisions by breaking problems into smaller pieces. If you think about the business planning process, you are going through a series of questions that help you answer the big question: Is this an attractive opportunity? Thus, you evaluate the industry, the competition, the customer, and so forth. Based on that analysis, you decide whether to launch the business or not. Constructing pro forma financials is part of this process. The place to start is the income statement. The other two statements are, in part, derived from the income statement. First, identify all of your revenue sources (usually, the various product offerings). Second, identify all of your costs. Once you have the business broken down into its component parts, the next step is to think about how much revenue you can generate in a year, but you can decompose this estimate as well.

Revenue Projections

Instead of visualizing what you will sell in a month or a year, break it down into a typical day. For example, if you were the entrepreneur starting The History Shoppe,[4] you would estimate how many customers you might serve in a particular day and how much they would spend per visit based on the types of books and artifacts they would buy (Exhibit 5.3). First, you detail your product mix and the average price for each item. As you can see, you expect to sell books, maps, and other historical artifacts. Second, you estimate the traffic that the store might draw on a typical day. You list your assumptions at the bottom of the schedule. Then, you estimate how many people who come into the store buy an item and how many items they might buy. The last column gives you total revenue per day by product category.

Exhibit 5.3 highlights critical revenue assumptions, or what might be termed *revenue drivers*. The thought process involved in generating the assumptions enhances your understanding of the business model. Going through this exercise tells you how you make money. It also helps you understand how you might be able to make more money. In other words, what revenue drivers can you influence? The History Shoppe might be able to increase its daily sales by increasing the traffic coming into the store (through advertising), how many people buy, and how much they buy (through "up selling"; "Can I get you anything else

EXHIBIT 5.3   Revenue worksheet.

Product/Service Description	Price	Units Sold/Day	Total Revenue
1. Historical Books	$ 20	75 visitors × 75% × 1.5 books	$1,687.50
2. Videos	30	75 visitors × 15% × 1 video	337.50
3. Maps	50	75 visitors × 10% × 1 map	375.00
4. Globes	100	75 visitors × 5% × 1 globe	375.00
5. Other (postcards, magazines, etc.)	5	75 visitors × 20% × 2 items	150.00
Totals			$2,925.00

Assumptions:
  Traffic −75 visitors a day
    —books −75% of visitors will buy 1.5 books each
    —videos−15% of visitors buy 1 video each
    —maps −10% of visitors buy 1 map each
    —globes−5% of visitors buy 1 globe each
    —other −20% of visitors buy 2 misc. items
50% of sales will happen during Christmas season
30% of sales will happen during summer tourist season (May through September)

today?"). Although this exercise is invaluable, the estimates are only as good as the assumptions.

How do you strengthen your assumptions? How can you validate the traffic level, the percentage of customers who buy, and so forth? The answer is through research. The first place you would start is by talking to people who know the business. You would talk to bookstore owners, book vendors, mall leasing agents, and others in the industry. A good way to interact with these participants is at industry tradeshows. The next thing you would do is visit a number of bookstores and count how many people come in, what portion buys, and how much they spend. Although you might feel conspicuous, there are ways to do this field research without drawing attention to yourself or interfering in the store's business. For example, you might sit outside a bookstore and count how many people enter the store and how many people come out of the store with a package. Finally, you could also talk to your expected customers, history buffs. Find out how often they buy history books or other history paraphernalia. Ask them how much they spend on these items a month and where they currently buy them. By going through several iterations of primary research, you will sharpen your estimates.

In addition to conducting the research yourself, you can seek secondary sources such as industry reports and Web sites. For example, The History Shoppe found a great reference book, *Manual on Bookselling* edited by Kate Whouley and published by the American Booksellers Association (ABA) in 1996. The ABA also publishes *1999 ABACUS Financial Study,* which provides detailed information on all sorts of financial metrics in the industry.

Once you are comfortable that your assumptions are sound, you can then multiply the typical day by the number of days of operation in the year. This exercise gives you yearly revenue estimates. This is a first cut. Clearly, a typical day varies by the time of the year. People do much of their shopping around the Christmas holiday. Therefore, most pro forma projections for new companies typically show monthly income figures for the first two years. This allows the entrepreneur to manage seasonality and other factors that might make sales uneven for the business.

Cost of Goods Sold

Once you have your revenue projections, you next consider costs. On an income statement, we see two categories of costs; cost of goods sold and operating expenses. Cost of goods sold (COGS), is the direct costs of the items sold. For The History Shoppe, COGS is the cost of inventory that is sold in that period. As a first cut, assume that COGS for a retail outlet would be around 50%

(assumes a 100% markup). Since your sales were approximately $3,000 per day, your COGS would be around $1,500.

As with revenue assumptions, sharpen your COGS assumptions. Use a similar schedule as in Exhibit 5.3 so that you can refine your COGS by product (see Exhibit 5.4). After some investigation at Hoovers.com, you find that the gross margin on books is only 27% for the likes of Amazon, Borders, Barnes & Noble, and Books a Million. On other items that you sell, other company's (MTS and TransWorld Entertainment) gross margins are around 31%. Although these margins are lower than estimated, these companies have a different business model; high volume, lower margins. The History Shoppe offers a premium shopping experience, meaning highly knowledgeable sales staff and unique historical artifacts. For the time being, keep your margin estimates, but would look for further validation as to whether they are achievable. Exhibit 5.4 shows the price per item, the gross margin (revenue minus COGS) per item, the revenues per item (from Exhibit 5.3), and then calculates COGS in dollar terms [Revenue $\times$ (1-COGS)]. Since the gross margins per items differ, the overall Gross Margin is 44%.

Operating Expenses

In addition to direct expenses, businesses also incur operating expenses, such as marketing, salaries, general administration (SG&A), rent, interest expenses, and so forth. The build-up method forecasts those expenses on a daily, monthly, or yearly basis as appropriate (see Exhibit 5.5). For example, The History Shoppe has been quoted a store rental price of $30 per/square foot per

EXHIBIT 5.4   Cost of goods worksheet.

Product/Service Description	Price	Gross Margin (%)	Revenue	COGS
1. Historical books	$ 20	40	$1,687.50	$1,012.50
2. Videos	30	50	337.50	168.75
3. Maps	50	50	375.00	187.50
4. Globes	100	50	375.00	187.50
5. Other (postcards, magazines, etc.)	5	50	150.00	75.00
Totals			$2,925.00	$1,631.25

Total Revenue	$2,925.00
COGS	1,631.25
Gross Profit	$1,293.75
Gross Profit Margin	44%

EXHIBIT 5.5   Operating expenses worksheet.

Expense	Daily	Monthly	Yearly	Total
Store rent			$90,000	$ 90,000
Manager salary			60,000	60,000
Assistant manager			40,000	40,000
Hourly employees	176			63,360
Benefits	21		12,000	19,603
Bank charges			10,530	10,530
Marketing/advertising		1,000		12,000
Utilities		333		4,000
Travel			1,000	1,000
Dues			1,000	1,000
Depreciation		833		10,000
Miscellenous			4,000	4,000
				0
Total				$315,493

Assumptions:

   Rent—3,000 sq ft. at $30/year = $90,000

   Hire 1 manager at $60,000/year

   Hire 1 assistant manager at $40,000

   Store is open from 9 A.M. to 7 P.M. daily, so 10 hours per day

   Need 2 clerks when open and 1 clerk an hour before and after open

   2 clerks × 10 hours × $8/hour + 1 clerk × 2 hours × $8/hour

   Benefits are 12% of wages and salaries

   Bank Charges about 1% of sales

   Advertising $1,000/month

   Travel—$1,000/year to attend trade shows

   Dues—$1,000/year for trade association

   Depreciation—$100,000 of leasehold improvements and equipment
      Depreciated straight line over 10 years.

year. The space is about 3,000 square feet so you put $90,000 in the yearly expense column. However, the rent will be paid on a monthly basis, so in the final income statement you would show a rent expense of $7,500 in the month-to-month income statement. At this point, however, you are just trying to get a sense of the overall business model and gauge whether this business can be profitable; showing it on a yearly basis is sufficient.

Based on the first cut, The History Shoppe is projecting operating expenses of approximately $315,000 per year. However, the devil is in the details as they say and one problem area is accurately projecting operating costs, especially labor costs. Constructing a headcount schedule is an important step in refining your labor projections (see Exhibit 5.6). Although the store is open on average 10 hours per day, you can see from the headcount table that Sunday is a shorter day and the store is open 11 hours on the other days. The store operates with a minimum of two employees at all times (including

EXHIBIT 5.6   Headcount table.

	Monday	Tuesday	Wednesday	Thursday	Friday	Saturday	Sunday	Total
Store Hours	10:00–9:00	10:00–9:00	10:00–9:00	10:00–9:00	10:00–9:00	10:00–9:00	11:00–5:00	
Hours Open	11	11	11	11	11	11	6	72
Shift 1	9:30–1:30	9:30–1:30	9:30–1:30	9:30–1:30	9:30–1:30	9:30–1:30	10:00–2:00	
Shift 2	1:30–5:30	1:30–5:30	1:30–5:30	1:30–5:30	1:30–5:30	1:30–5:30	1:00–5:00	
Shift 3	5:30–9:30	5:30–9:30	5:30–9:30	5:30–9:30	5:30–9:30	5:30–9:30		
Shift 1 hrs	4	4	4	4	4	4	4	
Shift 2 hrs	4	4	4	4	4	4	4	
Shift 3 hrs	4	4	4	4	4	4	0	
Total Shift Hours	12	12	12	12	12	12	8	80
Staff Headcount								
Shift 1	2	2	1	2	1	4	3	
Shift 2	1	1	0	1	1	4	4	
Shift 3	1	1	1	2	4	4	0	
Total Staff	4	4	2	5	6	12	7	40
Total Hours Worked								
Shift 1	8	8	4	8	4	16	12	
Shift 2	4	4	0	4	4	16	16	
Shift 3	4	4	4	8	16	16	0	
	16	16	8	20	24	48	28	160
Manager	0	0	8	8	8	8	8	40
Assisstant Manager	8	8	8	0	8	8	0	40

Total hourly employee hours/week = 160

Hourly rate $8/hour   8

Total wages per week $1,280

Total wages per year $66,560

either the assistant manager or store manager). During busier shifts, the number of employees reaches a peak of six people (afternoon shift on Saturday, including both managers). Looking at the calculation below the table, you see that the new wage expense is about $66,000, a bit higher than the first estimate. This *process* of examining and reexamining your assumptions over and over is what leads to compelling financials.

Just as you refined the hourly wage expense, do the same with other expenses. For example, you can see that The History Shoppe is projecting $12,000 in marketing expenses. Create a detailed schedule of how you plan on spending those advertising dollars. If you refer back to the business planning chapter (Chapter 4), you see in Exhibit 5.9 that we had already created a schedule of detailed expenses. This illustrates another point: Financial analysis is really just the mathematical expression of your overall business strategy. Everything you write about in your business plan has revenue or cost implications. As you read business plans, your mind should be putting together a mental picture of the financial statements, especially the income statement. If the written plan and the financials are tightly correlated, you have much greater confidence that the entrepreneur knows what she is doing.

The Preliminary Income Statement

Once you have forecasted revenues and expenses, you put them together in an income statement (see Exhibit 5.7). Looking at Exhibit 5.3, you forecasted average daily sales of almost $3,000. You need to annualize that figure. You expect the store to be open on average 360 days per year (assuming that the store might be closed for a few days a year, such as Christmas, Thanksgiving, etc.). Note that you lead with a line called Total Revenue and then show the detail that creates that total revenue line by itemizing the different revenue categories. COGS are handled in the same manner as revenues; you multiply the typical day by 360 days to get the annual total.

After adjusting the hourly wages per the headcount table (which also means adjusting employee benefits), take the operating expenses table (see Exhibit 5.5) and put it into the income statement (see Exhibit 5.7). If you believe that you can secure debt financing, put in an interest expense. For the initial forecast, you will leave out interest expense because you are still not certain what amount of financing you need to launch the business. Next, you compute taxes. Make sure to account for federal, state, and city taxes as applicable. Note that in the right hand column, you have calculated the expense percentage of total revenues. This is called a *common-sized income statement*. Although you have been rigorous in building up your statement, you can further validate by comparing your common-sized income statement to the industry standards.

EXHIBIT 5.7   Income statement.

Total Revenues	$1,053,000	100%
Historical books	607,500	
Videos	121,500	
Maps	135,000	
Globes	135,000	
Other	54,000	
Total COGS	$587,250	55.8%
Historical books	364,500	
Videos	60,750	
Maps	67,500	
Globes	67,500	
Other	27,000	
Gross Profit	$465,750	44.2%
Operating Expenses		
Store rent	90,000	
Manager salary	60,000	
Assistant manager	40,000	
Hourly employees	66,560	
Benefits	19,987	
Bank charges	10,530	
Marketing/advertising	12,000	
Utilities	4,000	
Travel	1,000	
Dues	1,000	
Depreciation	10,000	
Miscellaneous	4,000	
Total Operating Expenses	$319,077	30.3%
Earnings from Operations	$146,673	13.9%
Taxes	$58,669	
Net Earnings	$88,004	8.4%

Comparable Method

How can you tell if your projections are reasonable? The first thing to do is gauge whether your revenue projections make sense, and then see if your cost structure is reasonable. Comparables help you validate your projections. For instance, a good metric for revenue in retail is sales per square foot. The History Shoppe is projecting sales of $1 million in 3,000 square feet that equates to $351 per square foot. Secondary research into the average per bookstore[5] and also into what one or two specific bookstores achieve is a good place to start.[6] For example, $351 is in line with that of independent book stores ($350/square foot), but higher than Barnes & Noble ($243/square foot). The History Shoppe projection seems reasonable considering that it will be selling certain items (globes, maps, etc.) that have a much higher ticket price than books, but there are a couple of caveats to this estimate. First, it is likely to take The History Shoppe some time to achieve this level. In other words, the income statement might be more appropriate for the second or third year of operation. At that point, The History Shoppe will have built up a clientele and achieved some name recognition. Second, you would want to run some scenario analysis. Does this business model still work if The History Shoppe only achieves Barnes & Noble's sales per square foot ($243)? You would also run a few other scenarios related to higher foot traffic, recession, outbreak of war (sales of books on Islam increased with September 11 and escalating tensions in the Middle East). Having some validated metrics, such as sales per square foot, helps you run different scenarios and make sound decisions on whether to launch a venture in the first place, and then how to adjust your business model so that the venture has the greatest potential to succeed.

Other metrics that are easily obtainable for this type of establishment include sales per customer, or what is referred to as *average ticket price*. From Exhibit 5.3, The History Shoppe expects sales of $2,925 per day from 75 unique store visitors. That translates into an average transaction per visitor of $39. However, not every visitor will buy as many people will just come in and browse. In Exhibit 5.3, you assumed that 75% of the visitors would buy a book and lesser percentage of visitors would buy other items. If that percentage holds true, 56 people will actually purchase something each day. Thus, the average receipt becomes $52. This average ticket price is considerably higher than Barnes & Noble's rate of $27.

As with all your assumptions, you have to gauge whether a higher ticket price is reasonable. An entrepreneur might reason that The History Shoppe isn't discounting its books and is also selling higher priced ancillary goods (e.g., globes, maps). Run scenario analysis again to see if The History Shoppe survives if its average ticket price is closer to that of Barnes & Nobel. In other words, see what happens to the model overall when you change one of the assumptions, the average selling price in this case.

After you are comfortable with the revenue estimate, you next need to validate the costs. The best way is to compare your common-sized income statement with the industry averages or some benchmark companies. It is unlikely that your income statement will exactly match the industry averages, but you need to be able to explain and understand the differences. Exhibit 5.8 looks at the common-sized income statement for The History Shoppe and Barnes & Noble. The first discrepancy appears in the COGS. The History Shoppe projects COGS of 56% of revenue whereas Barnes & Noble is projecting 73%. Why would Barnes & Noble COGS be so much higher? On further investigation, you find that Barnes & Noble includes occupancy costs (rent, utilities, etc.) in

EXHIBIT 5.8   Comparable analysis.

	The History Shoppe		Barnes & Nobel (FY2002) (in millions)		Industry Average
Total Revenues	$1,053,000	100%	$4,871	100%	100%
Historical books	607,500				
Videos	121,500				
Maps	135,000				
Globes	135,000				
Other	54,000				
Total COGS	$587,250	55.8%	$3,557	73.0%	60.0%
Historical books	364,500				
Videos	60,750				
Maps	67,500				
Globes	67,500				
Other	27,000				
Gross Profit	$465,750	44.2%	$1,314	27.0%	40.0%
Operating Expenses					
Store rent	90,000				
Manager salary	60,000				
Assistant manager	40,000				
Hourly employees	66,560				
Benefits	19,987				
Bank charges	10,530				
Marketing/advertising	12,000				
Utilities	4,000				
Travel	1,000				
Dues	1,000				
Depreciation	10,000		150		
Miscellaneous	4,000				
Total Operating Expenses	$319,077	30.3%	$1,062	21.8%	37.5%
Earnings from Operations	$146,673	13.9%	$ 252	5.2%	2.5%
Taxes	$ 58,669				
Net Earnings	$ 88,004	8.4%			

COGS. If you add The History Shoppe's $90,000 rent plus $4,000 in utilities into COGS, COGS becomes 65% of revenue, still lower. However, COGS of 65% is in line with the specialty retail industry rate of 67%.[7] The reasoning for this discrepancy is similar to that of the higher ticket price. The History Shoppe's COGS is likely lower than Barnes & Noble because it is not a discount book seller (meaning it earns higher margins on every book sold than Barnes & Noble). Additionally, The History Shoppe also sells other retail items (i.e., globes, maps) that generate higher margins.

Since the gross profit margin is the inverse of COGS—revenue minus COGS—the explanation provided for COGS also holds for Gross Margin. Barnes & Noble gross margin is 27% versus 35% for The History Shoppe (with rent included in COGS).

When comparing the operating expenses between the two companies, we see that The History Shoppe is projecting operating expenses to be 29% of revenue versus 22% for Barnes & Noble. However, we must once again adjust for the occupancy expense because The History Shoppe is including occupancy in operating expenses whereas Barnes & Noble includes it in COGS. With that adjustment, The History Shoppe's operating expenses are about 21% of revenue, almost the same as Barnes & Noble.

Based on the comparable analysis, it appears that The History Shoppe's projections are reasonable. The History Shoppe's earnings from operations are higher (13.9%) than Barnes & Noble (5.2%) and the independent book store average (2.5%), but that may be explained by the higher gross margins and the fact that you haven't yet included any interest expenses. For example, if you use debt financing for any of your startup expenses, such as leasehold improvements, you will have an interest expense that would reduce your net income margin to be more in line with the comparable companies.

In this exercise, you have primarily used benchmark companies, but industry averages also provide useful comparable information. The *Almanac of Business and Industrial Financial Ratios* (Aspen Publishers, Inc.) or *Industry Norms and Key Business Ratios* (Dun and Bradstreet) are excellent sources to use as starting points in building financial statements relevant to your industry. These sources help entrepreneurs build income statements by providing industry averages for costs of goods sold, salary expenses, and interest expenses. Again, your firm will differ from these industry averages, but going through scenario analysis and understanding your business model, you should be able to explain why your firm differs.

BUILDING INTEGRATED FINANCIAL STATEMENTS

Once you have a baseline income statement, the next step is to construct monthly income and cash flow statements for two years (followed by years 3 through 5 on a yearly basis), and a yearly balance sheet for all five years. Five years is standard for many business plans because it usually takes new firms some time to hit their stride. It takes time to build sales and operate efficiently. Five years also gives the entrepreneur a sense of whether her investment of time and energy will pay off. Can the business not only survive, but provide the kind of financial return to make the opportunity costs of leaving an existing job worthwhile?

The income statement, cash flow and balance sheet are the core statements for managing any business. Changes in one statement affect all others. Understanding how these changes impact your business can mean the difference between survival and failure. Many entrepreneurs will find their business on the verge of failure, even if it is profitable, because they fail to understand how the income statement is related to the cash flow and balance sheet. How is that possible?

Entrepreneurs need to finance rapid growth. For example, The History Shoppe needs to buy inventory in advance of selling to its customers. The owner needs to ensure that he has enough books and other products on hand that he doesn't lose a sale because a customer is frustrated that the book or globe isn't in stock. Americans are notorious for wanting instant gratification. Yet, having inventory on hand drains cash. If The History Shoppe expects sales of $500,000 in December, then it must have $280,000 worth of inventory at the end of November ($500,000 × 56%—the average COGS). How does The History Shoppe pay for this? Internal cash flow? Vendor financing? Equity? Having strong pro forma financials helps the entrepreneur anticipate these needs far enough in advance so that the appropriate financing can be arranged. Failing to understand the numbers behind the business leads to ruin more often than not.

This example illustrates why a new business wants to show the income statement and cash flow on a monthly basis for the first two years; the most vulnerable period in a new venture's life. It takes time to build up your clientele (lower revenues), learn how to efficiently operate (higher costs), develop a track record so you can secure vendor financing (cash flow implications), understand seasonality (variance in demand), and many other issues. Monthly projections allow the entrepreneur to anticipate and understand any seasonality that might happen in the business. In addition to the financing issue discussed above, seasonality impacts other key operations and decisions. For example, The History Shoppe will need to hire more salespeople during the Christmas season. Integrated financials can help the entrepreneur plan for that hiring increase.

In sum, it is critical to show the first two years of pro forma projections on a monthly basis because this is when a company is most vulnerable to failure. Monthly forecasts help you understand these issues and prepare for them. For years three through five, yearly projections are sufficient because the further out one goes, the less accurate the projections become. Nevertheless, your longer term projections communicate your vision of the upside potential of your opportunity. The exercise of going through the projection process is more important than the accuracy of the projections. The process helps you gain a deeper understanding of the business and whether you should pursue the opportunity or not.

This example indicates how changes in one statement impact other statements. Exhibit 5.9 formally shows how the pro forma financials are integrated.[8] You can see that the income statement drives the balance sheet which drives the cash flow statement (although the cash from financing and uses of cash from the cash flow statement feed back into the balance sheet). We will briefly touch on how to move from our base income statement into a full set of financial pro forma projections, but going into a step-by-step process is beyond the scope of this chapter.

Income Statement

The base income statement you generated for The History Shoppe shows the level of operations that might be achievable in year three or four. Thus, we need to make a number of adjustments to generate the other years. First, we need to create monthly statements for the first two years. That means we need to understand the seasonality of our business and the sales cycle. One mistake that many entrepreneurs make is showing revenues from the first day they launch the business, but most new businesses incur expenses well in advance of generating revenue. Thinking in terms of The History Shoppe, you would consider the business launched soon after the first round of financing is closed. At this point, the entrepreneur can start spending money to establish the business. For instance, he might sign a lease, contract for equipment, and so forth. Show those expenses as incurred. Thus, The History Shoppe might show expenses for three months (the time to build-out the store before opening) before you show your first revenue.

The next consideration in generating your monthly forecasts is seasonality. Revenues in retail are not evenly spread across the 12 months. Exhibit 5.10 estimates how sales might be spread for a retail operation. The make or break season for The History Shoppe is Christmas as you see sales jumping dramatically in November and December. Another important season is the tourist season (The History Shoppe plans to locate near a major Revolutionary War site). Based on these projections, it makes sense to lease and build out the retail space in the January to March time frame when sales levels are expected to be low.

Another consideration is how long it will take The History Shoppe to build its clientele and ramp up its revenues. The History Shoppe is projecting sales of $350 per square foot once it hits its optimal operating position. In the first year of operation, that number might be significantly lower, say $200 per square foot, well below the Barnes & Noble average of $243 and the Independent Book Store average of $350. In year two, a reasonable estimate might be that average sales per square foot hit $250 and finally in year three you hit the

EXHIBIT 5.9 Interconnections among pro forma projections.

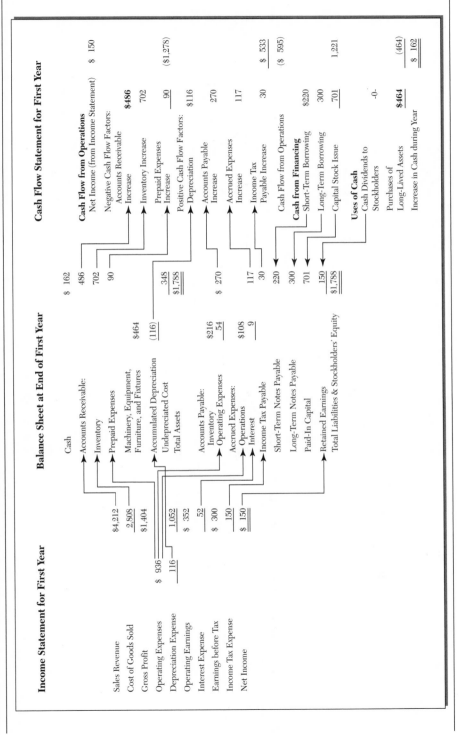

EXHIBIT 5.10 Seasonality projections (in thousands).

	Jan 3%	Feb 2%	Mar 3%	Apr 4%	May 6%	Jun 7%	Jul 9%	Aug 8%	Sep 5%	Oct 3%	Nov 10%	Dec 40%	Year 100%
Year 1	$22.5	$15.0		$24.0	$36.0	$42.0	$54.0	$48.0	$30.0	$18.0	$ 60.0	$240.0	$ 552.0
Year 2	$31.5	$21.0	$22.5	$30.0	$45.0	$52.5	$67.5	$60.0	$37.5	$22.5	$ 75.0	$300.0	$ 750.0
Year 3			$31.5	$42.0	$63.0	$73.5	$94.5	$84.0	$52.5	$31.5	$105.0	$420.0	$1,050.0

independent book store average of $350. Additionally, The History Shoppe is not generating sales for the first three months of year one due to the time it takes to build out the store, so you adjust the sales accordingly.

Balance Sheet

The balance sheet can be the most difficult to integrate into your other financial statements. For pro forma projections, yearly balance sheets are sufficient. Again, going into great detail is beyond the scope of this chapter, but there are a few items that often cause confusion.

First, will your business sell on credit? If so, it will record accounts receivable. Exhibit 5.9 shows how your sales from the income statement drive your accounts receivable on the balance sheet (some portion of those sales) that then drives accounts receivable increase on the cash flow. While you would record the sale when the customer took possession, you may not actually receive payment until some point in the future. Recording the sale would have a positive impact on your profitability, but would not affect your cash flow until the customer actually paid.

If your business is buying equipment, land, a plant, or in the case of The History Shoppe, adding leasehold improvements, you will have an asset of plant and equipment. A common error is to show this as a capital expense meaning that it appears in full on your income statement the moment you contract for the work. Doing so assumes that you will fully use that equipment within the year (or whatever length your income statement covers). To accurately reflect the acquisition of the asset, you show the full outflow of money as it occurs on your cash flow and then depreciate the cost per year of life of the asset on your income statement. You would also have an accumulated depreciation line item on your balance sheet showing how much of the asset has been used up. Referring back to Exhibit 5.5, you see that The History Shoppe is projecting leasehold improvements of $100,000, which it expects to use up over 10 years (10,000 per year or $833 per month).

Accounts payable acts in a similar manner to accounts receivable, except that this is a loan to your company from a supplier (see Exhibit 5.9). Once The History Shoppe is able to secure vendor financing on inventory, for example, you will show the COGS as you sell your books, but you may not have to pay the publisher until later (assuming that the book is a fairly fast-moving item). So the expense would show up on your income statement but not on your cash flow—until you paid for it. Until then, it is held in accounts payable on the balance sheet.

The final problem area is retained earnings. Entrepreneurs know that the balance sheet should BALANCE. A common error is to use the retained earnings line to make the balance sheet balance. Retained earnings is actually Previous Retained Earnings plus current period Net Income minus Dividends Paid that period.

If you find that your balance sheet isn't balancing, the problem is often in how you have calculated accounts receivable or accounts payable. Balancing the balance sheet is the most frustrating aspect of building your financial pro forma statements. Yet, hard wiring the retained earnings will ultimately lead to other errors, so work through the balancing problem as diligently as possible.

Cash Flow Statement

If you have constructed your financial statements accurately, the cash flow statement identifies when and how much financing you need. I coach the entrepreneurs that I work with to leave the financing assumptions empty until after they see how much the cash flow statement implies they need (see Exhibit 5.11). One of the many benefits of this process is that it helps you determine exactly how much you need so as to protect you from yielding too much equity or too much (or not enough) debt. The History Shoppe cash flow shows some major outlays as the store is gearing up for operation, such as inventory acquisition and equipment purchases. You can also see from the cash flow statement that the business is incurring some expenses prior to generating revenue ($17,000 listed as net earnings). This net earnings loss is reflected on the company's monthly income statement and is primarily attributable to wage expenses to hire and train its staff.

You can see that in the first 6 months, the cash position hits a low of $316,000. This is how much money The History Shoppe needs to raise to launch the business. For a new venture, most of the money will likely be in the form of equity from the entrepreneur, friends, and family. However, the entrepreneur may be able to secure some debt financing against his equipment (which would act as collateral if the business should fail). In any event, once you recognize your financing needs, you can devise a strategy to raise the money necessary to start the business. To provide some buffer against poor estimates, The History Shoppe might raise $350,000. This amount would show up on both the cash flow and balance sheet.

Integrating the Financial Statements

As the previous discussion implies, it can be difficult to integrate the statements unless you are a CPA and a spreadsheet wizard. Although I have my students go through the spreadsheet creation exercise, I recognize that entrepreneurs may not have the time or aptitude to build their spreadsheets from scratch. For those

EXHIBIT 5.11 The History Shoppe cash flow statement.

	Month 1	Month 2	Month 3	Month 4	Month 5	Month 6
Operating Activities						
Net earnings	(17,000)	(12,882)	(2,244)	(7,079)	(1,277)	8,394
Depreciation	1,115	1,115	1,115	1,115	1,115	1,115
Working capital						
Changes (Increase)/Decrease						
Accounts Receivable	0	(64)	(88)	40	(48)	(80)
(Increase)/Decrease						
Inventories	(104,562)	(19,605)	32,676	(39,211)	(65,351)	71,886
(Increase)/Decrease Other						
Current Assets	0	(230)	(316)	144	(172)	(287)
Increase/(Decrease) Accounts						
Payable & Accrued Expenses	0	3,215	4,421	(2,010)	2,411	4,019
Increase/(Decrease) Other						
Current Liabilities	0	3,445	4,737	(2,153)	2,584	4,306
Net cash provided/(used)						
by operating activities	(120,446)	(25,005)	40,301	(49,154)	(60,737)	89,354
Investing Activities						
Property & equipment	(101,000)	0	0	0	0	0
Other net cash used in						
investing activities	(101,000)	0	0	0	0	0
Financing Activities						
Increase/(Decrease)						
Short-Term Debt						0
Increase/(Decrease) Current						
Portion LTD						0
Increase/(Decrease)						
Long-Term Debt						0
Increase/(Decrease)						
Common Stock						0
Increase/(Decrease)						
Preferred Stock						0
Dividends Declared						0
Net Cash Provided/(Used)						
by Financing	0	0	0	0	0	0
Increase/(Decrease) in Cash	(221,446)	(25,005)	40,301	(49,154)	(60,737)	89,354
Cash at Beginning of Period	0	(221,446)	(246,451)	(206,150)	(255,304)	(316,041)
Cash at End of Period	(221,446)	(246,451)	(206,150)	(255,304)	(316,041)	(226,687)

of you who aren't spreadsheet proficient, I would suggest hiring an accountant. For those of you who are comfortable with spreadsheets but can't create your financial spreadsheets from scratch, I recommend using a fantastic template created by Frank Moyes and Stephen Lawrence at the University of Colorado.[9]

PUTTING IT ALL TOGETHER

Once the financial spreadsheets are completed, a two- to three-page explanation of the financials should be written and it should precede the statements. Although you understand all the assumptions and comparables that went into building the financial forecast, the reader needs the background spelled out. Describing the financials is also a good exercise in articulation. If your reader understands the financials and believes the assumptions are valid, you have passed an important test. If not, work with the reader to understand her concerns. Continuous iterations strengthen your financials and should give you further confidence in the viability of your business model.

The written explanation should have four subheadings: Overview, Income Statement, Cash Flow, and Balance Sheet. The overview section should highlight the major assumptions that drive your revenue and expenses. This section should map to several of the critical risks you identified in your written plan (see business plan chapter). The income statement description goes into more detail as to some of the revenue and cost drivers that haven't been discussed in the overview section. The cash flow description talks about the timing of cash infusions, accounts payable, accounts receivable. The balance sheet description illustrates how major ratios compare to industry standards and change as the firm grows.

CONCLUSION

Going through these exercises allows you to construct a realistic set of pro forma financials. It is difficult, but understanding your numbers enables you to articulate your business to all stakeholders so that you can build momentum toward the ultimate launch of your business. Just as the business plan is a live document (previous chapter), so are the financial statements live documents. The financials are obsolete immediately after they come off the printer. As you start your launch process, you can further refine your numbers, putting in actual revenues and expenses as they occur and adjusting projections based upon current activity. Once the business is operating, the nature of your financial statements change: They not only help you assess the viability of your business model, but also help you gauge actual performance and adjust how you operate based on that experience.

Although most entrepreneurs say that producing the financials causes some pain, they also concede that going through the process is gratifying and rewarding. They learn to master new management skills, build their business and protect their investment. So dig in.

6 VENTURE CAPITAL
William E. Wetzel Jr.

Venture Capital is a generic term that refers to equity and equity-linked financing for ventures ranging from seed and startup ventures to bridge financing for a few superstars preparing to move into the traditional capital markets, typically via a merger, acquisition, or IPO. Diverse investors with diverse objectives provide venture capital. Understanding differences among the sources and objectives of venture investors, and the markets in which they function, raises the odds that an entrepreneur's search for capital will be successful.

This chapter contains information useful for all entrepreneurs, but in particular, for those entrepreneurs pursuing sources of equity financing. The reasons are simple: Portfolios of equity investments in early stage ventures are illiquid for extended periods of time and entail extraordinary risks that justify the expectations of extraordinary rates of return, typically in the form of long-term capital gains. Less than 5% of ventures seeking capital offer the prospect of rates of return that justify such risks and lack of liquidity. You will save yourself time and grief if it becomes clear that you are among the 95%.

Two classes of investors make up the venture capital markets—venture capital funds and wealthy individuals, so-called *business angels*. We describe the basic characteristics of both classes, the dynamic markets in which they function, and provide suggestions for raising venture capital.

You will encounter a variety of industry statistics in this chapter. Some are based on verifiable empirical data. Others, where hard data are unavailable, are based on informed approximations. Where approximations are used, they are the best available and, more importantly, they best represent conditions in the venture capital markets. To provide entrepreneurs with practical guidelines, we use a number of generalizations about the diverse venture capital markets. Numerous exceptions to these generalizations are unavoidable.

VENTURE CAPITAL MARKETS

For entrepreneurs seeking capital, it's essential to have some familiarity with the extraordinary behavior of the venture capital markets in recent years. The past five years witnessed unprecedented changes, and as a result, raising capital for new ventures will be a daunting task for years to come. Here are some of the reasons:

• In 2002, venture capital disbursements fell to their lowest levels since 1997. According to PricewaterhouseCoopers/Venture Economics/National Venture Capital Association's *Money Tree Survey*, for the full year 2002, venture investing totaled $21.2 billion for 3,016 ventures. This was barely half of the $41.3 billion invested in 4,712 companies in 2001, and it's comparable to 1998, the last pre-dot-com bubble year. The year 2002 continued the decline from the run-up that peaked in 2000 when $106.6 billion was invested in 8,221 venture deals. In the space of two years, venture deals dropped 63%, dollars invested declined by 80% and the average deal size decreased by 46%, from $13 million to $7 million.

• Since three of every four venture deals represent follow-on financing for portfolio companies, a look at the pace of early-stage financings is instructive . . . and sobering. During 1995, $1.8 billion was invested in 513 early-stage deals. Five years later, during 2000, early-stage financing had grown to $26.3 billion invested in 2,888 deals—a multiple of 14 times the 1995 dollars invested in over five times as many deals. The average early-stage deal rose from $3.5 million to $9.1 million. During 2002, $4.1 billion was invested in 806 early-stage deals, making the average deal size equal to $5.1 million. Therefore, in two short years, early-stage deals dropped 72%, dollars invested decreased by 84%, and the average deal size decreased by 44%.

• Venture-backed company valuations have also plummeted, from an average of $80 to $90 million in 2000, to $30 to $40 million in 2002. As a consequence, "down rounds" are now the norm in follow-on deals. Fenwick & West LLP, a West Coast law firm, sampled 81 technology company deals that closed during the fourth quarter of 2002. Of these, 68% were down rounds. For example, to raise $120 million in 2002s largest deal, Caspian Networks, Inc., a

San Jose, California, producer of optical switch technology, took an 80.7% valuation cut from what it had been worth following an $82 million round in December 2000. The decimated valuation was great for the new money, but traumatic for investors in the earlier round.

- Liquidation preference multiples, which seldom exceeded an investor's original investment, have risen to over three times in some cases. In the Fenwick & West sample, 64% of the deals contained senior liquidation preferences, and over one-third had preference multiples ranging from > 1× to 2× (79%) to > 2× to 3× (14%) to > 3× (7%). A steady stream of "wash-out" deals, in which the equity stakes of early investors and entrepreneurs are either badly diluted or completely washed out, combined with perceptions of double and triple dipping liquidation preferences, are reviving old "vulture capital" stereotypes. According to Tom Claflin, founder of Claflin Capital, a Boston venture firm, the big problem with greedy term sheets is that they risk putting the motivation of entrepreneurs and investors at odds. At the end of the day, he explains, you want to "create a constructive environment in which management and investors are motivated to work together to develop a highly successful venture."

- The past two years produced seven consecutive quarters of negative returns on venture capital portfolios, putting a serious dent in long-term returns for the VC industry. Twenty-year portfolio performance for the private equity industry is now less than 15%, barely meeting the 15% to 20% returns that limited partners expected when they invested in venture funds.

- Venture capitalists had little reason to raise new money in 2002, particularly since the industry is sitting on $80 to $100 billion in funds left over from the boom days. In 2002, 108 venture funds raised $6.9 billion, a nine-year low and a fraction of their record total in 2000, when 653 funds raised $106.9 billion. The results were well below 2001 levels of $40.7 billion raised by 331 venture funds. When adjusted for the $5 billion refunded to investors by 108 funds, the net fund-raising total of $1.9 billion in 2002 represented the smallest inflow of venture capital since $1.6 billion was raised in 1981. One industry insider noted, "We are really at a standstill. I don't think you are going to see much money coming into the industry for three or four years."

- Exit windows for venture investors continued to shrink. The IPO market is at a virtual standstill and sales of portfolio companies to strategic buyers are harder to complete. Venture-backed IPOs fell from 441 in 2000 to 83 during 2002. The value of mergers and acquisitions of venture-backed companies fell 58% from 2001 to 2002, closing another door on early-stage investors looking to cash out their stakes. According to Thompson Venture Economics and the National Venture Capital Association, venture firms concluded 300 merger deals valued at $7.2 billion in 2002, compared to the prior year's 336 transactions for venture-backed companies, mainly among high-tech startups, valued at $17.1 billion.

Mark Heesen, president of the National Venture Capital Association, predicts the following: "It will likely take several years for short-term private equity performance to return to normal levels as it will take some time for company valuations to rise and the IPO and M&A markets to recover. Today venture capitalists are focused on building strong, sustainable businesses, so that when liquidity markets do emerge, they will be able to produce attractive returns for their investors."

Despite the double funk of the dot-com implosion and an ailing economy, don't abandon all hope of raising capital. In summing up the 2003 Venture Capital & Private Equity Conference, Sean Silverstone, an editor at *HBS Working Knowledge,* reported that the consensus among industry experts holds that today's back-to-basics approach to backing startups will soon payoff. Stewart Alsop, a venture investor and *Fortune* columnist is another optimist; he says, "Assuming we venture capitalists have relearned these lessons (no shortcuts to the hard work required to start new companies), this is one of the best of times to invest in startups. Entrepreneurs now take investments at low valuation. Executives now have been battle-tested. The stock market will, eventually, welcome new issues of startup stocks. In sum: These are the perfect conditions for venture capitalists looking to create great new companies."

WHEN NOT TO LOOK FOR VENTURE CAPITAL

Time runs a close second to cash on every entrepreneur's list of scarce resources. Don't waste valuable time thinking about raising venture capital until you have convinced yourself that your venture will generate substantial wealth for yourself and your investors. Your goal must be more than self-employment. You must have a burning desire to build an enterprise that will seize every opportunity for profitable growth and, ultimately, provide liquidity for your investors. Furthermore, the venture must be positioned in markets that provide such opportunities.

From an investor's perspective, there are three types of entrepreneurial ventures:

1. *Lifestyle ventures:* Lifestyle ventures account for over 80% of all startups. Typically, five-year revenue projections are well under $10 million. These ventures are fine for entrepreneurs driven by lifestyle motives, but they are of no interest to investors.

2. *Middle-market ventures:* Five-year revenue prospects for middle-market ventures can range from $10 million to $50 million. These ventures are also fine for entrepreneurs, but most will remain privately owned indefinitely or will be sold. They rely heavily on *bootstrap financing.* Those that grow faster than internal cash flows and retained earnings can support, may need outside equity-type financing. If the deal is properly structured, middle-market companies can offer acceptable capital gains and cash-out opportunities for investors, typically business angels.

3. *High-potential ventures:* One or two of every ten venture deals must be the homerun that every successful venture investor needs to cover the inevitable fatalities and bolster mediocre returns from the portfolio's living dead. Five-year revenue projections exceed $50 to $100 million. They typically require several rounds of six-, seven-, or even eight-figure financing and expect to be publicly traded or acquired within five years. They are the next generation Qualcom, Krispy Kreme, Macromedia, and eBay. Only high-potential ventures are candidates for financing from venture capital funds. They make up less than 1% of early-stage ventures.

In practical terms, at a minimum, your vision and your business plan must support expectations that within five years your venture will be generating revenues of at least $10 to $20 million and growing by at least 20% per year with a pretax profit margin of at least 15%. Ventures below these thresholds may provide comfortable incomes and perks for entrepreneurs, but the prospects for capital gains for investors are unattractive. At the other extreme, entrepreneurs will have the least trouble raising venture capital when their vision and financial projections support expectations of revenues in excess of $50 million within five years, growing at 30% to 50% or more per year and bringing down pretax profit margins of 20% or more.

There are no hard data on the number of startup and high-growth middle-market and high-potential ventures or their annual capital requirements. Educated guesses generated from data collected over 20 years by the Center for Venture Research at the University of New Hampshire place the number of companies growing at rates in excess of 20% per year at about half a million. Companies on the *Inc. 500* list of fastest growing private companies are leading examples. The number of startups with attractive capital gains potential is estimated to be in the neighborhood of fifty thousand per year. The annual equity financing requirements of these high-growth and startup ventures are estimated to total some $60 billion per year.

There are two primary sources of venture financing for entrepreneurs: one visible and one invisible.

Venture Capital Funds

The visible venture capital market is populated by the venture capital firms listed in *Pratt's Guide to Venture Capital Sources*. Choosing the right venture capital firms to approach is an important part of the fund-raising process. An entrepreneur who has not researched and targeted venture firms runs the risk of lengthening the search and overshopping the plan. Venture capitalists regularly exchange information, so rejection from one firm may influence others.

To target venture capital firms whose investment criteria match the characteristics of your venture, carefully examine *Pratt's Guide*. Published annually, it contains over 1,700 listings of venture capital firms. No more than 500 meet the requirements for membership in the respected National Venture Capital Association. The *Guide* includes:

- Complete contact data
- Capital under management
- Recent investment history
- Industry, project, geographic, and financing role preferences
- Helpful articles on raising funds and structuring deals

Pratt's Guide is an essential tool for targeting venture fund prospects. In the tradition of entrepreneurs everywhere, beg, borrow, or "steal" a copy.

Another guide, this one well worth buying is Dante Fichera's *Insider's Guide to Venture Capital, 2002*. In addition to detailed listings of over 400 active venture capitalists, Fichera's guide includes how-to essays by insiders, including how to:

- Find venture funds looking for companies like yours.
- Write—and pitch—a winning business plan.
- Decide what kind of funding you need and how to get it.
- Lead your company through its early growth stages.

According to PricewaterhouseCoopers, in today's market, a typical fund might close at $50 to $150 million and actively invest for three to five years. Many funds invest between $4 to $8 million in any one venture over a three- to five-year period and look for companies with market potential of $75 to $200 million. Venture capital firms have fixed costs that usually preclude their looking at deals under $5 million. Since a venture fund typically invests in only 20 to 30 companies, each investment must be screened carefully. Venture capitalists will be looking for a 30% to 40%, or more, annual return on investment and for a total return of 5 to 20 times their investment.

Every firm in venture fund portfolios started life in the *high-potential* category. Entrepreneurs most likely to succeed in their search for capital from venture capital funds will be looking for seven- or eight-figure financing and should be able to support most, if not all, of the following expectations:

- Gross revenues in excess of $50 million within 5 to 10 years
- Annual growth rates in excess of 30% to 40%
- Large and growing national or international market potential
- Competitive edges that can generate "obscene" profits
- Management teams with a record of building successful ventures
- Cash-on-cash return to investors of 40% to 50% per annum
- Depending on their holding period, capital gains multiples for investors of 5 to 20 times their investment

A typical round of financing from a venture capital fund is a later-stage deal in excess of $10 million. If your venture is looking for equity financing from institutional venture capital investors, you are on the wrong side of 100-to-1 odds. To save time knocking on the wrong doors, test your business plan against the *high-potential* venture criteria. If it flunks, take a close look at the invisible venture capital market.

Business Angels

The invisible venture capital market is by far the oldest and the biggest. It is made up of over two million individuals, most with a net worth well in excess of $1 million, excluding their personal residences. The majority of these individuals are self-made multimillionaires (first-generation money); in other words, they are individuals with substantial business and entrepreneurial experience. Over 60% of the *Forbes 400* richest people in America are self-made multimillionaires. Those inclined to bankroll entrepreneurs are known as *business angels* as mentioned earlier.

The Center for Venture Research at the University of New Hampshire estimates that about 250,000 angels invest $20 to $30 billion every year in over 30,000 ventures. Bill Gates, number one on the *Forbes 400* list, is Exhibit A on the angel list. For reasons he describes as intellectual as well as financial, Gates has bankrolled several startup ventures in the biotech field.

Entrepreneurs most likely to succeed in their search for capital from angels will be seeking low six- to low seven-figure financing. They will also be dealing with groups of individual investors willing to take positions in seed and startup deals, who demand competitive rates of return and exit opportunities but who often back ventures with less ambitious expectations than those required to grab the attention of venture funds.

For ventures with competent and committed management and a solid business plan, the odds of raising angel financing are much higher than the odds of raising capital from venture capital funds. A typical angel deal is an early stage round in the $100,000 to $500,000 range raised from six or eight investors. These coinvestors are usually trusted friends and business associates. Find one angel and you have found a choir.

The better odds are offset by the fact that angels are not easy to find. For obvious reasons, angels keep low profiles. There is no *Pratt's Guide to Angels*, and there are no public records of most angel deals. Informal networks of friends and business associates connect business angels to one another. They tend to meet on an ad hoc basis whenever a member of the group spots a promising investment opportunity. Entrepreneurs need to depend on ingenuity and tenacity in their pursuit of angel financing. Here are some tips on how to find prospective angels:

- Look close to home—most angels invest in ventures they can reach in less than a two-hour drive.

- Look for individuals familiar with your markets or technology—they are the most likely to be interested in your venture. Their experience can be more valuable than their capital.

- Many angels are active in charitable and civic affairs—look for their names in the local press and on the boards of directors and sponsors of such organizations.

- Most angels are risk-takers in their avocations as well as in their professions—many are private pilots and ocean sailors. Private aircraft and ocean-going sailboats must be registered with the FAA or the U.S. Coast Guard. These registrations are public information.

- Although it sounds bizarre, use your state motor vehicle department to find the owners of pricey performance cars.

- Use "gatekeepers," such as attorneys, accountants, and bankers who specialize in serving early-stage and high-growth ventures. Ask them for introductions to potential investors. Better yet, ask them to forward a copy of your business plan to their investor contacts.

- Above all, start building a roster of potential investors at least six months before you start your search for money.

Angel investors experience the entrepreneurial life vicariously meaning they are involved-but-not-immersed, bringing new ventures into the world but not as a full-time job. Many well-off baby boomers are expected to join the ranks of the angels as their careers wind down. They want to have an impact, but at their stage of life they don't want the hassle of managing day-to-day operations.

New organizational structures are emerging continually in the angel marketplace. Many of the new breeds of angel investors have organized into formal and informal groups. According to the Center for Venture Research at the University of New Hampshire, there were approximately 50 formal business angel groups in the United States five years ago. The Center estimates that now there may be as many as 170 formal and informal organizations located throughout leading technology and business regions in the United States and Canada. These groups typically have one or more of the following characteristics: loosely to well-defined legal structures; part-time or full-time management; standardized investment processes; a public face usually with a Web site and public relations activities; and, occasionally a traditionally structured venture capital/angel investing fund.

The number of organized groups has grown in response to a number of factors:

- A desire to attract better deals and generate higher returns than angels acting alone
- The growth of venture capital funds and the attraction of venture investing
- A widening "capital gap" between individual and institutional venture capital investors that has created a need and an opportunity for pooled investments
- The legal and economic complexity of these investments
- A large increase in the number of self-made, high net worth individuals who want to be more involved in their alternative asset management
- The volume of deal flow
- Social camaraderie among investors

These groups are far more organized and active than the investment clubs of the early 1990s. See the Kauffman Foundation's *Business Angel Investing Groups Growing in North America* for more details (available free on the Web at www.entreworld.org). Entrepreneurs have a better chance of finding interested angels when they are presenting to one of these groups. Further, when a deal is done, companies also stand to benefit from the collective expertise that such organizations offer.

One of the first angel alliances, Silicon Valley-based Band of Angels, dates back to 1995 and boasts seven initial public offerings and 15 acquisitions that have reaped double-digit returns. Startups must be located near the group's headquarters. The Band of Angels is a formal group of 150 former and current high-tech executives. Three startups are considered at each monthly meeting.

Companies that receive investment also receive the benefit of contacts and mentorship from the same people who helped build Silicon Valley.

The Carolina Angel Forum, now 50 investors strong, is striving to double its membership this year (2003), increasing the potential for young, local companies to raise $250,000 to $2 million in early stage funding. At their evening meetings, held four times annually, investors hear presentations from two entrepreneurs. Members can invest at will.

A new group has been formed to address the Midwest's angel shortage. The Midwest Angel Network Association includes three angel groups: Prairie Angels, Northern Illinois Angels, and Ceres Group. The Illinois Coalition, PricewaterhouseCoopers, the Chicagoland Chamber of Commerce, and Mayer, Brown, Rowe & Maw helped pull the group together.

Tech Coast Angels has about 200 members in its Los Angeles, Orange County, and San Diego chapters—a number that has risen slightly since 2000. Tech Coast Angels and Pasadena Angels, a group that meets in the San Gabriel Valley, recently invested $1 million in a venture that also landed $2 million from a New York venture capital firm. Tech Coast Angels counts 21 venture firms as *affiliate members,* meaning potential deals may be referred back and forth between the network and the VC firms. Tech Coast Angels see some 50 investment proposals a month. Two to four move to the due diligence phase, resulting in a second presentation at a group dinner. Usually, half of the finalists attract investors. Venture firms took part in the majority of the Tech Coast Angels' 11 investments during 2002.

Innovation Philadelphia is launching Mid-Atlantic Angel Group Fund I to bridge the gap between angel funding and institutional venture capital funding. The $5 million to $10 million fund will operate as a member-managed fund that provides its investors with an opportunity for active involvement in diversified venture capital investments throughout Southeastern Pennsylvania, Central and Southwestern New Jersey, and Delaware. The expected average investment will be between $250,000 and $500,000 in a $500,000 to $1.5 million round. The fund expects to invest in 8 to 12 companies.

John May and Cal Simmons, authors of *Every Business Needs an Angel,* helped organize or advise four angel clubs in the Washington, DC region managing over $50 million in investable assets, reaching 275 investors monthly, and making dozens of investments in early stage companies annually. One of the angel clubs they founded, The Dinner Club, is an organization of 60 individuals, each of whom contributed $80,000, creating a $5 million pool to back at least a dozen companies. The group meets monthly to hear pitches from entrepreneurs, does follow-up investigations, and makes early stage investments by majority vote.

Boston-based Common Angels, a 55-member group, has focused on software startups since its founding four years ago. Five members of the Massachusetts Software and Internet Council started the group. Common Angels, who hold monthly meetings over breakfast, have invested $32 million in software deals. Says managing director James Geshwiler, "There are as many different ways of investing as there are angels." He adds, "The people looking for quick killings have disappeared from the scene. The angels have grown up. They are now taking a very disciplined approach." Many angels don't want the responsibility for outside money and a huge portfolio. As Geshwiler sees it, "This is becoming a tier, an institutionalized tier of venture investing."

A directory of formal and informal angel groups around the country is available from the Center for Venture Research at the University of New Hampshire. Inc.com provides a briefer online Directory of Angel-Investor Networks. *Angel Investing: Matching Startup Funds with Startup Companies—A Guide for Entrepreneurs, Individual Investors, and Venture Capitalists* by Mark Van Osnabrugge and Robert Robinson is worth reading.

Electronic matching services are a distinctly different approach to improving the effectiveness of the invisible angel marketplace. The original computer-based matching service, Venture Capital Network, Inc. (VCN), was founded in 1984 as a not-for-profit affiliate of the Center for Venture Research at the University of New Hampshire. VCN moved to MIT in 1990, where it continues to function as The Technology Capital Network at MIT (TCN). A directory of similar networks around the country can be obtained from the Center for Venture Research at the University of New Hampshire.

VCN served as the prototype for ACE-*Net* (Access to Capital Electronic Network), a 1995 initiative of the SBA's Office of Advocacy. ACE-*Net* was developed in consultation with the U.S. Securities and Exchange Commission (SEC) and the North American Securities Administrators Association to promote entrepreneurs' access to seed and startup capital, to enhance the role of business angels in the venture capital market, and to reduce the cost of raising private equity capital through the use of standard interstate disclosure documents and policies.

Using a secure Internet database, ACE-*Net* is a national marketplace for entrepreneurial capital activity. ACE-*Net* operates in 46 states and Puerto Rico through 63 Network Operators affiliated with either the schools of business of state universities or state-based entrepreneurial centers. The national organization is responsible for all education and training activities, and oversees information technology and research contracts. A directory of the 63 Network Operators can be found on ACE-*Net*'s Web site. ACE-*Net* claims to have assisted over 2,500 entrepreneurs obtain financing.

The data contrasting angel and venture fund financing suggest that these two sources of capital complement each other. The complementary relationship is a function of the size and the stage of the deal. Angels are the most likely source of small amounts of early-stage financing. Venture capital funds are more likely to provide larger rounds of later-stage financing. At their intersection co-investing is not uncommon. Sychron, Inc., a provider of workload management software, received its initial round of funding led by Sigma Partners with Dot-EDU Ventures, First European American Ventures, and a number of angel investors.

THE HUNT FOR EQUITY FINANCING STARTS EARLY

A successful hunt for angel financing or financing from a venture capital fund normally will take at least six months from start to finish. The Center for Venture Research at the University of New Hampshire asked entrepreneurs who had raised venture financing how long it took to raise funds. The fund-raising process was divided into two stages:

Stage 1: the elapsed time between the decision to raise funds and the first meeting with an angel or managing partner of a venture capital fund

Stage 2: the elapsed time between the first meeting and the receipt of funds

In Stage 1, the median elapsed time was one month to find and meet the first angel, and 1.75 months to find and meet the first managing partner or senior investment professional of a venture capital fund. This result seems counterintuitive, given the relative obscurity of angels. However, although venture capital funds are easier to find, it may take more persistence to arrange an appointment with a venture capitalist than with an angel. One venture capitalist tests an entrepreneur's persistence by never returning the first three or four telephone calls.

A more significant difference was reported in the elapsed time between the first meeting and the receipt of funds (Stage 2). The median elapsed time was 2.5 months for angels and 4.5 months for venture capital funds. From start to finish, raising funds from angels consumed about four months compared to six months for capital raised from venture capital funds. In his critique of this section of the chapter, one battle-scarred entrepreneur/angel commented, "I do not believe this is correct. I believe this is revisionist hindsight. I would suspect 9 to 12 months from the concept to the check is much more realistic."

The shorter deliberation time for angels may be due to the fact that angel deals typically involve a close group of co-investors led by a successful entrepreneur who is familiar with the venture's technology, products, and markets. Typically, the lead investor will vary from deal to deal, and each angel's piece of the deal tends to be a relatively small percentage of an investors total assets. The average time angels spend conducting due diligence increased from three months in 2000 to four months today, according to Mike Franks, Managing Director of Goodman's Angel Network, a new Toronto-based angel group and an angel himself.

Venture capital funds, on the other hand, are involved in deals that represent a significant fraction of fund assets. Managing partners' carried interest in future profits and a fiduciary responsibility to their limited partners are powerful motivators of thorough due diligence. Organizational structure and decision-making authority involve more people in the approval process. In the post-dot-com economy, venture funds are taking more time to perform due diligence according to a Managing Partner of IDG Ventures. "In the heyday, you would see a proposal on Monday and have to present the term sheet on Friday." Now, he said, you have up to five months to perform due diligence. That time also allows a stronger relationship to build between VC and entrepreneur. (Not all entrepreneurs share this view of the virtues of protracted due diligence.)

Business Plans

A comprehensive, investor-oriented business plan will not guarantee success in raising funds, but lack of a business plan will ensure failure. Investors want the answers to three basic questions. Is there really an opportunity here? Can these people pull it off? Will the cash flow?

Preparing a winning business plan is a painful, but essential, exercise for two reasons:

1. The discipline of the process forces you to articulate your vision and how and when you expect to achieve it. Anticipate weeks of hard work to do the job right.
2. A clearly written and attractively packaged business plan raises the odds of getting the attention of investors. Because the business plan speaks for the venture, it must speak loud and clear. The ability to articulate goals, objectives, and a strategy for achieving them is characteristic of successful entrepreneurs. Investors look for entrepreneurs who can manage limited resources by objectives as well as by instinct. The Executive Summary is the most critical section in a business plan. This is your bait. To stand out

from the crowd, the Executive Summary must be crafted with care and flair. See Chapter 4 for a detailed discussion of business plans.

Professional Advice

You can't afford less than the best legal, accounting, banking, financial, and management advice. One word of caution: Don't confuse legal and accounting advice with business advice. Early-stage companies sometimes make the mistake of looking to attorneys to shape their businesses.

Be cautious about whom you choose for advisors. Ask for and check references. Here are several suggestions:

- *Attorneys:* Your attorney should be experienced in negotiating, pricing, and structuring venture financing and must also be familiar with state and federal securities regulations.
- *Bankers:* Picking the right banker is as important as picking the right bank. A commercial loan officer who has been through the financing of emerging companies more than once can be an invaluable source of financial advice and contacts.
- *Accountants:* Pick a respected CPA with a firm that specializes in the design of accounting and management information systems for emerging companies. The cost is high, but the sooner you have a full audit of your financial statements, accompanied by an unqualified opinion, the better.

Finally, know that successful entrepreneurs are your best source of counsel. Use several you respect on a working board of directors; listen to them and pay them if you can. The benefits are certain to exceed the costs.

THE RIGHT INVESTORS

Think of fund raising as a process of buying capital rather than selling stock. The difference is subtle but important. Venture capital is a commodity. It is available from a variety of sources on a variety of terms. For every venture, some combination of sources and terms will be more appropriate than others and will exert a powerful influence on the future of the venture. Besides the price, the following factors will influence the choice of sources:

- Investors' exit expectations
- The availability of future financing
- The quality of management assistance available from investors
- Investors' experience in dealing with illiquid, high-risk investments

The final deal should be a partnership of professionals with complementary resources and shared goals.

As part of a fund-raising strategy, always look for knowledgeable investors. They are the most likely to be attracted to your venture, and whether you ask for it or not, they will provide you with the benefit of their know-how—most of which they learned by making their own mistakes, the same way all entrepreneurs learn their most valuable lessons. The right investors are value-added investors. For first-time entrepreneurs, the know-how available from battle-tested investors can be more valuable than their capital.

Your best investor prospects will be familiar with your markets, products, and technologies. Often these investors have managed or financed a successful startup in a similar field. For your sake as well as theirs, these investors will stay in close touch with your venture. However, there is a fine line between a productive relationship and meddling. Your investors' professional qualifications are necessary but not sufficient for a healthy relationship. Interpersonal chemistry will determine the quality of the relationship. The fit must feel right, as well as look right.

Attention to chemistry and shared goals is especially important when dealing with individual investors. You are about to embark on a long journey together, a journey that will encounter some stormy seas. You will maximize your chances of surviving if your investment partners have the character, experience, and inclination to help you through it. You don't need to be dealing with investor fatigue when the going gets rough.

The following comments paraphrase the thoughts of one successful angel. For him, success is more than the numbers; it has to do with values and commitment to a shared vision. While he sits on the boards of directors of his portfolio companies, he describes his role as a coach and mentor, someone with whom the entrepreneur can share doubts, fears, and vulnerabilities. Creating a company that is so successful that he can sell his shares back to the founders at a reasonable profit is his idea of the ultimate achievement.

Create a compatible structure for investor relationships: a seat on a working board of directors, an informal consulting role, or full or part-time employment. Maintain frequent contact with all your investors. Quarterly financial statements accompanied by status reports from the CEO are bare minimums. Contact can mean a simple telephone call, e-mail, or faxed message. Investors like to be touched by short but frequent contacts.

The right investors will be aware of the risks involved in your venture and should be emotionally, as well as financially, able to bear those risks. You don't have time to deal with impatient, inexperienced investors (so-called doctor and dentist money) while trying to cope with the inevitable delays and problems that plague all entrepreneurs. Murphy (of Murphy's Law fame) will be your constant companion.

Unless your margins are truly exceptional (more than 20% after-tax), a rapidly growing venture will develop an insatiable appetite for cash. Ideally, your original investors will be prepared to provide the additional funds required to finance growth. If not, be sure that they anticipate the need and are realistic about the cost (dilution) of second- and third-round financing. Your pro forma financial statements provide the basis for discussing these issues with your initial investors.

DUE DILIGENCE

Once you and your prospective investors have reached a preliminary agreement, your investors will begin what is known as *due diligence*. Due diligence is the homework investors complete before a final decision is reached. The process includes background checks on the management team, industry studies, analysis of the competition, identification of major risks, and other reasons, often intangible, why the investment should not be made. In essence, due diligence is a detailed evaluation of your business plan. Expect at least two to three months to pass before the exercise is complete.

The most important variables in an investor's decision to finance a venture are the integrity, competence, and commitment of the entrepreneur and his or her management team. Be scrupulously honest about even the smallest details. One lie and it's over. One bluff and it's over. The key to raising capital is lowering risk, not hyping the upside.

But due diligence is a two-way street. Entrepreneurs should be equally concerned about the qualifications of their investors. Your banker, accountant, and attorney should know the local venture capital players cold. They will be glad to steer you toward the good guys and away from the bad. If your prospective investors don't have impeccable reputations, you need to look further. If you are dealing with angels, ask for references and bio-sketches describing their professional and educational backgrounds. Talk to each of the references.

Remember that you will be living with your investors through stressful times. Finding the right investors is worth the effort! The most valuable homework you can do is to talk to other entrepreneurs bankrolled by your potential investors. Ask your investors for a list of their portfolio company CEOs, including those that struggled. If they won't provide you with references, you've learned all that you need to know—keep looking. Call all the CEOs and ask the following questions:

- Have your investors been of any assistance to you beyond their money? How?
- How have they reacted when setbacks and disappointments came?
- If you had it to do over again and had some choices, would you bring them on board?

Given the challenges of turning dreams, blood, sweat, tears, and money into market leaders, you should not be surprised to hear a story or two which gives you pause. Companies do fail. CEOs do under perform for extended periods of time and over the course of multiple rounds of funding, ultimately straining relationships with any investor. But you should be hearing a vast preponderance of comforting stories—stories of support, contribution, patience, understanding, and mutual sacrifice, even friendship. If you do, you can be assured that your prospective investor is not a vulture capitalist.

These questions focus on the relationship between investors and the management they bet on. They are designed to help you decide whether your investors will make good partners. Satisfying yourself on these issues is part of the subtle distinction between buying capital and selling stock.

THE COST OF CAPITAL

Risk and, consequently, the cost of venture capital vary dramatically over the developmental stages of a new venture. The following generally accepted definitions of financing stages are taken from *Pratt's Guide to Venture Capital Sources*.

Early-Stage Financing

Seed Financing: A relatively small amount of capital is provided to an inventor or entrepreneur to prove a concept and to qualify for startup capital. If the initial steps are successful, this may involve product development and market research, as well as building a management team and developing a business plan.

Startup Financing: Capital provided to companies completing product development and initial marketing. Companies may be in the process of organizing, or they may already have been in business for one year or less, but not sold their product commercially. Usually such firms will have made market studies, assembled the key management, developed a business plan, and are ready to do business.

First-Stage Financing: Capital provided to companies that have expended their initial capital (often in developing and market-testing a prototype) and require funds to initiate full-scale manufacturing and sales.

Second-Stage Expansion Financing: Working capital for the initial expansion of a company that is producing and shipping and has growing accounts receivable and inventories. Although the company has made progress, it may not yet be showing a profit.

Third-Stage, or Mezzanine, Financing: Capital provided for major expansion of a company that has an increasing sales volume and that is breaking even or profitable. These funds are used for marketing, working capital, further plant expansion, or development of an improved product.

Bridge Financing: Financing needed when a company is between stages or when it plans to go public in six months to a year. Bridge financing is often structured so that it can be repaid from the proceeds of the next round or a public underwriting. It may involve restructuring of major stockholder positions through secondary transactions.

REQUIRED RATES OF RETURN

Despite every entrepreneur's confidence in his or her "sure thing," many more ventures fail than succeed. Investors need a few big winners to offset the losers. Depending on the stage of the financing and, therefore, the risks involved, compound rates of return from 25% to 60% or more are not unreasonable expectations. A representative range of risk/return relationships is shown in Exhibit 6.1.

The figures in Exhibit 6.1 are required *anticipated returns* (ex ante) going into a deal. Seasoned investors know that, no matter how thorough their due diligence, only one venture in 5 or 10 will meet or exceed their expectations. There is no average deal. Investors are fond of saying (with tongue in cheek) that they never made a bad investment—all their losers went south after the deal was made. In other words one or two big winners are required to offset the inevitable losers.

The rates in Exhibit 6.1 are rough approximations. The unique characteristics of each venture and investor will determine the appropriate rate. Recognize that the lower your investors' perceptions of risk, the lower will be their required return on investment (ROI); that is, the lower the share of equity you will have to give up to obtain any given amount of capital. Put another way, the longer you can survive on founders' capital, sweat equity, and bootstrap financing, the lower will be the cost of capital.

EXHIBIT 6.1   Risk-adjusted cost of venture capital.

Stage (Risk)	Expected Annual Return
Seed	80%
Startup	60
First stage	50
Second stage	40
Third stage	30
Bridge	25

Realized returns (ex post) on a successful investor's portfolio of venture deals seldom will be more than 5 to 10 points above the returns on a diversified portfolio of quality common stocks, that is, venture portfolio ROIs of 15% to 20%. Keep in mind that if a venture fails, investors typically incur bigger losses than founders—and if the venture succeeds, founders typically are bigger winners than their investors. For this reason alone, losing potential investors by quibbling over a few percentage points of ownership seldom makes sense.

Investors tend to think in terms of capital gain multiples—often called times return—rather than rates of return. The conversion is simple and can be done on most hand calculators. Exhibit 6.2 illustrates conversion relationships. To use Exhibit 6.2, select your investors' required rate of return in the ROI column. Next select the exit year that is the expected holding period between investment and cash-out. The capital gain multiplies corresponding to the required ROI are in the exit year column. For example, if the required ROI is 50% and the expected holding period is five years, the capital gain multiple is 7.6. A venture capitalist would say, "7.6× in 5 years."

EXHIBIT 6.2   Capital gain multiplies (times return)/ROI (rate of return) conversion table.

	Exit Year				
ROI	**3**	**4**	**5**	**7**	**10**
25%	2.0	2.4	3.1	4.8	9.3
30	2.2	2.9	3.7	6.3	13.8
40	2.7	3.8	5.4	10.5	28.9
50	3.4	5.1	7.6	17.1	57.7
60	4.1	6.6	10.5	26.8	110.0
80	5.8	10.5	18.9	61.2	357.0

NONFINANCIAL PAYOFFS

The influence of nonfinancial payoffs is another distinction between the venture capital fund and angel markets. Individual investors frequently look for nonfinancial as well as competitive financial returns from their venture investments.

Nonfinancial considerations fall into several categories. Some reflect a sense of social responsibility, and some are forms of *psychic income* (so-called hot-buttons) that motivate many individuals. The list of influential considerations includes:

- Generating jobs in areas with chronically high unemployment
- Developing socially useful technology (for example, medical, energy, and environmental technology)
- Assisting in the economic revival of urban areas
- Supporting female and minority entrepreneurs
- Personal satisfaction from assisting entrepreneurs to build successful ventures in a free enterprise economy

In addition to bringing a certain missionary zeal to the deal, angels (especially cashed-out entrepreneurs) typically look for fun in their investments. Most angels could be described as adventure capitalists.

Entrepreneurs sensitive to the match between the characteristics of their ventures and the idiosyncrasies of potential investors will be able to raise funds on terms that are attractive to both parties.

PRICING THE DEAL: THINK LIKE AN INVESTOR

Based on projected revenues, profits, growth rates, and future financing requirements (dilution), entrepreneurs and investors should arrive at a shared vision of the venture's value 5 to 10 years after financing, or at whatever exit date they agree on, and its exit strategy. Think in terms of dollars and value as opposed to ownership percentage. A business plan based on realistic assumptions is an entrepreneur's best friend at this point in the negotiations.

Four basic principles are involved in the pricing decision:

1. The division of ownership between founders and outside investors is determined by the expected future value of the venture and the share required to compensate investors at competitive rates—not by the relative dollar investments of the two parties.

2. The longer the track record of a new venture, the lower the perceived risk to an investor, the lower the cost of capital (see Exhibit 6.1), and the lower the share of equity required to purchase any given amount of capital.

3. The more a venture is expected to be worth at any point in the future, the lower the share of equity required to purchase any given amount of capital (see Exhibit 6.3).

4. The shorter the waiting period to cash out (that is, to harvest), the lower the share of equity required to purchase any given amount of capital. Holding periods are important to investors. Delays dramatically reduce realized ROIs.

Exhibit 6.3 illustrates how future values and holding periods affect the percentage of a venture's equity required to yield a 50% annual return on a $4 million investment. The impact is dramatic. An 11% stake would be required in a venture expected to be worth $80 million in two years. In a venture expected to be worth $80 million in seven years an 85% stake would be required. N/A indicates that over 100% of the equity would be required if holding periods are too long or future values too small, that is, no deal.

Most investors do not want a controlling interest in a venture. Some argue that no one investor should own a controlling interest, that it should take at least two people to effect a major change in the company's goals, direction, or financing. As Exhibit 6.3 reveals, investors seek more than 50% of a company only when needed to justify the capital invested. Investors expect you and your management team to run the company profitably. Beware of investors who are control freaks, including former operating managers who assume that they can run the company better than its management.

EXHIBIT 6.3   Percentage of ownership required to yield a 50% rate of return on a $4 million investment.

	Future Value of Company (in millions)					
Exit Year	$10	$20	$40	$60	$80	$100
2	90%	45%	23%	15%	11%	9%
3	N/A	68	34	23	17	14
4	N/A	N/A	51	34	25	20
5	N/A	N/A	76	51	38	30
7	N/A	N/A	N/A	N/A	85	68
10	N/A	N/A	N/A	N/A	N/A	N/A

N/A = Not applicable; investment would not be made.

PRICING MODELS

Pricing refers to the fraction of the equity your investors receive for the capital they provide. Deal pricing, the central mystery of venture capital, is part art, part science, and part Yankee horse-trading. Determining the value of a promising venture at the seed and startup stage is mostly "mystic art." In theory, investors attempt to estimate the value of the company at some time in the future, and then discount that figure to a present value using a desired rate of return. In practice, promising very early-stage deals are often valued by rules of thumb. One rule of thumb values a seed round between $2 million premoney minimum and $10 million premoney maximum. Start with $2 million then add for an experienced management team who've worked together before, large market opportunity, strategic partnership signed, real barriers to entry/competitors and investor interest.

Pricing models are powerful tools for negotiating and reaching agreement on the pricing of an investment. By focusing on pricing models and the assumptions that determine values in the capital markets, you can avoid some of the emotional biases that creep into negotiations when the stakes are high. A discussion of your investors' pricing model, its assumptions, and its probabilities will reveal the differences between your perceptions and your investors' perceptions. Reconciling these differences is essential. The following example employs traditional discounted cash flow techniques, except that it focuses on future values rather than present values using the risk-adjusted rates of return in Exhibit 6.1.

Assume that we are considering a $4 million first-stage round for a venture that expects to generate revenues of $40 million after five years with a 10% after-tax profit margin. Assume that after five years, the company expects to be growing annually at 20% or more and anticipates an IPO soon thereafter. Assume that publicly traded shares of companies of comparable size, risk, and growth rates in the same industry typically trade at P/E multiples around 15. Given these numbers and the investors' target ROI of 50% (7.6 times their investment in five years as shown in Exhibits 6.1 and 6.2), the founders must provide investors with a 51% stake in the company as shown in Exhibit 6.3.

This simple pricing model unfolds as follows: $40 million of revenues with a 10% margin yield after-tax profits of $4 million. Using a P/E ratio of 15, the equity will have a market value of $60 million. To earn a 50% ROI, investors need 7.6 times their investment of $4 million, that is, $30.4 million. For their investment to be worth $30.4 million, they will need to own 51% of the company's market capitalization of $60 million.

If $4 million represents 51% of the company, the implied post-money valuation of the company today is $7.8 million ($4 million/.51). Before the new money goes in, the venture has an implied pre-money valuation of $3.8 million ($7.8 – $4 million). This value is the result of the entrepreneur's recognition of a market opportunity and the capital and sweat equity invested to create a venture positioned to capitalize on that opportunity.

More sophisticated models (see Exhibit 6.4) include best case and worst case scenarios. Best case and worst case can be thought of as those assumptions and outcomes for which the probability of occurrence is one chance in 10. By focusing on the range of possible outcomes and their probabilities, entrepreneurs and investors can accomplish the difficult tasks of assessing financial risk and establishing the price of a round of financing with a minimum of subjective debate and hard feelings. Both parties should feel that the pricing outcome is fair and openly arrived at. Recognize, however, that, because of entrepreneurs' optimism and investors' skepticism, it is unlikely a real agreement will be reached on your projections. Most investors assume that an entrepreneur's worst case is, in fact, the best case.

EXHIBIT 6.4   Valuation model—Chicago method.

Capital invested $4,000,000
Required rate of return   50%

	Success	Sideways Survival	Failure
1. Revenue level after 5 years	$40 million		
2. Revenue level after 3 years		$10 million	
3. Revenue level after 2 years			$0
4. Exit strategy	IPO	Acquisition	Liquidation
5. After tax profit margin at liquidity°	10%	5%	0%
6. Earnings at liquidity°	$4 million	$500 thousand	$0
7. Price-earnings ratio at liquidity°	15	12	0
8. Value of company at liquidity°	$60 million	$6 million	$0
9. Present value of company using 50% discount rate above	$7.9 million	$1.8 million	$0
10. Probability of each scenario	60%	30%	10%
11. Expected present value under each scenario	$4.74 million	$540 thousand	$0
12. Weighted average present value of the company	$5.3 million		
13. Pre-money value	$3.3 million		
14. Percentage of ownership required to raise $4 million	76%		

°Liquidity refers to the point in the company's growth where the common stock can be sold by investors, either back to the company or to a third party.

Computer spreadsheets are indispensable tools for examining the implications of alternative assumptions, but beware of spreadsheet diarrhea. Investors are more interested in sales/marketing, management, production, and technology. Financial projections are the result of the vision, not vice versa.

TERM SHEETS—STRUCTURING THE DEAL

This is one place where entrepreneurs need help. A *term sheet* is a legal contract between an entrepreneur and investor describing the conditions under which money is provided. Since the plunge in valuations, term sheets have taken on even greater meaning for entrepreneurs and venture capitalists alike. Gary Glausser, partner and CFO of Birchmere Ventures, says, "When things were happening fast and furious, deals were being done with less attention to some of the details. The pendulum clearly was in favor of the companies because money was flowing. Now, the pendulum has swung the other way, and venture capitalists are dictating terms."

If you are dealing with a venture capital fund, after you have reached preliminary agreement on the amount and price of the deal, you will receive a nonbinding commitment letter and term sheet setting forth the following:

- The amount of the investment
- The form of the investment
- The share of the equity represented by the investment
- The terms and conditions to which you will be asked to agree

The types of securities used by venture investors range from common stock (typical of angel deals) to convertible preferred stock or subordinated debt with conversion features or warrants (typical of venture capital deals). Angel deals typically are less tightly structured than venture fund deals. Some angels won't do a deal if their agreement with an entrepreneur can't be captured in two pages. Venture fund term sheets often involve agreements that require 15 pages or more to cover everything the investors (and their well-paid attorneys) insist on reducing to written agreements.

Terms and conditions are legal obligations designed primarily to protect investors' interests. The preliminary term sheet is useful for identifying issues that could turn into deal killers if they are not resolved.

Before reviewing the proposed term sheet, do your homework! Never underestimate the wisdom to be found in interviews with other venture founders or the value of libraries, books, and seminars. *Term Sheets & Valuations— An Inside Look at the Intricacies of Venture Capital Term Sheets & Valuations* by venture capitalist Alex Wilmerding of Boston Capital Ventures is recommended reading. The book includes an actual term sheet from a leading law firm with line-by-line descriptions of each clause, identifying clauses favorable to entrepreneurs, clauses favorable to investors, neutral clauses, what can/should be negotiated, and the important points to pay attention to.

Virtually everything in a venture capital deal is negotiable, including the terms and conditions governing a venture investment. Don't go shopping for capital until you are familiar with the terms and conditions typically demanded by investors. These will be spelled out in the term sheet. Review the term sheet with your legal counsel and financial advisors before you start negotiations and don't hesitate to ask dumb questions. When it comes to term sheets, the only dumb question is the one you didn't ask. Concessions made under pressure to raise cash can lead to ruinous conflicts later. Since most terms are negotiable, it is essential that you understand the terms, identifying those that are most important to investors and those that are and are not acceptable to you. The ultimate contract should be one in which both parties feel that they have been treated fairly. Due diligence begins in earnest after you have signed off on the commitment letter and term sheet.

Term sheets in their entirety are too complex for treatment here. Terms and conditions deserving special attention include:

- *Liquidation preferences:* This is what investors want ahead of the other shareholders should the company be dissolved prematurely.
- *Antidilution protection:* Can have a big impact on shareholders if the company does a down round. Understand the implications of full ratchet versus weighted average forms of antidilution protection.
- *Voting rights:* Look for any special features, such as the right to veto a sale or merger of the company.
- *Board representation:* The composition of the board creates a dynamic that is critical for the future of the company.
- *Vesting provisions:* Should the founder and/or key employee stockholders leave the company, investors want the right to buy any unvested shares, usually at cost. Vesting can extend over three to four years.
- *Puts:* Terms under which investors can require the company to repurchase their shares after X years. Adds a "debt" feel to the deal.

HARVEST STRATEGY

Venture capital is *patient money.* Returns to investors take the form of long-term capital gains realized after an extended period during which the investment has little or no marketability (liquidity). Because expectations about timing and method of exit influence investment decisions, be prepared to discuss these issues early in your negotiations with investors. A harvest mentality based on the creation of substantial wealth for founders and investors is central to the fund-raising process.

Though each venture is unique and each industry is unique, successful companies require years to launch and build. The harvest strategy should reflect this fact of life by contemplating a medium-to-long time frame, at least three to five years for a high-potential venture and as long as seven to ten years for a middle-market company. A public stock offering, merger, or outright sale of the company are common exit strategies for high-potential ventures. Management and Employee Stock Ownership Plan (ESOP) buyouts are sometimes used as harvest strategies for investors in middle-market companies.

Patience and shared exit expectations are particularly critical for middle-market ventures, that is, ventures with limited prospects for a public offering or an acquisition by a larger firm within the 5- to 10-year exit horizon of most venture investors. If an investor expects to cash out by selling shares back to your venture or its management, be sure that the terms and conditions of the sale are tied to the operating performance and cash flow of the venture and not to some arbitrary multiple of the original investment. Your legal and financial advisors can help design acceptable "put" arrangements.

LESSONS FROM LOSERS

Most entrepreneurs learn the hard way—by making mistakes. However, entrepreneurs can learn some lessons from the mistakes of others. Reasons cited by investors for rejecting investment proposals can be instructive. Common reasons, gleaned from investor interviews, include:

- "In most cases, management did not seem adequate for the task at hand."
- "Unable to agree on price."
- "Unsatisfactory risk/reward ratios."
- "Too much wishful thinking."
- "Absence of a well-defined business plan."
- "Unfamiliar with business."
- "One of two key individuals not sufficiently committed—too involved with another activity."
- "Simply not interested in the proposed businesses. Saw no socioeconomic value in them."
- In the case of angels, the business was unattractive for whatever reason—including "Spouse refused."

CONCLUSION

Entrepreneurs and venture investors are at the heart of the free enterprise system. The last twenty years have seen the downsizing of large corporations and the emergence of the entrepreneur. All signs point to an acceleration of this "sea change" in the structure of the U.S. economy. This chapter is written for entrepreneurs with the integrity, competence, and commitment to build ventures that will create wealth for themselves and their investors, as well as the jobs, innovative products and services, export trade, and tax revenues of the future.

Business history in the United States is the history of equity financing. Raising equity is arduous. Multiple rejections are part of the process. But business history and the stock market pay tribute to the entrepreneurs who stuck it out.

7 DEBT AND OTHER FORMS OF FINANCING

Joel M. Shulman

RAISING CHEAP CAPITAL SUCCESSFULLY IS NOT THE SAME AS BEING SUCCESSFUL

Big companies have money . . . lots of money. In fact, large, publicly traded organizations have the cheapest capital of any company on the planet—by far. Inexpensive capital may be the single most significant comparative advantage that they have over small companies. It's a shame that they frequently squander it.

Fortune 500 companies have public stock, public debt, collateralized debt, debt with enhanced credit ratings, supplier financing, and in a few situations, commercial paper (short-term debt issued directly to the investor). This means large companies, in addition to all of their advantages with manufacturing economies of scale, intellectual property, R&D, and specialized management, can use the power of cheap capital to beat all others. They have the ability to approach the investor directly and can raise *billions* of dollars in a couple of hours simply by posting an interest rate on a Telerate, Reuters, or Bloomberg terminal. Some companies such as Ford Credit or General Electric Credit do this *every* day. Entrepreneurs running small companies need to borrow against their cash reserves or stretch their credit card balances. Others appeal to family and friends for risk capital.

Financial giants can bypass the financial intermediaries altogether and save on high transaction fees by placing their money directly with the investor.

195

In summary, major companies have more funding sources, lower interest rates, lower transaction fees, and immediate access compared to small entrepreneurial companies. Large, publicly traded companies have funding sources that small companies can only dream about. Yet, despite these enormous advantages, large companies frequently fail. Being successful at raising cheap capital is not the same as being successful. There is more to the equation than just getting money. Large companies need to have good investment opportunities and an efficient structure to manage their investors' capital. Otherwise an abundance of capital spent recklessly will only create losses. It will just be a matter of time before losses creep in and capital flows cease to exist. Entrepreneurs running small companies tend to have the opposite problem. They don't have excess resources to waste so they are very careful with each dollar that they put to work.

Given the same opportunity among large and small companies, we would expect small companies, owing to their difficulty and cost in raising risk capital, to be more efficient with spending. Moreover, since small firms are likely to be managed by watchful owners/entrepreneurs there may be a higher likelihood that waste of company assets will be lower among nonowner/managers. This suggests that the returns among efficiently managed small entrepreneurial firms might potentially be higher than the returns generated among similar ventures in the large organization. The potential of bringing together the cheap capital from large companies coupled with the efficiencies incorporated in small companies provides the makings of a great combination. However, thus far, it's been easier said than done. Entrepreneurs running small companies need to scrape together their risk capital from a variety of equity and debt sources. In this chapter, we explore some of the traditional methods of financing along with some market recent innovations. Much of what we discuss addresses issues of just being efficient in working capital operations. Successful entrepreneurs don't really need lessons in this area. They live the experience every day.

GETTING ACCESS TO FUNDS—START WITH INTERNAL SOURCES

Entrepreneurs requiring initial startup capital, funds used for growth, and working capital generally seek funds from *internal* sources. This contrasts with managers or owners of large, mature firms who have access to profits from operations, as well as funds from external sources. Internal funds are distinguished from external funds in that internal funding sources do not require external analysts or investors to independently appraise the worthiness of the capital investments before releasing funds. Moreover, since external investors and lenders do not share the entrepreneur's vision, they may view the potential risk/return trade-off in a different vein and may demand a relatively certain return on their investment after the firm has an established financial track record.

Exhibit 7.1 shows a listing of funding sources and the approximate timing of the firm's usage. In the embryonic stages of the firm's existence, much of the funding comes from the entrepreneur's own pocket. For example, in the beginning entrepreneurs consume their personal savings accounts, credit cards, and other assets such as personal computers, fax machines, in-home offices, furniture, and automobiles.

Soon after entrepreneurs begin tapping their personal fund sources, they may also solicit funds from relatives, friends, and banks. Entrepreneurs would generally prefer to use other people's money (OPM) rather than their own because if their personal investment turns sour, they still have a nest egg to feed themselves and their families. The nest egg phenomenon may be particularly acute if the entrepreneur leaves a viable job to pursue an entrepreneurial dream on a full-time basis. The costs to the entrepreneur in this case include the following:

- The opportunity cost of income from the prior job.
- The foregone interest on the initial investment.
- The potential difficulty of being rehired by a former employer (or others) if the idea does not succeed.

EXHIBIT 7.1   Sources of outside funding.

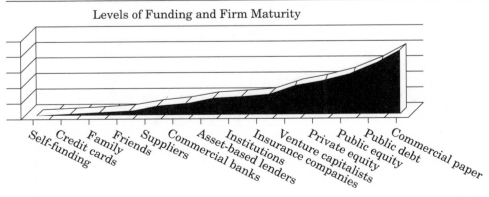

Levels of Funding and Firm Maturity

Self-funding, Credit cards, Family, Friends, Suppliers, Commercial banks, Asset-based lenders, Institutions, Insurance companies, Venture capitalists, Private equity, Public equity, Public debt, Commercial paper

Add to this the embarrassment of having to beg for a new job while paying off old debts and the prospective entrepreneur quickly realizes that the total cost of engaging in a new venture is very high.

Family and friends may volunteer to fund the entrepreneur's project in the early stages, and often will do so without a formal repayment schedule or specified interest cost. However, the funds are far from free.

Total costs, including nonfinancial indirect costs—such as family pressure, internal monitoring, and strained relations—are extremely high. Moreover, family and friends make poor financial intermediaries since they have limited financial resources, different repayment expectations, and narrow loan diversification. This contributes to the entrepreneur's desire to get outside funding from a traditional source as soon as possible. The question is: Where can entrepreneurs go before banks will give them money?

EARLY STAGE INVESTMENTS EXPERIENCE NEGATIVE CASH FLOW

Entrepreneurs in the early stages of their high-potential ventures (HPV) tend to lose money. This makes it extremely difficult to get traditional sources of funding (i.e., bank debt). The graph in Exhibit 7.2, known as the *J-curve*, shows the typical cash flow and return cycle for a risky project. Companies lose money in the first few years (with the losses often increasing in the second

EXHIBIT 7.2   The J-curve phenomenon.

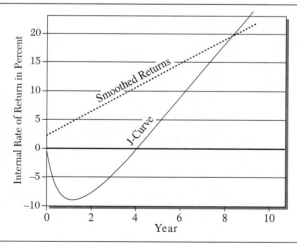

and third years) and then become positive a few years later. If during the low cash-flow period, the project/firm does not get refinanced or an additional cash flow injection, the ballgame is over. The HPV at this stage has an incomplete venture with nontransferable intellectual capital that is nearly impossible to get refinanced. This represents one of the primary reasons why many small businesses fail within the first five years. Since the project/firm usually has a limited operating history and few creditworthy assets, banks won't lend money. Consequently, if the venture capitalists or risk capital providers withhold future investments the ventures have insufficient capital to continue. They run out of funds during this early, critical period and terminate the business.

Institutional investors and high net worth individuals recognize the risk inherent in these new ventures and invest anyway. They figure that it takes only one or two good deals out of 10 investments to compensate for the other mediocre investments and losers. They operate on a *portfolio* approach. They evaluate many deals and invest in a small fraction. Within their investment base, they diversify their holdings so that, on average, they hope to make a good rate of return. Their orientation is completely different from traditional investors. However, the vast majority of entrepreneurs cannot get venture financing. This means that they need to be clever with the handling of their working capital requirements. Perhaps the best way is to manage their receivables and inventories in a manner that makes them cash-flow positive before they need their funds. This allows entrepreneurs to finance their operations, and in some cases, become cash-flow positive, despite relatively low profit margins.

WORKING CAPITAL—GETTING CASH FROM RECEIVABLES AND INVENTORIES

The timing of receivables collection and payment of accounts payable are key determinants in whether a firm is cash rich or cash poor. For example, an increase in net working capital (that is, current assets minus current liabilities) does not necessarily translate into an increase in liquidity. One reason for this is that increases in net working capital often result from increases in operating assets, net of increases in operating liabilities. These operating assets, such as accounts receivable and inventory, are usually tied up in operations and are not commonly liquidated (prematurely) to pay bills. Bills are typically paid with liquid financial assets, such as cash and marketable securities. Thus, only the liquid financial assets can be used to assess a firm's liquidity. Companies can improve their cash flow position by accelerating cash inflows and delaying out-flows. For example, companies that experience tight cash flows may request to their customers that they need to pay up-front. This will help finance the firm's operations, yet still provide the product or service to the customer. Presumably, the customer receives a discount or preferred service as a result of this early payment. In the absence of an accelerated cash receipt from the customer, the firm needs to borrow or receive credit from its suppliers.

Corporate insolvency usually results when the firm fails to service debt obligations or callable liabilities in a timely manner. Consequently, corporate liquidity can be estimated fairly accurately by taking the difference between liquid financial assets and callable liabilities. This is referred to as the *net liquid balance.*

Exhibit 7.3 shows how the net liquid balance is actually a part of net working capital. *Net working capital* is easily calculated in one of two ways:

1. Take the difference between current assets and current liabilities (as de-scribed earlier)
2. Take the difference between long-term liabilities, including equities, and long-term assets (such as fixed assets)

EXHIBIT 7.3   Integrative approach to working capital management.

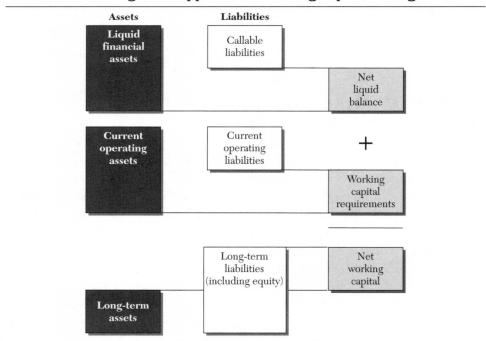

The first formula is often misinterpreted to be the difference between two liquid components, whereas the second definition suggests that the residual of long-term liabilities minus long-term assets is used to finance current assets, some of which may be liquid. The second definition also enables you to analyze the current assets and liabilities as consisting of both liquid financial/callable components and operating components.

Net working capital is actually the sum of working capital requirements balance. This suggests that only a part of net working capital is liquid. As a small firm grows, current operating assets increase. If current operating liabilities do not increase at the same rate as the increase in current operating assets (which is true when an entrepreneur pays suppliers before receiving payment from customers), then the entrepreneur will find that the firm's net liquid balance will decrease (assuming the firm does not increase its long-term funding arrangements). This may be true even though the firm is generating paper profits. As long as the increase in working capital requirements *exceeds* the increase in profits (*Note:* Profits are included in the long-term liabilities part of Exhibit 7.3 due to increase in stockholders' equity), then the firm will find itself reducing its liquidity levels.

This highlights one of the fundamental weaknesses of the traditional liquidity ratios, such as the current ratio or quick ratio. These ratios include both liquid financial assets and operating assets in their formula. Since operating assets are tied up in operations, inclusion of these assets in a liquidity ratio is not very useful from an ongoing concern perspective. Note the difference between a liquidity perspective and a liquidation perspective. A *liquidation perspective* assumes that in the event of a crisis assets may be sold off to meet financial obligations, while a *liquidity perspective* assumes the firm's financial obligations are met without impairing the viability of future operations. From an ongoing perspective, a new *ratio-net liquid balance* to *total assets* may be more indicative of liquidity than either the current ratio or the quick ratio.

SOURCES OF SHORT-TERM CASH—MORE PAYABLES, LESS RECEIVABLES

Entrepreneurs usually do not have all the cash they need all the time. Very often, an entrepreneurial firm needs to build up its inventory, thus reducing cash levels. Or an entrepreneur's customers may place unusually large orders, thus increasing accounts receivable financing or reducing company cash levels. There are many ways entrepreneurs can obtain additional short-term cash to restore their cash balances to the required levels.

As a rule, entrepreneurs look for short-term cash at the lowest possible rates. If they cannot obtain cash at no cost or at a very small cost, they begin to explore more expensive sources of cash. For example, an entrepreneur faced with a cash shortage might look first to her company's suppliers and her customers. She would look to suppliers because they extend credit to the company by collecting for goods and services after those goods and services are supplied. The entrepreneur can enlarge this credit by paying bills more slowly. The entrepreneur may also obtain additional cash by collecting from her company's customers more quickly.

Short-Term Bank Loans

If these relatively low-cost options are unavailable (or if their cost is too high because of the ill-will generated), the entrepreneur may next turn to the company's bank for a short-term loan. Entrepreneurs faced with a severe cash shortage may also try to convert into cash two of their working capital assets—accounts receivable and inventory. An entrepreneur may pledge her accounts receivable to a finance company in exchange for a loan, or she may sell them to a factoring company for cash. Similarly, an entrepreneur may pledge her inventory (often using a warehousing system) in exchange for a loan.

Trade Credit

Trade credit is one important and often low-cost source of cash. Nearly all entrepreneurs make use of trade credit to some degree by not paying suppliers immediately for goods and services. Instead, companies bill the entrepreneur, and the entrepreneur pays in 10 days, 30 days, or more. From the time when the supplier first provides the goods or services to the time when the customer finally pays for them, the supplier has, in effect, loaned the entrepreneur money. The sum of all these loans (bills) represents an entrepreneur's trade credit. By paying bills more slowly, an entrepreneur can increase the amount of these loans from his suppliers.

One way an entrepreneur can take more time to pay for his bills (or stretch his payables) is to stop taking discounts. For example, if his company normally takes advantage of all prompt-payment discounts, such as 2% for payment within 10 days, he can increase his company's cash by passing up the discount and paying the bill in the expected 30 days. Of course, this is an expensive source of cash. If he loses a 2% discount and has the use of the funds for 20 more days, he has paid approximately 36% interest (annual rate) for using the money.

However, he might argue that, in practice, the interest cost would not really be 36% because by forgoing discounts and aggressively stretching payables, the company would not pay the bill in 30 days. Instead, such a company would stretch out this payable as long as possible and perhaps attempt to pay in 60 days. Now, the equivalent interest rate is only about 15% (50 days' extra use of the money for 2%).

This brings up the subject of late payments. Many entrepreneurs do not consider 30 days (or any other stated terms) a real deadline. Instead, they try to determine the exact point at which further delay of payment will have a penalty. For example, if a company pays too slowly, the supplier may take one of the following actions:

- Require payment in full on future orders
- Report the company to a credit bureau, which would damage the company's credit rating with all suppliers
- Bring legal action against the company

Many cash managers believe, however, that as long as they can pay company bills just before incurring any of these penalties, they maximize their company's cash at little or no cost. The *hidden costs* of this approach include such risks as damaged reputation, lower credit limit from suppliers, higher prices from suppliers to compensate for delayed payment, and the risk of exceeding the supplier's final deadline and incurring a penalty.

Negotiating with Suppliers

If an entrepreneur wants more credit and would like to stretch out her payables, she does not always have to incur the risks just described. Very often, she can negotiate with her suppliers for more generous credit terms, at least temporarily. If she and her supplier agree on longer credit terms (say 60 or 90 days), she can get the extra trade credits she needs without jeopardizing her supplier relations or credit ratings. It's important to bear in mind that suppliers are trying to build up their businesses and must compete with other suppliers. One way these suppliers compete is through credit terms, and that fact can be used to the entrepreneur's advantage. Just as the entrepreneur solicits several price quotes before placing a major orders, she nay also want to encourage competition among suppliers for credit terms.

Some suppliers use generous terms of trade credit as a form of sales promotion. This is especially likely where a distributor is trying to enter a few geographical areas and is faced with the need to lure customers away from established rivals. In such circumstances, generous credit may well be more effective than an intensive advertising campaign or a high-pressure sales team. The credit may be a simple extension of the discount or net terms, or it may take a modified form such as an inventory loan.

Seasonal Business Credit Terms

If the entrepreneur is in a highly seasonal business, such as many types of retailing, he will find large differences in credit terms in different seasons. For example, as a retailer, he might be very short of cash in the fall as he builds up inventory for the Christmas selling season. Many suppliers understand this and willingly extend their normal 30-day terms.

Furthermore, some suppliers offer exceedingly generous credit terms to smooth out their own manufacturing cycle. Consider a game manufacturer that sells half its annual production in the few months before Christmas. Rather than produce and ship most of the games in the late summer, this manufacturer would much rather spread out its production and shipping schedule over most of the year. To accomplish this, the manufacturer may offer seasonal dating to its retail store customers. Seasonal dating provides longer credit terms on orders placed in off-peak periods. For example, the game manufacturer might offer 120-day terms on May orders, 90-day terms on June orders, and so on. This encourages customers to order early, and it allows the game manufacturer to spread out production over more of the year.

Advantages of Trade Credit

Trade credit has two important advantages that justify its extensive use. The first advantage is convenience and ready availability; because it is not negotiated, trade credit requires no great expenditure of executive time and no legal expenses. If a supplier accepts a company as a customer, the usual credit terms are automatically extended even though the maximum line of credit may be set low at first.

The second advantage (which is closely related to the first) is that the *credit available from this source automatically grows as the company grows.* Accounts payable are known as a spontaneous source of financing. As sales expand, production schedules increase, which in turn means that larger quantities of materials and supplies must be bought. In the absence of limits on credit, the additional credit becomes available automatically simply by placing orders for the extra material. If the manufacturing process is long and the supplier's payment is reached before the goods have been sold, some additional source of credit will also be needed. But the amount required will be much less than it would have been if no trade credit had been available.

Tightening Up Accounts Receivable Collections

Rapidly growing accounts receivable tie up a company's money and can cause a cash squeeze. However, these same accounts receivable become cash when they are collected. Some techniques—such as lockboxes and wire transfers—enable firms to collect receivables quickly and regularly. However, the question is: How can the rate of collection of receivables be increased temporarily during a cash shortage?

The most effective way to collect receivables quickly is simply to *ask for the money.* If the entrepreneur just sends a bill every month and shows the amount past due, the customer may not feel a great pressure to pay quickly. But if the entrepreneur asks for the money, either with a handwritten note on the statement of account, a phone call, or a formal letter, the customer will usually pay more quickly. To take an extreme case, a customer receiving several calls a week from an aggressive entrepreneur may pay the bill just to get the entrepreneur to stop bothering him. Of course, these more aggressive collection techniques also have costs, such as loss of customer goodwill, scaring away new customers, loss of old customers to more lenient suppliers, and the generation of industry rumors that the company is short of cash and may be a poor credit risk.

Stretching out accounts payable and collecting accounts receivable more quickly are really two sides of the same issue. Most entrepreneurs attempt to stretch out their bill payments as long as reasonably possible and to collect their own bills as quickly as competitively possible. The entrepreneur's objective is to maximize company cash, using both techniques, without antagonizing either suppliers or customers so much that his working relationship with them suffers.

Although the fastest way to collect receivables is to ask for the money regularly, the entrepreneur can also *change his sales terms* to collect cash more quickly. The entrepreneur has several options, including:

1. *Introduce discounts:* A company can initiate a discount for prompt payment (for example, a 2% discount for payment within 10 days). Similarly, a company with an existing discount may increase the discount (for example, increase discount from 1% to 2%).
2. *Reduce credit terms:* If competitively possible, an entrepreneur may require payment in full in 15 days, a deposit when the order is placed, COD orders (in which the customer must pay for goods on delivery), or even full payment with the order. Companies will have difficulty instituting these measures if competitors offer significantly more lenient credit terms.
3. *Emphasize cash sales:* Some entrepreneurs, particularly those selling directly to consumers, may be able to increase their percentage of cash sales.

4. *Accept credit cards:* Sales made on bank credit cards or on travel or entertainment cards are convertible within a couple of days into cash. The credit card companies charge 3% to 7% of the amount of the sale for this service.

5. *Impose a penalty for late payment:* Some companies now charge 1.0% or 1.5% of the unpaid balance per month as a penalty for late payment. Again, competitive conditions may make this approach unlikely.

OBTAIN BANK LOANS THROUGH ACCOUNTS RECEIVABLE FINANCING

One approach an entrepreneur can take to free up working capital funds is to convert his accounts receivable into cash more quickly through aggressive collection techniques. However, when the entrepreneur fears that aggressive collection may offend customers and cause them to take their business to competitors, the entrepreneur may decide to convert his accounts receivable to cash through a finance company. In this form of financing, the entrepreneur can choose between two methods: *pledging* and *factoring.* The following sections describe both methods. In practice, finance companies or banks offer many variations on these two financing methods.

Pledging

Pledging means using accounts receivable as collateral for a loan from a finance company or bank. The finance company then gives money to the borrower, and as the borrower's customers pay their bills, the borrower repays the loan to the finance company.

With this form of accounts receivable financing, the borrower's customers are not notified that their bills are being used as collateral for a loan. Therefore, pledging is called *nonnotification financing.* Furthermore, if customers do not pay their bills, the borrower (rather than the finance company) must absorb the loss. Thus, if the customer defaults, the lender has the right of recourse to the borrower.

In general, a finance company will not lend the full face value of the accounts receivable pledged. In determining what fraction of the face value of receivables to lend, the finance company considers three factors:

1. The credit rating of the borrower's customers (because bills that may be paid slowly, or not at all, obviously do not make good collateral).

2. The quantity and dollar value of the accounts receivable (because a small number of large dollar-value receivables is easier to control).

3. The borrower's credit rating (because the finance company prefers having the loan repaid to taking possession of the collateral). Typically, a company can borrow 75% to 90% of the face value of its accounts receivable if it has a good credit rating and its customers have excellent credit ratings. Companies with lower credit ratings can generally borrow 60% to 75% of the face value of their receivables.

Pledging receivables is not a cheap source of credit. Moreover, an additional charge is often made to cover the lender's expenses incurred in appraising credit risks. Therefore, this source of financing is used mostly by smaller companies that have no other source of funds open to them.

Factoring

Factoring is defined as selling accounts receivable at a discount to a finance company (known as the *factor*). There are many variations of factoring, but the following example covers the main points. With factoring, a company usually transfers the functions of its credit department to the factor. That is, the factor takes over credit checking and collection. If the factor rejects a potential customer as an unacceptable credit risk, the company must either turn down the order or insist on cash payment.

An example will demonstrate how this process works. Suppose the W. Buygraves Inc. company (buyer) orders $10,000 worth of exotic wood and marble from the Saleman Company (seller). The Saleman Company calls its factor to report the order. The factor checks the credit rating of the Buygraves Company and, if all is satisfactory, calls the Saleman Company with an approval. The Saleman Company then ships the goods and sends an invoice to the Buygraves Company. The invoice instructs the Buygraves Company to pay the factor. At the same time, the Saleman Company sends a copy of the invoice to the factor, and the factor sends approximately 85% of the invoice amount ($8,500 in this case) to the Saleman Company. The factor must now collect the $10,000 from Buygraves. When the factor actually collects the bill, it may send the Saleman Company a small additional amount of money to recognize collections being higher than original estimates.

The fees that factors charge vary widely. These fees include:

- An interest charge, usually expressed on a daily basis (for the time the bill is outstanding) and equivalent to a 15% to 30% annual interest rate

- A collection fee, usually in the range of an additional 6% to 10% annual rate
- A credit checking charge, either a percentage of the invoice or a flat dollar amount

The factor keeps a hold-back amount (which is not immediately paid to the Saleman Company) to more than cover these various fees and charges, deducts the total from the hold-back amount, and sends the remainder to the Saleman Company.

OBTAINING LOANS AGAINST INVENTORY

An entrepreneur's inventory is an asset that can often be used as collateral for a loan. In this way, entrepreneurs can get the cash they need while still retaining access to their inventory. There are four basic ways to use inventory as security for a loan, depending on how closely the lender controls the physical inventory. These four ways are:

1. *Chattel mortgage,* in which specific inventory is used to secure the loan
2. *Floating (or blanket) lien,* in which the loan is secured by all the borrower's inventory
3. *Field warehousing,* in which the lender physically separates and guards the pledged inventory right on the borrower's premises
4. *Public warehousing,* in which the lender transfers the pledged inventory to a separate warehouse

Each method is discussed in detail.

Chattel Mortgage

A *chattel (or property) mortgage* is a loan secured by specific assets. For example, a borrower might pledge 5,000 new refrigerators as collateral for a loan. To guarantee the lender's position as a secured creditor (in case of bankruptcy), a chattel mortgage must precisely describe the items pledged as collateral. In the case of the refrigerators, the loan agreement would include the serial numbers of the specific refrigerators pledged by the borrower. If the borrower sells some of these refrigerators or receives a new shipment of refrigerators, the chattel mortgage must be rewritten to include these changes specifically.

Because the chattel mortgage describes the collateral so specifically, it offers fairly high security to a lender. Lenders further reduce their risk by lending only a fraction of the estimated market value of the collateral. This fraction depends on how easily the assets can be transported and sold. In the case of refrigerators, which are easy to sell, a borrower might obtain as much as 90% of their wholesale cost. But a borrower with a highly specialized inventory, such as bulldozer scoops, might get 50% or less of their fair market value because the lender would have difficulty selling the bulldozer scoops to recover the money. Because chattel mortgages describe the collateral so specifically, lenders limit their use to high-value items.

Floating Lien

Instead of naming specific items of inventory to secure a loan, borrowers may pledge all of their inventory. This is *floating, or blanket, lien.* Because such an arrangement does not describe specific items of inventory, it does not have to be rewritten each time the borrower sells an item from inventory or receives new items into inventory. However, this flexibility makes it extremely difficult for the lender to maintain the security for the loan. For example, the borrower might sell most of the inventory and not leave enough to secure the loan. For this reason, banks and finance companies will usually lend only a small fraction of the inventory's market value when using a floating lien.

Field Warehousing

Field warehousing was invented to fully protect the lender's security. Under a field warehousing arrangement, the borrower designates a section of the premises, often a room or a specific area of the regular warehouse, for the use of the finance company. The finance company then locks and guards this field warehouse area and stores in it the actual inventory that the borrower is using as collateral. The finance company gives the borrower the agreed-on fraction of the fair market value of the inventory and receives in return a warehouse receipt, which gives the finance company title to the inventory. Companies use field warehousing when the inventory is especially bulky or valuable, such as structural steel, bulk chemicals, or diamonds.

Whenever the borrowing firm needs some of the inventory, it repays part of the loan, and the finance company releases part of the inventory. In this way, the finance company guarantees that there is sufficient collateral at all times to secure the loan.

Public Warehousing

Public warehousing is similar to field warehousing except that the actual inventory is moved to an independent warehouse away from the borrower's plant. As with field warehousing, the finance company releases inventory as the borrower repays the loan. Again, this ensures that the collateral is always sufficient to cover the loan.

There are many variations of warehousing. For example, some bonded warehouses accept checks in payment for loans and then forward these checks to the finance company while releasing the appropriate amount of inventory to the borrower. If such an arrangement is acceptable to all parties, it helps the borrower regain title to the inventory more quickly.

Costs of Warehousing

Warehousing companies collect both a service charge and interest. The service charge is usually a fixed amount plus 1% to 2% of the loan itself. This service charge covers the cost of providing field warehousing facilities or of transferring inventory to a public warehouse. In addition, the warehouse company charges interest, usually 10% or more. Because of the high fixed costs of setting up a warehousing system, this form of financing is practical only for inventories larger than about $500,000.

OBTAINING "FINANCING" FROM CUSTOMER PREPAYMENTS

As we discussed earlier, some companies are actually financed by their customers. This situation typically occurs on large, complex, long-term projects; it includes defense contractors, building contractors, ship builders, and management consulting firms. These companies typically divide their large projects into a series of stages and require payment as they complete each stage. This significantly reduces the cash these companies require, compared to firms that finance an entire project themselves and receive payment on completion. In some companies, customers pay in advance for everything they buy. Many mail order operations are financed this way.

CHOOSING THE RIGHT MIX OF SHORT-TERM FINANCING

The entrepreneur attempts to secure the required short-term funds at the lowest cost. The lowest cost usually results from some combination of trade credit, unsecured and secured bank loans, accounts receivable financing, and inventory financing. Though it is virtually impossible to evaluate every possible combination of short-term financing, entrepreneurs can use their experience and subjective opinion to put together a short-term financing package that will have a reasonable cost. At the same time, the entrepreneur must be aware of future requirements and the impact that using certain sources today may have on the availability of short-term funds in the future.

In selecting the best financing package, the entrepreneur should consider the following factors:

- The firm's current situation and requirements
- The current and future costs of the alternatives
- The firm's future situation and requirements

For small firms, the options available may be somewhat limited, and the total short-term financing package may be less important. On the other hand, larger firms may be faced with a myriad of possibilities. The short-term borrowing decision can become quite complex, but the selection of the right combination can be of significant financial value to the entrepreneur's firm.

Traditional Bank Lending: Short-Term Bank Loans

After an entrepreneur has fully used her trade credit and collected her receivables as quickly as competitively possible, she may turn to a bank for a short-term loan. The most common bank loan is a *short-term,* unsecured loan made for 90 days. Standard variations include loans made for periods of 30 days to a year and loans requiring collateral. Interest charges on these loans typically vary from the prime rate (the amount a bank charges its largest and most financially strong customers) to about 3% above prime.

Very often, an entrepreneur doesn't immediately need money but can forecast that she will have a definite need in, say, six months. The entrepreneur would not want to borrow the required money now and pay unnecessary interest for the next six months. Instead, the entrepreneur would formally apply to her bank for a *line of credit* that is, an assurance by the bank that, as long as the company remains financially healthy, the bank will lend the company money (up to a specified limit) whenever the company needs it. Banks usually review a company's credit line each year. A line of credit is not a guarantee that the bank will make a loan in the future. Instead, when the company actually needs the money, the bank will examine the company's current financial statements to make sure that actual results coincide with earlier plans.

Banks also grant *guaranteed lines of credit.* Under this arrangement, the bank guarantees to supply funds up to a specified limit, regardless of circumstances. This relieves the company of any worries that money may not be available when it is needed. Banks usually charge extra for this guarantee, typically 1% a year on the unused amount of the guaranteed line of credit. For example, if the bank guarantees a credit line of $1 million and the company borrows only $300,000, the company will have to pay a commitment fee of perhaps $7,000 for the $700,000 it did not borrow.

In return for granting lines of credit, banks usually require that an entrepreneur maintain a compensating balance (that is, keep a specified amount in its checking account without interest). For example, if an entrepreneur receives a $1 million line of credit with the requirement that she maintain a 15% compensating balance, the entrepreneur must keep at least $150,000 in her demand account with that bank all year. The bank does not pay interest on this demand account money; so the use of this money is the bank's compensation for standing ready to grant up to $1 million in loans for a year. When the bank actually makes loans during the year, it charges the negotiated rate of interest on the loan.

Maturity of Loans

The most common time period, or maturity, for short-term bank loans is 90 days; however, an entrepreneur can negotiate maturities of 30 days to one year. Banks often prefer 90-day maturities, even when the entrepreneur will really need the money for longer than 90 days, because the three-month maturity gives the bank a chance to check the entrepreneur's financial statements regularly. If the entrepreneur's position has deteriorated, the bank may refuse to renew the loan and, therefore, avoid a future loss.

Entrepreneurs, on the other hand, prefer maturities that closely match the time they expect to need the money. A longer maturity (rather than a series of short, constantly renewed loans) eliminates the possibility that the bank will refuse to extend a short-term loan because of a temporary weakness in the entrepreneur's operations.

Interest Rates

The rates of interest charged by commercial banks vary in two ways:

1. The general level of interest rates varies over time
2. At any given time, different rates are charged to different borrowers

The base rate for most commercial banks traditionally has been the *prime rate,* which is the rate that commercial banks charge their very best business customers for short-term borrowing. It is the rate that the financial press puts in the front page every time it is changed. Congress and the business community speculate about the prime's influence on economic activity because it is the baseline for loan pricing in most loan agreements.

Historically, the prime was a base line for loan pricing; "prime plus two" or "2% above prime" was a normal statement of interest rate on many loan contracts. However, as the banking industry has begun to price its loans and services more aggressively, the prime is becoming less important. Along with the change in the prime, *compensating balances* (that is, the borrower's agreeing to hold a certain percentage of the amount of the loan in a noninterest-bearing account) are becoming less popular.

The current trend in loan pricing is *to price the loan at a rate above the marginal cost of funds* as typically reflected by the interest rates on certificates of deposit. The bank then adds an interest rate margin to the cost of funds, and the sum becomes the rate charged to the borrower. This rate changes daily in line with the changes on money market rates offered by the bank. As liability management becomes more of a way of life for bankers, the pricing of loans will become a function of the amount of competition, both domestic and international, that the banker faces in securing loanable funds. As a result of this competition for corporate customers and enhanced competition from the commercial paper market, large, financially stable corporations are often able to borrow at a rate below prime.

Interest represents the price that borrowers pay to the bank for credit over specified periods of time. The amount of interest paid depends on several factors:

- The dollar amount of the loan
- The length of time involved
- The nominal annual rate of interest
- The repayment schedule
- The method used to calculate the interest

The various methods used to calculate interest are all variations of the simple interest calculation. *Simple interest* is calculated on the amount borrowed for the length of time the loan is outstanding. For example, if $1 million is borrowed at 15% and repaid in one payment at the end of one year, the simple interest would be $1 million times 0.15, or $150,000.

When the *add-in interest* method is used, interest is calculated on the full amount of the original principal. The interest amount is immediately added to the original principal, and payments are determined by dividing principal plus interest by the number of payments to be made. When only one payment is involved, this method is identical to simple interest. However, when two or more payments are to be made, the use of this method results in an effective rate of interest that is greater than the nominal rate. In this example, if the $1 million loan were repaid in two six-month installments of $575,000 each, the effective rate is higher than 15% because the borrower does not have the use of funds for the entire year.

The *bank discount method* is commonly used with short-term business loans. Generally, there are no immediate payments, and the life of the loan is usually one year or less. Interest is calculated on the amount of the loan, and the borrower receives the difference between the amount to be paid back and the amount of interest. In the example, the effective interest rate is 17.6%. The interest amount of $150,000 is subtracted from the $1 million, and the borrower has the use of $850,000 for one year. If you divide the interest payment by the amount of money actually used by the borrower ($150,000 divided by $850,000), the effective rate is 17.6%. If the loan were to require a compensating balance of 10%, the borrower does not have the use of the entire loan amount; rather, the borrower has the use of the loan amount less the compensating balance requirement. The effective rate of interest in this case would be 20%—the interest amount of $150,000 divided by the funds available, which is $750,000 ($1,000,000 minus $150,000 interest and minus a compensating balance of $100,000). The effective interest cost on a revolving credit agreement includes both interest costs and the commitment fee. For example, assume the TBA Corporation has a $1 million revolving credit agreement with a bank. Interest on the borrowed funds is 15% per annum. TBA must pay a commitment fee of 1% on the unused portion of the credit line. If the firm borrows $500,000, the effective annual interest rate is 16% [(0.15 × $500,000) + (0.01 × $500,000) divided by $500,000].

Because many factors influence the effective rate of a loan, when evaluating borrowing costs, only *the effective annual rate* should be used as a standard of comparison to ensure that the actual costs of borrowing are used in making the decision.

Collateral

To reduce their risks in making loans, banks may require collateral from entrepreneurs. Collateral may be any asset that has value. If the entrepreneur does not repay the loan, the bank owns the collateral and may sell it to recover the amount of the loan.

Typical collateral includes both specific high-value items owned by the company (such as buildings, computer equipment, or large machinery) and all items of a particular type (such as all raw materials or all inventory). Banks use blanket liens as collateral where individual items are of low value, but the collective value of all items is large enough to serve as collateral.

The highest level of risk comes in making loans to small companies, and it is not surprising to find that a high proportion of loans made to small companies—probably 75%—is secured. Larger companies present less risk and have stronger bargaining positions; only about 30% of loans made to companies in this class are secured.

One aspect of protection that most banks require is *key person insurance* on the principal officers of the company taking out the loan. Because the repayment of the loan usually depends on the entrepreneur or managers running the company in a profitable manner, if something should happen to the entrepreneur or key managers, there may be some question about the safety of the loan. To avoid this uncertainty, a term insurance policy is taken out for the value of the loan on the life of the entrepreneur or key managers. If the officer or officers die, the proceeds of the policy are paid to the bank in settlement of the loan.

When making loans to very small companies, banks often require that the owners and top managers personally sign for the loan. Then, if the company does not repay the loan, the bank can claim the signer's personal assets, such as houses, automobiles, and stock investments.

Applying for a Bank Loan

To maximize the chances of success in applying for a bank loan, an entrepreneur should maintain good banking relations. Personal visits by the entrepreneur and other senior officers, as well as quarterly delivery of income statements, balance sheets, and cash flow statements, are useful means of sustaining such relations.

The actual process of obtaining bank credit (whether a line of credit or an actual loan) must be conducted on a personal basis with the bank loan officer. The loan officer will be interested in knowing the following information:

- How much money the company needs
- How the company will use this money
- How the company will repay the bank
- When the company will repay the bank

Entrepreneurs should be able to fully answer these questions and support their answers with past results and realistic forecasts; if so, they stand an improved chance of obtaining the line of credit or loan that they need.

Restrictive Covenants

Bank term loans are negotiated credit, granted after formal negotiations take place between borrower and lender. As part of the terms agreed to in these negotiations, the bank usually seeks to set various restrictions, or *covenants,* on the borrower's activities during the life of the loan. These restrictions are tailored to the individual borrower's situation and needs; thus, it is difficult to generalize about them. This section introduces some of the more widely used covenants and their implications. All of these covenants are (at least to some degree) negotiable; it is wise for the financial executive to carefully review the loan contract and to attempt to moderate any overly restrictive clause a bank may request.

The restrictive covenants in a loan agreement may be classified as:

- *General provisions* are found in most loan agreements and are designed to force the borrower to preserve liquidity and limit cash outflows.
- *Routine provisions* are also found in most loan agreements and are normally not subject to modification during the loan period.
- *Specific provisions* are used according to the situation and are used to achieve a desired total level of protection.

The following sections describe these restrictions in more detail.

General Provisions

Most common of all general provisions is a requirement relating to the *maintenance of working capital.* This may simply be a provision that net working capital is to be maintained at or above a specified level. Alternatively, when the company is expected to grow fairly rapidly, the required working capital may be set on an increasing scale. For example, the bank may stipulate that working capital is to be maintained above $500,000 during the first 12 months of the loan, above $600,000 during the second, above $750,000 during the third, and so on. If the borrower's business is highly seasonal, the requirement for working capital may have to be modified to reflect these seasonal variations.

The provision covering working capital is often set in terms of the borrower's current ratio—current assets divided by current liabilities—which must be kept above, for example, 3 or 3.5 to 1. The actual figure is based on the bank's judgment and whatever is considered a safe figure for that particular industry.

Working capital covenants are easy to understand and very widely used. Unfortunately, they are often of rather doubtful value. As discussed in this chapter, a company may have a large net working capital and still be short of cash.

Another widely used covenant is *a limit on the borrower's expenditures for capital investment.* The bank may have made the loan to provide the borrower with additional working capital and does not wish to see the funds sunk into capital equipment instead. The covenant may take the form of a simple dollar limit on the investment in capital equipment in any period. Alternatively, the borrower is often allowed to invest up to, but not more than, the extent of the current depreciation expense. Such a provision may prove to be a serious restriction to a rapidly growing company. Any company will find such a covenant damaging if the maximum expenditure is set below the figure needed to maintain productive capacity at an adequate and competitive level.

Most term loan agreements include *covenants to prevent the borrower from selling or mortgaging capital assets without the lender's permission.* This may be extended to cover current assets other than the normal sale of finished goods, in which case the borrower is prohibited from factoring accounts receivable, selling any part of the raw-material inventory, or assigning inventory to a warehouse finance company without the bank's express permission.

Limitations on additional long-term debt are also common. The borrower is often theoretically forbidden to undertake any long-term debt during the life of the term loan, though in practice the bank usually allows new debt funds to be used in moderation as the company grows. The provision is often extended to prevent the borrower from entering into any long-term leases without the bank's authorization.

One type of covenant that clearly recognizes the importance of cash flows to a growing company is a *prohibition of or limit to the payment of cash dividends.* Again, if dividends are not completely prohibited, they may be either limited to a set dollar figure or based on a set percentage of net earnings. The latter approach is obviously the less restrictive.

Routine Provisions

The second category of restrictive covenants includes routine provisions found in most loan agreements that usually are not variable. The loan agreement ordinarily includes the following requirements:

- The borrower must furnish the bank with periodic financial statements and maintain adequate property insurance.
- The borrower agrees not to sell a significant portion of its assets. A provision forbidding the pledging of the borrower's assets is also included in most loan agreements. This provision is often termed a negative pledge clause.
- The borrower is restricted from entering into any new leasing agreements that might endanger the ability to pay the loan.
- The borrower is restricted from acquiring other firms unless prior approval has been obtained from the lender.

Specific Provisions

Finally, a number of restrictions relate more to the borrowing company's management than to its financial performance. For example:

- Key executives may be required to sign employment contracts or take out substantial life insurance.
- The bank may require the right to be consulted before any changes are made in the company's top management.
- Some covenants prevent increases in top management salaries or other compensation.

Restrictive covenants are very important in borrowing term loans. If any covenant is breached, the bank has the right to take legal action to recover its loan, probably forcing the company into insolvency. On the other hand, it may be argued that the covenants protect the borrowing company as well as the lender, in that their intention is to make it impossible for the borrower get into serious financial trouble without first infringing on one or more restrictions, thus giving the bank a right to step in and apply a guiding hand. A bank is very reluctant to force any client into liquidation. In the event that restriction is infringed on, however, the bank may use its very powerful bargaining position to demand even tighter restrictions—and some control over the borrower's operations—as the price of continuing the loan.

OBTAINING FUNDS FROM HOME EQUITY LOANS

In recent years, many entrepreneurs have been borrowing against their home equity as a line of credit. While the general intent of this funding is made available for home improvements, the savvy entrepreneur sees this line of credit to be a convenient, competitively financed vehicle to finance a business venture. With the rise of real asset values throughout the United States (particularly the East and West Coasts) the ability to finance risky ventures in this manner has grown appreciably. In many respects the use and availability of home equity lines of credit have replaced (and certainly have buffeted) the use and application of small firm loans. Presumably the increased efficiency and availability of such financing will only serve to make this form of financing more popular for future generations of entrepreneurs.

EQUIPMENT FINANCING

Capital equipment is often financed by intermediate-term funds. These may be straightforward term loans, usually secured by the equipment itself. Both banks and finance companies make equipment loans of this type. The nonbank companies charge considerably higher interest whereas capital equipment is often financed by intermediate-term funds. These may be straightforward term loans, usually secured by bank term loans.

As with other types of secured loans, the lender will evaluate the quality of the collateral and advance a percentage of the market value. In determining the repayment schedule, the lender ensures that the value of the equipment exceeds the loan balance. In addition, the loan repayment schedule is often made to coincide with the depreciation schedule of the equipment.

One further form of equipment financing that should be considered is the *conditional sales contract*, which normally covers between two and five years. Under such a contract, the buyer agrees to buy a piece of equipment by installment payments over a period of years. During this time, the buyer has the use of the equipment, but the seller retains title to it until the payments are completed. Companies that are unable to find credit from any other source may be able to buy equipment on these terms. The lender's risk is small because the equipment can be repossessed at any time if an installment is missed. Equipment distributors who sell equipment under conditional sales contracts often sell the contract to a bank or finance company, in which case the transaction becomes an interesting combination of equipment financing for the buyer and receivables financing for the seller.

The credit available under a conditional sales contract is less than the full purchase price of the equipment. Typically, the buyer is expected to make an immediate down payment of 25% to 33% of the full cash price, and only the balance is financed. The cost of the credit given may be quite high. Equipment that is highly specialized or subject to rapid obsolescence presents a greater risk to the lender than widely used standard equipment, and the interest charged on the sale of such specialized equipment to a small company may exceed 15% to 20%.

OBTAINING EARLY FINANCING FROM GOVERNMENT SUPPORTED PROGRAMS

Many government supported programs are sources of financing for small businesses, including startups. Many entrepreneurs get money for startups and growing companies with loans guaranteed by the Small Business Administration (SBA). Some get capital from Small Business Investment Companies (SBIC), which the SBA licenses and regulates and also loans money. Details of SBA programs and other government support for entrepreneurs are provided in the next chapter.

LARGE COMPANIES HELP SMALL COMPANIES— NEW MODEL OF FINANCING

In a perfect world (from a large company's perspective), the world's most efficient capital user would also be the company that has the best projects and the lowest cost of funds. This efficient model of an organization would grow larger, more efficient, and more profitable. In fact, the basic premise of large, central-managed organizations operates under this premise. Large firms grow bigger and more powerful over time and dominate all others. Entrepreneurs running small shops wouldn't stand a chance.

However, this does not happen normally in the real world. Despite the implied advantages available to large organizations, they often fail to capitalize on their strategic advantage. The problem therefore has little to do with the cost of funds and everything to do with its successful allocation. Who gets the funds and at what price? Large companies win and small firms lose. This is true at least with respect to funds access.

However, CEOs of large companies realize that they need a better way to distribute their inexpensive risk capital. Small firms are constantly seeking new ways in which to gain strategic advantages while being independent in operation. Both firms have a distinct advantage over the other: Large companies have access to cheap funds and small companies have a more efficient orientation. Thus, a practical solution is now being developed between large, public companies and small entrepreneurial firms. Large companies can benefit from a better growth model that allows them to grow through investments in small companies. In turn, small companies can gain access to inexpensive financing from the large firm along with strategic partnering benefits. This approach is being developed, but has not yet brought in more than a trickle of funds to small companies. But it appears to be an interesting development. Meanwhile, small, entrepreneurial companies need to learn how to put their cash conversion cycles to best use and attempt to minimize outlays while taking advantage of inherent funding sources. This chapter addressed the latter. Hopefully, in the context of all funding sources, this approach will help entrepreneur's odds of survival.

EXTERNAL ASSISTANCE FOR STARTUPS AND SMALL BUSINESSES

8

Elizabeth J. Gatewood

There is a wealth of external assistance out there about which you have probably never heard. Federal, state, and local governments and nonprofit institutions offer a bewildering array of helpful resources. This chapter offers a map for the varied terrain of entrepreneurial assistance.

WHY YOU SHOULD CONSIDER EXTERNAL ASSISTANCE PROGRAMS

External sources of assistance are certainly useful and probably necessary for almost all entrepreneurs, because the successful creation of a startup company, or the management of a small, growing company, is a highly complex, time-consuming, and difficult process. You need all the help you can get.

The stereotypical entrepreneur—the so-called rugged individualist who doesn't need help—may still wince at the thought of government assistance. Some entrepreneurs believe that government regulations (especially in the areas of taxation, employee benefits, and environmental controls) may hinder small business. Nevertheless, many agencies of the government are committed to assisting entrepreneurship, usually because of the potential of small businesses to create jobs.

According to the U.S. Small Business Administration (SBA), small businesses create three out of every four new jobs, produce more than half of the private gross domestic national product, and invent 55% of the nation's technological innovations. Over 25 million small companies (constituting 99.7% of all businesses in the United States) provide work and income for more than 50% of the private U.S. workforce, and inspire further entrepreneurial activity. Small businesses are central to the U.S. economy, despite the dominance in the business and general press of the corporate giants that make up the *Fortune* 500.

Not all successful companies have required external assistance in their early stages. But many successful entrepreneurs have built their companies with government-guaranteed startup loans, lucrative government contracts, or government-sponsored advice on business plan development. Here are some examples:

- Electronic Data Systems (EDS), built by Ross Perot, had early contracts with the state of Texas and the federal government's Medicare programs.
- Apple Computer, Inc. and Cray Research, Inc. received Small Business Investment Companies (SBIC) capital during their early stages.
- Nike, Federal Express, Compaq Computer, Winnebago Industries, T.J. Cinnamons, and Godfather's Pizza were all assisted by SBA-sponsored programs.

External assistance programs have helped entrepreneurs at all phases of small company growth, in all sectors of industry, at all income levels, of all races, and of both genders.

You should consider external assistance programs because they are available, free, or inexpensive, and often effective in delivering useful services. They can also give you a competitive advantage in the difficult and complex project of starting up a new company or building a small company.

EXTERNAL ASSISTANCE AVAILABLE TO ANYONE IN THE UNITED STATES

Getting Advice: Business Development Programs

Most small business owners or would-be entrepreneurs begin with a need for business development assistance. This may involve managerial or technical assistance, for example, identifying and accessing relevant business and technical information, or using such information to evaluate new products, business concepts, and business plans. Many turn to the SBA.

THE U.S. SMALL BUSINESS ADMINISTRATION

Recognizing the importance of entrepreneurial initiative, Congress in 1953 created the Small Business Administration, an independent federal agency, to promote small business. The SBA is the primary federal agency charged with aiding, counseling, assisting, and protecting the interests of small business, although other federal agencies also provide services to this diverse economic constituency. In 2003, the agency had 70 district offices and numerous branch offices spread throughout the United States and its territories, and annual loan guarantee authorization of over $12.3 billion.

A small business must meet certain size criteria to be eligible for the SBA's services. These services include not only business development programs carried out by the SBA's Resource Partners (discussed later in this chapter), but also loans, procurement assistance, and international trade assistance. The Small Business Administration Act of 1953 defines a small business as "one which is independently owned and operated and not dominant in its field of operation." For statistical purposes, the SBA defines a small business as one with fewer than 500 employees. For business development assistance, loans, and other services, the SBA defines eligibility either by employment size or annual revenue criteria that vary by industry and change periodically.

The SBA uses the North American Industry Classification System (NAICS) manual to define industries, and it periodically reorganizes and clarifies eligibility criteria. The SBA sales and employment size criteria in 2002 were as follows:

- *Services and retailing.* Small if annual sales are not over $6.0 to $24.5 million, depending on the specific industry.
- *Wholesaling.* Small if number of employees does not exceed 100.
- *Manufacturing.* Small if average employment in the preceding four calendar quarters did not exceed 500, including employees of any affiliates; large if average employment was more than 1,500. If employment is between 500 and 1,500, the SBA decides based on a size standard for the particular industry.
- *Construction.* Small if average annual sales for three years preceding application did not exceed $28.5 million, except for specialty contractors, for whom sales may not have exceeded $12 million.
- *Agriculture.* Small if average annual sales range from $0.75 to $10.5 million, depending on the industry.

The SBA has gradually reduced its provision of management and technical assistance to small business firms via its own field representatives. Technical and management assistance is now primarily provided through several innovative partnerships, collectively called the SBA's *Resource Partners,* described next. SBA provides information about their services and tips on how to start and manage your business on their Web site.

Where to Find the SBA

For your district SBA office, look in the Blue Pages, under the "U.S. Small Business Administration," or consult the following Web page www.sba.gov /regions/states.html, or call the 24-hour SBA answer desk at (800) 827-5722 (800-UASK-SBA). Send e-mails to: answerdesk@sba.gov. For the hearing-impaired, the TDD number is (703) 334-6640. Web address: http://www.sba.gov.

As mentioned, the SBA also supports business development efforts through the following Resource Partners:

- The Small Business Development Center (SBDC) program.
- The Service Corps of Retired Executives (SCORE) program into which the former Active Corps of Executives (ACE) program was merged in 1982.

These SBA Resource Partners assisted more than a million clients and training attendees in fiscal year 2002 alone. That's still less than 5% of the 25 million small businesses in the country—clearly, they're waiting to hear from you!

Small Business Development Centers (SBDCs)

Congress initiated the SBDC pilot program in 1977 to make management assistance and counseling more widely available to present and prospective small business owners. Congress enacted the SBDC program into law in 1980 and granted the SBA oversight for the program.

SBDCs offer one-stop assistance to small businesses and startups by providing a wide variety of information and guidance in central and easily accessible locations. They offer free counseling services and reasonably priced seminars and workshops to new and existing businesses. There are now more than 1,100 service locations organized into 58 SBDC territories—one or more in each of the 50 states (Texas has four), the District of Columbia, Guam, Puerto Rico, Samoa, and the Virgin Islands.

In each state, there is a lead organization (often within a state university and sometimes within the state government itself), endorsed by the governor, which sponsors the SBDC and manages the program. The lead organization coordinates program services offered to small businesses through a network of subcenters and satellite locations in each state. Subcenters are located at colleges, universities, community colleges, vocational schools, chambers of commerce, and economic development corporations.

SBDC assistance may be divided into two main areas: free one-on-one counseling and inexpensive classroom-style training. Customized counseling services range from informal detailed evaluations of business plans by an industry-experienced counselor to advising growing companies on expansion plans for new territorial or product markets to assistance in putting together loan packages.

SBDCs sometimes supplement their free counseling services by making referrals on specialized accounting, legal, or technical subjects to professional business services. One SBDC, at the University of Houston, has negotiated a reduced-fee program for these services. The service also offers referrals to potential advisory board members for the small business owner.

SBDC training seminars are usually priced at substantial discounts off commercial rates (i.e., $30 to $60 for a four-hour mini-course on how to write a business plan). They are offered by SBDC staff or recognized local experts. Training seminars cover topics such as:

- Strategic planning
  — Business planning
- Market analysis and strategy
  — Marketing to the government
  — International trade
- Product feasibility and development
  — Technology access
- Organizational analysis
- Financial control
  — Loan assistance
  — Cash management
  — Bookkeeping and accounting

Some SBDCs also feature specialized centers that provide assistance in the following areas:

- Government contracting (procurement).
- International trade (for existing businesses looking for international expansion, or startups focused on international trade).

- Technology transfer and product development—Guidance in commercializing new products or services may include advice on royalty agreements, patent research, and new product evaluations.

Each SBDC center has full-time and part-time employees and recruits qualified volunteers from professional and trade associations, the legal and banking communities, academia, and chambers of commerce to counsel clients. Many SBDCs also use paid consultants, consulting engineers, and testing laboratories from the private sector to help clients who need specialized expertise.

SBDCs maintain strict client confidentiality. Only counselors directly working with you learn details of your company's operations. All advisors—whether staff, paid consultants, or volunteers—have to sign a conflict-of-interest agreement. This prohibits disclosure of information about any client to any nonSBDC personnel or any other client, solicitation or acceptance of gifts from clients, or investment in SBDC clients.

The SBA provides 50% or less of the operating funds for each state SBDC. The matching-fund contributions come from state legislatures, private sector foundations and grants, state and local chambers of commerce, state-chartered economic development corporations, public and private universities, vocational and technical schools, and community colleges. The success of SBDCs is reflected in the increasing tendency of sponsors' contributions to exceed the minimum 50% matching share. Unlike SCORE (described in the next section of this chapter), which is totally funded by the SBA, SBDCs are freer to develop programs and services independently of the SBA.

Where to Find SBDCs

The SBA has offices located throughout the country. For the one nearest you, consult the telephone directory under "U.S. government," or call the SBA answer desk at (800) 827-5722 (800-UASK-SBA) or (202) 205-7064 (fax). For the hearing impaired, the TDD number is (202) 205-7333 http://www.sba.gov/sbdc/sbdcnear.html.

The Association of Small Business Development Centers (ASBDC) is located at:

8990 Burke Lake Road
Burke, Virginia 22015
Phone: (703) 764-9850
Fax: (703) 764-1234
E-mail: info@asbdc-us.org
Web address: http://www.asbdc-us.org

Service Corps of Retired Executives (SCORE)

SCORE, a volunteer organization founded in 1964, numbers more than 10,500 retired and active executives and small business owners who volunteer their professional management expertise to help current and future business owners and managers. Most SCORE volunteers are retired, but some are still in the workforce. SCORE provides business information and management help through confidential counseling, training, and workshops.

SCORE provides the following information and advisory services:

- Short-term startup counseling.
- Longer term counseling for established clients.
- Team counseling, when several experts are desirable.

SCORE clients have included a wide variety of businesses—for example, graphic arts companies, archaeological consulting firms, and security systems stores. Counseling may occur at a SCORE office, at the client's place of business, or online. On average, 70,000 individuals visit www.score.org each month. In fiscal year 2002, 49,399 entrepreneurs engaged in SCORE e-mail counseling, which is available 24 hours a day, 7 days a week.

SCORE offers a prestartup seminar, one of many topics covered in the 5,500 workshops SCORE provided nationwide for 387,938 people in 2001. SCORE is also an active participant in the operation of Business Information Centers (BICs). In 2003, there were more than 80 BICs nationwide, primarily in major cities. BICs typically have a video library; computer services, including online research capabilities and applications software; and other business library services for entrepreneurs.

Where to Find SCORE

For your district SBA office, look in the Blue Pages, under the "U.S. Small Business Administration." Or call the 24-hour SBA answer desk at (800) 827-5722 (800-UASK-SBA). For the hearing impaired, the TDD number is (703) 334-6640. E-mail counseling is available from the SCORE Web site at www.score.org

The National SCORE Office (NSO) is located at:

409 Third St., SW
Sixth Floor
Washington, DC 20024
(800) 634-0245
Web address: http://www.score.org

SCORE has helped nearly 4.5 million people since 1964. In fiscal year 2002 its $5 million budget supported 800 counseling locations, providing assistance through its network of 389 chapters.

Summary of SBA Resource Partner Activities

Exhibit 8.1 shows that for 2001, SBDCs and SCORE counseled almost 400,000 small business owners and prospective small business owners. In the same year, they provided training events that attracted almost 450,000 attendees.

Getting Money: Financial Assistance from the SBA

Debt fuels growth. The entrepreneur promoting a new business venture through a well-prepared business plan and the successful small business proprietor both face the challenge of finding money for startup operations, for working capital, and for expansion and growth. A variety of institutions respond to these needs.

The SBA's financial assistance programs for small companies and startups complement its business development programs. SBA guarantees loans made by lending institutions to small businesses, provides venture capital through its Small Business Investment Company Program and provides loans to nonprofit organizations to fund small loans to small businesses.

The financial contribution of the SBA to small business growth in the United States has been significant. From 1991 through 2000, the SBA helped almost 435,000 small businesses get more than $94.6 billion in loans, more than in the entire history of the agency before 1991. No other institution in this country—perhaps no other in the world—has been responsible for as much small business financing as the SBA has.

EXHIBIT 8.1 **Business development programs: SBA's resource partners (fiscal year 2001).**

	SBDCs	SCORE	Total
Counseling			
Clients counseled	228,424	165,387	393,811
Counseling hours	1,158,916	1,020,139	2,179,055
Hours/client	5.07	6.17	11.24
Training units	18,481	4,291	22,772
Attendees	341,148	103,491	444,539
Training hours	1,610,217	441,978	2,052,195
Attendees/unit	18	24	20

In fiscal year 2001, the SBA backed more than $16.5 billion in financing to America's small businesses; approved more than 50,000 small business loans totaling almost $12.2 billion; and invested $4.5 billion in small businesses through its venture capital program. Many SBA loan programs are targeted to specific groups and needs. Borrowers can use different SBA financial assistance programs simultaneously, typically up to the SBA's loan guarantee limit of $1 million. In some SBA programs the limit may actually be larger.

Loan Guarantees

The 7(a) General Loan Guarantee

This is the SBA's principal way of financially promoting small business creation and growth. (The 7(a) name refers to a section of the original SBA law.) It represents more than 83% of the agency's total loan effort. 7(a) loans are made by private lenders to small businesses that cannot obtain credit without an SBA guarantee and are then guaranteed by the SBA for up to 75% (85% if total loan is $150,000 or less) of the amount provided by the commercial lender.

Effective December 2000, a maximum loan amount of $2 million has been established for the 7(a) program, however, the maximum amount that the SBA will guarantee is $1 million. Although the maximum loan amount is $2 million, the average loan amount is significantly smaller—$220,000. The maximum repayment period for loans is 25 years for land, buildings, and equipment; typically seven years for working capital. Funds can be used for working capital; to construct, expand, or convert facilities; to purchase machinery or equipment; to buy land and buildings; for a seasonal line of credit; and for inventory. In some cases, the loan may be used for refinancing certain types of debt.

A study by PricewaterhouseCoopers reported that businesses that got loan guarantees showed higher growth than comparable businesses. Perhaps only companies with very strong business plans and founding teams can pass the screens of a primary lender and the SBA guarantee evaluation.

The Low Doc Program

This program has extended the SBA's guaranteed lending efforts to loans that most banks previously would have been reluctant to make because they would have considered them too small to be profitable. The Low Doc Program encourages conventional lenders to make loans of $150,000 or less by reducing the amount of paperwork lenders must submit to the SBA. SBA will guarantee up to 85% of these smaller loans, as opposed to 75% of loans greater than $150,000. Loan proceeds may be used for purposes specified for 7(a) loans, except for certain types of existing debt. The maximum repayment period is 25 years for real estate and equipment and generally 7 years for working capital. Businesses that are startups, or have annual sales of $5 million or less for the past three years, or have 100 or fewer employees qualify for Low Doc loans. Lending decisions are based on applicant character and credit history.

The CAP Lines Program

This program is designed to improve small business access to working and short-term capital. SBA provides guarantees up to 75% (85% if total loan is $150,000 or less) on lines of credit extended by commercial lenders for up to five years. The maximum loan guarantee amount is $1 million. Interest rates are negotiated between the lender and the borrower but are subjected to an SBA maximum of 4.25 percentage points above prime. Proceeds from the loan can be used for seasonal capital needs, as advances against inventory and accounts receivables during peak seasons, financing the direct labor and material costs associated with contracts, financing direct labor and materials construction and renovation costs, and consolidating short-term debt.

The 504 Certified Development Company Loan Program

This program finances fixed assets with long-term, low-interest funds through certified development companies (CDCs). The typical structure for a CDC funding project would include 50% conventional bank financing, 40% CDC second mortgage, and 10% owner's equity. CDCs are nonprofit economic development agencies, certified by the SBA and licensed by the state to operate in designated counties only. In 1996, there were approximately 270 CDCs nationwide. CDCs raise their funds by selling 100% SBA-guaranteed debentures to private investors.

These loans are generally up to $1 million (up to $1.3 million in some cases) at 10- to 20-year maturities. Funds can be used for purchasing land or buildings; constructing, renovating, or expanding buildings; or buying machinery or long term equipment. Collateral and personal guarantees are required. Interest rates are based on 5- and 10-year U.S. Treasury issues plus an increment. Fees are approximately 3% of the debenture and may be financed with the loan proceeds. To be eligible for the 504 program, a business must have a tangible net worth less than $7 million and average net income less than $2.5 million after taxes for the previous two years. Businesses engaged in speculative investments or investments in rental real estate are not eligible. CDCs consider jobs generated or jobs saved in choosing projects to fund.

Defense Loan and Technical Assistance (DELTA) Program

The Delta Program, a joint effort of SBA and the Department of Defense (DOD), provides funding to small companies affected by cutbacks in defense. The loans can be through the 7(a) loan program or a Certified Development Company (CDC). The maximum loan amount for a 7(a) Delta loan is $2 million, the maximum for a CDC Delta loan is $1.3 million (up to 40% of a project). If both types of loans are used, or if the company already has a SBA loan, the total amount that SBA will guarantee is $1.25 million. Proceeds from a DELTA loan may be used for acquisition of assets, raw materials, inventory, renovations, leasehold improvements, plant expansions, retooling, and refinancing of current debt.

Pollution Control Loans Program

SBA provides loan guarantees under the 7(a) program to small businesses that are planning, designing, or installing a pollution control facility. The facility must abate, control, prevent, or reduce pollution. The maximum guarantee amount is $1 million. However, if the company has an existing SBA loan guarantee, this amount is reduced by the outstanding guarantee.

Other Loans

Disaster Loans

The SBA offers two types of loans for businesses located in disaster areas designated by the president or the SBA administrator. Businesses suffering uninsured property damage or economic losses from the disaster can obtain long-term recovery loans at low interest rates. Property damage to real estate, machinery, equipment, supplies, or inventory is eligible for physical disaster loans of up to $1.5 million to nonfarm businesses of all sizes damaged in a disaster. Loans of up to $1.5 million for economic losses, for working capital until normal operations resume after the physical disaster, are available to small businesses and agricultural cooperatives that are not able to access credit elsewhere. Interest rates for physical disaster loans are 3.189%, 6.378% for business with other sources of credit (rates as of January 14, 2003). Economic injury disaster loans for working capital cannot exceed 4%. Terms are negotiated with the borrower with a maximum of 30 years; however, businesses with other credit sources are limited to three-year terms. Businesses damaged by Hurricane Andrew and the Midwest floods were beneficiaries of SBA disaster loans.

Micro-Loans

The SBA's experimental Micro-Loan Program was distributed through 101 non-profit organizations (e.g., community service and church groups) in 48 states, Washington, DC, and Puerto Rico in 1996. These micro-loans are targeted at women, low-income, and minority entrepreneurs, especially those in areas that have suffered economic downturns. They help entrepreneurs form or expand small, often home-based, enterprises. Individuals should have the skills but not the capital needed to operate a small business.

Micro-loans may range from a few hundred dollars up to $35,000. The average loan is $10,500. Funds may be used for working capital, inventory, supplies, furniture, fixtures, machinery, and equipment. The maximum term of the loan is six years. Interest rates vary, depending on the intermediary lender and costs to the intermediary from the U.S. Treasury.

The Surety Bond Guarantee Program

The SBA provides guarantee bonds for qualified small contractors who are unable to obtain surety bonds through regular bonding markets. For a contractor to be eligible for the program, average annual revenues for the past three fiscal years cannot exceed $6 million.

The SBA guarantees bonds for contracts up to $2 million. The guarantees are for 80% or 90%, depending on the amount of the contract or the status of the contractor. Approved socially or economically disadvantaged contractors receive a 90% guarantee for contracts regardless of the contract size; other contractors receive a 90% guarantee for contracts not exceeding $100,000 and an 80% guarantee for those over $100,000.

The small business pays the SBA a guarantee fee of $6.00 per thousand of the contract amount, and when the bond is issued, it pays the surety company's bond premium. In fiscal year 2001, the SBA provided surety bond guarantees to 6,320 contractors with construction contracts worth more than $1.4 billion.

Small Business Investment Company (SBIC) and Specialized Small Business Investment Companies (SSBIC) Program

SBICs and SSBICs are privately owned and managed investment firms that are licensed and regulated by the SBA. They augment their own funds by borrowing at favorable rates with SBA guarantees and by selling their preferred stock to the SBA. They provide equity capital and long-term loans to small businesses. To be eligible, you must qualify as a small business using SBA criteria (see earlier section).

SSBICs operate similarly to SBICs but received additional leverage from the federal government because they provide capital to small businesses owned by individuals classified as socially or economically disadvantaged. (The Small Business Program Improvement Act of 1996 repealed Section 301(d) and as a result, no new SSBIC licenses are being issued. However, existing 301(d) licensees were "grandfathered" and are still in operation.) There were approximately 200 SBICs and 100 SSBICs. These organizations made 3,836 regular SBIC and 168 SSBIC financings in 2002.

SBA Interest Rate Policy

Interest rates on guaranteed loans are negotiated between borrowers and lenders, although rates cannot be higher than levels set by SBA regulations. Interest rates may be fixed or variable. For fixed rate loans, maturing in less than seven years, rates may not exceed 2.25% plus prime, maturing in seven years or more, rates may not exceed 2.75%. For loans less than $25,000, the maximum is 4.25% and 4.75%. For loans between $25,000 and $50,000, the maximum is 3.25% and 3.75%.

Variable rate loans are based on the lowest prime rate or the SBA optional peg rate, which is calculated quarterly and published in the Federal Register. The lender and borrower negotiate the amount that will be added to the base rate. All guaranteed loans require payment of a guarantee fee by the lender, which varies with the type of loan and may be passed on to the borrower.

How to Apply for an SBA Loan Guarantee

The SBA has the following general credit requirements:

1. The applicant must be of good character and have a good credit history.
2. The applicant must have experience in business management and demonstrate the commitment necessary for a successful operation.
3. The applicant must have enough funds—including the SBA-guaranteed loan plus personal equity capital—to operate the business on a sound financial basis. If the company is a new business, this means enough cash to fund startup expenses and sustain expected losses during the early stages of operation.
4. If the company is an existing business, it must have a past earning record and future prospects to show repayment ability.

5. If the company is a new business, the startup entrepreneurs must provide at least one-third of the total startup capital needed. Therefore, the loan requested should be no more than twice the value of the owner's equity capital in the business.

Borrowers must fully secure the loan with collateral and provide personal guarantees. The SBA normally takes about two weeks to process a request.

Finding an SBA-Approved Lender

About 7,000 lenders nationwide made at least one SBA loan in 1995. Over 950 of these lenders have been designated as either SBA-preferred or SBA-certified lenders. It is worth your while to identify SBA-preferred lenders in your area because they are empowered to apply an SBA loan guarantee to a loan without consulting the SBA in advance. The benefit of dealing with an SBA-certified lender is that the SBA will normally decide whether to guarantee a bank loan within three days. To find out which lenders are preferred or certified, call your SBA district office.

Where to Find an SBA-Approved Lender

For your district SBA office, look in the Blue Pages, under "U.S. Small Business Administration." Or consult the Web page www.sba.gov/regions/states.html. Or call the 24-hour SBA answer desk at (800) 827-5722 (800-UASK-SBA). Send e-mails to: answerdesk@sba.gov. For the hearing-impaired, the TDD number is (703) 344-6640. Web address: http://www.sba.gov.

Selling to the Government: The Art of Procurement

The federal government is a big customer. It buys billions worth of goods and services every year from U.S. businesses. In 2001, government agencies awarded 105,000 of the 177,000 prime contracts to small businesses, or almost 60%. Total government procurement in 2001 was almost $235 billion. Of this amount, 38% or almost $90 billion went to small prime contractors or small subcontractors. The majority of contracts are fairly large. In 1997, only 23% of all procurement contracts were for $25,000 or less, totaling $727 million but, comprising only 0.4% of all spending on procurement.

PRO-Net

The Small Business Act provides for preferential treatment to be granted to small business concerns in the award of government procurement contracts. The SBA has developed cooperative programs with major government purchasing agencies under which proposed purchases are reviewed by purchasing officials and suitable items are set aside, wholly or partially, for small business bidders. This system of preferences in contract awards is known as *set-asides*. They are aimed at small businesses, disadvantaged small businesses, and small businesses owned by women.

The law also requires large prime government contractors to subcontract work to small businesses. The SBA accordingly develops subcontracting opportunities by negotiating the amounts to be subcontracted to small business concerns by prime contractors undertaking major federal projects.

To achieve these goals, the SBA maintains PRO-Net, a computerized database of more than 195,000 small, disadvantaged, 8(a), HUBZone, and women-owned businesses, as an electronic gateway for procurement information. It is open to all small firms that are interested in seeking federal, state, and private contracts. PRO-Net provides a search engine for contracting officers, a marketing tool for small firms, and a link for small firms to procurement opportunities. The PRO-Net system can search for businesses by NAICS codes, key words, location, quality certifications, business type, ownership race or sex, and a number of other criteria.

Doing business with the federal government has the following advantages:

- A wide range of purchasing needs—variety
- Creditworthiness
- Potential long-term contracts
- Detailed bidding procedures designed to ensure fairness

On the other hand, disadvantages include the competitive nature of the bidding process that may reduce profit margins, and its bureaucratic aspects which require painstaking attention to involved procedures.

The SBA and Minority Subcontracting

The SBA is authorized under Section 8(a) of the Small Business Act to enter into contracts with other federal agencies for goods and services and then to subcontract the work to firms owned by socially and economically disadvantaged persons. The 8(a) program is a business development program that helps socially and economically disadvantaged individuals enter the economic main-stream partially through access to federal contracts. The SBA must approve the firms who participate in the 8(a) program after they demonstrate the nature and source of their disadvantage. The maximum period of eligibility is nine years from initial program certification.

More than half of all federal procurement through disadvantaged firms is channeled through the 8(a) program. In fiscal year 2001, a total of 6,942 businesses participated in the 8(a) program. A total value of $4.3 billion of new contracts and modifications were awarded to active program participants and an additional $2 billion to graduates of the program. In addition the SBA is authorized under Section 7(j) of the act to provide management and technical assistance to 8(a) clients and small businesses in areas of high unemployment. (See Exhibit 8.1 for details on the type of assistance offered by various programs.)

Procurement Assistance Programs Sponsored by the U.S. Department of Defense

Congress has created a national policy stating that a fair proportion of the products and services used by the DOD should be purchased from small businesses and small disadvantaged businesses. This policy is grounded in the need to maintain a strong, diversified industrial base and increase competition in defense-related procurement. Defense purchasing officials, therefore, maintain contact with small business firms, small disadvantaged business firms, and small business firms owned by women.

The DOD accordingly supports various procurement counseling services under the Defense Procurement Technical Assistance (PTA) program. The PTA is a cooperative program in which the DOD shares the cost of the services with state and local governments and nonprofit organizations. These services (which go by different names in different states) can help entrepreneurs seeking to sell goods and services to the DOD. They also help small businesses identify government agencies—federal, state, county, and municipal agencies that may buy their goods and services—and identify bid opportunities that are currently or prospectively available.

PTAs may offer procurement assistance in the form of technical data, drawings, and the counseling know-how to complete a bid package. They may maintain a library of relevant government specifications, standards, and regulations, including the *Federal Acquisition Regulation* (which describes the basic contracting rules for all federal agencies) and key supplements, plus military specifications and standards. PTAs may access technical data and generate pricing histories on parts, help the client develop quality control manuals, and match by computer the client's business capabilities and products with the millions of items and services purchased by government agencies. PTAs may use computer software to scan the *Commerce Business Daily,* which lists many government bid requests, contract awards, and leads on subcontracting, and the *U.S. Government Purchasing and Sales Directory,* which lists the military and civilian agencies that tend to buy particular products and services. PTAs also assist businesses implementing electronic data interchange (EDI) for the bidding process.

How to Get SBA and DOD Procurement Help

For your district SBA office, look in the Blue Pages, under "U.S. Small Business Administration." Or call the National SBA answer desk at (800) 827-5722 (800-UASK-SBA). For the hearing-impaired, the TDD number is (703) 344-6640.

To find whether a PTA program is available in your area, call the nearest Defense Contract Management District (DCMD), administered by the DOD's Defense Logistics Agency:

East: 495 Summer St.
Boston, MA 02210-2184
Phone: (617) 753-4318
Toll-free: (800) 321-1861

West: 18901 So. Wilmington Ave.
Carson, CA 90746-2856
Phone: (310) 900-6025

International: 8725 John J. Kingman Dr., Ste. 3221
Ft. Belvoir, VA 22060-6221
Phone: (703) 428-1766

Selling Abroad: International Business in the Global Village

According to the SBA, every billion dollars in U.S. exports generates about 30,000 jobs. Small firms account for almost a quarter of all exporters. Because of the importance of small business in export, the SBA, the SBA's Resource Partners, the U.S. Department of Commerce, the U.S. Export-Import Bank, and the Overseas Private Investment Corporation (OPIC) have business development and financial assistance programs to help companies involved in exporting.

Export Business Development Programs

U.S. Export Assistance Centers (USEACs)

USEACs are located in major cities in the United States. They integrate services provided by the U.S. Small Business Administration, the U.S. Department of Commerce, the Foreign Commercial Service, the Export-Import Bank, and local international trade programs by providing a single location for access.

The USEACs provide one-on-one counseling to firms to assist them in identifying target markets and developing international marketing strategies. They also provide assistance in areas relating to export finance.

In 2002, there were 20 USEACs located in Atlanta, Baltimore, Boston, Charlotte, Chicago, Cleveland, Dallas, Denver, Detroit, Los Angeles, Miami, Minneapolis, Newport Beach, New Orleans, New York, Philadelphia, Portland, San Jose, Seattle, and St. Louis.

The Small Business Automated Trade Locator Assistance System (ATLAS)

ATLAS, sponsored by the OIT, provides a computerized service useful to exporters. ATLAS provides international marketing and trade information by scanning several large databases. ATLAS can identify the largest markets for specific products ranked by unit sales and dollar volume, five-year trends within those markets, and major sources of foreign competition. The ATLAS system is designed to be useful to businesses that have already identified their target markets. The more specific you are in delineating your product and geographic markets, the more useful the information you will receive.

ATLAS is available free of charge through SBA regional and district offices. SBA will pilot providing the ATLAS information on the Internet through the SBA Web site. It will be called Export Access and will be listed under the Office of International Trade. Under an agreement between the SBA and the Federal Bar Association, the Export Legal Assistance Network (ELAN) offers free initial consultations with an experienced international trade attorney on topics ranging from contract negotiation to agent/distributor agreements, export licensing requirements, and credit collection procedures.

International Trade Centers

The SBA's Resource Partners have a special mission in international trade. Six hundred SCORE members have international trade experience and many SBDCs offer international trade assistance through their International Trade Centers. These centers can help the client:

- Evaluate the potential for company and product exports.
- Analyze and research potential export markets.
- Define market entry strategies.
- Select distribution networks.
- Manage the logistics of export.

The International Trade Administration

The U.S. Department of Commerce (USDOC) also helps companies expand their international trade capabilities through the International Trade Administration (ITA). ITA operates domestic and overseas programs designed to stimulate the expansion of U.S. exports. Major programs include export counseling and assistance.

Through ITA, a U.S. business can tap into a worldwide network of:

- Trade specialists who can provide export counseling on a variety of products and industries
- Country specialists versed in international economic policies and specific markets
- Industry specialists who help develop trade promotion programs
- Import trade specialists who can advise domestic industries with regard to unfair trade practices

The ITA's U.S. Commercial Service can access a network of some 1,800 trade experts located in 83 countries, 103 U.S. cities, and Commerce Headquarters in Washington, DC. This network covers 96% of the global markets for U.S. goods and services.

The following services are available through your U.S. Commercial Service offices. These services are not free: They range from $50 for the National Trade DataBank discs to $1,400 to $6,100 per country for the Customized Market Analysis.

- Developing export expertise:
  — The *Export Qualifier Program* helps firms evaluate their readiness to export through a computerized diagnostic questionnaire.
- Identifying target markets:
  — The *National Trade DataBank* includes over 190,000 trade-related documents, product-specific market research reports, and trade statistics. Information is collected by 20 agencies, updated monthly, and issued on two CD-ROM disks. The databank is also available at federal

depository libraries and can be accessed through the Internet at STAT-United States' Web site (www.stat-usa.gov).

— The *Customized Market Analysis* can assess the competitiveness of your product in a specific market. It involves intensive custom research involving product-specific interviews or surveys. Although potentially useful, this service may be cost prohibitive for small businesses.

- Finding potential partners:
    — The *Agent/Distributor Service* can help you locate up to six foreign representatives who, after looking at your product literature, may be interested in marketing your product.

    — *International Company Profile* will help you evaluate potential partners overseas, in terms of reliability, creditworthiness, and standing in the local business community.

    — *Commercial News United States* is a catalog of new U.S. products and services sent to 120,000 potential overseas buyers, agents, and distributors in more than 145 countries.

    — The *International Buyer Program* brings delegations of overseas buyers from around the world to your exhibit at participating U.S. trade shows.

    — The *Trade Opportunities Program* identifies timely sales leads overseas and provides them to U.S. business.

    — *Catalog and video/catalog exhibitions* are organized every year for certain industries in selected markets. The Department of Commerce shows U.S. exporter catalogs and videos to potential agents, distributors, and other buyers in each market. Participating exporters often receive up to 50 leads from each exhibition.

    — *Trade mission/trade shows* organized with state, local, or private groups help U.S. companies that have representatives visiting their targeted overseas export market to introduce and market their products there.

    — *Matchmaker delegations* are introductory missions for firms entering export markets. The Matchmaker program visits more than 15 countries each year. Matchmaker organizers evaluate a product's potential for a market and make introductions to potential buyers or licensees. This program is also for entrepreneurs who are visiting their export market.

    — The *Gold Key Service* provides the following services to U.S. businesspeople who are visiting their export market:

    Market orientation briefings

    Specialized market research

    Introductions to potential partners

    Interpreter for meetings

Commercial officers located at overseas posts organize all services. Typically this service costs $500 for the first day and $250 for each additional day for in-country time. You need to notify the commercial officer at least six weeks in advance of your arrival.

The Department of Commerce's Bureau of Export Administration issues licenses for the shipment of controlled exports, especially in the areas of computers, electronics, communications, and biotechnology.

Export Financial Assistance

The SBA offers two types of export loan guarantees that protect the lender from default by the exporter. Both must be collateralized with U.S.-based assets. The SBA guaranteed 425 export related loans for $167 million made by commercial lenders in fiscal year 2001.

Export Working Capital Loan Guarantees

These are short-term loan guarantees available to small businesses based in the United States that are at least one year old. Loans provide working capital to acquire inventory, pay for direct manufacturing costs, to purchase goods and services for export, or to support standby letters of credit. The SBA can guarantee up to the lesser of $1 million or 90% of the loan amount. An Export Working Capital loan guarantee may be combined with an International Trade loan guarantee. Loan maturities match a single transaction cycle or generally one year.

International Trade Loan Guarantees

These are guaranteed loans through private lenders that help U.S.-based facilities that engage in international trade or are recovering from the effects of import competition. The fixed-asset portion of the loan cannot exceed $1 million and the nonfixed asset portion cannot exceed $750,000. Proceeds may not be used for debt refinancing. The SBA's guarantee may not exceed 75% (85% if total loan is $150,000 or less) of the loan. Loan maturities are up to 25 years for facilities and equipment and up to three years for working capital. The proceeds from the loans may be used for the purposes specified by the 7(a) loan program (see earlier section).

The Export-Import Bank of the United States (Ex-Im Bank)

Ex-Im Bank has three export finance programs of interest to small businesses: working capital guarantees, export credit insurance, and guarantees and loans extended to finance the sale of U.S. goods and services abroad. In the last five years, Ex-Im Bank assisted nearly 12,000 companies in their export activities, over 87% of these were small businesses. Ex-Im transactions benefiting small businesses in 2002 totaled $1.8 billion. This was 86% of all Ex-Im Bank transactions for that year.

Working Capital Guarantees

This Ex-Im Bank program is very similar to the SBA's Export Working Capital loan guarantees (see page 243). The guarantees cover loans to provide working capital to acquire inventory or pay for direct manufacturing costs, to purchase goods and services for export, or to support standing letters of credit. Guarantees may be for a single transaction or a revolving line of credit. Terms are generally for 12 months and are renewable. Companies need to be based in the United States and in business for at least one year to be eligible for this program. Unlike the SBA, Ex-Im Bank does not require the business to meet the SBA definition of a small business. Ex-Im Bank will guarantee 90% of the loan amount and sets no limit on loan size.

Export Credit Insurance

Ex-Im Bank offers a variety of insurance policies to protect U.S. exporters from foreign buyers default on payment because of commercial or political risks. One program, geared for the small exporter, offers a short term (up to 180 days) policy that covers 95% of commercial risks and 100% of political risk. The exporter is required to insure all export credit sales, not just specific sales. The program is open to businesses that have an average annual export credit sales volume of less than $5 million in the previous two years and meet the SBA definition of a small business.

Direct Loans and Guarantees

Ex-Im Bank provides direct loans and guarantees of commercial financing to foreign buyers of U.S. capital goods and related services. The loans and guarantees cover up to 85% of the U.S. export value, with repayment terms of one year or more. However, there are very few direct loans or guarantees provided each year.

The Overseas Private Investment Corporation (OPIC)

In general, OPIC encourages U.S. business to invest in developing countries and newly emerging democracies and free market economies. OPIC offers a number of programs to ensure U.S. investment against political violence, expropriation, and currency risks. It also provides medium- to long-term financing through direct loans and loan guarantees for new investments, privatizations, and expansions and modernizations of existing plants by U.S. investors. If investors contribute additional capital for modernization and expansion, acquisitions of existing operations are also eligible.

Direct loans, generally from $2 to $10 million, are earmarked for projects significantly involving small businesses or cooperatives. Loan guarantees are generally for loans above $10 million and can go as high as $250 million. In 2002, there were more than 150 countries or areas on the OPIC program list.

Where to Find International Trade Assistance

For your district SBA office and SCORE, look in the Blue Pages, under "U.S. Small Business Administration," or call the toll-free hotline at (800) 827-5722 (800-UASK-SBA). Web address: http://www.sba.gov.

The Department of Commerce's (800) USA-TRAD is a clearinghouse of international trade sources. For the hearing impaired, the TDD number is (703) 344-6640 (800-TDD-TRAD). Web address: http://www.doc.gov.

You can find Department of Commerce industry and country desk officers at:

U.S. Department of Commerce
International Trade Administration
14th and Constitution Avenue, NW
Washington, DC 20230
(202) 482-2867

Contact the Export-Import Bank of the United States at:

811 Vermont Avenue, NW
Washington, DC 20571
(202) 565-3946
Export Hotline: (800) 565-EXIM
Web address: http://www.exim.gov

Contact the Overseas Private Investment Corporation at:

1100 New York Avenue, NW
Washington, DC 20527
ATTN: Small Business Center
E-mail: smallbiz@opic.gov
Call Toll Free: (800) CALL-SBC
Local Phone: (202) 336-8700
Fax: (202) 336-8701

EXTERNAL ASSISTANCE FOR SPECIAL GROUPS, LOCATIONS, AND INDUSTRIES

Business Assistance Programs for Women

According to the Center for Women's Business Research, the number of majority-owned, privately held, women businesses reached 6.2 million in 2002. Sales for these businesses were estimated at $1.15 trillion; they employed some 9.2 million people. The SBA estimates that women ran an additional 314,000 C corporations. The SBA estimates that by the year 2005, women will own half of all businesses.

Despite this explosive growth, few special support programs are aimed solely at women. This has fueled a debate about whether women need special programs or whether they are better served by accessing business assistance programs aimed at the general population.

All SBA offices have a staff member designated as a Women's Business Ownership Representative, whose duty is to discuss resources that are available for women and to provide assistance for accessing those resources. A program available in nearly all 50 states, designated the *Women's Network for Entrepreneurial Training (WNET),* provides mentoring for small business owners. The mentoring program matches a successful woman business owner with at least five years experience to a woman business owner who has been in business for at least one year and has shown potential for growing her business. The mentoring relationship is for one year.

Another program for women, called the *Demonstration Projects,* has established centers for potential or current women business owners in a number of states. The centers offer counseling and training in management, marketing, and

---

Where to Find SBA Help for Women

For your district SBA office, look in the Blue Pages, under "U.S. Small Business Administration," or call the 24-hour SBA answer desk at (800) 827-5722 (800-UASK-SBA) for your district SBA office. Speak to a Women's Business Ownership Representative. For the hearing-impaired, the TDD number is (703) 344-6640:

Office of Women's Business Ownership
Small Business Administration
409 Third Street SW, Fourth Floor
Washington, DC 20416
(202) 205-6673
E-mail: owbo@sba.gov

finance. Although open to all women, the program was developed for women who might not normally use services provided through traditional channels.

Assistance Programs for Minority-Owned Businesses

Recent statistics on business ownership from the Bureau of the Census show the changing face of small business in America (Exhibit 8.2). Although the number of minority-owned small businesses in America is still a small percentage of the total business population, just over 3.1 million of 25 million in 1997, the growth rate in the number of minority-owned businesses far exceeds that of nonminority-owned businesses. The overall growth rate for minority-owned business was 57% between 1992 and 1997 compared to nonminority-owned at 15%. This fast growth rate was expected to continue into the future.

The *Minority Business Development Agency (MBDA)*, an agency of the U.S. Department of Commerce, is the only federal agency specifically created to establish policies and programs to develop the U.S. minority business community. The MBDA sponsors a network of approximately 50 Minority and Native American Business Development Centers (MBDCs/NABDCs), located throughout the country in areas with the largest minority populations.

Each center develops and maintains a listing of existing minority-owned firms for inclusion in the agency's Automated Business Enterprise Locator System (ABELS). The ABELS system is used by government and private industry purchasing officials to identify minority vendors qualified to supply the goods and services they need. To qualify for ABELS, you must certify that your firm is a nonretail business that:

- Is at least 51% owned, controlled, and actively managed by minority persons
- Can provide products or services to other businesses, private organizations, and government agencies

The centers cannot make or underwrite loans because the MBDA has no loan-making authority. MBDCs/NABDCs do engage in business development

EXHIBIT 8.2   Growth in minority-owned business, 1992–1997.

	1992	1997	Increase (%)
African-American	621,000	823,500	33
Hispanic	772,000	1,200,000	55
Asian and Pacific Islander	603,500	913,000	51
American Indian and Alaskan Native	102,300	197,300	93

EXHIBIT 8.3   MBDC/IBDC fees.

Gross Sales	Cost per Hour
< $100,000	$10
$100,000 to $299,999	20
$300,000 to $999,999	30
$1,000,000 to $2,999,999	40
$3,000,000 to $4,999,999	50
$5,000,000+	60

counseling for a fee. The fee ranges from $10 to $60 per hour depending upon the gross sales of the business (Exhibit 8.3). Services typically offered include loan packaging, business planning, marketing, and financial analysis.

The maximum federal funding of each MBDC/IBDC (Indian Business Development Center) represents not more than 85% of the total cost of the project. Each center is expected to provide the other 15% through private sources of support.

Other minority assistance programs are discussed in the section on procurement.

Where to Find the MBDA

The U.S. Department of Commerce
Minority Business Development Agency
14th and Constitution Avenue, NW
Room 5053
Washington, DC 20230
To contact the MBDA by phone: (888) 324-1551
To contact the MBDA by e-mail: help@mbda.gov

Business Assistance Programs for Veterans

The SBA has a special mission to help veterans get into business and stay in business. In each local SBA office, there is a staff person designated the Veterans Affairs Officer, specially trained to guide the veteran seeking business assistance. In addition to SBA Resource Partners' normal business development counseling and training courses (which veterans are welcome to attend), the SBA and its resource partners at times conduct special business training conferences for veterans.

For example, during the Persian Gulf War, SCORE set up workshops to teach businesspeople called up by the Reserves how to cope with sudden and long absences from their businesses. SCORE members also mentored family members and others chosen to manage businesses during the reserves' absences.

Where to Find SBA Help for Veterans

For your district SBA office, look in the Blue Pages, under "U.S. Small Business Administration." Or call the 24-hour SBA answer desk at (800) 827-5722 (800-UASK-SBA) for your district SBA office. Speak to the Veterans Affairs Officer. For the hearing-impaired, the TDD number is (703) 344-6640. Web address: http://www.sba.gov.

Business Assistance for Rural and Agricultural Entrepreneurs

Before describing programs for this group, it should be pointed out that rural is not synonymous with *agricultural*. Not all rural entrepreneurs are engaged in the traditional rural occupation of agriculture. Consider different potential sources of assistance based on your location and your line of business. For example, the U.S. Department of Agriculture (USDA) offers programs that provide management and technical assistance, guaranteed and other loans, and grants and cooperative agreements in areas not limited to traditional agricultural enterprises.

The Agricultural Extension Service

This is the outreach arm of the USDA. Although the Agricultural Extension Service has agents in all land-grant universities and nearly all the nation's 3,150 counties, services of interest to businesses vary dramatically by location. It sometimes provides management and marketing assistance to rural businesses, including agricultural and natural-resource-based enterprises, manufacturers, retail businesses, and service businesses. The services are aimed at increasing the profitability and growth of existing businesses, as well as identifying neglected market segments.

How to Find the Cooperative Extension Service

To find what services are available in your area, look under the Blue Pages for "U.S. Department of Agriculture" or the Blue Pages (County) for "County Extension Office."

The U.S. Department of Agriculture's Rural Business-Cooperative Service (RBS) Business and Industry Guaranteed Loan Program

This program offers loan guarantees similar to the SBA's for individuals, public or private organizations, and federally recognized Indian tribal groups (excludes charitable, religious, or fraternal institutions or organizations) located outside cities with populations of 50,000 or less, however, priority is given to applications for loans in rural communities of 25,000 or less. Funds can be used for working capital; equipment purchases; improvement, construction, or acquisition of fixed assets (including land and buildings); and, in some cases, debt refinancing.

The maximum loan amount is $10 million. A minimum of 10% of total capital is required in the form of equity for existing businesses (20% for startups). The terms are up to 30 years for land and building, 15 years for machinery and equipment, and 7 years for working capital. RBS loan guarantees do not require that you prove your inability to get credit without the guarantee. Interest rates may be fixed or variable and are at competitive banking rates.

The RBS Intermediary Relending Program

This program makes loans to nonprofit organizations, which in turn lend funds to small businesses in their service area. Funds may be used to start a new business or expand an existing one. The nonprofit organization may provide up to 75% of each project's cost up to $150,000. The RBS has the following requirements:

- Projects must create new jobs or retain old jobs.
- Funds must be used in rural areas including cities with 25,000 or fewer people.
- Applicants must have been turned down by at least two other sources before applying for this program.
- Applicants must certify that they are unable to finance the project.

The interest rate to the nonprofits is 1% for up to 30 years. The interest rate charged to the ultimate recipients must be reasonable and is negotiated by the intermediary and the recipient.

How to Find Help for Rural and Agricultural Entrepreneurs

Look under the Blue Pages for "U.S. Department of Agriculture" or the Blue Pages (County) for "County Extension Office."

Business Assistance for Urban Entrepreneurs

The U.S. Department of Housing and Urban Development (HUD) offers a *Community Development Block Grant (CDBG) Entitlement Program* that awards grants annually to entitled metropolitan cities and urban counties. Cities designated as central cities of metropolitan statistical areas (MSAs), other cities with populations of at least 50,000, and qualified counties with populations of at least 200,000 (excluding the population-entitled cities) are eligible to receive grants. The amount of grants for each community is determined by a formula using several measures of community need, such as the poverty level.

Communities receiving grants are free to develop programs that meet local needs in housing, public works, economic development, public services, acquisition, clearance or redevelopment of real property, or administration and planning concerning urban needs, as long as the activities meet the national objectives of the program. The national objectives are to benefit low- and moderate-income persons, to prevent or eliminate slums or blight, or to meet other urgent community needs. Some communities establish revolving loan pools that may be accessed by startups and small businesses.

Total funds budgeted for the program in fiscal year 2003 were $4.7 billion; however, only about 10% of these funds will probably be used for economic development projects, and an even smaller percentage of funds will directly benefit for-profit businesses.

Where to Find HUD

Businesses should contact their city or county planners to determine whether a CDBG revolving loan pool exists or could be started for funding their projects. City or county planners should contact HUD (look in the Blue Pages under U.S. Government) for more information:

U.S. Department of Housing and Urban Development
451 Seventh Street, SW
Washington, DC 20410
Telephone: (202) 708-1112
TTY: (202) 708-1455
Web address: www.hud.gov

Business Assistance for Entrepreneurs in Distressed Areas

The U.S. Department of Commerce, through its Economic Development Administration (EDA), provides assistance for entrepreneurs in economically distressed areas.

For More Information

Businesses should contact their city or county planners to determine whether a Title IX revolving loan pool exists or could be started for funding their projects. City or county planners should contact EDA for more information:

U.S. Department of Commerce
Economic Adjustment Program
14th and Constitution Avenue, NW
Washington, DC 20230
(202) 482-2659

The Economic Adjustment (Title IX) Program (EAP) provides funds to communities that have suffered from long-term economic decline (chronic distress) or from a sudden and severe event, such as a hurricane or plant closing that has undermined the economic stability of the community. In either case, to be eligible for Title IX funding, the community must demonstrate very high unemployment or very low per capita income. The EAP funding to the community must be used for planning or implementing economic rebuilding.

Some communities have chosen, as part of their rebuilding efforts, to establish revolving loan pools. The funds are then available for targeted small business startups and expansions, business and job retention projects, and the redevelopment of blighted land and vacant facilities.

Engineering and Technical Assistance

According to the SBA, U.S. small businesses in the twentieth century have invented the airplane, the aerosol can, double-knit fabric, the heart valve, the optical scanner, the pacemaker, the personal computer, the soft contact lens, and the zipper. Although building a better mousetrap may not automatically trigger a stampede to your door, technological innovation is a valuable competitive advantage. Recognizing this, a variety of federal initiatives have promoted technological innovation. Unfortunately, these federal technological assistance programs are highly fragmented, the result of many different initiatives over many years.

The federal government provides both business development programs and financial assistance programs. Development programs for technologically oriented businesses include the following:

- Small Business Development Centers
- National Innovation Workshops

- Manufacturing Extension Partnership Program
- The Federal Laboratory Consortium for Technology Transfer
- NASA Regional Technology Transfer Centers
- National Technology Transfer Center
- The National Technical Information Service
- Federal Research in Progress Database

Financial assistance programs for technologically oriented businesses include:

- The Small Business Innovation Research Program
- The Small Business Technology Transfer Program
- The Advanced Technology Program

All of these programs are discussed in detail in the following sections.

- Energy Related Inventions Program
- Innovative Concept Program

Small Business Development Centers (SBDCs)

SBDCs provide technical services to startups and small businesses. These services provide assistance in product licensing or small business formation based on new product development. Several SBDCs around the nation provide innovation assessments designed to determine a new product idea's potential for commercialization.

More than 80% of SBDCs provide assistance to small businesses in developing Small Business Innovation Research proposals (discussed in the next section). All SBDCs provide links to federal, state, and local sources of technology and technical information.

National Innovation Workshops

The Departments of Energy and Commerce, in partnership with SBDCs, sponsor six to seven innovation workshops each year around the country. The two-day workshops are targeted at inventors and technology-based businesses. The workshops provide information on:

- The availability of federal R&D funding through Small Business Innovation Research and other programs at the federal or state level.
- Technical assistance available through federal laboratories.
- Federal and state sources of technical information.

They also provide more generic business assistance information.

For More Information

To find the times and places of the next National Innovation Workshops, contact:

The Association of Small Business Development Centers (ASBDC)
8990 Burke Lake Road
Burke, Virginia 22015
Phone: (703) 764-9850
Fax: (703) 764-1234

Manufacturing Extension Partnership

The Department of Commerce and the National Institute of Science and Technology (NIST) fund regional Manufacturing Technology Centers to help small and mid-sized manufacturers compete in the global marketplace. The Centers encourage the adoption of modern technologies and business practices that result in greater productivity, efficiency, and profitability.

In 2002, there were over 400 manufacturing extension centers covering all 50 states and Puerto Rico. Each center is a partnership with federal, state, and local governments, industry, and educational institutions.

Services vary depending upon the local client base and regional needs. In general, centers provide in-depth assessments of manufacturing and technology needs, assistance in selecting appropriate technologies and processes, and plans for integrating these technologies into company operations. Manufacturing extension centers have a variety of software useful to manufacturers, including computer-aided design (CAD), computer-aided manufacturing (CAM), computer-aided assessment and bench marking tools, as well as PC based hardware systems.

Since 1989 more than 149,000 firms have received assistance ranging from factory floor layout to invoice-handling procedures.

For More Information

Manufacturing Extension Partnership
National Institute of Standards and Technology
100 Bureau Drive, Stop 3460
Gaithersburg, MA 20899-3460
Phone: Just call the toll-free number (800) 637-4636 (800 MEP 4 MFG) and your call will be automatically routed to the MEP center that serves your region. Web address: http://www.mep.nist.gov.

The Federal Laboratory Consortium for Technology Transfer (FLC)

Federal research and development laboratories received approximately $25 billion in fiscal year 2000 (which was about 38% of total federal R&D investment for that year). Federal laboratories may enter into agreements with individuals or companies to conduct cooperative research. The U.S. government also holds thousands of patents available for licensing. The key to entrepreneurial success may be deciding how to access these resources given the number of federal laboratories and the complexity of their technological resources.

Many individual federal laboratories, such as Los Alamos and Sandia, have outreach programs to help small and medium-sized manufacturers. These programs are subject to annual budget reauthorizations, but they are part of a trend to increase the laboratories' budgets to provide enhanced outreach services. This trend recognizes the need for technology transfer to the private sector from the large number of federal laboratories that are potential sources of technology. Consortium members include all major federal R&D laboratories and their parent organizations, comprising some 700 laboratories belonging to 17 federal departments and agencies.

The FLC provides access for entrepreneurs and small businesses to technology, top-notch scientists and engineers for problem solving, and state-of-the-art laboratory equipment and facilities. FLC members devote approximately 5% of their total laboratory budget to transferring technology out of the laboratories.

For More Information

Federal Laboratory Consortium
(888) 388-5227
Web address: http://www.federallabs.org

A request for assistance flows from the entrepreneur or small business person to an FLC regional coordinator to a laboratory representative, and then to the actual technologist who can solve the problem or supply the resource. There is no cost for any of the services.

NASA Regional Technology Transfer Centers (RTTCs)

The RTTC mission is to transfer and assist in the commercialization of NASA and other federal technology. RTTC consultants assist in the identification, evaluation, acquisition, and adaptation of technology to meet specific business needs.

The six RTTCs, which are linked to the NASA field centers, are affiliated with 60 universities and other not-for-profit organizations. They provide access to approximately one million documents in the NASA data bank and to more than 400 other computerized databases. The databases include selected contents for some 15,000 scientific and technical journals.

For More Information

To contact your RTTC, call (800) 472-6785

National Technology Transfer Center (NTTC)

The NTTC helps businesses access NASA and other federal technology resources by matching specific needs of the business with the appropriate NASA or federal resource. The NTTC will search NASA and federal databases and will expedite communication with NASA or federal laboratory experts who may assist with solutions. The NTTC works closely with the Federal Lab Consortium, the NASA Regional Technology Transfer Centers, and other organizations interested in technology transfer for commercialization purposes.

The NTTC also operates a national electronic bulletin board service for the public and private sectors. The free service includes announcement of new technologies, answering of questions on technical problems, and notices of technology transfer conferences and meetings. The bulletin board also includes a number of searchable databases.

For More Information

The National Technology Transfer Center
Wheeling Jesuit University
316 Washington Ave.
Wheeling, WV 26003
Phone: (800) 678-NTTC
Fax: (304) 243-4388
Web address: http://www.nttc.edu

The National Technical Information Service (NTIS)

This is an agency of the U.S. Department of Commerce. NTIS is a national and international information system for technical, engineering, and business-related information. NTIS serves as the central source for federally generated computerized data files, databases, and software. The online database system is accessible by modem.

For More Information

U.S. Department of Commerce
Technology Administration
National Technical Information Service
Springfield, VA 22161
(703) 605-6000
Web address: http://www.ntis.gov

Federal Research in Progress Database (FEDRIP)

FEDRIP is a program of the Department of Commerce. The database contains summaries of U.S. government-funded research projects.

For More Information on FEDRIP

Online access for a fee can be obtained by filling out the online form located at http://www.nisc.com/grc/grcsub.htm and mailing it to:

NTIS Subscription Dept.
ATTN: GRC
5285 Port Royal Road
Springfield, VA 22161
Fax: (703) 605-6880

In 2002, it included over 218,000 preliminary, ongoing, or final project reports. Each FEDRIP entry includes title, principal investigator, performing and sponsoring organization, detailed abstract, project objectives, and sometimes intermediate findings and funding amount. The summaries provide up-to-date research progress in specific technical areas before technical reports or journal articles are published. Updates to the database are done monthly.

The Small Business Innovation Research (SBIR) Program

Many high-technology companies started up with a government research and development (R&D) contract. If your company has the ability to do technological research and development, you should consider applying to the SBIR program.

The SBIR program is a multiagency federal research and development program coordinated through, but not managed by, the SBA. The SBIR program began in 1982 with the enactment of the Small Business Innovation Development Act. The act required agencies of the federal government with budgets for externally contracted R&D in excess of $100 million to establish SBIR programs. Funding for the program is derived from a fixed percentage of each agency's R&D budget. Under the SBIR program, federal agencies set aside 2.5% of certain research and development funds for use by small firms.

The SBIR program aims to fund scientifically sound research proposals that will, if successful, have "significant public benefit." SBIR's threefold objectives are:

- To increase small firm participation in federal R&D
- To foster commercial applications from applied federal research
- To encourage innovation for public benefit

The SBIR program involves a competitive three-phase award system that provides qualified small business concerns with opportunities to propose innovative studies that meet the specific R&D needs of the various agencies of the federal government:

- Phase I: SBIR awardees receive up to $100,000 to evaluate the scientific merit and technical feasibility of an idea. The period of performance normally does not exceed six months. Only Phase I awardees are eligible for consideration in Phase II.
- Phase II: Awardees receive up to $750,000 to develop prototypes, finalize products, and further expand on the research results of Phase I. The period of performance normally does not exceed two years.
- Phase III: Firms try to commercialize the results of Phase II. Despite its classification as Phase III, this stage requires the use of private or non-SBIR federal funding. No SBIR funds are utilized in Phase III. However, Phase III may involve production contracts with a federal agency for future use by the federal government.

The SBIR program has experienced explosive growth since its inception in 1983. In that first year of awarding activity, the program made 686 Phase I awards for $44.5 million to small high technology firms. In 2001, the program produced 3,215 Phase I awards and 1,533 Phase II awards for approximately $1.5 billion dollars.

In 2002, there were 10 federal agencies that participated in the SBIR program:

1. Department of Agriculture
2. Department of Commerce
3. Department of Defense
4. Department of Education
5. Department of Energy
6. Department of Health and Human Services
7. Department of Transportation
8. Environmental Protection Agency
9. National Aeronautics and Space Administration
10. National Science Foundation

SBIR proposals should be 25 pages or fewer and should follow the specified agency format. Proposals should demonstrate:

- A hypothesis that rests on sufficient evidence
- Clear use of technical information
- Familiarity with recent literature or methods
- Adequate experience or training
- A realistic proposed effort
- Technological innovation
- Good potential commercial application

Awards have covered a broad range of scientific research, from human habitability and biology in space to airborne datalink cockpit management, and from neural-network-based speech identification to aquacultures.

To be eligible to compete, a business concern must be for profit, at least 51% owned and controlled by individuals who are citizens of, or lawfully admitted permanent residents of, the United States, and, including affiliates, may not have more than 500 employees. The principal researcher for the project must be employed by the business.

The Small Business Technology Transfer (STTR) Program

The STTR program is a relatively new effort of the federal government that encourages innovation by fostering partnership between small businesses and nonprofit research institutions. It is similar to the SBIR program in that it is co-ordinated through but not managed by the SBA. Five federal agencies are re-quired by STTR to set aside a portion of their R&D budget for awards to small business/nonprofit research institution partnerships. Participating agencies are the Department of Defense, Department of Energy, Health and Human Services, National Aeronautics and Space Administration, and National Science Foundation (see the box on page 261).

The STTR, like the SBIR program, involves a competitive three-phase award system.

1. STTR awardees receive up to $100,000 for the exploration of the scien-tific, technical, and commercial feasibility of an idea or technology. The period of performance is approximately one year. Only Phase I awardees are eligible for Phase II awards.

2. Awardees receive up to $500,000 to expand R&D results and commercial potential. The period of performance is a maximum of two years.

3. Firms try to commercialize the results from Phase II. No STTR funds are available for Phase III, however awardees may pursue other federal agency funding.

To be eligible for STTR funding, the business must be for-profit, at least 51% owned and controlled by individuals who are citizens of, or lawfully admit-ted permanent residents of, the United States, and including affiliates, may not have more than 500 employees. The nonprofit research institution must be lo-cated in the United States. The principal researcher, unlike the SBIR program, does not have to be an employee of the business. The STTR Pilot program began making awards in FY 1994. In that year, 198 awards were issued for ap-proximately $19 million to small high technology businesses that collaborated with nonprofit research institutions to undertake R&D projects. In FY 2001, Federal participating agencies awarded 224 Phase I awards and 113 Phase II awards totaling just over $78 million dollars.

The Advanced Technology Program (ATP)

The Department of Commerce and the National Institute of Standards and Technology also make awards to businesses or to industry-led joint ventures of businesses, universities, federal laboratories, and nonprofit independent re-search organizations. These awards are for innovative research and develop-ment of cutting-edge, generic technologies that have the potential to improve U.S. economic growth and productivity. Generic technologies underlie a wide range of potential applications for a broad range of products or processes. The

How to Apply for an SBIR or STTR Award

Although the SBA sponsors various SBIR/STTR conferences and seminars in every state, the agency does not distribute copies of SBIR or STTR solicitations. The participating federal agencies responsible for generating SBIR and STTR topics and conferring awards release their own solicitation announcements. However, the SBA collects solicitation information from participating agencies and publishes it quarterly in its electronic Pre-Solicitation Announcement (PSA). PSAs provide the following information:

- The research topics of current interest to each participating agency.
- The opening and closing dates of each solicitation.
- Whom to contact for a copy of the agency solicitation.

For more information contact:

U.S. Small Business Administration
Office of Technology
409 Third Street, SW
Washington, DC 20416
(202) 205-6450
Web address: http://www.sba.gov

Technical abstracts of past SBIR awards are available through an online service of the U.S. Department of Commerce National Technical Information Service (NTIS) known as the Federal Research in Progress (FEDRIP) database (described earlier in this chapter). FEDRIP is also accessible through DIALOG or Knowledge Express, the private information services. About 16,500 projects are currently listed in this database.

Information on each past SBIR project typically includes:

- Company name, address, and telephone number
- Sponsoring federal agency
- Funding awarded for Phase I and Phase II
- A 200-word abstract describing the technical work
- Commercialization potential

Free copies of the FEDRIP Search Guide (PR-847) are available by calling (703) 487-4650. For information on the DIALOG Online Service, call (800) 3-DIALOG; on Knowledge Express, call (800) 529-5337.

technologies can be from any scientific area.

Past awards have ranged from ceramics to metal processing, from optical data storage systems to tissue engineering. The awards support the development of laboratory prototypes and proof of technical feasibility, not commercial prototypes, proof of commercial feasibility, or product development.

Awards to individual firms are limited to $2 million over three years to cover direct R&D costs. Awards to joint ventures are for five years, and the dollar amounts are limited only by available funding. However, NIST funding to joint ventures is capped at less than 50% of total R&D costs. Support for the ATP program has increased over time from the initial appropriation of $10 million in 1990. To date over $2 billion has been dispersed.

How to Find ATP

Proposals must be submitted to specifically dated solicitations. To get your name on the mailing list for solicitation announcements contact:

Advanced Technology Program
National Institute of Standards and Technology
100 Bureau Drive, Stop 4701
Gaithersburg, MD 20899-4701
(800) ATP-FUND
E-mail: atp@nist.gov
Web address: http://www.atp.nist.gov

The awards are based on business and technical merit and the potential benefit to U.S. industry. They are highly competitive. Only 642 awards have been made from 5,451 proposals as of late 2002. About 60% of the almost $2 billion total ATP funding went to 195 joint ventures of two or more firms or organizations, of this amount 32% were led by small businesses of less than 500 employees. The remaining 40% of funding went to 447 single company projects, of which 65% were small businesses. In addition small businesses make up a significant percentage of membership in ATP joint ventures led by large businesses.

Innovative Concepts (Inn Con) Program

This Department of Energy program provides seed money to individuals, small companies, and university researchers to allow them to determine if their innovative energy saving ideas and inventions are technically and economically feasible. It also provides linkages to potential technical or commercial partners and other possible funding sources. Inn Con chooses an energy-related topic and solicits proposals for funding in 1 to 2 year cycles. Up to 15 projects per cycle are awarded seed money at two levels: up to $75,000 for early development projects and up to $250,000 for more developed projects moving toward prototype development and commercialization. To add your name to the mailing list for proposal solicitation announcements contact:

> U.S. Department of Energy
> Inventions and Innovations Program
> 1000 Independence Avenue, SW
> Washington, DC 20585-0121

EXTERNAL ASSISTANCE AVAILABLE PRIMARILY TO STATE AND LOCAL RESIDENTS

State Resources

State, local, and regional development agencies imitate, support, and expand federal efforts to help startups and small businesses. Like the federal agencies, their services target business development, startup and small business financing, procurement, and international trade. Their clients include women, minorities, entrepreneurial ventures in rural or depressed areas, and technologically oriented startups.

Your first stop should be your state department of commerce, a useful starting place for finding other resources, such as those national programs described in this chapter, and other state, regional, and local-sponsored management assistance and financial support programs. This management and technical assistance may range from business planning to licensing, helping firms locate capital, and finding state and federal procurement opportunities. They typically offer state certification programs for businesses owned by minorities and women.

Local Resources

Chambers of Commerce

These are city-based groupings of local businesses that often provide assistance for firms wishing to relocate or start operations in the city. Chambers often provide information packages on local regulations and taxes. They also work closely with economic development organizations to lobby the city government for more favorable business conditions. They have traditionally provided a setting for business leaders, including entrepreneurs, to network and discuss common problems.

Incubators

These organizations nurture several fledgling firms that share services and equipment and occupy building space at a reduced rate. Nationwide there are about 800 incubators, up from 12 in 1980. Businesses starting out in incubators have an 87% success rate, which is higher than the average startup success rate. In addition to low-cost shelter and services, one of the biggest benefits provided by incubators is the support and counsel provided by a network of business assistant professionals.

Where to Find Incubators

National Business Incubation Association
20 E. Circle Dr., Suite 190
Athens, OH 45701
(614) 593-4331
Web address: http://www.nbia.org

University Libraries

Although they have no direct charter to assist startups, many university business libraries, particularly those at public universities, are dedicated to serving the information needs of business. They offer reasonably priced information services, including:

- Photocopies or book loans
- Government publications
- Company reports-annual or 10K
- Scientific or technical information
- Business management information
- Market or product studies
- Reviews of computer hardware or software
- Tax or legal information searches
- Patent and trademark searches

- Technical standards and specifications
- Consumer profiles and census data
- Corporate financial information
- Mailing labels
- Other search help

Public Libraries

The business sections of city-funded public libraries also provide useful resources.

9 LEGAL AND TAX ISSUES

Richard P. Mandel

Tony and Jennifer had both worked for the same manufacturer of computer disk drives since their college graduations some five years ago. Their employer manufactured and sold a variety of drives that were powered by the company's own proprietary software. These products sold fairly well, but the company regularly received complaints regarding the slow response time of these drives relative to the computers to which they were linked.

Tony worked in sales at the company and was acutely aware of these complaints. He had spoken often about this problem with Jennifer, who was employed in engineering. After considering the problem for some time, Jennifer was convinced she could solve the problem through new software that could be loaded into these or any company's drives by the end-user.

One night, after work, the two budding entrepreneurs decided to establish their own company to develop and sell this software. Jennifer estimated it would take her six months to develop and perfect the software, and Tony thought he could develop significant sales volume within eight months after that. Tony was additionally convinced he could obtain enough money from his wealthy Uncle Max to keep them going until then. However, they both recognized that when it came time to market and distribute their product on a large scale, they would probably need both bank and investor financing. Furthermore, although the two of them could probably perform all necessary tasks in the short run, they expected that additional programmers, sales professionals, and packing and shipping personnel would be necessary in the long run. Both of them knew of fellow employees who would be perfect for these positions. Excited about their plans, Jennifer and Tony prepared to submit their resignations.

This chapter covers legal issues that an entrepreneur must consider before leaving a position to start a new venture (e.g., whether the new firm can legally compete with the former company). The chapter then discusses issues that need to be resolved before initiation of the new venture, including how to choose the legal form of the business (such as a corporation or partnership), how to name the business, and how to avoid potential tax pitfalls related to the initial founders' investments (such as how to negotiate stockholder agreements and handle the disposition of stock). The legal and tax issues involved in hiring employees are covered, as are insurance considerations and tax issues related to financing the venture.

LEGAL ISSUES INVOLVED IN LEAVING A POSITION

Enthusiastic entrepreneurs may be so excited about where they are going that they forget to consider where they have been. Many are surprised to learn that serious limitations arising out of their former employment may be imposed on their freedom of action. Some of these limitations may be the result of agreements the entrepreneur signed while in the former position. Others may be imposed as a matter of law, without any agreement or even knowledge on the part of the employee.

The Corporate Opportunity Doctrine

The corporate opportunity doctrine is an outgrowth of the traditional obligation of loyalty owed by an agent to a principal. In its most common form, *it prohibits an officer or director of a corporation, a partner in a partnership, or a person in a similar position from identifying a business opportunity that would be valuable to his company and using that information for his own benefit or the benefit of a competitor.*

Thus, a corporate director who discovers that one of the corporation's competitors may shortly be put on the market cannot raise money and purchase the competitive company himself. To discharge his legal obligation to the corporation of which he is a director, he would be required to disclose the opportunity to his board and allow the board to decide (without his participation) whether the corporation will make the purchase. Only after the corporation has been fully informed and has decided not to take advantage of the opportunity may the director use that information for himself. Even then, as the new owner of a competitor, he would be required to resign from his former corporation's board.

The scope of this *duty of loyalty* is normally adjusted by the law to reflect the individual's position within the business. Although the president and members of the board may be required to turn over knowledge of all opportunities that may be in any way related to the business of the company, lower level employees probably have such an obligation only with regard to opportunities that are directly relevant to their positions. Thus, arguably, a sales manager may be required to inform her company of any sales opportunities she may encounter that are relevant to the company's products. She may not be required to inform the company of a potential business acquisition.

Tony and Jennifer must consider the corporate opportunity doctrine because the opportunity to create a product that more quickly drives the devices made by their employer is directly relevant at least to Jennifer's job. Yet both Jennifer and Tony probably have positions low enough in the company hierarchy that their obligations in this regard are very limited. In addition, the slow pace of the company's disk drives and the fact that such a problem might be solved by more sophisticated software appears to be well known by the company's officers, who have shown little interest in the software side of the business.

Recruitment of Employees from the Former Employer

As Jennifer and Tony delved more deeply into their dreams, they began to identify certain fellow employees who might wish to join their company sometime down the road. This, too, can in some circumstances be problematic.

Another aspect of the duty of loyalty owed by an employee to an employer is the legal requirement that *the employee cannot knowingly take action designed to harm the employer's business.* This is, perhaps, pure common sense. After all, the employee is collecting a paycheck to perform tasks that advance the employer's interests. We would not expect the law to countenance a paid salesperson's regularly recommending that customers patronize a competitor, nor would we expect the law to endorse an engineer's giving his best ideas to another company. Similarly, courts have held that it is a breach of the duty of loyalty to solicit and induce fellow employees to leave their jobs.

Once again, the likelihood that a court would enforce this obligation depends to some extent on the nature of the employee's activities and his or her position in the company. Neither Tony nor Jennifer need fear reprisals for their having convinced each other to leave. Nor would there be much likelihood of liability if they convinced another employee to leave with them, especially if these conversations took place after working hours.

However, if either Tony or Jennifer worked in the human resources department, where their job descriptions would include recruiting and retention of employees, this activity might well expose them to liability. Furthermore, if their plan included the wholesale resignations of a relatively large number of employees, *such that the company's ability to continue to function efficiently might be compromised,* a court would be more likely to intervene with injunctive or other relief. This is especially true if the defendants' job descriptions included maintaining the efficient operation of the departments they were involved in destroying.

Use of Proprietary Information

Another potential complication involves Tony and Jennifer's use of information or technology belonging to their former employer. Such information need not be subject to formal patent or copyright protection to be protected. *Any information that gives the company a competitive advantage, which the company has taken reasonable steps to keep confidential and that is not otherwise known to outsiders, is likely to be protected by law as a trade secret.* Such information may include inventions and technology, but it may also include such other valuable information as customer lists, pricing strategies, and unique operating methods.

In this case, if Jennifer had developed the software concept that solves the speed problem as part of her job, that concept might well belong to the company and be unavailable to Jennifer and Tony for their new enterprise. It is not enough for the concept to be developed by or for the company; the concept must be unique and unknown to software engineers outside the company, and the company must have taken steps to keep it that way.

Thus, the company should label any physical manifestations of the information as "confidential" and should restrict its distribution to those who have either a legal or contractual obligation to keep such information private. If, on the other hand, the company had deliberately or carelessly allowed the distribution of the information to outsiders, it has likely lost the right to restrict its use.

Many companies require employees to sign agreements that spell out the employees' obligation to protect trade secrets. Indeed, this is one of the "reasonable steps" it should take to maintain confidentality. This has led some employees to believe that such an obligation applies only to those who have signed such an agreement. This is a misconception. *The obligation to respect an employer's trade secrets and keep them confidential is imposed by law and is not dependent upon contract.* Furthermore, that obligation continues after the employment relationship has been terminated, for whatever reason, and continues indefinitely until the information makes its way into the public domain.

Employers who require a confidentiality agreement from their employees are generally not misinformed about the general applicability of the law but are simply making sure that the employees are aware of their responsibilities in this regard. After all, if an employee, under a mistaken belief about his rights, releases proprietary information to outsiders, it is small comfort to the employer to have the right to sue the employee for damages.

Fortunately for Jennifer and Tony, they appear to have merely identified a need that is known generally to the industry; they have not begun to develop the specific software solution to the problem. On that set of facts, it is extremely doubtful that their new enterprise will make use of any information that legally belongs to their former employer.

Protecting Proprietary Information in the New Business Venture

By the time Jennifer and Tony have developed a product that meets the identified need, they will have created a body of proprietary information of their own. At that point they will be forced to consider the variety of means at their disposal to protect that information from use by competitors and end-users who have failed to pay for the privilege.

A measure of protection is available from the copyright laws and, depending on the nature of their product, from a patent. Both of these options require disclosure of the information in exchange for the protection granted by the government; thus, they present the risk that others may engineer around the patent or reconfigure the software around the copyright. In such a case, Tony and Jennifer would be unlikely to have resources adequate to bring the necessary lawsuits to protect their rights.

Thus, they may choose to forgo statutory protection and protect their asset by a policy of nondisclosure as a trade secret, accompanied by very tight licensing agreements with customers. Further discussion of these issues and of the relative advantages and risks of these various modes of intellectual property protection is contained in Chapter 10.

Noncompetition Obligations to the Former Employer

Related to the obligation not to disclose proprietary information is *the obligation not to compete with one's employer.* Like most of the obligations discussed already, this is derived from the fiduciary relationship between employer and employee, specifically, the duty of loyalty. How can an entrepreneur justify accepting a paycheck from his or her employer when he or she is simultaneously establishing, working for, or financing a competing business?

The law imposes this duty not to compete on all employees, officers, directors, partners, and so on, while their association with the employer remains in effect. Unlike the obligation to protect proprietary information, however, this obligation does not extend to the period after termination of the relationship. Extension of this obligation requires the contractual promise of the employee. Thus, in the absence of a contract, as soon as Tony and Jennifer quit their present jobs (but not before), they are free to go into direct competition with their former employer, so long as they do not make use of any of the employer's proprietary information.

Noncompetition agreements can be analyzed using many different measurements. To begin with, the scope of the obligation must be examined. In an extreme case, an employee may have agreed not to engage in any activity that competes with any aspect of the business his former employer engaged in, or planned to engage in, at the time of the termination of the employee's association with the company. At the other end of the spectrum, the employee may have agreed only to refrain from soliciting any of the former employer's customers or (somewhat more restrictively) from dealing with any of them no matter who initiated the contact. Such agreements also may be measured based on the length of time they extend beyond the termination of employment and by the size of the geographic area they cover.

Such measurements are important because, in the employment context, many states take the position that such agreements contravene basic public policies, such as encouraging competition and allowing each individual to make the best use of his or her talents. A few such states actually refuse to enforce all such noncompetition agreements. Most, however, purport to enforce only those agreements that are deemed reasonable under the circumstances. Thus, these public policies are balanced against the employer's recognized interest in protecting its business and goodwill. Only those restrictions that are limited to the extent necessary to prevent harm to the employer's legitimate interests will be enforced.

For example, a medical practice that does business only with customers located within a 25-mile radius would probably not be able to enforce a noncompetition agreement that extends much beyond that geographic area. Furthermore, although a manufacturer may be able to enforce such an agreement against an officer, salesperson, or engineer who has either direct contact with customers or knowledge of the company's processes and products, it might not be able to enforce the same agreement against a bookkeeper, whose departure would have little effect on the company's goodwill. Even the officer, salesperson, or engineer might be able to resist an agreement that purports to remain in effect beyond the time the employer might reasonably need to protect its goodwill and business from the effects of new competition.

Another factor that may affect the enforceability of a noncompetition agreement is whether the employer agrees to continue part or all of the former employee's compensation during the noncompetition period. In addition, a noncompetition agreement that might be unenforceable against an employee might nonetheless be enforceable against the seller of a business or a major stockholder having his stock redeemed. Finally, employers in some states can take comfort in the fact that some courts that find the scope or length of a noncompetition agreement objectionable, nonetheless enforce the agreement to the maximum extent they deem acceptable. Others take an all-or-nothing approach.

Since in Tony and Jennifer's case there is no indication that they have signed a noncompetition agreement, they need only resign from their current positions before taking any affirmative steps to establish their new enterprise. After resigning, they are under no further noncompetition restrictions.

CHOOSING AN ATTORNEY AND ACCOUNTANT

There is a natural reluctance to incur what are perceived to be unnecessary expenses in beginning a new venture, and many people perceive engaging an attorney and accountant as just such expenses. However, as may already be evident from the discussion so far, the earlier these professionals can be consulted, the more likely the business will be to avoid costly mistakes. One is tempted to repeat the old cliche, "Either pay me now or pay me later," the latter alternative being much more costly.

Choose a Lawyer Who Is Experienced in Small Business Startups

The choice of an appropriate attorney is complicated by the fact that American law does not officially recognize legal specialties. Thus, in virtually all states, there is only one form of licensing, and, once licensed, an attorney can practice in all areas of the law. In practice, however, the American legal profession has become highly specialized, with many attorneys confining their practices to one or two areas of expertise. Thus, most patent attorneys do very little else, and most good litigation attorneys concentrate on litigating. Few very good corporate attorneys know their way around a courtroom. Just as these legal areas are practiced mainly by specialists, the representation of startups and small businesses is a specialty as well.

Tony and Jennifer would do well to ask their prospective attorney to describe his or her experience in representing small businesses. The local generalist may not be sufficiently aware of the many technical matters identified in this chapter (and elsewhere in this book). Also, an attorney experienced in the problems of startups will be familiar with the unique cash-flow problems of such ventures. A business's need for legal services may never be so great in comparison with its ability to pay than at the outset. The attorney may be willing to work out installment payments or other arrangements to avoid postponing essential early planning.

Some attorneys practicing in this area have adopted a policy of accepting equity in the new business as part of the fee arrangement. Interestingly, many such attorneys do not lower their fee in exchange for equity but justify taking equity as the price of accepting the risk that their fee may not be paid if the business does not succeed. Such an arrangement may lead to dangerous conflicts of interest in the future, when legal advice affects the value of the company's stock. For example, how can an entrepreneur be confident of an attorney's advice regarding the suitability of the company for a public offering when such an offering would have the effect of creating a market for the same attorney's stock? This type of arrangement has become less common since the demise of the dot-com era.

Choose a Small, Local Accounting Firm

Many of the same considerations inform the choice of an accountant. Although the level of expertise in the national and international firms is unmatched, most of them have little experience with startups such as that proposed by Tony and Jennifer, since their fee structures are inappropriate for the size of such businesses. Many local firms have all the skills necessary to serve the startup and can be sensitive to the cash-flow issues mentioned earlier.

It is important to engage the accountant as early as possible so he or she can establish the information management systems and recommend the computer software that will get the company's records off on the right foot. This gives the entrepreneur the tools necessary to gauge the success of his or her efforts against his or her budget before it is too late to adapt, and it prevents the expensive and frustrating task of reconstructing the company's results from fragmented and missing records at the end of the year.

CHOOSING THE LEGAL FORM OF YOUR BUSINESS

Business Forms

One of the first issues Jennifer, Tony, and their attorney and accountant will confront, after weaving their way through the thicket of issues associated with leaving their current jobs, is what legal form they should choose for their new venture. Many choices are available.

The Sole Proprietorship

The most basic business form (and the one that will apply unless an individual entrepreneur chooses otherwise) is the sole proprietorship. This is a business owned and operated by one individual, who is in total control. No new legal entity is created; the individual entrepreneur just goes into business, either alone or with employees, but without any co-owners. This is the simplest of entities but one that will not be attractive to Jennifer and Tony unless one of them chooses to forgo ownership and act only as an employee.

The Partnership

The default mode for Tony and Jennifer is the partnership. This is the legal form that results when two or more persons go into business for profit, as co-owners, sharing profits and losses. Since Tony and Jennifer clearly contemplate sharing ownership and control, they will find themselves in a partnership unless they choose otherwise.

A Corporation

Another choice available to our subjects is the corporation. This form is created by state government, as a routine matter, on the entrepreneur's filing an application and paying a fee. It is a separate entity, with legal existence apart from its owners, the stockholders. Jennifer and Tony might well choose to form a corporation, dividing its stock between them.

The Subchapter S Corporation

A variation of the corporate option is the so-called subchapter S corporation. If a corporation passes a number of tests, it may elect to be treated as such. However, it is essential to understand that such election affects only the tax status of the corporation. In all other respects, a subchapter S corporation is indistinguishable from a standard corporation. For reasons discussed later in this chapter, Jennifer and Tony may also find this business form attractive.

The Professional Corporation and Limited Liability Partnership

The professional corporation is another variation of the corporate form. This choice is typically available only to businesspeople who intend to render professional services, such as medical or legal practitioners, accountants, architects, and social workers. It was created primarily to allow these professionals to take advantage of certain tax opportunities once available only to corporations, without granting them the limited liability afforded to normal business corporations.

Over time, however, many of the tax advantages formerly available only to corporations have been extended to sole proprietorships and partnerships, and some of the limited liability formerly associated with business corporations has been extended to professional corporations. Thus, the differences among these forms have narrowed considerably. In addition, many states now allow groups who have practiced as partnerships to obtain limited liability by registering as limited liability partnerships. In any case, Tony and Jennifer will not be practicing a profession, so these business forms will not be attractive to them.

The Limited Liability Company

In recent years, all states have enacted legislation enabling businesses to be conducted as *limited liability companies*. These entities are owned by "members," who either manage the business themselves or appoint "managers" to run it for them. All members and managers have the benefit of limited liability (as they would in a corporation) and, in most cases, are taxed similar to a subchapter S corporation without having to conform to the S corporation restrictions described later.

The Limited Partnership

Another possible legal form is a hybrid of the corporate and partnership forms known as the limited partnership. Such a business has one or more general partners (who conduct the business) and one or more limited partners (who act as passive investors, similar to stockholders with no other interest in the business). Because both Tony and Jennifer intend to be actively involved in the business, neither would qualify as a limited partner. But Uncle Max may well qualify if he is willing to fade into the background once he has made his investment.

The Nonprofit Entity

A summary of available business forms should not omit the nonprofit entity. Typically, such a business will take the form of a corporation or trust and will elect nonprofit status as a tax matter. Although many startups do not make a profit, nonprofit (or, more accurately, *not-for-profit*) status is available only to certain types of entities, such as churches, educational institutions, social welfare organizations, and industry associations. If an organization so qualifies, its income is exempt from taxation (as long as it doesn't stray from its exempt purpose), and if certain additional tests are met, contributions to it may be tax deductible. Since Tony and Jennifer do not intend to operate a qualifying business, they need not explore this option.

Choosing the Form

Faced with all these choices, the budding entrepreneur will want to compare these various business forms on a number of parameters relevant to the needs of his business. Both the attorney and accountant for the business can be extremely helpful at this juncture.

Although these forms may be compared on the basis of an almost endless list of factors, those normally most relevant include control issues, exposure to personal liability, tax factors, and administrative costs. These issues are discussed in detail in the following sections, and Exhibit 9.1 provides an overview of the issues and how they affect each business form.

Control Issues

The *sole proprietorship* is the simplest and most direct with regard to the subject of control. Since there is only one principal in the business, this individual wields total control over all issues. However, that option is not available to Tony and Jennifer.

The simplest option available to them is the *partnership*. In that form, control is divided among the principals in accordance with their partnership agreement. Although a written agreement is normally not legally required, this issue and many of the others that arise in a partnership argue for a written agreement to encourage specificity. The parties may agree that all decisions must be made by unanimous vote, or they may adopt a majority standard (making Uncle Max the swing vote). More likely, they may require unanimity for a stated group of significant decisions and may allow a majority vote for others. In addition, Jennifer and Tony may delegate authority for certain types of decisions to one or both of the active partners.

EXHIBIT 9.1 Comparison of various business forms.

	Control	Liability	Taxation	Administrative obligations
Sole proprietorship	Owner has complete control	Unlimited personal liability	Not a separate taxable entity	Only those applicable to all businesses
Partnership	Partners share control	Joint and several unlimited personal liability	Not a separate taxable entity	Only those applicable to all businesses
Corporation	Control distributed among shareholders, directors, and officers	Limited personal liability	Separate taxable entity unless subchapter S election	Some additional
Limited partnership	General partners control, limited partners do not	General partners: joint and several unlimited personal liability, limited partners: limited personal liability	Not a separate entity	Some additional
Limited liability company	Members share control or appoint managers	Limited personal liability	Not a separate entity unless affirmatively chosen	Some additional

Regardless of how this power is allocated in the partnership agreement, however, third parties are allowed to rely on the authority of any partner to bind the partnership to contracts relevant to the ordinary course of the partnership's business. Thus, no matter what may have been agreed among them, Uncle Max will have a free hand with third parties, subject only to the consequences of his breaching his agreement with the others. This is also true for the consequences of torts committed by any partner acting in the course of partnership business. The looseness of this arrangement may well be enough to discourage Jennifer and Tony from choosing the partnership option.

A *corporation*, whether professional or business, and regardless of whether it has elected subchapter S status, is controlled by three levels of authority. Broadly speaking, the stockholders vote, in proportion to the number of shares owned, on the election of the board of directors, sale or dissolution of the business, and amendments to the corporation's charter. In virtually all cases, these decisions are made either by the majority or by two-thirds of the shares. Thus, if Tony, Jennifer, and Uncle Max each owned one-third of the issued stock, unless Uncle Max had provided otherwise when he invested, Tony and Jennifer (if they voted together) could elect the entire board and sell the business over the objections of Uncle Max. Uncle Max would not even be entitled to a minority position on the board. He would, however, be the swing vote should Jennifer and Tony ever disagree, perhaps prompting them to consider nonvoting stock or some similar device for him.

The board of directors, in turn, makes all the long-term and significant policy decisions for the business, as well as electing the officers of the corporation. Votes are virtually always decided by majority. The officers, consisting of a president, treasurer, and secretary at minimum, run the day-to-day business of the corporation and, as such, are the only level of authority that can bind the corporation by contract or in tort.

In this case, one would expect either Tony or Jennifer to be president and the other, perhaps, to be executive vice president and treasurer. Other commonly used titles are chief executive officer, chief operating officer, and various vice presidents. It is not uncommon for the corporation's attorney to act as secretary, since the attorney presumably has the expertise necessary to keep the corporate records of the company in an accurate manner. We might also expect that Tony and Jennifer would convince Uncle Max not to insist on a title, thus eliminating his power to deal with third parties on the corporation's behalf.

The *limited liability company* can be operated much like a general partnership. All members can share in control to the extent set forth in a members agreement. However, most states allow the members of a limited liability company to appoint one or more "managers" (usually, but not necessarily members) to control most of the day-to-day operations of the business. In the case of Jennifer, Tony, and Uncle Max, we might expect the three members to appoint Jennifer and Tony as managers to avoid giving Uncle Max the authority to deal with outsiders on behalf of the business.

The *limited partnership* concentrates all control in the general partners, who exercise that control as set forth in the limited partnership agreement (just as such control is allocated in a partnership agreement). Limited partners have virtually no control, unless the limited partnership agreement has granted them some influence over very significant issues such as sale of the business or dissolution. Only the general partners have the apparent authority to bind the partnership in contract or tort with third parties. Since the limited partnership is required to file the names of its general partners with the state, third parties are deemed to know that limited partners (whose names do not appear) cannot have such authority.

Based on control issues alone, therefore, Tony and Jennifer would likely be leaning away from a general partnership and toward the limited partnership, limited liability company, or corporation. Their decision will, however, be greatly affected by considerations of personal liability.

Personal Liability Issues

If the business should ever incur current liabilities beyond its ability to pay, must the individual owners make up the difference? If so, this could easily result in personal bankruptcy for the owners on top of the loss of their business. And this unhappy result need not occur as a result of poor management or bad business conditions. It could just as easily be brought about by an uninsured tort claim from a buyer of the product or a victim of a delivery employee's careless driving.

For both the *partnership* and the *sole proprietorship,* the business is not recognized as a legal entity separate from its owners. Thus, the debts of the business are ultimately the debts of the owners if the business cannot pay. This unlimited liability is enough to recommend avoidance of these forms for virtually any business, with the possible exception of the one-person consulting firm, for which all liability will be the direct result of the wrongdoing of its owner in any case.

If this unlimited liability is uncomfortable for Jennifer and Tony, imagine what it means to Uncle Max, who apparently has significant assets to lose and who will likely be excluded from meaningful control over the business. This is made even worse because all partnership liabilities are considered joint and several obligations of all partners. Thus, Uncle Max will be responsible for full payment of all partnership liabilities if Tony and Jennifer have no significant assets of their own.

Uncle Max can gain solace because in trading away his influence over the operation of the business in a *limited partnership,* he is granted limited liability for its debts. Thus, if the limited partnership cannot meet its obligations, Uncle Max will lose his investment, but his personal assets will not be exposed to partnership creditors except to the extent that he made promises of future investment.

However, the limited partnership does not afford this protection to the general partners. They retain unlimited exposure. Tony and Jennifer may believe they can afford to take this risk, especially if they have no significant assets. Yet even if that is so today, it may not be the case at the time liability is incurred.

The solution to all this lies in the *corporation* and the *limited liability company,* both of which afford limited liability to all owners. None of the three participants in our enterprise would have personal liability for its debts. If the business ultimately becomes insolvent, its creditors will look only to business assets for payment and will absorb any shortfall.

This solution is not quite as simple as it sounds. To begin with, creditors know these rules as well as the entrepreneurs. Thus, large or sophisticated creditors, such as banks and other financial institutions, will insist on personal guarantees from the owners before extending credit. In addition, the law has developed a number of theories that allow creditors of corporations to "pierce the corporate veil" and go after the stockholders of a failed corporation under certain conditions. Although it is still early in the history of limited liability companies, it is reasonable to assume that courts will adopt similar theories applicable to them. Generally, these theories fall into one of two categories.

The first of these covers businesses that were initially underfunded, or "thinly capitalized." A business should start out with a combination of capital and liability insurance adequate to cover the claims to which it might normally expect to be exposed. As long as the capital was there at the outset and has not been depleted by dividends or other distributions to stockholders, the protection of the separate entity survives, even after the capital has been depleted by unsuccessful operation.

The second situation that may result in the piercing of the separate entity is the failure of the owners to treat the corporation or limited liability company as an entity separate from themselves. This may be manifest by the entrepreneurs acting in one or more of the following ways:

- Failing to use Inc., Corp., LLC, or a similar legal indicator when dealing with third parties
- Commingling business and personal assets in a personal bank account or allowing personal use of business assets
- Failing to keep business and legal records and to hold regular directors, stockholders, or member meetings

After all, why should creditors be required to respect the difference between the business and its owners when the owners themselves have not?

Assuming, however, that Tony and Jennifer will avoid conduct that would expose them to such personal liability, both the corporate and limited liability company forms should look rather attractive to them. No significant business decision should be made, however, without a look at the tax consequences.

Taxation Issues

Once again, the business form that is simplest to understand in regard to income taxation is the *sole proprietorship*. The financial results of the business are calculated, and the profit or loss appears on the tax return of the sole owner. He can eliminate much of the profit by taking it out of the business as salary, but that has no tax effect, as it simply increases taxable wages by the exact amount that it lowers profit. The tax rate applied to any profit would be the maximum marginal rate to which the taxpayer is exposed by the combination of this profit and his or her other taxable income. If there is a loss, the results of the business act as a sort of tax shelter by offsetting an equal amount of the owner's other taxable income, if any.

As one might expect, the *partnership* acts in a manner very similar to that of the sole proprietorship. Since a partnership is not recognized as a separate taxable entity, it pays no taxes itself (although in many cases it is required to file an informational return). Its profit or loss is reported by its partners. The only complication is allocating the percentage of this profit or loss to be reported by each partner. This is normally determined by the allocations of profit and loss set forth in the partnership agreement by the partners themselves, so long as that allocation reflects a "substantial economic reality."

The *limited partnership* is taxed in exactly the same way as the partnership, with profit and loss allocated among *all* partners, both general and limited, in accordance with the limited partnership agreement. Since the business contemplated by Jennifer and Tony is likely to lose money at the outset, the tax-sheltering aspects of both the partnership and limited partnership may be attractive to Uncle Max, who surely has other sources of income he would like to shelter.

Of the two, the limited partnership would be preferable, since by accepting limited partner status, Uncle Max can have his shelter without being exposed to personal liability. He may be tempted to request that the agreement allocate 99% of the losses to him, since he likely needs the shelter more than Jennifer and Tony do. However, unless he is contributing 99% of the capital and will receive a similar percentage of profit (both operating and capital gain), such an allocation will require close attention to the rather technical "substantial economic reality" test.

A further obstacle to Uncle Max's taking advantage of the possible tax shelter of early losses is presented by the passive loss rules of the Internal

Revenue Code. Simply stated, if Uncle Max is not "materially participating" in the business (which would, by definition, be the case if he were a limited partner), any losses distributable to him from the business could be used to offset income generated only by other passive activities (such as investments in other limited partnerships). The losses could not shelter income from salaries, interest, or dividends from traditional portfolio investments.

Were the business to be organized as a *corporation,* Tony and Jennifer would doubtless be warned about the bugaboo of "double taxation." This fear results because a corporation is recognized as a separate legal entity for income tax purposes, and, thus, it pays a separate corporate level of income tax. Double taxation arises when the corporation makes a profit, pays tax on it, and distributes the remainder to its stockholders as a dividend. The stockholders must then pay income tax on the dividend, resulting in double taxation of the same money.

The same would be true if the corporation paid tax on its profit and then retained the remainder for operations. When the corporation or its stock is eventually sold, the increased value caused by that retention of earnings would be taxed to the selling stockholders as a capital gain.

In reality, however, double taxation is more a myth to the small business than a legitimate fear. In fact, in most cases, it presents an opportunity for significant economic savings. To begin with, most small corporations reduce or even eliminate profit by increasing salaries and bonuses for their owners. This can be done up to the point where the compensation of these individuals is deemed unreasonable by the Internal Revenue Service. If profit is eliminated in this way, the owners will have removed their money from the corporation and will pay only their own individual income tax on it.

On the other hand, if it is necessary to retain some of these earnings, the corporation will pay income tax at a *lower* rate than the stockholders would have, since tax will be imposed at the lowest marginal corporate rate, rather than the stockholders' highest rate. When the corporation or its stock is later sold, the stockholders will be taxed at favorable capital gain rates, and the corporation will have had the use of the money in the meantime to create greater value. Thus, it is the rare small corporation that will actually pay the much-feared double tax.

Furthermore, if the corporation meets certain eligibility requirements, it can elect (under subchapter S of the Internal Revenue Code) to be taxed essentially as if it were a partnership. Whatever profit or loss it generates will appear on the tax returns of the stockholders in proportion to the shares of stock they own, and the corporation will file only an informational return. To take advantage of this option, the corporation must have 75 or fewer stockholders, all of whom are individuals (in most cases) and either resident aliens or citizens of the United States. The corporation can have only one class of stock and is ineligible to participate in most multiple entity corporate structures.

The *subchapter S* election can be very useful in a number of circumstances. For example, if the business is expected to be profitable and Uncle Max insists on a share of those profits, Tony and Jennifer could not avoid double taxation by increasing salaries and bonuses. Since Uncle Max performs no services for the business, any compensation paid to him would automatically be deemed unreasonable. But under subchapter S, since there is no corporate tax, a dividend to Uncle Max would only be taxed at his level.

If the business were to become extremely successful, Tony and Jennifer could reap the rewards without fear that their salaries might be attacked as unreasonable, since, in effect, there are no corporate compensation deductions to disallow. Furthermore, if the business is expecting losses in the short term, Uncle Max can use his share of the losses (determined by his percentage of stock) as a shelter (subject to the passive loss considerations described previously). Even Tony and Jennifer could use their losses against the salaries from their former jobs earlier in the year or against salaries earned by their spouses, if any. An early subchapter S election can also avoid double taxation should the corporation eventually sell all its assets and distribute the proceeds to the stockholders in liquidation. On the other hand, Jennifer and Tony will find that a subchapter S election (and for that matter, use of a limited liability company) will make it difficult to receive tax-free employee benefits and exclude a portion of their capital gains if they should ultimately sell their stock.

In a perfect world, Tony, Jennifer, and Uncle Max could form a corporation, elect subchapter S treatment, and arrange their affairs such that Uncle Max could make as much use of short-term losses as could be supported by "economic reality" and the passive loss rules. However, since profits and losses in an S corporation must be allocated in accordance with stock ownership, and only one class of stock is allowed, any disproportionate allocation of losses to Uncle Max would be accompanied by a disproportionate allocation to him of corporate control and later profits. More creative allocations of profit, loss, and control could be accomplished in a general or limited partnership, but one or more of the parties would have to accept exposure to unlimited liability.

Limited liability companies were designed for just this circumstance. If structured carefully, they afford the limited liability and tax treatment of the S corporation, while avoiding the S corporation's restrictive eligibility requirements. Freed from these restrictions, limited liability companies can make use of creative allocations of profit and control that would constitute prohibited classifications of stock in the S corporation context. However, since limited liability companies are required to calculate their income and loss in accordance with partnership tax rules (as opposed to S corporations, which use corporate tax rules), there may be some negative effects from this choice. For example, certain tax-free methods of selling the company may not be available to a limited liability company. On the other hand, in some circumstances, the limited liability company may allow greater losses to pass through to Uncle Max.

After consideration of these factors with their lawyer and accountant, Jennifer and Tony may still favor the limited liability company for the conduct of their business. Such an entity would shield them from personal liability, and, as managers, allow them to exercise control free from undue influence from Uncle Max. And, as long as the company is properly structured, Uncle Max can have the advantage of the maximum amount of short-term loss available under applicable tax rules. Only an undue administrative burden would seem to be sufficient to reverse this decision.

Administrative Obligations

Certain administrative obligations will be required no matter which business form Jennifer and Tony choose. For example, upon entering business, they should obtain a federal identification number for their business. This will facilitate interaction with the federal government, including the filing of tax returns (real or informational) and the withholding of income and payroll taxes.

On the state level, the business should obtain a sales and use tax registration number, to facilitate reporting and collection of such taxes and to qualify for exemption from such taxes when it purchases items for resale. A nonprofit entity has 18 months to file for and secure nonprofit status from the Internal Revenue Service. Furthermore, as described earlier, all business entities will incur a certain amount of additional accounting expense, specifically for the calculation and reporting of taxable profit and loss.

Corporations, limited liability companies, and limited partnerships, however, bring some additional administrative burden and expense. All three must file an annual report with the state government in addition to a tax return. This document usually reports only the business' current address, officers, directors, managers, general partners, and similar information, but it is accompanied by an annual maintenance fee. The fee, in addition to any minimum income tax that the state may levy, must be paid to avoid eventual involuntary dissolution by the state.

In addition, corporations are sometimes formed under the laws of one state while operating in another. In particular, the state of Delaware has acquired the reputation of having a corporate law that is particularly sympathetic to management in its dealings with stockholders. Although this is a questionable advantage in the context of a small business, many corporations nonetheless form in Delaware merely for the appearance of sophistication. In such cases, the corporation must pay initial fees and annual maintenance fees not only to the state of Delaware (or whichever state is chosen for formation) but also to each state in which it actually operates. Many large, national businesses pay these fees in virtually all 50 states.

Although Jennifer and Tony could avoid these fees by operating as a partnership, it is likely they will conclude that the advantages of the corporate or limited liability company forms are worth the price.

CHOOSING A NAME FOR THE BUSINESS

The choice of a name for a business may at first seem to be a matter of personal taste, without many legal ramifications. However, since a business's name is ultimately the repository of its goodwill, the entrepreneur must take care to choose a name that will not be confused with the name of another business. If he or she does not exercise such caution, the entrepreneur may discover sometime in the future that he or she has expended considerable money and effort enhancing the goodwill of another entity. Worse yet, he or she may be sued for infringement of another's rights.

Even apart from these concerns, an entrepreneur choosing to operate in the corporate, limited liability company, or limited partnership form must clear her choice of name with the state of organization. Although partnerships and sole proprietorships need not do so, corporations, LLCs, and limited partnerships obtain their existence by filing charters with the state. As part of this process, each state will check to see if the name chosen by the potential new entity is "confusingly similar" to a name used by another entity currently registered with that state. This includes entities formed under that state's laws and foreign entities qualified to do business there. Some states will also deny the use of a name they deem misleading, even if it is not similar to the name of another entity.

Passing this test is far from sufficient for the protection of goodwill, however. Because no other entity is using your name in your state does not mean that others are not using it in other states. Furthermore, passing the corporate, LLC, or limited partnership name check doesn't guarantee that no one is using or will use your name for a partnership, sole proprietorship, or product or service name, in your state or elsewhere.

Fortunately, it is possible to discover whether your chosen name is being used by others and to protect it from later use. A number of companies have compiled databases that contain the names of a wide range of entities and products. Virtually all such services contain all corporate, LLC, and limited partnership names from all U.S. jurisdictions. Others add trade and service mark registrations from around the country. Most lawyers have access to a particularly comprehensive data base that includes the preceding lists as well as names from major trade directories, big-city telephone directories, and similar sources. Once a name has passed this test, you can be relatively sure that it is yours if you protect it.

A limited form of protection can be obtained relatively inexpensively by filing the name (and any associated logo or slogan) with the *state trademark registry* in any state in which you intend to use the name, logo, or slogan. If your business provides a service rather than sales of goods, the same protection can be provided by the state's *service mark registry.* The protection provided by these registries extends only throughout the state and will be preempted elsewhere by any federal registration existing or later obtained. Thus, at best, state registration is merely evidence of your prior use of a mark, resulting perhaps in a later federal registrant's being required to allow your continued use of the mark in a limited market area.

The most effective form of protection is a *federal registration,* which is available only for marks that are being used in interstate commerce. Such a registration bars future use of the mark within the relevant class of goods or services anywhere in the United States by anyone who has not established rights through prior use. Since this protection is rather draconian, it is not granted without serious examination by the U.S. Patent Office. Registration can be denied if the name or mark is already in use by others. Protection can also be denied if the name is excessively generic, such that it describes all goods or services in a particular class instead of identifying the goods and services of a particular market participant. Thus, the name Disk Drive Software would likely be denied protection in the case of Jennifer and Tony's business. (Other legal doctrines relevant to trademark registration are described in Chapter 10.)

Once Jennifer and Tony have chosen a name for their business and product and have selected a level of protection they are comfortable with, they can turn their attention to the initial funding of their enterprise.

POTENTIAL TAX PITFALLS RELATED TO THE INITIAL INVESTMENT OF THE FOUNDERS

Left to their own devices, Tony and Jennifer would likely arrange the issuance of their equity in the company for no tangible investment whatsoever. After all, they intend to look to Uncle Max for working capital in the short run, and their investment will be the services they intend to perform for the business in the future.

Historically, in the corporate form such a plan would have run afoul of some rather anachronistic corporate legal restraints that required consideration for stock issuances to take the form of present property or cash and to at least equal the par value of the stock issued. These requirements were based on a theory of protection for corporate creditors, who could be assured that the corporation had assets at least equal to the aggregate par value of the shares of its stock that had previously been issued. Stock issued for less than par value was considered "watered stock" and exposed the holder and the directors issuing it to personal liability for the shortfall.

Much of the protection provided by these rules has been eroded over the years, however, by a number of developments. For example, it has long been commonplace to authorize stock with minimal par value (such as $0.01 per share) or even no par value at all. The corporation then issues stock for what it believes to be fair value without risk of failing to cover the aggregate par. In addition, it has long been possible to issue stock in exchange for intangible assets such as past services rendered. However, stock issuance for future services remains illegal under most corporate statutes, although many proposals have been made to legitimize it.

Of more practical concern than these corporate problems, however, is that any property (including stock) transferred to an employee in exchange for services is considered *taxable income* under the Internal Revenue Code. Thus, even were it possible for Tony and Jennifer to be issued stock in exchange for future services under corporate law, they would face an unexpected tax liability as a result.

The solution to all this may be to require Tony and Jennifer to reach into their limited resources and contribute some minimal cash amount to the business in exchange for their ownership. This would avoid the corporate and tax problems associated with issuance for future services. However, as noted previously, if their minimal investment was the full extent of the business's initial capitalization, the corporate veil might well be in danger.

Jennifer and Tony have no reason to fear exposure to personal liability since, at the same time they will be making their minimal investment, Uncle Max will be putting in the real money. Yet the participation of Uncle Max exposes Jennifer and Tony to a danger they may believe they have successfully avoided. Since Uncle Max will be paying substantially more for his equity than Jennifer and Tony are paying for theirs, the Internal Revenue Service will likely take the position that they are being afforded the opportunity for a bargain purchase in exchange for the services they are providing to their employer. Thus, once again, Tony and Jennifer may face an unexpected income tax on the difference between the price of Uncle Max's equity and the price of theirs.

One way to solve this problem is to postpone Uncle Max's investment until a time sufficiently remote from the date of Tony and Jennifer's investment that an argument can be made for an increase in the value of the equity. However, in addition to the essentially fictional nature of this approach, Jennifer and Tony cannot wait that long. To solve this problem, the parties must design a different vehicle for Uncle Max's investment.

In the corporate form, it may seem immediately advisable to create some sort of senior security for Uncle Max, such as *preferred stock* with a liquidation preference of approximately the amount he invested. A similar preferential position can be devised in an LLC. Assuming for a moment that the initial plan was to split the equity equally among the parties, Uncle Max may well insist on such a security; otherwise, Tony and Jennifer could dissolve the business immediately after its formation and walk away with two-thirds of Uncle Max's investment. In addition to having a preference on liquidation, Uncle Max might insist that he share in the company's growth, but this could be accommodated by allowing him to participate in profits remaining for distribution after dividend and liquidation preferences have been paid.

Demonstrating the sometimes frustrating interrelated character of tax and corporate law, however, is that the issuance of preferred stock to Uncle Max would render the corporation ineligible for subchapter S status because it would then have more than one class of stock. As discussed previously, the LLC is not bound by any such restriction.

Another solution could lie in the *utilization of debt securities*. If Uncle Max pays for his equity the same price per share as Jennifer and Tony paid, and if he injects the remainder of his investment in the form of a loan, his fellow owners will not face taxable compensation income, and the business will retain the opportunity to benefit from subchapter S, if desired.

Investment as debt also affords Uncle Max the potential for future nontaxable distributions from the company in the form of debt repayment, and he gains priority as a creditor should the company be forced to liquidate. All the while, he protects his participation in growth through his additional ownership of equity.

As with all benefits, it is possible to get too much of a good thing. Too high a percentage of debt may expose all the owners to the accusation of thin capitalization, resulting in the piercing of the corporate veil. And abusively high debt/equity ratios or failure to respect debt formalities and repayment schedules might induce the Internal Revenue Service to reclassify the debt as equity, thus imposing many of the adverse tax results described earlier.

NEGOTIATING STOCKHOLDER, MEMBER, AND PARTNERSHIP AGREEMENTS

The results of the negotiations among Jennifer, Tony, and Uncle Max regarding their respective investments would normally be memorialized in a stockholders' or members' agreement. In the unlikely event that this business were to be organized as a partnership or limited partnership, very similar provisions allocating equity interests and rights to distributions of profit and cash flow would appear in a partnership agreement. In each case, however, the parties would be well advised to go beyond these subjects and reach written agreement on a number of other potentially thorny issues at the outset of their relationship.

Negotiating Employment Terms

For example, Tony and Jennifer should reach agreement with Uncle Max on the extent of their *commitment to provide services* and the *level of compensation* for doing so. It would be very unusual for persons in the position of Tony and Jennifer to forgo compensation solely to share the profits of the business with their investor. For one thing, what would they live on in the interim? For another, the profits of the business are properly conceived of as the amount left after payment of the costs of capital (interest on Uncle Max's note) and the expenses of the business (including reasonable compensation to its employees). Thus, Jennifer and Tony should negotiate *employment terms* into the agreement, setting forth their responsibilities, titles, compensation, and related issues.

This is especially important in this case, since each of the three owners holds only a minority interest in the business. Both Tony and Jennifer may wish to foreclose the possibility that Uncle Max may ally with one of them and employ a majority of the voting power to remove the other as a director, officer, manager, or employee of the company. Given the lack of any market for the equity of this company, such a move would essentially destroy any value the equity had for the holder in the short run.

Although a concise description of each party's obligations and rewards is still advisable to avoid dispute, the negative scenario just outlined would be illegal in a *partnership* (in the absence of serious misconduct by the party being removed) since the majority partners would be violating the fiduciary duty of loyalty of each partner toward the others imposed under partnership law. Although no such duty formally exists among stockholders in a *corporation*, many states have extended the fiduciary duties of partners to the relationship among founders of a closely held corporation. Similar doctrines may be expected in LLCs. Thus, in many states, were Jennifer to be removed without cause from her employment and corporate positions by Tony and Uncle Max, she would have effective legal recourse even in the absence of an agreement.

Negotiating Disposition of Equity Ownership Interests

As for other items that might be covered in the agreement among Jennifer, Tony, and Uncle Max, many such agreements address the disposition of equity held by the owners under certain circumstances.

Transfer to Third Parties

To begin with, it is probably not contemplated by any of these persons that their equity will be freely transferable, such that new "partners" may be imposed on them by a selling stockholder or member. Although sale of equity in a closely held corporation or LLC is made rather difficult by federal and state securities regulation and the lack of any market for the shares, transfers are still possible under the correct circumstances. To avoid that possibility, stockholders' and members' agreements frequently require that any owner wishing to transfer equity to a third party must first offer it to the company or the other owners, who may purchase the equity, usually at the lower of a formula price or the amount being offered by the third party.

Disposition of Equity on the Owner's Death

Stockholders' and members' agreements should also address the disposition of each party's equity in the event of death. Again, it is unlikely that each owner would be comfortable allowing the equity to fall into the hands of the deceased's spouse, children, or other heirs. Moreover, should the business succeed over time, each owner's equity may well be worth a significant amount at the time of death. If so, the Internal Revenue Service will wish to impose an estate tax based on the equity's value, even though it is an illiquid asset. Under such circumstances, the deceased's estate may seek the assurance that some or all of such equity will be converted to cash so that the tax may be paid. If the agreement forbids free transfer of the equity during one's lifetime and requires that it be redeemed at death for a reasonable price, the agreement may well be accepted by the IRS as a binding determination of the equity's value, preventing an expensive and annoying valuation controversy.

Any redemption provision on the death of the owner, especially one that is mandatory at the instance of the estate, immediately raises the question of the availability of funds. Just when the company may be reeling from the loss of one of its most valuable employees, it is expected to scrape together enough cash to buy out the deceased's ownership. To avoid this disastrous result, many of these arrangements are funded by insurance policies on the lives of the stockholders or members. This would be in addition to any key person insurance held by the company for the purpose of recovering from the effects of the loss. In structuring such an arrangement, however, the parties should be aware of two quite different models.

The first, and traditional, model is referred to as a *redemption agreement.* Under such an agreement, the company owns the life insurance policies and is obligated to purchase the owner's shares on his death. The second model is referred to as a *cross-purchase agreement* and provides for each owner to own insurance on the others and to buy a proportional amount of the deceased's equity. Exhibit 9.2 illustrates the primary differences between the two agreements.

The second arrangement poses some serious mechanical problems, but it may be quite advantageous. To begin with, the cross-purchase agreement becomes quite complicated if there are more than a few owners or members, since each owner must own and maintain a policy on each of the others. There must be a mechanism to ensure that all these policies are kept in force and that the proceeds are actually used for their intended purpose. Complicated escrow arrangements are often necessary to accomplish this. In addition, if the ages of the owners are materially different, some owners will be paying higher premiums than others. You might ignore this difference on the basis that those who pay most are most likely to benefit from this arrangement, since their insureds are likely to die sooner. An alternative is to equalize the impact of the premiums by adjusting the parties' compensation from the company.

If these complications can be overcome, however, the cross-purchase agreement provides some significant benefits over the redemption agreement. For example, if Uncle Max were to die and the company purchased his equity,

EXHIBIT 9.2   Comparison of stock redemption agreement and stock cross-purchase agreement.

	Effect on tax basis	**Effect on alternative minimum tax**	**Need for adequate corporate surplus**
Redemption agreement	No stepped-up basis	Risks accumulated current earnings preference for corporations	Need adequate surplus
Cross-purchase agreement	Stepped-up basis	No effect	Surplus is irrelevant

Tony and Jennifer would each own 50% of the company, but their cost basis for a later sale would remain at the minimal consideration originally paid for their equity. In a cross-purchase arrangement, they would purchase Uncle Max's equity directly. This would still result in 50-50 ownership, but their cost basis for later sale would equal their original investment plus the amount of the insurance proceeds used to purchase Uncle Max's equity. On later sale of their equity, or the company as a whole, the capital gain tax would be significantly lowered.

Another benefit of the cross-purchase agreement is that although the receipt of life insurance proceeds is exempt from income taxation, it can result in a *tax preference item* for a corporation not electing subchapter S treatment. This would expose the corporation to the alternative minimum tax. This tax preference item does not apply to individuals and is thus avoided by use of the cross-purchase model. It also does not apply to S corporations and LLCs.

Finally, the cross-purchase model eliminates the possibility that the corporation will not have sufficient surplus to fund a buyout on the death of a stockholder. Similar restrictions would be imposed by an LLC's obligations to its creditors. It would be highly ironic if the deceased's life insurance merely funded an earnings deficit and could not be used to buy his equity.

Disposition of Equity on Termination of Employment

Stockholders' and members' agreements normally also address disposition of equity on events other than death. Repurchase of equity on termination of employment can be very important for both parties. The former employee, whose equity no longer represents an opportunity for employment, would like the opportunity to cash in the investment. The company and its other owners may resent the presence of an inactive owner, who can capitalize on their subsequent efforts. Thus, partnership, members', and stockholders' agreements normally provide for repurchase of the interest of a stockholder, member, or partner who is no longer actively employed by the company. This applies only to stockholders, members, or partners whose efforts on behalf of the company were the basis of their participation in the first place. Such provisions would not apply to Uncle Max, for example, since his participation was based entirely on his investment.

This portion of the agreement presents a number of additional problems peculiar to the employee-owner. For example, the company cannot obtain insurance to cover an obligation to purchase equity on termination of employment. Thus, it may encounter an obligation to purchase the equity at a time when its cash position cannot support such a purchase. Furthermore, in addition to the corporate requirement of adequate surplus, courts uniformly prohibit repurchases that would render the company insolvent. Common solutions to these problems involve committing the company to an installment purchase of the equity over a period of years (with appropriate interest and security) or committing the remaining owners to make the purchase personally if the company is unable to do so for any reason.

Furthermore, these agreements frequently impose penalties on the premature withdrawal of a stockholder, member, or partner. In our example, Uncle Max is relying on the efforts of Tony and Jennifer in making his investment, and Tony and Jennifer are each relying on the other's efforts. Should either Tony or Jennifer be entitled to a buyout at full fair market value if he or she simply decides to walk away from the venture? Often, these agreements contain *vesting provisions* that require a specified period of service before repurchase will be made at full value. For example, a vesting provision might state that unless Tony stays with the venture for a year, all his equity will be forfeited on his departure. After a year, one-fifth of his equity will be repurchased for full value, but the rest will be forfeited. Another 20% will vest at the end of each ensuing year.

Such provisions, in addition to providing incentive to remain with the company, have complicated tax implications. As discussed earlier, if an employee receives equity for less than fair market value, the discount would be considered taxable compensation. The Internal Revenue Code provides that compensation income with regard to unvested equity is not taxed until the equity is vested. But at that time, the amount of income is measured by the difference between the price paid for the equity and its value *at the time of vesting*. The only way to avoid this result is to file an election to pay the tax on the compensation income measured at the time of the purchase of the equity, even though the equity is not then vested. For Tony and Jennifer, this provision acts as a trap. Although they have arranged the initial investments of the parties such that there is no compensation income at the time the equity is purchased, if it is not then fully vested, their taxable income will be measured at the end of each future year as portions of the equity vest. Thus, they must file the election to have their income measured at the time of purchase to avoid a tax disaster, even though there is then no income to measure. And that election must be filed within 30 days of their receipt of the equity, not at the end of the year, as they might think.

Some agreements go beyond vesting provisions and give incentive to the founders by imposing further penalties on owners who leave voluntarily or are terminated for cause. Thus, the agreement applicable to Jennifer and Tony might provide that vested equity be repurchased for full fair market value if they are terminated involuntarily (including as a result of disability or death) and for only half of fair market value if they leave for any other reason.

Involuntary termination without cause is a somewhat remote possibility because of the expansion of the concept of fiduciary loyalty mentioned earlier.

Negotiating Distributions of Company Profits

Stockholders', members', and partnership agreements may also include numerous other provisions peculiar to the facts and circumstances of the particular business. Thus, partnerships, LLCs, and subchapter S corporations often provide for mandatory distributions of profit to the partners, members, or stockholders, at least in the amount of the tax obligation each will incur as a result of the profits of the business. If Uncle Max agreed to accept nonvoting equity, the agreement might include provisions to resolve deadlocks between Tony and Jennifer on significant issues; otherwise, the 50-50 split of voting power might paralyze the company. Various types of arbitration provisions might be employed to prevent this problem.

Negotiating Repurchase of Equity

Further, some agreements provide an investor like Uncle Max with the right to demand repurchase of his equity at some predetermined formula price at a designated future time, so that he will not be forever locked into a minority investment in a closely held company. Conversely, some agreements provide the company with the right to repurchase such equity at a predetermined price (usually involving a premium) should the capital no longer be needed. The presence or absence of these provisions depends on the relative negotiating strength of the parties.

LEGAL AND TAX ISSUES IN HIRING EMPLOYEES

From the beginning of this venture, Tony and Jennifer have known that if they are successful, they will have to hire employees for both the engineering and the marketing and sales functions. Thus, they should consider some of the issues raised by the presence of employees.

Obligations of Employees as Agents of the New Company

It should be understood that employees are agents of the company and as such are governed by many of the agency rules that define the relationships of partners to the partnership and officers to the corporation. Thus, employees have the previously described duty of loyalty to the company and obligations to respect confidentiality, to account for their activities, and not to compete.

Yet Jennifer and Tony are probably more interested in the potential of their employees to affect the business's relationships with third parties, such as customers and suppliers. Here the rules of agency require that a distinction be drawn between obligations based on contractual liability and those resulting from noncontractual relationships such as tort actions. Exhibit 9.3 provides an overview of these employee obligations.

Employees can bind their employers to contracts with third parties if such actions have either been expressly or implicitly authorized. Thus, if Tony and Jennifer hire a sales manager and inform him that he has the authority to close any sale up to $50,000, he may wield that authority without further consultation with his principals. He also has the implied authority to do whatever is necessary to close such deals (such as sign a purchase order in the company's name, arrange delivery, and perhaps even alter some of the company's standard warranty terms).

However, the employee's authority often extends beyond that expressly or implicitly given him. To illustrate this, suppose Tony and Jennifer's sales manager decides to close a sale for $100,000 worth of goods. This goes beyond his express authority and is not within his implied authority, since it was expressly prohibited. Yet from the point of view of the customer, the company's sales manager appears to have the authority to close all sales transactions. A customer

EXHIBIT 9.3   Comparison of employee obligations based on contractual liability and tort action.

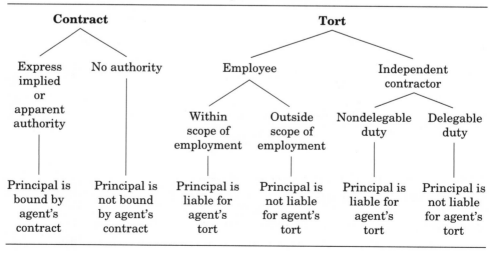

who has not been informed of the limitation imposed on the employee has no reason to think that anything is wrong. The law vindicates the customer in this situation by providing that the employee has apparent authority to conclude contracts within the scope of authority he appears to have. Since he was put into that position by his employer, and the employer has not informed the customer of the limits imposed on the employee, the employer is bound by the employee's actions.

Outside of the contract arena, the employee's power to bind the employer is based on similar considerations. Under the doctrine of *respondeat superior* (or *vicarious liability*), the employer is responsible for any actions of the employee occurring within the scope of his employment. Thus, if the sales manager causes a traffic accident on the way to a sales call, the employer is responsible for damages. This imposition of liability is in no way based on the employer's fault; it is *liability without fault,* imposed as a result of the economic judgment that employers are better able to spread losses among customers and insurance companies. Consistent with this approach, employers are normally not liable for the torts or criminal actions of employees outside the scope of their employment, such as actions occurring after hours or while the employee is pursuing his or her own interests. Furthermore, an employer is normally not liable for the torts or criminal actions of agents who are not employees (so-called independent contractors) since they are more likely to be able to spread these costs among their own customers and insurance companies.

However, employers should not take this as an invitation to avoid all liability by wholesale hiring of independent contractors. The labeling of a potential employee as an independent contractor is not necessarily binding on the courts. They will look to the level of control exerted by the employer and other related factors to make this determination. In addition, many activities of employers are considered nondelegable (such as disposal of hazardous waste). Employers cannot escape the consequences of such activities by hiding behind independent contractors.

Laws Prohibiting Employment Discrimination

In addition to these common law considerations, there are a number of statutory rules of law that govern the employer-employee relationship. Perhaps the most well known of these are the laws prohibiting employment discrimination. These laws, which include Title VII of the Civil Rights Act of 1964, the Age Discrimination in Employment Act, and laws protecting disabled and pregnant employees, collectively prohibit employment discrimination on the basis of sex, race, national origin, religion, age, and disability. Interestingly, they do not yet prohibit discrimination on the basis of sexual orientation, although a number of state and local laws do.

Prohibited discrimination applies not only to hiring but to promotion, firing, and conditions of employment. In fact, sexual discrimination has been found in cases of sexual harassment unconnected to hiring, promotion, or firing, but simply involving the creation of a so-called hostile environment for the employee.

These statutes are exceptions to the age-old common law concept of *employment at will,* which allowed employers to hire and fire at their whim, for any reason or for no reason at all. This rule is still nominally in force in situations not covered by the discrimination acts and not involving employment contracts. Notwithstanding the rule, however, courts in many states have carved out exceptions to employment at will for reasons of public policy, such as cases involving employees fired for refusing to perform illegal acts or employees fired in bad faith to avoid paying commissions or other earned compensations to the employee. Furthermore, courts in some states have been willing to discover employment contracts hidden in employee manuals or personnel communications that employers may not have thought legally binding.

Other Employment Statutes

When they begin taking on employees other than themselves, Tony and Jennifer will encounter a variety of other statutes that regulate the employment relationship and the workplace itself. For example:

- ERISA and the Internal Revenue Code closely regulate the form and amounts of any tax-qualified pension, profit-sharing, or welfare plans that employers may wish to maintain, generally prohibiting discrimination in favor of owners and highly paid employees.
- OSHA and the regulations adopted under that act closely regulate safety and health conditions in the workplace, imposing heavy fines for violations.
- The Fair Labor Standards Act provides minimum wages and overtime pay for employees in nonexempt (generally nonexecutive) positions, as well as prohibiting child labor and other practices.
- Social security and unemployment compensation—The company will find itself contributing to both these funds for each of its employees, as well as withholding social security and income taxes from its employees' wages. With regard to unemployment compensation, the amount of the contribution may depend on the number of employees laid off over the years,

causing Jennifer and Tony to contest claims from employees who may have left voluntarily or been fired for cause.

- Worker's compensation—The company will probably be required to carry worker's compensation insurance to cover claims under that system. Although the premiums may seem burdensome, worker's compensation was, at the outset, a welcome compromise between the interests of employers and those of employees. In exchange for avoiding the costs and uncertainties of litigation, employees were assured payment for job-related injuries but lost the opportunity to sue for increased amounts based on pain, suffering, and punitive damages. Employers gave up many common law defenses that formerly could be used against employees but were able to avoid the disastrously high judgments available under common law.

Employment Agreements

In addition to the common law and statutory considerations common to the hiring of all employees, the hiring of persons for professional positions in engineering, marketing, and sales presents a new set of issues. Such persons are likely to demand employment agreements and a piece of the action in some form.

Negotiating the Term of Employment

The attractiveness of employment agreements stems, in the main, from protection against *firing without cause.* Thus, a major item of negotiation will likely be the term of the contract. Although you might think that, for the employee, the downside of such a provision is that he or she must make a commitment to stay with a company he or she may come to dislike, courts have universally held that an employee cannot be forced to work for an employer against her will. Any contrary ruling would, it has been said, amount to a form of slavery! Thus, an employment contract is essentially a one-way street. The employee is promised employment for a period of time, with accompanying salary, bonus, and incentive provisions; but he or she can leave the company at any time without consequence. As a result, Tony and Jennifer would be well advised to avoid employment agreements whenever possible and, if forced to grant one, at least obtain some benefit for the company.

Negotiating Employee Obligations

Such benefit usually comes in the form of the *noncompetition* and *proprietary information covenants* discussed at the beginning of this chapter. For example, an engineer may promise, in exchange for a two-year employment agreement, not to work in the software industry for a year after termination of his or her employment. Yet, as mentioned earlier in the context of Tony and Jennifer's former employment, proprietary information obligations exist apart from any employee agreement, and it is quite possible that courts would refuse to enforce noncompetition provisions against the employee. Although you could make the argument (in a state that will listen) that the company needs some protection against a former sales manager soliciting the company's customers for a competitor, the argument appears more difficult when applied to a software engineer. This is especially true when you realize that such an engineer's use of proprietary information learned or developed under a former employer would in any case be prohibited by common law and by contractual prohibitions on the use of proprietary information.

Negotiating Equity Sharing with Employees

In addition to demands for job security, higher level employees will frequently ask to share in the company's success. This can be easily accomplished by a grant of equity, but Jennifer and Tony would be well advised to resist such a demand, which could upset the company's balance of power and expectations of economic return among the major equity holders. These demands can often be satisfied by an incentive bonus plan tied to the success of the company or, more effectively, to the accomplishment of individual goals set for the employee.

If this is unacceptable to the employee, his return could be tied to the fortunes of the company by the use of *phantom stock, stock appreciation rights,* or similar devices in the LLC context, which simulate the benefits of equity without requiring actual equity ownership. These plans grant the employee bonuses equal to any distributions that would have been made if he had owned a certain percentage of equity, while also rewarding him through payment of any increase in value such equity would have experienced. However, even this type of plan might not be acceptable to an employee with significant negotiating leverage because it does not give him voting rights. In addition, because the employee does not actually own equity (a capital asset), he cannot report the increase in value as capital gain at lower federal income tax rates. Thus, in certain cases it may be necessary to grant the employee equity in some form.

As previously mentioned, a direct grant of equity to an employee is considered a taxable event. The employee pays income tax on the difference between the value of the equity and the amount paid for it, if any. However, as previously described, the imposition of tax can be postponed if the equity is forfeitable, for example, on the employee's leaving the the company before the passage of a designated period of time. No doubt Tony and Jennifer would condition the grant of equity to any employee on his or her remaining employed for a substantial period, so this rule would apply.

The negative side of this rule is that in the absence of an election to pay tax at grant, when the equity is finally vested, the taxable income is measured by the difference between the amount paid, if any, and the value of the equity *at the time of vesting*. Worse yet, this tax will be payable before the employee has received any cash with respect to this transaction. Cash will be available on sale of the equity; but typically, the employee will not wish to sell at this time, and there will be no market for equity in a closely held company in any case.

Offering Stock Options to Employees

In a corporation, the issuance of stock options is often thought of as a solution to the tax problem. The employee is given the right to purchase stock in the corporation at a fixed price for a significant period of time. Thus, without investing any money, the employee can watch the value of this right increase as the value of the stock increases relative to the amount he would have to pay to purchase it. This right would be much less valuable if the grant of the option to the employee were a taxable event, but, unless the option is transferable and there is a recognized market for it (which is extremely unlikely in a case like Tony and Jennifer's), the grant of the option is not taxable.

Unfortunately, however, when the employee ultimately exercises the option and purchases the stock, the Internal Revenue Code requires recognition of income in the amount of the difference between the amount paid and the value of the stock at that time. Again, this occurs at a time when the employee has received no cash and likely has little desire or ability to sell.

Recognizing this problem, Congress has provided more favorable tax treatment for employee incentive stock options that meet a number of requirements:

- Incentive stock options (ISOs) must be issued pursuant to a stock option plan approved by the corporation's stockholders.
- The exercise price must be the fair market value of the stock at the time of issuance.
- Each option cannot last more than 10 years, and no more than $100,000 of exercise price may become exercisable in any one year.
- Perhaps most significant, the employee must hold any stock purchased pursuant to the option for the longer of one year after exercise or two years after the grant of the option.

If these requirements are met, unless he is subject to the alternative minimum tax, the employee is not taxed until he actually sells the stock acquired under the option (and has cash to pay the tax). The income is then taxed at favorable long-term capital gain rates.

The corporation can still require the employee to sell such shares back to the corporation on termination of employment. From the corporation's point of view, the only drawback is that the corporation loses any deduction that would otherwise be available to an ISO for compensation paid to employees. Tony and Jennifer might find this plan to be an attractive way to grant the requested incentive to their key employees in a corporate context. It is unfortunately *not* available to a limited liability employer.

Exhibit 9.4 compares various ways of handling equity sharing with employees.

INSURANCE

The expenses associated with beginning a business are considerable. The fees demanded by the state and the costs associated with retaining attorneys and accountants have already been described. As employees are added to the organization, social security, unemployment compensation, and other costs increase. As previously mentioned, worker's compensation insurance is required by many states. But this is not the only insurance that should be considered.

EXHIBIT 9.4   Comparison of equity sharing methods.

	Date of Grant	Risk Removed	Sale of Equity
Vested equity	Ordinary income	No income	Capital gain
Risk of forfeiture	No income	Ordinary income	Capital gain
Risk of forfeiture Sec. 83(B) election	Ordinary income	No income	Capital gain

	Date of Grant	Date of Exercise	Sale of Stock
Nonqualified stock option with readily ascertainable value	Ordinary income	No income	Capital gain
Nonqualified stock option with no ascertainable value	No income	Ordinary income	Capital gain
Incentive stock option (ISO)	No income	No income	Capital gain

Property Insurance

To begin with, Tony and Jennifer should consider property insurance for any equipment or inventory that they may have on hand. Should they ever obtain a loan for their business, the lender will likely take inventory and equipment as collateral and insist that it be insured (with the proceeds payable to the lender).

Liability Insurance

Tony and Jennifer should also consider purchasing liability insurance to cover claims against them for product liability and other possible tort claims. As mentioned before, the presence of such insurance often mitigates against claims of undercapitalization by plaintiffs attempting to pierce the corporate veil. Automobile liability insurance is required by many states as a condition for registration of a car. And the dangers of tort liability caused by employees have been discussed earlier.

Key-Person Life Insurance

The advisability of purchasing life insurance to cover equity redemptions under cross-purchase or redemption agreements has been discussed. Yet, this is not the only role for life insurance in a business. Consider what would result from Tony's untimely death. Not only may Jennifer or the company be required to repurchase his equity, but the operations of the company would likely grind to a standstill while it searched for a new sales manager. If the company owned additional insurance on Tony's life (known as "key-person" insurance), it would have funds to tide it over during this business slowdown as well as money to apply to the search for and compensation of Tony's successor.

Business Interruption Insurance

Similar in effect to key-person insurance, is so-called business-interruption insurance, which, in many cases of catastrophic business shutdown, will replace some of the company's cash flow. Such a policy is usually quite expensive, however, and may not be within the reach of a typical startup.

Group Life, Disability, and Health Insurance for Employees

As the company grows and adds employees, there will be increasing demand for insurance as part of the employee benefit package. Many companies provide group life insurance or group disability insurance for their employees. The latter can help the business avoid the moral dilemma caused by an employee who is too sick to work. Cutting off his salary may seem unthinkable, but paying another full salary for a long-term replacement may be more than the company can afford. Purchasing a policy with a significant deductible (such as 90 to 180 days) may solve this problem at very reasonable cost. Furthermore, in many industries it has become routine for the employer to provide health insurance as an employee benefit.

These three group policies may be provided to employees tax free, and the company may deduct the costs of premiums. The only exceptions to this favorable tax result are for the partner in a partnership, member of an LLC, and significant shareholder of a subchapter S corporation, all of whom must report these benefits as taxable income. Thus, one negative aspect of the choice of a LLC or subchapter S for Tony and Jennifer is that any group life, disability, or health insurance provided to them by the company would be included in income. Currently, 70% of their group health insurance is then deductible.

RAISING MONEY

Thoughts of future hirings will inevitably bring Tony and Jennifer to consider another challenge to the company. Although Uncle Max's money may be sufficient for the short term, other sources of investment will eventually have to be identified. Although financing new businesses is discussed in detail in Chapters 4 through 8, this section describes potential legal and tax implications.

Loans

One source of financing that leaps to mind is debt financing from a commercial bank or other institutional lender. Although these institutions are notoriously loathe to advance loans to startup companies, such a loan may be possible if sufficient collateral or guarantees are available. The loan may take the form of a term note, a line of credit, or some sort of revolving credit plan, depending on the circumstances. It will almost certainly be the case, however, that the lender will insist on security for the loan.

Liens

At a minimum, this security will consist of an interest in all of the borrower's assets. In Jennifer and Tony's case, the lender will perfect a lien under Article 9 of the Uniform Commercial Code on the company's property, including:

- Machinery and equipment (computers, filing cabinets, desks, and so on)
- Inventory (copies of their software as well as blank disks, paper, pencils, and so on)
- Accounts receivable
- All intangible property (copyrights, patents, and trade secrets relating to their product)

Notice of such security interest will be filed under the Code wherever appropriate to perfect this interest such that no future potential lender or purchaser will be misled.

Under the provisions of the Code, such filing will perfect the lender's lien on any new property, including:

- New machinery or equipment purchased after the loan is made, unless such new items are purchased on credit and a lien is granted to the seller or lender.
- Accounts receivable that arise later.
- All new inventory, but any inventory sold to customers in the ordinary course of business will be automatically freed from the lien.

Any further amounts advanced by the lender to the company in the future will be similarly secured.

If the loan ultimately goes into default, the lender may take possession of the collateral and arrange its sale. The proceeds are then applied to the costs of repossession and sale and the amount unpaid under the loan. Any additional amounts would be turned over to any lower priority secured creditor and ultimately to the borrower or its bankruptcy estate.

Although such a lien might seem to provide adequate security, most lenders will insist on guarantees from additional parties. In some cases, guarantees from governmental agencies such as the Small Business Administration may be available (see Chapter 8 for information on how to obtain such guarantees). However, in almost every case, the lender will insist upon personal guarantees from the major owners of the borrower. In our case, this will certainly include Tony and Jennifer, and probably also Uncle Max because of his large share of the company's equity and obviously deep pockets. In many cases, the lender further demands that such guarantees be backed by collateral interests in the private property of the guaranteeing stockholders. Thus, Uncle Max may find that his signature is required both on a personal guarantee and on a second mortgage on his home. Or he may be required to pledge securities held in his personal brokerage account.

These personal guarantees circumvent the limited liability that entrepreneurs hope to achieve through use of the corporate and LLC forms. The abandonment of this protection is unavoidable, however, and extends only to the particular lender. The owners remain protected against other trade creditors and tort plaintiffs.

Tax Effects

As a matter of strategy, the form in which a guarantee is given can have serious negative tax effects if insufficient care is given to structuring the loan transaction. For example, if Tony, Jennifer, and Uncle Max were to approach a small, local bank, they might find that the bank is reluctant to lend to a company under any circumstances. Under these conditions, the three stockholders may choose to borrow the money personally and invest the proceeds in the company themselves. Repayment of the loan would then be made out of the company's profits when they are distributed to its stockholders. As a result of this arrangement, however, the stockholders of a corporation would receive taxable distributions from the corporation (in the form of either salary or dividends) but would receive no compensating deduction for the repayment of a personal loan.

It would be better if they could convince the bank to lend to the corporation and take personal guarantees. Then the corporation could repay the loan directly (deducting the interest on a business loan), and the money would never pass through the hands of the stockholders. Alternatively (but with some additional risk), the stockholders could borrow directly from the bank but grant it a second mortgage as collateral, thereby potentially rendering the interest deductible for them as mortgage interest.

Ironically, if the corporation elects subchapter S treatment, strategy considerations may point in the opposite direction. Since Uncle Max, especially, will wish to see the corporation's short-term losses appear on his personal return, he will be concerned that the amount of loss he may use is limited to his tax basis in his investment. Such basis consists of the amount he paid for his stock, plus any amount he has loaned directly to the corporation. If the company were to borrow from the bank and Uncle Max were merely to guarantee the loan, the amount of the loan would not increase his basis (or his allowable loss) in a subchapter S corporation (although his LLC basis would be increased, even in the absence of a guarantee, at least to some extent). If he were to borrow the money from the bank and lend it to an S corporation himself, his basis would be increased. In either event, the amount of loss he can use may be limited by the passive loss rules discussed earlier.

Legal Issues in the Sale of Securities to Outside Investors

As an alternative to institutional lending, Jennifer, Tony, and Uncle Max may turn to outside investors. Although it may be difficult to attract venture capitalists to such a small startup, other sources of capital, in the form of neighbors, friends, doctors, lawyers, dentists, and other individuals or entities with an interest in ground-floor investing, may be available. If they choose this route, it is crucial that they take note of two common misconceptions.

Although most businesspeople are aware that both federal and state law regulates the offer and sale of securities, most believe that these statutes apply only to the offerings of large corporations and that small companies are exempt. This is one of the dangerous misconceptions held by many people like Tony, Jennifer, and Uncle Max. These laws (specifically, the Federal Securities Act of 1933, the Federal Securities Exchange Act of 1934, and state "Blue Sky" statutes) apply to all issuers.

Further, even many businesspeople who are aware of the scope of these acts believe that they apply only to issuers of equity securities, mainly stock. This, too, is a misconception. These statutes apply to all issuers of "securities," not just issuers of stock. Securities include, in addition to stock, most debt (other than very short-term loans), options, warrants, LLC memberships, limited partnership interests, and all other forms of investment in which the investor buys into a common enterprise and relies on the efforts of others for the investment's success. Thus, such disparate items as orange groves, Hawaiian condominiums, and even worms have been held to be regulated securities under the circumstances of their respective cases.

The wide scope of these statutes led some to assert that they include the offering of *franchise opportunities.* Those offering franchises argued that the success of a franchisee is not normally determined solely by the efforts of the franchisor but requires significant effort on the part of the franchisee. This debate has been rendered moot, however, by the adoption by the Federal Trade Commission of regulations requiring disclosure by franchisors of virtually the same range of information as is required under a securities registration statement. Many states have enacted similar franchise registration laws, requiring dual federal and state registration in most franchise offerings. (Further discussion of franchising can be found in Chapter 11.)

In general, then, the securities laws prohibit the offering of securities to the public without prior (and very expensive) registration with an appropriate government authority such as the federal Securities and Exchange Commission. They also punish fraudulent activities in connection with such offerings, including not only affirmatively false statements, but also mere nondisclosure of material facts about the investment. Because of the complexity and expense of registration, these laws allow exceptions to the registration requirement in specific circumstances, but even these are subject to the antifraud provisions of the laws. Thus, the challenge to our three entrepreneurs is to identify provisions in the securities laws that will offer them an *exemption from registration,* with the understanding that they must still provide sufficient disclosure to potential investors (often, in the form of a so-called offering circular) to avoid antifraud liability.

One such exemption contained in the Securities Act of 1933 is the *intrastate offering exemption.* Based on the general principle that the federal government can constitutionally regulate only *interstate* commerce, the statute necessarily exempts offerings that are purely local. However, the scope of this exemption is relatively narrow. Not only must all persons who purchase the securities reside in one state, but all offerees must be resident there as well. Furthermore, the company offering the securities must be formed under the laws of that state and do most of its business there. These restrictions, this exemption may be useful only for the smallest of offerings. Besides, the exemption excuses the offering only from registration with the Securities and Exchange Commission (SEC). The state's securities laws may still require expensive and time-consuming state registration.

The more popular exemption from registration under the federal act is the *private placement exemption,* which excuses transactions "not involving a public offering." Over the past decade, the SEC has relied on this exemption, and other provisions in the law, to issue regulations designed to facilitate the raising of capital by small businesses in small offerings. Thus, as of this writing, Regulation D under the act exempts from registration any offering of under $1 million worth of securities. Above that amount, the regulation requires increasing levels of disclosure (still short of full registration, however) and limits the number of offerees to 35 plus an unlimited number of so-called accredited investors. For these purposes, accredited investors include certain institutions, as well as individuals with net worth or annual income levels that indicate a need for less protection. Even apart from the regulation, however, issuers can argue that offerings made to relatively sophisticated investors with prior relationships to the issuer qualify as transactions "not involving a public offering."

Exemption from registration under the federal act *does not* grant exemption under a state act. Offerings made to investors in a number of states require adherence to the Blue Sky statutes of each state. Fortunately, however, virtually all state statutes allow similar exemptions for private placements, typically excusing offerings to 25 or fewer persons.

Thus, Tony and Jennifer will likely be able to seek out the investment they will need without having to register with the federal or state government.

However, it cannot be overemphasized that they remain subject to the *antifraud provisions* of these acts. Thus, they will be well advised to seek professional assistance in drawing up a comprehensive offering circular disclosing all that an investor would need to know about their company to make an intelligent investment decision. (See Chapter 6 for further discussion of venture capital.)

CONCLUSION

Considering all the legal and tax pitfalls described in this chapter, one is tempted to ask whether Tony, Jennifer, or any other entrepreneur would choose the road of the startup if she were fully aware of all the potential complications lying in wait. This would surely be an overreaction. Yet, not to be aware of these matters is to consciously choose to play the game without knowing the rules. These issues are there whether one chooses to prepare for them or not. Surely, Tony and Jennifer are much more likely to succeed in their venture for having taken the time to become aware of the legal issues facing the entrepreneur.

INTELLECTUAL PROPERTY

10

Joseph S. Iandiorio

One of the most valuable and fundamental assets of a new small business is its intellectual property. Intellectual property is defined as a business's intangible assets, including patents, trademarks, copyrights, and trade secrets. The rights to such property can be used to prevent competitors from entering your market and can represent a separate source of revenue to the business. All too often, however, they are overlooked or misunderstood, and they are nearly always undervalued. To fully protect and utilize these assets, every entrepreneur, small business owner, and manager, as well as advisors such as management, financial, and technical consultants; lawyers; accountants; bankers; and venture capitalists, must be aware of what these rights are and how they are protected and preserved. This awareness is becoming even more critical in a world of global competition and international markets where ideas and information are fast becoming more valuable than products and things. The adoption of two international treaties, the North American Free Trade Agreement (NAFTA) and the General Agreement on Tariff and Trade (GATT) underwrite this concern.

THE BASICS: WHAT IS PROTECTABLE AND HOW SHOULD IT BE PROTECTED?

When a new idea is conceived or a new product or method is designed, the first questions that arise are: Can I protect this? Can I keep competitors from

With grateful acknowledgment to Kirk C. Teska for new additions, updates, and edits.

311

copying this? There are very practical reasons for protecting a new idea. Investors are reluctant to put money into a venture that cannot establish a unique product niche. Stockholders will challenge a corporation's investment of its resources in a program that can be easily copied once it is introduced to the market. All the time, effort, and money invested in perfecting the idea, as well as advertising and promoting it, may be wasted if imitators can enter the market on your heels with a product just like yours. Moreover, the imitators can cut prices because they have not incurred the startup expenses you had to endure to bring the idea from conception to a mass-producible, reliable, and appealing product or service.

Here are some examples of things that may be protected:

- A new product and its name
- A new method
- A process
- A new service and its name
- A new promotional or merchandising scheme or approach
- New packaging
- A new design

Once it has been determined that a new idea, product, or method is eligible for one or more forms of protection—a patent, trade secret, trademark, or copyright—the rights should be secured as quickly as possible. Each form of protection is obtained in a different manner and provides a different set of rights. The various forms are discussed in the following sections.

For example, consider a typical modern product—a microprocessor-based hand-held device. It bears the name of the manufacturer and a brand name and is accompanied by a user's manual. What is protectable, and how should you protect it? The next sections help answer these questions.

Patents

There are three kinds of patents: utility, design, and plant. *Utility patents* are the kind commonly considered when one seeks to protect an invention. They are granted for any new and useful process, machine, manufacture, or composition of matter, or improvement thereof, including new uses of old devices or new combinations of well-known components. *Design patents* cover only the industrial design of an object—its ornamental appearance. Patents have become much more important with the growth of new business methods and biotechnology inventions in the past few years, especially regarding the protection of human-engineered life forms. Most of the following discussion focuses on utility patents, though some special considerations of design patents are also provided. *Plant patents* are available for inventions or discoveries involving asexual reproduction of distinct and new varieties of plants.

Utility Patents

Utility patents cover three classes of inventions:

- *Chemical inventions* include new compounds, new methods of making old or new compounds, new methods of using old or new compounds, and new combinations of old compounds. Assays, biological materials and methods, drugs, foodstuffs, drug therapy, plastics, petroleum derivatives, synthetic materials, pesticides, fertilizers, and feeds are all protectable.
- *General/mechanical inventions* include everything from gears and engines to tweezers and propellers, from zippers to fur-lined keyhole appliqués to Jacque Cousteau's scuba regulator. For example, complex textile-weaving machines, space capsule locks and seals, and diaper pins are all protectable.
- *Electrical inventions* include everything from lasers to light switches, from the smallest circuit details to overall system architectural concepts.

   Computer software is patentable in various forms:

- Application programs, such as the software that controls a chemical-processing plant or a rubber-molding machine, are patentable.
- Software for running a cash management account at a brokerage house or bank is patentable.
- The microcode in a ROM that embodies the entire inventive notion of a new tachometer is patentable.
- Internal or operations programs that direct the handling of data in the computer's own operations are patentable.

A common misconception is that software, internet-based business ideas, and so-called "business methods" are not patentable. The truth is software has long been patentable. And, in 1998, the high patent court put to bed the notion that business methods were an exception to patentable subject matter when Signature Financial Group's patent for its mutual fund administration system was upheld as valid. Another well-known example is Amazon's "One-Click" patent (No. 5,960,411) litigated in 1999 against Barnes & Noble.

Obtaining a Utility Patent

The basic requirement for a utility patent is that the idea be new and that it be embodied in a physical form. The physical form may be a thing or a series of steps to perform.

Patent protection is established only when a patent is issued for an invention. The owner of the patent has the right to exclude others from making, using, and selling, offering for sale, or importing the patented invention during the term of the patent. Historically, the term of a U.S. patent was 17 years from the date of issue. No longer. Patents issuing from patent applications filed after June 8, 1995, have a term of 20 years from the date of filing. Patents issued before June 8, 1995, maintain their 17-year term. Those patents that issue after June 8, 1995, based on patent applications filed before June 8, 1995, have either 17 years from issuance or 20 years from filing, whichever is longer.

The effort begins when the inventor or inventors conceive the invention. Typically a registered patent attorney on their behalf prepares a patent application and files it in the U.S. Patent and Trademark Office. From the date that the application is filed, there is a *patent pending*. Full protection applies if and when the Patent and Trademark Office agrees that the invention is patentable and issues the patent.

The patent application must contain a complete and understandable explanation of the invention. It does not have to be a nuts-and-bolts instruction manual. It is enough to convey the inventive concept so that a person skilled in the art to which the invention relates can make and use the invention without undue experimentation. Further, the explanation must contain a full description of the best mode known by the inventor for carrying out the invention. For example, the inventor cannot use the second best embodiment of the invention as an illustration for the patent application disclosure and keep secret the best embodiment. That will make the resulting patent invalid.

The *timing* of the filing of the patent application is critical. In the United States, the application must be filed within one year of the first public disclosure, public use, sale, or offer for sale of the invention, or the filing will be barred and the opportunity to obtain a patent forever lost. This is known as the *one-year period of grace*. This may change in the future to a system in which there is no period of grace (the application must be filed *before* any activity), to conform with the laws of most other countries.

A description of the invention in a printed publication constitutes a public disclosure. A mere announcement is not sufficient, unless it contains an explanation of the invention. It does not matter that only a few copies of the publication were made available, so long as it was an unrestricted distribution.

Market testing, exhibitions, or even use by the inventor himself can be a public use sufficient to activate the one-year period. An exception is a public use for experimental purposes. The test for whether a public use was an experimental use is rigorous. The inventor must show that it was the operation and function of the invention that was being tested, not the appeal or marketability of the product employing the invention. Further, some evidence of the testing should be established. For example, if samples were sent to potential customers for evaluation, it would be good to show that the customers returned filled-out evaluation forms and that the inventor considered and even made changes based on those evaluations.

A sale more than a year before the application will generally bar a patent even if the invention is embedded so deeply within a larger system that it could not ever be discovered. If the device containing the invention is sold, that is enough. The idea is that an inventor should be given only one year in which to file his patent application after he has begun to commercially exploit or to attempt to commercially exploit his invention. Thus, for an invention embodied in a production machine installed in a locked, secure room, the one-year period for filing a patent application begins the first time a device produced by that machine is sold even though the machine may never be known to or seen by anyone other than the inventor. And it is not just an actual sale that triggers the one-year period: an offer for sale is sometimes enough, even if the sale is never consummated.

Criteria for Obtaining a Utility Patent

A patent application contains three basic parts:

1. Drawings show an embodiment of the invention
2. A written description of the invention that refers to the drawings
3. One or more claims

Sometimes (often in chemical cases), the drawings are omitted. The definition of the patented invention, the protected property, is not what is disclosed in the drawings and specification portion of the application; this is only the description of one specific embodiment. The coverage of the patent is defined by the third part of the application, the claims.

To qualify for a patent, the claims must be novel and unobvious. *Novelty* is a relatively easy standard to define: if a single earlier patent, publication, or product shows the entire claimed invention, the invention is not novel. *Obviousness* is somewhat more difficult to grasp. Even though an invention may be novel, it may nevertheless be obvious and therefore unpatentable. The test for obviousness is fairly subjective: Are the differences between the invention and all prior knowledge (including patents, publications, and products) such that the invention would have been obvious to a person having ordinary skill in the art to which the invention pertains at the time the invention was made? If so, the invention is not patentable even if it is novel.

Obviousness is a somewhat subjective determination but many ideas have ultimately been deemed patentable even though an examiner of the U.S. Patent and Trademark Office originally rejected them as obvious. In one notable case, an inventor came up with the idea of a leaf bag configured to look like a giant Halloween style pumpkin when stuffed with leaves. The U.S. Patent and Trademark Office concluded that since leaf bags were well known and pumpkins were well known, the idea of a pumpkin leaf bag was obvious and therefore not patentable. Not so said the Court of Appeals for the Federal Circuit: the Patent Office failed to prove there was any motivation to combine the idea of a Halloween pumpkin with a leaf bag. As a result, the patent for the leaf bag pumpkin issued. Obviousness rejections are to be expected from the Patent Office.

The meanings of *novelty* and *unobvious* in the area of patentability can be better understood with an example. Suppose a person is struggling to screw a wood screw into hard wood, and he realizes that the problem is that he cannot supply enough twisting force with the blade of the screwdriver in the slot in the head of the screw. So he gets the idea of making the slot a little deeper, so that the screwdriver blade can bite a little deeper and confront more surface area of the slot, thus applying more force to turn the screw. This is a good idea, but it creates another problem. The deeper slot extends much closer to the sides of the screw head. There is less support, and fatigue lines develop, which eventually cause the screw head to crack. The inventor then gets the idea to use a new screwdriver with two shorter, crossed blades, which will give increased surface area contact with two crossed slots in the head of the screw.

But a problem still exists. Although the twin blades do not require such deep slots, there are now twice as many slots, and the screw head is seriously weakened. Now the inventor sees another path: keep the double-blade configuration, but chop off the corners, so that the slots need not extend out so close to the edge of the new screw head.

The result: The inventor has invented the Phillips head screwdriver, for use with a Phillips head screw. Certainly the invention is "novel": no one else had made that design before. It is also "unobvious" and thus patentable. The addition of the second blade and elimination of the corners has resulted in a wholly new screwdriver concept. The concept is patentable.

Now suppose another party, seeing the patent issued on this double-blade Phillips head, comes up with an improvement of her own. Her invention is to use three crossed blades (cutting the head of the screw into six equal areas), with their corners removed. This design may not be patentable. Certainly it is novel, but is it unobvious? Not likely. Once the first inventor has originated the idea of increasing the number of blades and eliminating corners, it may be obvious to simply add more blades.

Drafting the Patent Claims

Once it is decided that a patentable invention exists, it must be protected by properly drafted patent claims. It is the claims that the U.S. Patent and Trademark Office examiner analyzes and accepts or rejects in considering the issuance of the patent. It is the claims that determine if someone has infringed a patent. It is the claims that define the patent property.

Claims are the most important part of a patent. It is useless to have claims that covers the inventions yet do not protect your product or process from being copied by competitors. Does this sound contradictory? Study the following example and you will understand.

Suppose an inventor meets with a patent attorney and shows the attorney a new invention for carrying beverages on the slopes while skiing. The invention eliminates the risk of smashing glass, denting metal, or squashing a wineskin, and it also eliminates the need to carry any extra equipment: It's a hollow ski pole. The ski pole has a shaft, a chamber, and a handle. The handle has a threaded hole that communicates with the hollow shaft. Partway down the inside of the hollow shaft is a plastic liner that creates a chamber for holding liquids; this plastic liner is attached to the shaft. The chamber is closed by a threaded plug, which engages the threaded hole. The inventor wants to patent the pole, so he assists the patent attorney in writing a description of the ski pole. They write the following claim:

A hollow ski pole for carrying liquids, comprising:

- A hollow shaft;
- A liner sealing the hollow inside of the shaft to define a chamber for containing liquid;
- A handle on the shaft;
- A threaded hole in the handle communicating with the chamber in the hollow shaft; and
- A threaded plug for engaging the threaded hole.

The patent application is filed. The U.S. Patent and Trademark Office examines the application and issues the patent with that claim. The inventor is happy for only a short time because a competitor comes out with a similar hollow ski pole that doesn't use a liner. The competitor simply welds a piece of metal across the inside of the shaft to make a *sealed* chamber. The competitor has avoided infringing the patent, because there is no liner, which was one of the limitations of the first patent claim. Another competitor replaces the threaded plug with an upscale mahogany stopper. Again the patent is not infringed, because there is no threaded plug.

To infringe a patent, a competitor must infringe a claim of the patent. To infringe a claim of the patent, the infringing process or product must include *every* element of the claim.

This problem can be avoided by exploring the various ways in which the product can be built. This may require input from sales, marketing, engineering, and production people as well as the inventor. After a thorough study, a better claim might have been:

A hollow ski pole for carrying liquids, comprising:

- A hollow shaft;
- A chamber formed in said hollow shaft for containing a liquid;
- A handle on the shaft having a hole communicating with the chamber in the hollow shaft; and
- A means for closing the hole in the handle.

Someone could still design around this claim by leaving out the means for closing the hole; the skier could use her thumb and hope she doesn't fall. Practically speaking, however, the claim would be good enough to keep others from making a meaningful competing product without infringing. There is a limit to how broadly the claim can be worded, however. Eventually, if the claim becomes broader and broader, and does not specify the ski pole or hollow shaft, it may apply to a bottle or a pot with a cover, and the patent will not be obtainable—it is not new. Careful claim drafting is critical.

Inventorship

Another important area is *inventorship*. In the United States, the inventor(s) and no one else must file a patent. The inventor is the originator of the inventive concept. A project leader is not by his supervisory position alone an inventor of an invention. Neither is a technician or engineer who may have built the first working model. The inventor may have sold or assigned the patent application to someone else—his employer, a partner in some enterprise, a company he has newly formed, or another inventor. Thus, the original inventors may not be the owners of the patent, but it must still be filed in their names. Usually, the inventors assign the patent rights when the application is filed.

Provisional Patent Applications

A new type of patent application, referred to as a *provisional patent application,* is now available. A provisional application requires only a written description of the invention and drawings; unlike a conventional application no claims or oath are required. Its purpose is to allow companies to get something on file quickly and inexpensively to establish an early filing date that can be relied on by the full patent application, which can be filed up to one year later. Some doubt their effectiveness for either purpose. Provisional applications will be regarded as abandoned in 12 months. The full conventional patent applications must be filed within the 12 months and must refer to the provisional application in order to assume the benefits of the earlier filing date. The provisional application, however, must be complete enough to support the disclosure of the later filed full patent application. Otherwise, the filing date is lost and there is a risk of the patentable subject matter falling into the public domain.

In one case, a product embodying an invention was sold in the spring of 1996, a provisional application was filed in the spring of 1997 for the product, and a full patent application was filed in the fall of 1997. But, the provisional failed to adequately describe the invention actually claimed in the full patent application. The result? The patent was held invalid because the provisional failed to provide the necessary disclosure. When the patent owner sued a competitor for patent infringement, the Court found the resulting patent claims contained detailed information not present in the provisional patent application. As a result, the patent was invalidated and the competitor was free to use the patented invention. Provisionals have found favor because they are typically less expensive than full patent applications and allow companies to advertise "patent pending." In 2002, over 80,000 provisional patent applications were filed. But, as this case proves, provisionals are only as good as the details they contain. Provisionals should contain all of the details of the invention. The claims for the invention, if not actually drafted, should at least be envisioned to ensure that the provisional application adequately supports the later filed claims in the full application.

Design Patents

Hockey uniforms, ladies' dresses, computer housings, automobile bodies, buildings, shoes, and game boards are all protectable with design patents. But this type of patent covers only the *appearance,* not the idea or underlying concept. What you see is what you get. *Design patents* are generally less expensive than utility patents and in some cases are the only protection that is needed or obtainable.

Design patents have a life of only 14 years from the date of issue but are otherwise generally subject to the same rules as other patents. That is, the new and original ornamental design to be patented must be novel and unobvious and must be filed within one year of the first public use, publication, sale, or offer for sale.

Trade Secrets

Trade secrets cover everything that patents cover and much more. A trade secret is knowledge, which may include business knowledge or technical knowledge that is kept secret for the purpose of gaining an advantage in business over your competitors. Customer lists, sources of supply of scarce material, or sources of supply with faster delivery or lower prices may be trade secrets. Certainly, secret processes, formulas, techniques, manufacturing know-how, advertising schemes, marketing programs, and business plans are all protectable.

There is no standard of invention to meet as there is with a patent. If the idea is new in this context, if it is secret with respect to this particular industry or product, then it can be protected as a trade secret. Unlike patents, trademarks, and copyrights, there is no formal government procedure for obtaining trade secret protection. Protection is established by the nature of the secret and the effort to keep it secret.

A trade secret is protected eternally against disclosure by all those who have received it in confidence and all who would obtain it by theft for as long as the knowledge or information is kept secret. In contrast to patent protection, there are no statutory requirements for novelty or restrictions on the subject matter.

The disadvantage of trade secrets compared with patents is that there is no protection against discovery by fair means, such as accidental disclosure, independent inventions, and reverse engineering. Different persons developed many important inventions, such as the laser and the airplane, more or less simultaneously. Trade secret protection would not permit the first inventor to prevent the second and subsequent inventors from exploiting the invention as a patent would.

The distinction between patents and trade secrets is illustrated in a case in which a woman who designed a novel key holder immediately filed a patent application. It was a simple design and could easily be copied. While the patent was still pending, she licensed it to a manufacturer for a 5% royalty, with the agreement that if the patent didn't issue in five years, the royalty would drop to 2%. The patent never issued, and the royalty was dropped to 2%. Over the next 14 years, on sales of $7 million, the manufacturer's edge eroded as others freely copied the design. The manufacturer repudiated the royalty contract on the ground that it required payment forever for the small jump that the manufacturer got on its competitors, whereas the patent, had it issued, would have allowed only 17 years of exclusivity. The court held the manufacturer to its requirement to pay. The ruling allowed the inventor to receive 2% royalty for as long as the manufacturer continued to sell the key holder. Had the patent issued, royalties would have lasted only 17 years!

Many companies use both approaches, filing a patent application and, during its pendency, keeping the invention secret. When the patent is ready to issue, the company reevaluates its position. If the competition is close, they let the patent issue. If not, the patent application is allowed to go abandoned and trade secret protection is relied on. But following a change in the patent law, patent applications are published 18 months after their earliest filing date voiding trade secret protection unless active steps are taken by the inventor or his assignee to prevent publication, for example, agreement not to file an application for the invention in any foreign country.

Certain trade secrets have been appraised at many millions of dollars, and some are virtually priceless. For example, the formula for Coca-Cola is one of the best-kept trade secrets in the world. Known as Merchandise 7X, it has been tightly guarded since it was invented 100 years ago. It is known by only two persons within the Coca-Cola Company and is kept in a security vault at the Trust Company Bank in Atlanta, Georgia, which can be opened only by a resolution from the company's board of directors. The company refuses to allow the identities of those who know the formula to be disclosed or to allow them to fly in the same airplane at the same time. The company elected to forego producing Coca-Cola in India, a potential market of 550 million people, because the Indian government requires the company to disclose the secret formula as a condition for doing business there. While some of the mystique surrounding the Coca-Cola formula may be marketing hype, it is beyond dispute that the company possesses trade secrets that are carefully safeguarded and are extremely valuable.

Secrecy is essential to establishing trade secret rights; without it there is no trade secret property. There are four primary steps for ensuring secrecy:

1. Obtain confidential disclosure agreements with all employees, agents, consultants, suppliers, and anyone else who will be exposed to the secret information. The agreement should bind them not to use or disclose the information without permission.

2. Take security precautions to keep third parties from entering the premises where the trade secrets are used. Sturdy locks, perimeter fences, guards, badges, visitor sign-in books, escorts, and designated off-limits areas are just some of the ways that a trade secret owner can exercise control over the area containing the secrets.

3. Stamp specific documents containing the trade secrets with a confidentiality legend and keep them in a secure place with limited access, such as a safe, locked drawer, or cabinet.

4. Make sure all employees, consultants, and others who are concerned with, have access to, or have knowledge about the trade secrets, understand that they *are* trade secrets, and make sure they recognize the value to the company of this information and the requirement for secrecy.

Trade secret owners rarely do all of these things, but enough must be done so that a person who misappropriates the secrets cannot reasonably excuse his conduct by saying that he didn't know or that no precautions were ever taken to indicate that something was a trade secret. This is important because, unlike patents, trade secret protection provides no "deed" to the property.

Since there is no formal protection procedure, the necessary steps for establishing a trade secret are often not taken seriously until the owner brings a lawsuit against one who has misappropriated them. In each specific case, the owner must show that the precautions taken were adequate.

Trade secret misappropriations generally fall into one of two classes: someone who has a confidential relationship with the owner violates the duty of confidentiality, or someone under no duty of confidentiality uses improper means to discover the secret.

Trade secret theft issues frequently arise with respect to the conduct of ex-employees. Certainly, a good employee will learn much about the business during his employment. And some of that learning will go with him as experience when he leaves. That cannot be prevented. The question is: Did he come smart and leave smarter, or did he take certain information that was exclusively the company's?

For example, in one case, a company that had been making widgets for the government for many years did not get its annual contract renewed. When the company questioned the loss of the contract, it was explained that a competitor was supplying widgets of equal quality at a lower price. Upon investigation, the company determined that the competitor was located in the same town, that the competitor's widgets were uncannily identical in every dimension, and that the competitor was owned by an ex-employee of the company who had left over a year before. Amicable approaches failed, and a lawsuit was instituted during which the company discovered that the ex-employee had copied their detailed engineering drawings to make the widgets. This eliminated all engineering and design costs and enabled the competitor to sell the widgets to the government at a much lower price. But the ex-employee had not stolen anything. The man knew that every year his ex-employer reissued important engineering drawings that had become torn and tattered or that needed updating, and threw out the old ones. The ex-employee testified that while driving by the plant one day, he saw the old drawings sticking out of the dumpster. He drove in, took them out of the dumpster, put the ones he wanted in his car, and chucked the rest back in the dumpster. That's how he got a widget with identical dimensions. The court held him liable for misappropriation of trade secrets. He had trespassed to obtain the drawings, and he had learned of the ex-employer's practice of disposing of old drawings while an employee with a duty of confidentiality to the company. The court granted an injunction preventing the ex-employee from selling widgets for a period of months equal to the jump he got by not having to develop his own engineering drawings.

But what if the ex-employee had not trespassed to obtain the drawings from the trash? What if he had waited for the trash collector to remove them and then asked if he could go through the trash? Or what if he had gone to the dump and picked the drawings out of the trash? When does the owner part with ownership of trade secret materials dumped in the trash?

Trade secrets are extremely valuable, often more so than patents, and can form the basis for lucrative licensing programs. Care should be taken to identify and protect them early and consistently.

Trademarks

Trademark protection is obtainable for any word, symbol, or combination thereof that is used on goods to indicate their source. Any word—even a common word such as "look," "life," or "apple"—can become a trademark, so long as the word is not used descriptively. Apple for fruit salad might not be protectable. Apple® for computers certainly is.

Common forms such as geometric shapes (circles, triangles, squares), natural shapes (trees, animals, humans), combinations of shapes, or colors may be protected. Even the color pink has been protected as a trademark for building insulation. Three-dimensional shapes such as bottle and container shapes and building features (e.g., McDonald's golden arches) can also be protected.

While people generally only speak of trademarks, that term encompasses other types of marks. A trademark is specifically any word or symbol or combination of the two that is used on goods to identify its source. However, a *service mark* is a word or symbol or combination used in connection with the offering and provision of services. Blue Cross/Blue Shield, Prudential Insurance, and McDonald's are service marks for health insurance services, general insurance services, and restaurant services. Ownership is established by advertising the mark in conjunction with the service, as opposed to trademarks, where advertising is insufficient—the mark must be used on the goods or their packaging in commerce.

There are also other types of protectable marks. A *collective mark* indicates membership in a group, such as a labor union, fraternity, or trade association. A *certification mark* is used to indicate that a party has met some standard of quality; Quality Court Motels, Underwriter's Laboratory, and Good Housekeeping's Seal of Approval are familiar examples.

If you use any such name or feature to identify and distinguish your products, then think trademark protection. Ownership of a trademark allows you to exclude others from using a similar mark on similar goods that would be likely to confuse consumers as to the source of the goods. This right applies for the duration of ownership of the mark, which is as long as the owner uses the mark.

Trademarks can be more valuable to a company than all of its patents and trade secrets combined. Consider the sudden appearance and abrupt increase in the worth of trademarks such as Cuisinart, Haagen-Dazs, and Ben & Jerry's. Consider also the increased value that a trademark name such as IBM, Microsoft, or General Electric brings to even a brand new product.

A trademark, unlike a patent, can be established without any formal governmental procedure. Ownership of a trademark is acquired simply by being the first to use the mark on the goods in commerce, and it remains the owner's property as long as the owner keeps using it. And keep using it you must, for nonuse for a period of three years may constitute abandonment.

If a name is too descriptive, it cannot be registered and may freely be used as is or in a slightly modified form by competitors. The more descriptive the mark, the less advertising required to inform consumers what the product is for. But, such a mark enjoys a much lower level of protection. On the other hand, a highly protectable arbitrary mark (Exxon®, Kodak®) requires significant expenditures in advertising dollars to inform consumers what a product or service covered by the mark actually is. Pick trademarks that are suggestive enough to adequately inform consumers but which are not too descriptive. Examples of marks held to be too descriptive include "Beer Nuts," "Chap-Stick," "Vision Center" (for an optical clinic), "Professional Portfolio System" (stock valuations), "5 Minute" (glue which sets in five minutes), "Body Soap" (body shampoo), "Consumer Electronics Monthly," "Light Beer," and "Shredded Wheat."

The mark should not be descriptive of the goods on which it is used, although it may be suggestive of the goods. However, it is best to select a mark that is arbitrary and fanciful with respect to the goods. This is because every marketer, including a competitor, has the right to use a descriptive term to refer to its goods. Therefore, exclusive rights to such a mark cannot be secured.

A trademark owner should also take care to prevent the mark from becoming generic, as happened to Aspirin, Cellophane, Linoleum, and other product names. Thus, it is not proper to refer to, for example, simply a Band-Aid, Jello, or Kleenex. The correct form of description is Band-Aid adhesive bandages, Jell-O fruit-flavored gelatin dessert, or Kleenex facial tissues.

It is wise to have a search done for a proposed new mark to be sure that the mark is available to adopt and use on the goods, that is, to verify that no one else is already using or has registered the same or a similar mark on the same or similar goods. It is confusing to customers and expensive to change a mark and undertake the costs of all new printing, advertising, and promotional materials when you discover that another has already used your new trademark.

Registering a Mark

Although it is not required to register a trademark, there are significant benefits associated with registration that make it worthwhile. Registration may be made in individual states, or a federal registration may be obtained. A state registration applies only in the particular state that granted the registration and requires only use of the mark in that state. A federal registration applies to all 50 states, but to qualify, the mark must be used in interstate or foreign commerce. A distinct advantage of federal registration is that even if a mark is used across only one state line, that is, if goods bearing the mark are in commerce only between one state and another state or country, that is enough to establish federal protection in all 50 states. Thus, if you are using your mark in Massachusetts, New Hampshire, and Rhode Island, for example, but do not register it federally, you may later be blocked from using your mark in all other states if a later user of the same mark, without knowledge of your use of the mark, federally registers it. That later user would then have the rights to the mark in all other 47 states even though its actual use may have been only in Oregon and California.

While your common law rights to a trademark or service mark last as long as you properly use the mark, registration must be periodically renewed. Federal registrations extend for 10 years; terms for states vary, but 10 years is typical.

Over the history of trademark law in the United States, registration in the U.S. Patent and Trademark Office followed the common law. That is, to establish ownership of a trademark one had to use the mark on the goods in commerce, and to register the mark in the U.S. Patent and Trademark Office you had to establish that the mark was indeed in use.

That has changed somewhat. Now an application can be filed to register a mark that is not yet in use but is intended to be used. After the U.S. Patent and

Trademark Office examines the application and determines that the mark is registerable, the applicant is required to show actual use within six months. The six-month period can be extended if good cause is shown. Nevertheless, before registration, even before actual use, the mere filing of the application establishes greater rights over others who actually used it earlier but did not file an application for registration.

Ownership of a Mark

Care must be taken with trademark properties. A trademark cannot simply be sold by itself or transferred like a desk or car, or a patent or copyright. A trademark must be sold together with the business or goodwill associated with the mark, or the mark will be abandoned. Further, if a mark is licensed for use with a product or service, provision must be made for quality control of that product or service. That is, the trademark owner must require the licensee to maintain specific quality levels for products or services with which the mark is used, under penalty of loss of license. The owner must actually exercise that control through periodic inspection, testing, or other monitoring that will ensure that the licensee's product quality is up to the prescribed level.

Ownership of a mark is most important in a business. When Cuisinart started selling its food processors, it promoted them vigorously under the trademark Cuisinart. A good part of the business's success was due to the fact that the machines were sturdily made by a product, quality-conscious French company, Robot Coupe, who had been making the machines for many years before they became popular among U.S. consumers under the mark Cuisinart. When price competition reared its head, Cuisinart found cheaper sources. Robot Coupe owned no patents and had no other protection. When Cuisinart began selling brand X under the name Cuisinart, a wild fight ensued through the courts and across the pages of major newspapers in the United States, but to no avail. The whole market had been created under the name Cuisinart, and Cuisinart had the right to apply its name to any machine made anywhere by anyone it chose. Robot Coupe, whose machine had helped create the demand for food processors, was left holding its chopper.

European Trademark

A European trademark registration is now available, known as a Community Trade Mark (CTM), wherein a single registration will cover the entire European Union: with the benefit of a single filing plenary protection is provided. However, there are certain drawbacks. For example, a single user in any country of the European Union could block registration everywhere and cost considerations make a CTM filing uneconomical generally unless trademarks are sought in at least three countries. Soon, registration will be possible simultaneously in the United States and other foreign countries via a new treaty, known as the *Madrid Protocol.*

Copyright

Copyrights cover all manner of writings, with the term *writings* being very broadly interpreted. It includes books, advertisements, brochures, spec sheets, catalogs, manuals, parts lists, promotional materials, packaging and decorative graphics, fabric designs, photographs, pictures, film and video presentations, audio recordings, architectural designs, and even software and databases. Software and databases are protected not only in written form but also as stored in electronic memory.

A utilitarian object such as a hypodermic needle, a hammer, or a lamp base cannot be the subject of a copyright. Yet stained glass windows, software, piggy banks, and a sculpture useful as a lamp qualify for copyright protection.

A copyright does not protect a mere idea; it protects the *form* of the expression of the idea. But this is broadly interpreted. For example, you can infringe a book without copying every word; the theme may be protected even though on successive generalizations the theme will devolve to one of seven nonprotectable basic plots. This is apparent in the software area, where using the teachings of a book to write a program has resulted in copyright infringement of the book by the computer program. In another case, a program was infringed by another program even though the second program was written in an entirely different language and for an entirely different computer. The form of the expression protected was not merely the actual writing, the coding, but the underlying concept or algorithm—the flow chart. Copyright is a very strong and readily achievable source of protection.

A copyright has a term extending for the life of the author plus 70 years. For corporate "authors" or works made for hire, the period is 95 years from first publication or 120 years from creation, whichever is shorter. During the life of the copyright, the owner has the exclusive rights to reproduce, perform, display the work, and to make derivative works.

Establishing Copyright

Historically, under law a copyright was established by publishing the work—a book, painting, music, software, instruction manual—with copyright notice, typically "Copyright," "Copr.," or © followed by the year of first publication and the name of the owner. The notice may appear on the reverse of the title page of a book, on the face of a manuscript or advertisement, or on the base of a sculpture. It had to be visible and legible, but it could be placed so as not to interfere with the aesthetics of the work. If more than a few copies of the published work appeared without the notice, the copyright was forfeited forever. Works that were unpublished did not need notice. They were protected by virtue of their retention in secrecy. Publication with notice was all that was required; registration with the Copyright Office was not always immediately necessary.

Under the laws enacted in 1976, publication without notice can be rectified if the notice is omitted from only a small number of copies, registration of the work with the Copyright Office is effective within five years, and an effort is made to add the notice to those copies published without it. Notice must be on the work in all its forms. For example, for software the notice should appear on the screen, in the coding, on the disk, and on the ROM, wherever the software is resident or performing. In one case an infringer got away with reading out copyrighted software from a ROM because there was no notice on the ROM, although there was notice elsewhere.

Now, no notice is required at all. To become a member of an international copyright treaty known as the *Bern Convention,* the United States had to abolish all formalities required to establish copyright in a work. Now the simple fact that a work was created, whether published or not, is enough to establish the copyright. It is not clear that this removal of the need for notice is retroactive. Thus, new works after March 1989 need not have notice, but those that were required to bear notice before the amendment should, in the exercise of prudence, continue to bear the notice.

Although notice is no longer compulsory, it is a valuable and worthwhile practice since it provides actual notice that the work copied was copyrighted.

Registering a Copyright

Copyright registration is not compulsory, but it, too, bestows valuable additional rights. If the copyright owner has registered the copyright, statutory damages can be recovered without proof of actual damages. This can be a real advantage in copyright cases where actual damage can be difficult and expensive to prove.

Registration requires filling out the proper form and mailing it to the Copyright Office with the proper fee and a deposit of two copies of the work for published works, or only one copy if the work is unpublished. Accommodations are made for filing valuable or difficult deposit copies: Deposit for three-dimensional works can be effected using photographs, and deposits for large computer programs can be effected using only the first and last 25 pages.

Further, if the program contains trade secrets, there is a provision for obscuring those areas from the deposit.

Summing Up

Now consider the question posed at the beginning of this chapter: What parts of a handheld microprocessor-based product are protectable, and how can they be protected? The data stored in memory, the circuits, and programming of the microprocessor, as well as its architecture, could be protected by patents or trade secrets. All of the other software could be protected by patent, too. The software and screen displays could also be protected by copyright and trade secret (software protection is discussed in detail later in this chapter). The user's manual could also be protected by copyright. The company name and the product name could be trademarks. And, a design patent could protect the housing of the device.

THE INTERNET

Internet activity is placing new pressures on intellectual property practice. Uploading and downloading of copyrighted material on the Internet can be copyright infringement. Copyright infringement has also been found in some cases against bulletin board operators and administrators who have received and stored such material.

Domain names are taking on some of the characteristics of trademarks. Further, there have been some instances where a party has incorporated a well-known name or mark of another in his own domain name resulting in 'infringement. There is now a domain name dispute resolution system offering trademark owners a less expensive alternative to court when pursuing cybersquatters.

INTERNATIONAL PROTECTION FOR INTELLECTUAL PROPERTY

Obtaining protection for patents, trademarks, and copyrights in the United States alone is no longer sufficient in the modern arena of international competition and global markets. International protection often needs to be extensive and can be quite expensive, but there are ways to reduce and postpone the expense in some cases. Protection must be considered in countries where you intend to market the new product or where competitors may be poised to manufacture your product.

A patent in one country does not protect the invention in any other country: A separate patent in each country must protect a novel product or method. In addition, each country has different conditions that must be met, or no patent protection can be obtained. The first and most important restriction is the *time* within which you must file an application to obtain a patent in a country or else *forever lose your right to do so.*

Patent Filing Deadlines

Not all countries are the same with respect to filing deadlines. For example, as previously noted, in the United States an inventor may file an application to obtain a patent on an invention up to one year after the invention has become public through a publication explaining the invention, a public use of the invention, or the sale or offer for sale of the invention—the period of grace.

There is no period of grace in most other countries, such as Great Britain, West Germany, Sweden, France, Italy, Switzerland, Belgium, Austria, the Netherlands, Australia, and Japan. Each country has a slightly different view of what constitutes making an invention public. In Japan, for example, public use of an invention before the filing of an application bars a patent only if the public use occurred within Japan, but in France any public knowledge of the invention anywhere bars the patent.

Thus, whereas the United States allows a business *one full year* to test market its new product, most other countries require that the patent application be filed *before any public disclosure,* that is, before the owner can even begin to determine whether the new product will be even a modest success. And meeting this requirement is not inexpensive, especially when the U.S. dollar is down against the currencies of other major countries.

How to Extend Patent Filing Deadlines

However, there are ways around having to file immediately in foreign countries, as provided for by the *Paris Convention.* If you file in the United States and then file in any country that is a party to the convention within one year of the date on which you filed in the United States, the U.S. filing date applies as the filing date for that country. In this way, by filing one application for the invention in the United States, you can preserve your initial U.S. filing date for up to one year. This means that you can file an application in the United States, and then immediately make the invention public by advertising, published articles, and sales. If within one year the product appears to be a success, you can then file in selected foreign countries, even though the prior public use of the invention would ordinarily bar your filing in those countries.

There are other options that allow you to postpone the cost of foreign filings while preserving your right to file. Another, more recent treaty known as the *Patent Cooperation Treaty* (PCT) permits a delay of up to 20 or even 30 months before the costs of filing in individual countries are incurred. The PCT option is available if you file and request PCT treatment within one year of your U.S. filing date.

Thus, by filing a PCT application in a specially designated PCT office within one year of your U.S. filing, and by designating certain countries, you can preserve your right to file in those countries without further expense for 20 or 30 months after the U.S. filing date. That will provide an additional 8 or 18 months for test marketing the product. This does introduce the extra cost of the PCT application filing, but if you are considering filing in, say, six or more countries, the extra PCT filing may be well worth the cost for three reasons:

1. It delays the outflow of cash that you may not presently have or may require for other urgent needs.
2. It provides for a uniform examination of the patent application.
3. If the product proves insufficiently successful, you can decide not to file in any of the countries designated under the PCT and save the cost of all six national application filings.

Another cost-saving feature of international patent practice is the *European Patent Convention* (EPC), which is compatible with the Paris Convention and the PCT and which enables you to file a single European patent and designate any one or more of 17 European countries in which you wish the patent to issue.

There are a number of international treaties that affect trademark rights and copyrights as well.

LICENSING AND TECHNOLOGY TRANSFER

A license is simply a special form of contract or agreement. Each party promises to do or pay something in return for the other party doing or paying something. Contracts that deal with the transfer of technology, or more broadly, intellectual property—patents, trade secrets, know-how, copyrights, and trademarks—are generally referred to as licenses. The licensed property can be anything from the right to use Mickey Mouse on a T-shirt or to make copies of the movie *Star Wars,* to the right to operate under the McDonald's name, to use a patented method of making a microchip, or to reproduce, use, or sell a piece of

Sometimes the boiler-plate provisions of a license or other technology agreement can come back to haunt one or both of the parties. A court held that the contractual language "jurisdiction for any and all disputes arising out of or in connection with this agreement is California" was permissive rather than mandatory allowing the defaulting company to file suit in a location remote from the licensor. In other cases, courts have found inconsistencies between various boiler-plate provisions placing important contractual rights in jeopardy. Even the contractual boiler-plate is important and should be carefully thought out and drafted.

software. Software licenses are just one of the many types of licenses. The basic considerations are the same as for any other license, but specific clauses and language are tailored to the software environment.

Common Concerns and Clauses

The term *license* is typically used to refer to a number of different types of contracts involving intellectual property, including primarily an assignment, an exclusive license, and a nonexclusive license. This broad reference is used in this section.

An assignment is an outright sale of the property. Title passes from the owner, the assignor, to the buyer, the assignee. An assignment can take a number of forms:

- It can cover an entire patent, including all the rights under the patent.
- It can apply to an undivided fractional portion of all the patent rights (such as 30% undivided interest).
- It can include all the rights embraced by a patent limited to any geographical part of the United States.

A license is more like a rental or lease. The owner of the property, the licensor, retains *ownership*; the buyer, the licensee, receives the *right to operate* under the property right, be it a patent, trade secret, know-how, copyright, or trademark. An *exclusive license* gives the licensee the sole and exclusive right to operate under the property to the exclusion of everyone else, even the licensor. A *nonexclusive license,* in contrast, permits the licensee to operate under the licensed property but without any guarantee of exclusivity. The licensor can try to find more licensees and license them, there may be others who are already licensed, and the licensor can also operate under the property.

By definition, an assignment is exclusive since the assignee acquires full right and title to the property. Many licensees prefer an assignment or exclusive license because they want a clear playing field with no competitors in order to maximize their revenue from the property and justify the license cost.

Within either of these forms—exclusive license or nonexclusive license—may be included a right to *sublicense,* which is the right of the licensee to license others. This removes part of the licensor's control over the property and extends the licensee's liability to the conduct and payment of all sublicensees. A sublicense is an important and valuable right that is not automatically conveyed with the primary license right; it must be expressly granted. The term *transferable* in a license means that the license can be transferred as a whole along with the part of the licensee's business to which the license pertains; it does not confer the right to sublicense.

Licensors often prefer a nonexclusive license because it spreads their royalty income over a number of diverse licensees, increasing the chances of a successful return. In addition, if the property is freely available to all credible businesses, no one is left out or disadvantaged. All have an equal chance to compete, and the chances of a lawsuit from a rejected potential licensee are reduced.

Defining the Property Being Licensed

Great care must be exercised to clearly define the property being licensed. For example, consider the following questions:

- Is it more than one patent, just one patent, or only a part of one patent?
- It is just the trademark, or the entire corporate image—names, advertising, and promotional scheme and graphics?
- If it concerns copyright, does it cover just the right to copy a book or other printed material in the same print form, or does it include any of the following rights?
  — Translation into another language
  — Adaptation for stage, screen, or video
  — Creation of derivative works
  — Merchandising its characters and events on T-shirts and toys?
- If it involves know-how or trade secrets, where are they defined?

Licensees must be sure that they are getting what they want and need. A licensor must make clear the limits of the grant. In a software license if the grant is only to use the software, not to modify it or merge it with other software, that must be expressly stated.

Limitations on Licenses

A license may have numerous, different limitations, including time, the unit quantity, and the dollar value of products or services sold. The license can also be limited geographically. Field-of-use limitations are quite common, too. This limitation restricts the licensee to exploit the licensed property only in a designated field or market.

Assigning Value to a License

Perhaps the most universal concern in negotiating a license is assigning a dollar value to intellectual property? First, determine what it *cost* to acquire that property, to build that property. For example, all of the following are hard costs that go into creating a property:

- The research and development cost involved in coming up with a new invention
- The design cost of coming up with a new trademark or copyrighted work
- The costs of commercializing the invention
- The cost of advertising and promoting the trademark or copyrighted work, which can run into millions of dollars a year
- Incidental costs, such as legal costs, engineering costs, and accounting costs

Second, determine how this intellectual property affects the profitability of the product or the business. Can you charge more because the product has a famous name or because of the new features the invention has bestowed on the product? Can your costs be cut because of the new technology of the invention? If so, determine dollar values for those figures.

You might also determine how much the intellectual property increases gross revenues by opening new markets or by acquiring a greater percentage of established markets. All of these figures can be converted into dollar amounts for valuation.

Royalty Rates

A typical royalty rate for a nonexclusive license to a patent, trade secret, or know-how is 5%, but that rule is breached as often as it is honored. Nonexclusive license royalty rates in patent licenses can be 10%, 20%, 25%, or even higher. And exclusive license royalty rates tend to be higher because the licensee receives total exclusivity and the licensor is at risk if the licensee does not perform. Exclusive licensors generally demand initial payments for the same reason. In determining a reasonable royalty as a damage award in an infringement suit, courts have considered the following factors:

- The remaining life of the patent
- The advantages and unique characteristics of the patented device over other, prior devices
- Evidence of substantial customer preference for products made under the patent
- Lack of acceptable noninfringing substitutes
- The extent of the infringer's use of the patent
- The alleged profit the infringer made that is credited to the patent

Negotiating License Agreements

In any commercial agreement in which the consideration promised by one party to the other is a percentage of profits or receipts or is a royalty on goods sold, there is nearly always an implied promise of diligent, careful performance and good faith. But licensors generally seek some way to ensure that the licensee will use its best efforts to exploit the property and maximize the licensor's income. One approach is simply to add a clause in which the licensee promises to use its "best efforts." Another approach is to compel certain achievements by the licensee. The license may require a minimum investment in promotion and development of the property, which may be expressed in dollars, human labor hours, or even specific stated goals of performance or sales. Or the simpler approach of a minimum royalty can be employed: The licensee pays a certain minimum dollar amount in running royalties annually, whether or not the licensee's sales actually support those royalties—not a pleasant condition for the licensee but one that provides a lot of peace of mind for the licensor.

Perhaps the best assurance of performance is a competent, enthusiastic licensee. A little preliminary investigation of the licensee (in terms of net worth, credit rating, experience, reputation, manufacturing/sales capability, and prior successes/failures) can assuage a lot of fears and eliminate risky licensees. A *reverter clause,* which evicts the licensee and returns control to the licensor in the event of unmet goals, is the ultimate protection. Often the licensor's greatest concern is that the licensee might now or later sell one or more competing products, leading to a plain conflict of interest. A *noncompetition clause* can prevent this, but antitrust dangers are raised by such clauses, and licensees do not like this constraint on their freedom. Other approaches are safer, such as specified minimum performance levels.

Confidential disclosure clauses are necessary in nearly all license agreements, especially those involving trade secrets, know-how, and patent applications. Such clauses are necessary to protect not only the property that is the subject of the license, but also all of the technical, business, financial, marketing, and other information the parties will learn about each other during the license term, and even during negotiations before the license is executed.

Foreign Licenses

The aforementioned clauses and concerns pertain generally to all licenses, domestic United States as well as foreign. In addition, there are other clauses more peculiarly suited to foreign agreements.

Geographic divisions are important because of the somewhat different treatment of intellectual property in each country. The manufacture and use of the product related to the patent, trade secret, or know-how may be limited to the United States, but sales may be permitted worldwide. Payment must be defined as to the currency to be used as well as to who will pay any taxes or transfer charges. The parties must provide for government approval of the transfer of royalties and repatriation of capital.

A license agreement is a special form of contract in which each party promises to do something in exchange for promises by the other party. It is based on a business understanding between the parties and common sense applied to the attainment of business goals. But it is more complex than a normal contract because of the uniqueness of its subject matter, intellectual property—patents, trademarks, copyrights, trade secrets, and know-how. These properties require special action for their creation and maintenance. Great care is necessary in licensing such properties to maximize their returns and prevent their loss.

SOFTWARE PROTECTION

Protection for computer software has been the subject of debate for many years. At one time, there was strong opposition to the awarding of patents for inventions embodied in or involving software. That is no longer the case. Now software is commonly patented. Trade secret protection was formerly available, but only if you kept the software secret, which made it awkward to embrace copyrights. Now the Copyright Office has a procedure whereby software copyrights can be registered yet trade secrets contained in the software can be specifically preserved.

Software "law" is really a collection of many different Federal and State laws: patent law broadly protecting the functionality of the software, copyright law protecting the code itself and, to a limited extent, the structure of the code, trademark law protecting the commercial name given the software, trade secret law (in some cases), contract law for licenses associated with the software (click wrap licenses, shrink wrap licenses, user agreements, development agreements, and other software agreements), tort law (you want to disclaim warranties in all licenses), and even criminal law. The Digital Millenium Copyright Act further defines what is and what is not permissible in the area of reverse engineering and breaking access protection schemes.

Patents for Software

Broad patent protection is available for software. The scope of patent protection extends beyond the coding or routines, beyond the structure and organization, beyond the user interface and menus of the program, to the broad underlying concept of algorithm. All manner of software is protectable by patent regardless of how it is perceived—as controlling industrial equipment or processes, as effecting data process, or as operating the computer itself.

For example, software implementation of steps normally performed mentally may be patentable subject matter. In one case the software implementation of a system that automatically transferred a customer's funds among a brokerage security account, several money funds, and a Visa/checking account automatically upon the occurrence of preset conditions, was held to be patentable subject matter. Also, a software method of translating from one language to another (Russian to English) was found to be protectable.

Many patents have been issued on software; the following are some examples:

- The "one-click" Amazon patent
- A system for registering attendees at trade shows and conventions
- A securities brokerage cash management system
- An automated securities trading system
- An insurance investment program for funding a future liability
- Software for managing an auto loan
- Software for optimization of industrial resource allocation
- Software for automatically determining and isolating differences between text files (word processing)

- Software for returning to a specified point in a document (word processing)
- Software for determining premiums for insurance against specific weather conditions

Software specific to the operation of the computer itself is patentable, too. For example, patents have issued on:

- Software for converting a source program to an object program
- Programs that translate from one programming language to another
- A cursor control for a pull-down menu bar
- Software that displays images in windows on the video display
- A computer display with window capability

The software may be composed of old routines as long as they are assembled in a different way and produce a different result; it is well established in patent law that a combination of old parts is patentable if the resulting whole is new. Indeed, most inventions are a new assembly of well-known parts or steps.

Design patents have also been used to protect software. Design patents have been issued for visual features produced on the screen by the computer software, such as various display icons; one example is an icon for a telephone display.

One approach to exposing copiers is to include a short routine that does nothing. Then, if a competitor copies the program as is or even codes it in another language, it will be easier to prove infringement if the "do-nothing" routine ends up in the competitor's product. A company desiring to develop a software program that competes with an existing product should employ "clean-room" techniques wherein the company's programmers are given functional specifications but have no access to the competitor's program or code.

Software Copyrights

Copyright protection for software, though not as broad as patent protection, is nevertheless quite broad although courts do differ on the breadth of copyright protection.

All forms of programs are protectable by copyright flow charts, source programs, assembly programs, and object programs. And it makes no difference whether the program is an operating system or an applications program. No distinction is made concerning the copyrightability of programs that directly interact with the computer user and those that, unseen, manage the computer system internally. Protection is also afforded microcode or microprograms that are buried in a microprocessor, and even programs embedded in a silicon chip. Even databases are sometimes protected by copyright.

More subtle copyright problems have occurred regarding databases. The purveyor of a computer program that permits users to access and analyze the copyrighted database of another was found liable for copyright infringement because to analyze the data, the program had to first copy portions of the database.

Software Trade Secret Protection

Software may also be protected through a trade secret approach, separately or in conjunction with patent and copyright protection. Normally, all information disclosed in a published copyrighted work is in the public domain. However, the U.S. Copyright Office fully recognizes the compatibility of copyright and trade secret protection, and its rules provide special filing procedures to protect trade secrets in copyrighted software.

HOW TO AVOID THE PRELIMINARY PITFALLS OF PROTECTING INTELLECTUAL PROPERTY

Frequently, when people think of protecting a new idea or product, they turn to patents, trade secrets, and copyrights. But the game can be won or lost long before you have the opportunity to establish one of those forms of protection. That is why the fundamental forms of protection—confidential disclosure agreements, employment contracts, and consultant contracts—are so important. Whether or not an idea or product is protectable by an exclusive statutory right such as a patent or copyright, there still is a need at an early stage, before such protection can be obtained, to *keep the basic information confidential* to prevent public use or disclosure that can result in the loss of rights and inspire others to seek statutory rights before you.

Confidential disclosure agreements, employment agreements, and consultant agreements have some things in common. They define the obligations of the parties during the critical early stages of development of a new concept, product, or process. They are usually overlooked until it's too late, after the relationship is well under way and a problem has arisen. For proper protection of the business, there must be agreements with employees, consultants, and in some cases, suppliers and customers to keep secret all important information of the business and to assign to the business all rights to that information.

It is commonly thought that only technical information can be protected. This is not so. All of the following can be protectable information:

- Ideas for new products or product lines
- A new advertising or marketing program
- A new trademark idea
- The identity of a critical supplier
- A refinancing plan

And all of these can be even more valuable than the technical matters when it comes to establishing an edge over the competition and gaining a greater market share.

Employment contracts, consultant contracts, and confidential disclosure agreements all should be in writing and signed before the relationship begins, before any work is done, before any critical information is exposed, and before any money changes hands. A business must not be in such a rush to get on with the project that it ends up without full ownership of the very thing it paid for. And the employees, consultants, or other parties must not be so anxious to get the work that they fail to understand clearly at the outset what they are giving up in undertaking this relationship.

Preparing Employment Contracts

Employment contracts must be fair to both parties and should be signed by all employees, at least those who may be exposed to confidential company matters or may contribute ideas or inventions to the business. They should also be short and readable if they are ever to be effectively enforced.

Employment contracts, like all agreements, must have considerations flowing both ways. If I agree to paint your house for $3,000, my consideration to you is the painting of your house. Your consideration to me is the $3,000. In an employment contract, the consideration from the employee includes all promises to keep secrets and assign ideas and inventions; the consideration from the business is to employ the employee. Thus, it is best to present these contracts to the prospective employee well before he or she begins work.

After the job has begun, the consideration will be the employee's "continued" employment, and that sounds a bit threatening. Although "continued" employment is certainly proper consideration, in construing these contracts, courts can easily see that the employer usually has the superior bargaining position, and so they generally like to know that when the contract was offered for signature, the employee had a fair opportunity to decline without suffering severe hardship. It is not a good idea to present the employment contract in a packet of pension, hospitalization, and other forms to be signed the day the employee shows up to begin work after having moved the entire family across the country to take the job.

Transfer of Employee Rights to Company Innovations

One of the most important clauses in an employment contract is the agreement by the employee to transfer to the company the entire right, title, and interest in and to all ideas, innovations, and creations. These include designs, developments, inventions, improvements, trade secrets, discoveries, writings, and other works, including software, databases, and other computer-related products and processes. The transfer is required whether or not these items are patentable or copyrightable. They should be assigned to the company if they were made, conceived, or first reduced to practice by the employee. This obligation should hold whether the employee was working alone or with others and whether or not the work was done during normal working hours or on the company premises. As long as the work is within the scope of the company's business, research, or investigation or it resulted from or is suggested by any of the work performed for the company, its ownership is required to be assigned to the company.

This clause should not seek to compel transfer of ownership for everything an employee does, even if it has no relation to the company's business. For example, an engineer employed to design phased array radar for an electronics company may invent a new horseshoe or write a book on the history of steeplechase racing. An attempt to compel assignment of ownership of such works under an employment agreement could be seen as overreaching and unenforceable. The same may be true of a clause that seeks to vest in the employer ownership of inventions, innovations, or other works made for a period of time after employment ends or before employment begins.

Ancillary to this transfer or assignment clause is the agreement of the employee to promptly disclose the inventions, innovations, and works to the company or to any person designated by the company, and to assist in obtaining protection for the company, including patents and copyrights in all countries designated by the company. The employee at this point also agrees to execute:

- Patent applications and copyright applications
- Assignments of issued patents and copyright registrations
- Any other documents necessary to perfect the various properties and vest their ownership clearly in the company

If these activities are called for after the employee has left the company, she is still obligated to perform but must be paid for time and expenses.

Employee Moonlighting Might Compromise Confidentiality

Another important concern is moonlighting. While a company that sells CAD/CAM workstations doesn't care if its programmers drive fish delivery trucks on their own time, there are extremely sensitive situations that the company as well as the employee must take care to avoid. In one case, a CAD/CAM company discovered huge telephone charges for various lengthy periods from 3:00 P.M. to 8:00 P.M. on most days of the week, including Saturdays and Sundays. The company challenged the telephone bill and found that the calls were indeed made from the company's own phones to a major computer manufacturer many miles away. The computer manufacturer claimed ignorance. But after a lengthy investigation it was discovered that an employee of the company had been hired on a consulting basis by a middle manager at the manufacturer to develop a software system. The employee had been doing his consulting for the computer manufacturer over the telephone lines from his computer terminal while sitting at his desk in his company office. The employee was not shortchanging the company as far as hours were concerned; he was working long hours to make up for his moonlighting, and the software he was developing was not in the company's CAD/CAM area. But the revelation was chilling. The mere awareness that an information line existed between this giant computer manufacturer and the company, and what might have transpired over that line, haunted the company's officers and managers for some time afterward.

To prevent this, the employee should agree in the employment contract that during employment by the company there will be no engagement in any employment or activity in which the company is now or may later become involved, nor will there be moonlighting on the company's time or using the company's equipment or facilities.

Noncompetition Clauses

A closely related notion is a noncompetition provision whereby the employee agrees not to compete during his employment by the company and for some period after leaving the company's employ. This is a more sensitive area. It may be perfectly understandable that a company does not want its key salesperson, an officer, a manager, or the head of marketing or engineering to move to a new job with a competitor and have the inside track on his ex-employer's best customers, new product plans, manufacturing techniques, or new marketing program. But the courts do not like to prevent a person from earning a livelihood. Courts do not compel a lifelong radar engineer, for example, to turn down a job with a competitor in the same field and instead take a job designing cellular phones. A person who has spent a lifetime marketing and selling drapes and curtains cannot be made to sell floor coverings or used cars.

However, the higher up and more important a person is in the operation of the company, the greater is the probability that that person will be prevented from competing if the employment agreement provides for it. Officers, directors, founders, majority stockholders, and other key personnel have had such provisions enforced against them, but even then the scope of the exclusion must be fair and reasonable in terms of both time and distance. A few months, a year, or even two years could be acceptable, depending on how fast the technology and market is moving. Worldwide exclusion might be acceptable for a salesperson who sells transport planes. In the restaurant business, a few miles might be all that is necessary. A contract that seeks to extend the exclusion beyond what's fair will not be enforced.

One way to ensure that an ex-employee does not compete is to allow the company to employ the person on a consultant basis over some designated period of time. In this way, the employee's involvement in critical information areas can gradually be phased out, so that by the time the employee is free to go to a competitor there is no longer a threat to the company, and at the same time the employee has been fairly compensated.

Bear in mind, however, that even if ex-employees are free to compete, they are not free to take with them (in their memories or in recorded form) any trade secrets or any information confidential or proprietary to the company or to use it or disclose it in any way. To reinforce this, the employment contract should provide that the employee will not, during employment by the company or at any time thereafter, disclose to others or use for her own benefit or for the benefit of others any trade secrets or any confidential or proprietary information pertaining to any businesses of the company—technical, commercial, financial, sales, marketing, or otherwise. The restriction could also protect such information pertaining to the business of any of the company's clients, customers, consultants, licensees, affiliates, and the like.

Along with this, the employment contract should provide that all documents, records, models, electronic storage devices, prototypes, and other tangible items representing or embodying company property or information are the sole and exclusive property of the company and must be surrendered to the company no later than the termination of employment, or at any earlier time upon request of the company. This is an important provision for both the employer and employee to understand. In some states, the law imposes serious criminal sanctions and fines for the removal of tangible trade secret property.

Preventing Employee Raiding

Another potential area of conflict is employee raiding, the hiring away of employees by an ex-employee who is now employed by a competitor or who has founded a competing business. This is a particularly sensitive situation when the ex-employee holds a position of high trust and confidence and was looked up to by the employees she is now attempting to hire. It is particularly damaging when the employees being seduced are critical to operations either because of their expertise or their sheer numbers. In all circumstances, such an outflow of employees is threatening because of the potential loss to a competitor of trade secrets and know-how. This can be addressed by a clause prohibiting an employee, during her employment period and for some period thereafter, from hiring away fellow employees for another competing enterprise.

Employee Ownership of Copyright

One of the most hazardous areas of ownership involves the title to copyrights. If a copyrighted work is created or authored by an employee, the company automatically owns the copyright. But the employee must be a bona fide employee. That is, there must be all the trappings of regular employment. If a dispute arises over ownership between the company and the author, the courts will seek to determine whether the author was really an employee. Was this person provided a full work week, benefits, withholdings, unemployment insurance, worker's compensation, and an office or workspace? If the author was anything less than a full employee, the copyright for the work belongs to the person. It does not belong to the company!

This means that if the company hires a part-time employee, a consultant, a friend, or a moonlighter, that person may end up owning the copyright for the work. Thus, when the nonemployee completes the software system that will revolutionize the industry and bring income cascading to the enterprise, the employee, not the company, will own the copyright. The company will own the embodiment of the system that the employee developed for the company, but the employee will own the right to reproduce, copy, and sell the system over and over again. It has happened. A company that spent hundreds of thousands of dollars to develop a software system owned the finished product but not the copyright in the product. The nonemployee owned the copyright and had the right to reproduce the product without limit and sell it to those who most desire it—typically the company's competitors and customers.

This is a chilling scenario but one that is easy to avoid with a little fore-thought. The solution is easy: Simply get it in writing. Before any work starts, payment changes hands, or plans are revealed, *have the proposed author sign a written agreement* specifying that, whether or not the author is subsequently held to be an employee or a nonemployee, all right, title, and interest in any copyrightable material is assigned to the company. The lack of such a clear un-derstanding in writing can wreck great dreams, ruin friendships and partner-ships, and hamstring businesses to the point of insolvency while the parties fight over who owns the bunny rabbit, the book, the software, the poster, or the videotape on how to be a successful entrepreneur.

Moral Rights of Authors or Artists

Another area that must be considered is the moral rights of authors in their works. In the United States, moral rights of artists in their visual works are protected. Moral rights are variously defined as the rights of attribution and integrity, or the rights of paternity and integrity. What this means is that an artist has a right to insist that his name be associated with the work, or to refuse to have his name associated with the work if it is mutilated in the artist's opinion, and also to insist that the work not be mutilated; that is, the integrity of the work must be maintained. The moral rights doctrine has been invoked, for example, in an attempt to prevent the removal of a wall contain-ing a painted mural.

The law in the United States that established the moral rights doctrine provides that the artist's moral rights may not be transferred, but may be waived by the artist in a written statement that specifically identifies the work and the uses to which the waiver applies.

Therefore, in every agreement dealing with copyrights, it is prudent to in-clude a clause in which the artist in writing specifically refers to the work or works and waives the moral rights for all uses of all the works. It probably would also be wise to refer to Section 106(a) of the Copyright Act, which em-bodies the moral rights doctrine.

Rights of Prior Employees

There is another issue to consider under employment contracts. When a new employee is to be hired, obtain a copy of the employment contract with the last employer or the last few employers to determine whether this employee is free to work for this company now, in the capacity the employee seeks. Prior employers have rights, too, that can conflict, rightly or wrongly, with the employee's new employment.

Consultant Contracts

Consultant contracts should contain provision similar to those in an employment contract, along with some additional provisions. A consultant agreement should clearly define the task for which the consultant is hired—for example, to research a new area; to analyze or solve a problem; design or redesign a product; set up a production line; or assist in marketing, sales, management, technical, or financial matters. This is important to show:

- Why the consultant was hired
- What the consultant is expected to do
- What the consultant may be exposed to in the way of company trade secrets and confidential and proprietary information
- What the consultant is expected to assign to the company in the way of innovations, inventions, patents, and copyrights

A company hiring a consultant wants to own the result of whatever the consultant was hired to do, just as in the case of an employee. But a consultant's stock in trade is the expertise and ability to solve problems swiftly and elegantly in a specific subject area. Sharp lines must be drawn as to what the consultant will and will not assign to give both parties peace of mind.

Consulting relationships by their nature can expose each of the parties to a great deal of the other party's trade secrets and confidential and proprietary information. The company can protect itself with clear identification of the pertinent information and by employing the usual safeguards for trade secrets. It also must limit disclosure to the consultant to what is necessary to do the job, and also limit the consultant's freedom to use the information in work for others and to disseminate the information. Consultants must protect themselves in the same way to prevent the company from misappropriating the consultant's special knowledge, problem-solving approaches, and analytical techniques.

An often overlooked area is the ownership of notes, memos, and failed avenues of investigation. False starts and failures can be as important as the solution, especially to competitors. Related to this is the question of the ownership of the raw data. Raw data may be extremely valuable in their own right but also may be used to easily reconstruct the end result of the consultant's work, such as a market survey.

Confidential Disclosure Agreements

Whenever an idea, information, an invention, or any knowledge of peculiar value is to be revealed, a confidential disclosure agreement (a/k/a nondisclosure agreement) should be signed by the receiving party to protect the disclosing party. The disclosure may be necessary for any of the following reasons:

- To interest a manufacturer in taking a license to make and sell a new product
- To hire a consultant to advise in a certain area
- To permit a supplier to give an accurate bid
- To allow a customer to determine whether or not it wants a product or wants a product modified
- To interest investors to invest in the business

Disclosure agreements are important not only to protect the knowledge or information itself, but also to preserve valuable related rights such as *domestic and foreign patent rights.* These agreements should be short and to the point.

Basically, the receiver of the disclosure should agree to keep confidential all information disclosed. Information is defined as all trade secrets and all proprietary and confidential information, whether tangible or intangible, oral or written, and of whatever nature (e.g., technical, sales, marketing, advertising, promotional, merchandising, financial, or commercial).

The receiver should agree to receive all such information in confidence and not to use or disclose the information without the express written consent of the discloser. It should be made clear that no obligation is incurred by the receiver for any information that it can show was in the public domain, that the receiver already knew, or that was told to the receiver by another party.

The receiver should be limited to disclosing the information to only those of its employees who need to know in order to carry out the purposes of the agreement and who have obligations of secrecy and confidentiality to the receiver. Further, the receiver should agree that all of its employees to whom any information is communicated are obligated under written employment agreements to keep the information secret. The receiver should also represent that it will exercise the same standard of care in safeguarding this information as it does for its own, and in no event less than a reasonable standard of care. This latter phrase is necessary because some businesses have no standard of care or a very sloppy attitude toward even their own important information.

Provision should be made for the return of all tangible embodiments of the confidentially disclosed information, including drawings, blueprints, designs, parameters of design, monographs, specifications, flow charts, sketches, descriptions, and data. A provision could also be included preventing the receiving party from entering a competing business or introducing a competing product or service in the area of the disclosed information. Often a time limit is requested by the receiver, after which the receiver is free to disclose or use the information. Such a time period could extend from a few months to a number of years, depending on the life cycle of the information, tendency to copy, competitive lead time, and other factors present in a particular industry. Strong, clear language should be used to establish that no license or any other right, express or implied, to the information is given by the agreement.

While such confidential disclosure agreements between the discloser and receiver are the ideal, they are not always obtainable. The receiver may argue that no such agreement is necessary, saying in effect, "Trust me." Or the receiver may flatly refuse on the grounds that it is against its policy. Some large corporations turn the tables and demand that their own standard *nonconfidential* disclosure agreement be signed before the disclosure of any information.

Under a nonconfidential disclosure agreement, often referred to as *idea submission agreements,* the discloser gives up all rights to the information except as covered by a U.S. patent or copyright. Outside of those protections the receiver is free to use, disclose, or do whatever it wishes with the information. This is not due simply to arrogance or orneriness. A large corporation has many departments and divisions where research and development of new ideas are occurring unknown to other areas of the corporation. In addition, in a number of cases courts have held corporations liable for misappropriation of ideas and information when no written agreement existed, and even where a *nonconfidential* disclosure agreement purported to free the receiver from any restriction against dissemination and use of the idea.

If no agreement can be reached or if the nonconfidential disclosure agreement counter offer occurs, the discloser must decide whether to keep the idea under the mattress or take a chance on the honesty of the receiver; however, in such a case it is wise to reduce the initial disclosure to a minimum to cut the losses should a careless or unscrupulous receiver make public or misappropriate the idea.

A middle ground that courts have recognized is an *implied* confidential relationship evidenced by the actions of the parties. In one case, a letter soliciting a receiver's interest in a particular field and indicating that the matter was confidential resulted in a face-to-face meeting between the discloser and receiver, where the full idea was revealed. Later, when the receiver came out with a product using the idea, the discloser sued and won. The letter set up a confidential relationship that the receiver did not reject, but rather accepted by meeting with the discloser and accepting the idea without any comment or exclusion. The receiver did not sign the letter, but it bound the company nevertheless under the totality of the circumstances.

CONCLUSION

These basic forms of protection—employment contracts, consultant contracts, and confidential disclosure agreements—need not be complex or lengthy, but they are essential at the earliest stages of idea generation to protect and preserve for the business some of its most valuable and critical property.

11 FRANCHISING

Stephen Spinelli

In the United States in the year 2003, almost 600,000 franchised outlets had total sales nearing $1 trillion, accounting for 35% of all retail sales. There are another 80,000 franchised outlets internationally. Public franchise companies outperformed the Standard & Poor's 500 in the decade of the 1990s. Between 1972 and the present, franchising has shown real growth in every year. Because each franchise company typically represents an extensive network of related companies, they are poised for even greater growth in the next decade. The sheer size of what is called franchising makes it worth investigating.

WHAT IS FRANCHISING?

Over the years, franchising has been described as anything from a pyramid scheme to just another form of employment. Robert T. Justis, Professor of Franchising at the University of Nebraska, defines franchising in general as a business opportunity by which the owner, producer, or distributor (franchisor) of a service or trademarked product grants exclusive rights to an individual (franchisee) for the local distribution of the product or service, and in return receives a payment or royalty and conformance to quality standards.

Business format franchising is defined as a contractual, ongoing business relationship between a franchisor and franchisee. The business format concept includes a marketing plan, documented and enforced procedures, process assistance, and business development and innovation. Business format franchising is an overall method of doing business and is a more complex relationship than franchising solely for the purpose of product distribution. The relationship in a business format franchise must be as dynamic as the marketplace to survive.

HISTORICAL BACKGROUND

Few business practitioners or students have not heard about the McDonald's story and its founder, Ray Kroc. Although their contribution to franchising is monumental, the history of franchising dates much further back.

The extensive "pub" network in the United Kingdom may be the oldest franchise system in the world. During the Roman occupation of Britain, the major supplier of food, drink, and accommodations for the traveler was the Church. Religious tenets of the time dictated that two days' food and lodging be supplied free to any traveler. Abuses of these privileges resulted in the growth of commercial enterprises around 740 to 750.

By 957, King Edgar decided there were too many alehouses and decreed a limit of one per village. As a part of that decree, some common standards were instituted. The business format required a standard measure, limited quantities, and a prohibition of sales to priests. A monitoring system was established and fines levied against violators. Franchising was born.

The population steadily grew, and evolving consumer and economic realities forced consolidation of the industry. The national brewers recognized a need to secure market share. "Publicans grappled with the difficulty of keeping pace with fast-moving events and the ever-increasing demands of various kinds." More and more pub owners allied with brewers. By the early nineteenth century, half of all alehouses were tied by some form of agreement. The House of Commons Committee on Public Breweries in 1818 noted that tied houses were "of much higher order" than free houses. Franchising was here to stay.

Franchising in the United States began in the 1840s and continues to grow today. Two distinct types of franchises have developed. The first, *product franchising,* was created by makers of complex durable goods who found existing wholesalers either unwilling or unable to market their products. These manufacturers built their own distribution systems and created franchise systems as alternatives to the high cost of company-owned outlets. The second type, *business format franchising,* was created in the 1950s when it became evident that the outlet itself could be a vehicle for entrepreneurial activity.

A franchise system can be a combination of franchisor-operated outlets and franchisee-operated outlets or only franchisee-operated outlets. Of the outlets,

87% in U.S. franchise systems are operated by franchisees. Types of businesses generally included in business format franchising are restaurants, food and non-food retailing, and business services. The flowering of the Internet spawned a new array of franchised service companies. Not included in business format franchising are gas stations and soft drink bottlers, for example. Midas and Dunkin' Donuts are two examples of business format franchises. A consumer electronics retailer of Sony would be a product franchise.

BECOMING A FRANCHISEE VERSUS STARTING A STAND-ALONE BUSINESS

The keys to success in a franchise are the same as for any other business. The difference is that the array of factors responsible for a franchise's success is tried and true, and there is a proven ability to transfer this system of excellence to varied and dispersed locations. Therefore, the franchise model is predicated on the assumption that *value has been developed* through the careful operation, testing, and documentation of a commercially viable idea. Given that this has been accomplished (which your own diligence must verify), the initial success of the system lies in the ability of the franchisor to communicate this system to qualified franchisees. The long-term success of the system is uniquely tied to the franchisor's ability to receive and assimilate process feedback from the franchisees and use this feedback to modify the system.

The choice of becoming a franchisee or starting a stand-alone business hinges on your answers to two important questions:

1. Is risk sufficiently mitigated by the trademark value, operating system, economies of scale, and support process of the franchise to justify a sharing of equity with the franchisor (vis-à-vis the franchise fee and royalty payments)?
2. Is my personality and management style amenable to sharing decision making responsibilities in my business with the franchisor and other franchisees?

To quantify the choice between a franchise and a stand-alone business, use the following:

Franchise fee + PV of royalty = PV of the increased net income from the
value of the franchise trademark

where PV is the present value of a sum of money. (For an explanation of PV, see Chapter 14 and the glossary.) If your analysis reveals this equation to be true, or if the right-hand side of the equation is greater than the left-hand side, the franchise decision is appropriate.

Much of this chapter focuses on the quantity and quality of the services and systems that a franchise offers. The choice of a franchise versus stand-alone startup is a question of due diligence, of evaluating the competitive advantages offered by the franchise. Those advantages must exist in sufficient quantity to justify the cost in franchise fees, royalties, and management encumbrances. The key to performing due diligence is in the contract between the franchisee and franchisor.

THE FRANCHISE CONTRACT

The most refined franchise relationship develops into a partnership between the franchisor and the franchisee, and among the franchisees. However, a contract is necessary to ensure an understanding between the parties of their rights and obligations and the associated costs. In franchising, this contract is usually called a license agreement or a franchise contract. Because of the degree of regulation of franchising in the United States, the license agreement has become the definitive statement if litigation occurs.

In a mature franchise, the trade name and trademark are the most valuable assets owned by the franchisor. In the business format franchise, the documented operating system is integral to the trade name and trademark. Together they are responsible for the market value of the franchise. In some cases, building specifications, equipment design, and secret formulas or recipes may be important parts of the franchisor's assets. (For example, the Colonel adamantly believed his "secret recipe" was integral to the product and image of Kentucky Fried Chicken.) Some assets may be patented or copyrighted.

Consideration of franchising by a company or due diligence by a franchise prospect requires an intimate understanding of the license agreement. Franchising is a legal specialization, and some firms concentrate their entire practice in this field. An attorney's review of the license agreement is a necessary cost of franchising. As a part of the legal review, the attorney should, prepare a lay-language brief of the license agreement. In the development or review of a license agreement, business issues will be woven into the legalese. The more practical the detail in the license agreement, the better the chance for a healthy long-term relationship. However, implementing the license agreement will require the franchisor to incur monitoring costs, which must be considered along with other costs of the relationship such as litigation expense and quality concerns.

We use the license agreement, or franchise contract, as a guide to the due diligence process. Understanding the terms of the license agreement is an integral part of the risk management process vital to all franchise endeavors. The following sections highlight the normal operating parameters in a franchise contract with special attention to the pitfalls. Remember, proper evaluation of the franchise opportunity rests in assessing the value and cost of the franchise in relation to expected profits from going it alone.

Services Provided by the Franchisor

This section of the contract is invariably briefer than that detailing the franchisee obligations. However, a few key references will be sufficient to indicate the franchisor's positive intent and obligation. The services provided by the franchisor are separated into initial and continuing services. The type of business will heavily influence the services the franchisor supplies. As a rule of thumb, the prospective franchisee should discount any personal knowledge or experience in the industry and then ask the question, will the magnitude of the initial services establish the franchisee business in a manner appropriate to efficient operation on the day of opening and beyond?

Real Estate Development

Because many business format franchises include a real estate ingredient, site selection and construction specification and supervision are extremely important. Adages such as "Location, location, location," "Just around the corner from success," and "a B site will get you an F in profitability" are not exaggerations. The real estate on which an outlet is located is often both the point of sale and the physical foundation for the service delivery system. It usually cannot be changed without severe economic stress. Most franchisors will approve the location, but not all will actually search for a site. Even fewer will take *responsibility* for finding a site.

The key aspects of site location include a thorough understanding of the primary target audience (PTA), your most likely customer, and the propensity of the PTA to patronize your franchise under varying environmental conditions. An important part of the franchisor's value lies in the accumulation and processing of data from the operating units. Although the franchisor cannot and should not give out information regarding specific stores, compilations with analysis are usually available. This is how the PTA information is gathered. If it is the franchisee's responsibility to locate a site, there must be clearly documented processes linking the PTA to the location specifics. General location parameters include cost, population, traffic volume, traffic patterns, visibility, zoning and permits, and ingress and egress.

Cost

A Holiday Inn franchise requires at least a $2 million investment, much of which is in the real estate. In fact, real estate often requires the majority of the capital required to open a franchise. Even a long-established retail venture that decides to franchise must perform a thorough analysis of the site characteristics to reveal location standards for successful expansion. Because real estate is so important to most franchises, the occupancy cost should be constantly re-evaluated in your financial model. Changing demographics and infrastructure and growth into varying regions might drastically affect your ability to be profitable.

Contact a large commercial real estate broker and review your site specification needs. Gather examples of recently sold or leased property with comparable specifications. Do the property or occupancy costs correlate with the franchisor guidelines for operating a profitable outlet? This process should also be followed by the franchisor, especially when expansion into new geographic territories is contemplated. Even if purchase prices are the same, lease terms and conditions can vary over time and among regions. Make sure that the *capitalization (cap) rates* used in calculating lease cost are comparable. The cap rate is the percentage return the landlord can expect her property to yield on the value of the asset (in this case, land and building) that is being leased. The term of a lease, the amount of time the lessee contractually holds the property, should match the term of the license agreement.

Population

How many targeted customers, PTA—not members of the general population—in how wide a market area, is prescribed by the franchisor? For example, Service-Master lawn care tracks dual-income homes in their trade areas. Cross reference the minimum PTA number with the franchisor pro forma market share and sales projection:

> 3-mile radius
> 50,000 population, 20,000 PTA
> 10% market share
> 2,000 PTA × 3 visits per year = 6,000 customers
> Franchisor's sales projections/6,000 = Average ticket price

Do a spreadsheet analysis ramping up volume to track these sample numbers. Are your projections reasonable and in line with the numbers projected by the franchisor? Will existing outlets' performance validate these projections?

Traffic Volume

Volume is quoted as pedestrians or vehicles per day. Many franchisors will prescribe a minimum volume, usually quoted on a 12- or 24-hour basis. Take note of the outlets the franchisor has singled out or the outlets of franchisees who have expressed satisfaction with their sales volume. Most state departments of motor vehicles, registry, or public works have traffic flow information.

Traffic Patterns

Corner location, the home-bound versus work-bound side of the road, and speed of traffic are but a few of the critical issues related to traffic patterns; A donut or coffee franchise may require the work-bound side of the road. Customers are less likely to stop for morning coffee if they must cross traffic when rushing to their jobs. This is an example of the fine distinction between a marginal return and a substantial return—or worse, the difference between failure and success.

Visibility

Visibility is especially important for products bought on impulse. When it is noon and you are hungry, you may react on impulse to a fast-food sign. Finding a preschool (a growing area of franchising) is probably a more considered choice and not an impulse purchase.

Visibility is a three-prong issue, including the signage, building, and property entrance. At the top speed of the vehicles traveling the road of the proposed location (not to be confused with the posted speed), how many feet and seconds pass from the first view of each of these criteria to the entrance of the site? Is there sufficient time from the initial sighting of the location variable for a driver to comfortably turn into the location? A location that provides adequate turning time with respect to all three visibility variables has the highest ranking in this area.

Seasonality has an impact on visibility. A site as viewed in the winter may yield dramatically different results from the same site in the spring, with trees in full leaf.

Zoning and Permits

The cost and time requirements relating to zoning can vary dramatically from state to state and among local municipalities. Often a land use attorney is required for the process, as well as architects, surveyors, civil engineers, and traffic specialists. Increasingly, environmental impact studies are mandated by state regulation. Estimate the cost of these professionals as a part of due diligence.

Usually the franchisee is required to bear these costs up front. If the franchisor bears the costs, they are often capitalized in the real estate development expense and will be reflected in the outlet rent. In particularly complicated zoning affairs, the cost may inflate the project well beyond the ultimate market value and potentially beyond the occupancy cost projected in the franchisor's financial pro forma.

Ingress and Egress

This is real estate jargon for entrance to and exit from the site. Checkers drive-in restaurant, launched in 1986, requires most site plans to have two drive-through windows in the flow of ingress and egress. Planning boards frequently modify a site plan even at the last minute. A quick change in entrance and exit layout can dramatically alter site acquisition criteria.

Summing Up: Don't Ignore Location Success Factors

If franchising is the vehicle chosen by a currently operating firm for expansion, it is critical to match the existing location success factors to the business format developed for sale to a franchisee. To neglect this is a fatal flaw, especially if the franchisee is responsible for finding the new location. It is extremely difficult to overcome location flaws and often impossible to change them.

In rapidly growing franchise systems, there is a greater propensity to compromise on the development of individual stores in a rush to gain market share. Often the decision to franchise is made as a result of the desire to grow quickly. This cannot be allowed to dominate good business practice if long-term stability is an objective.

It is mutually beneficial to the franchisor and franchisee to have franchisor professionals provide detailed input in the real estate development. Some franchises typically locate in a mall—T-Shirt Plus, for example. The same attention to location and demographic issues applies. A successful outlet will yield profit for the franchisee and capital for expansion. The franchisor will gain larger royalty payments. If the franchise is operated poorly and it ultimately fails, the franchisor can turn over the unit quickly, operate it as a company store, or sell the property to an unrelated third party only if the real estate has been carefully acquired and developed.

Investing in the real estate is a separate business venture from the franchise for both the franchisor and the franchisee. In evaluating the franchise opportunity, calculate the occupancy cost on a market *rental rate.* This can be done by multiplying the market square footage rental cost by the size of the proposed project. Alternatively, use the *market lease factor*—8% in a sluggish market (New England in 2003), 12% in an expansive market (New York, 2000)— applied to the total project cost. The market lease factor is the rate the landlord will charge based on the current demand in the marketplace.

A franchisor who wishes to be the realty holder or lessor will need to negotiate the rental relationship. Some franchisors use what is called *percentage rent* to calculate the occupancy cost for the franchisee. There are a number of methods to implement percentage rents. The simplest is to charge a constant percentage of top-line sales. This can be beneficial in the startup phase but can result in above-market rents for the exceptionally performing location. This is particularly true for businesses with rapidly escalating costs and pricing, and can result in squeezed franchisee margins. This rental formula may seem attractive at the outset but could become burdensome. The variations in the use of percentage rents are limitless. Other methods include charging base rent, a minimum amount each month plus a smaller amount of top-line sales, or an amount slightly less than market rent plus a percentage of top-line sales over the projected break-even sales volume. Some franchisors will offer a variety of options; some will not. The franchisee should negotiate the options as a result of pro forma analysis and in congruence with risk mentality.

Established expertise in interpreting crucial real estate variables is included as part of the franchise purchase. Therefore, the franchisee must be sufficiently convinced that the necessary expertise is in place, available, and utilized.

Construction Specification and Supervision

Upon preliminary qualification of the site, the franchisor should integrate its construction department into the process. The franchisor usually has a standard set of blueprints. Most states require modification to meet state building code with the stamp of an architect from that state. Local municipalities may require further modification. Some franchisors modify plans even to the local level, but most do not. The level of sophistication of the model plans will greatly impact modification cost and efficiency. Very general plans leave much room for architectural inventiveness, resulting in diminished standardization, loss of efficiency, and reduced market value of the real estate.

Beyond the physical blueprints, the franchisor may provide construction supervision. Bidding contracts, draw approvals, construction monitoring, and final punch list are the categories of construction supervision. Beware of the franchisor that controls the construction process without independent bidding.

There is nothing wrong with construction as a profit center if it also accrues benefits to the franchisee. This is best monitored through the marketplace of contractors. The franchisee should be involved in the construction process even if it is totally supervised by the franchisor. The franchise operator will understand the building better and live with it in greater harmony. Minor examples of building aspects the operator must be familiar with include the heating, ventilation and air conditioning, and basement sump pump operation.

Training

Training is a vital initial service and is also helpful on a continuing basis. The license agreement must define the *specific* form in which this franchisor responsibility will be carried out. It should extend significantly beyond a manual and the classroom. Training will vary with the specifics of the franchise but invariably should include organized and monitored on-the-job experience. Well-established and stable franchise systems require operational experience in the system for as long as a year prior to the purchase of a franchise. However, this is not the norm. Once the franchise is operational, the franchisee may be expected to do much or all of the on-site training. Manuals, testing, training aids such as videos and certification processes are often provided by the franchisor.

As discussed previously, the trade name and mark are the most valuable assets in a franchise system. This is the result of delivery of the product on a consistent basis to consumers who acknowledge the value through paying a price that includes a profit margin. A poor training regimen will inevitably dilute the standardized, consistent delivery of the product and reduce trade name value.

Preopening Support

The foundation of the support services program is the level and sophistication of preopening support. Preopening support is a concentrated, multifunctional program to launch the new franchise. Inventory and equipment purchase and setup, staff hiring and training, and startup marketing are key variables. Built on a sound location program, preparedness at launch can create the momentum for success. The franchisor who has the expertise in place to provide sophisticated startup assistance likely has the capability to provide the contractually required continuing services. A poor opening experience is an ominous sign concerning the quality of the franchise.

Continuing Services

Many license agreements define royalties as payment for the use of intellectual property. However, the continuity of the franchise relationship often rests on the cost/value rationalization of the royalty payment by the franchisee to the franchisor. Not only must the franchisor create a marketplace basket of services, but also in the provision of services the system must be sustained and nurtured.

The actions of each franchisee affect the value of the trademark and thus the value of each individual franchise. The actions of the franchisor also affect franchise value. Both parties are necessarily interdependent and have a vested interest in actively supporting the system. A franchise agreement that acknowledges and addresses this interdependence is advantageous. The franchisee's performance is somewhat dependent on the quantity and quality of franchisor support. Conversely, the degree of franchisor support is usually inversely related to franchisee performance; more attention is usually provided the underperforming franchisee. Although this is a reasonable response to a threat to trademark value, balance in the application of franchisor resources is a key ingredient for success.

Performance and Standards Monitoring

By developing an array of statistical and financial monitoring devices, the franchisor can identify both the exceptional performer and the potential failure. Application of resources against identified problems maintains a stable system. Operational systems or marketing programs are often changed in a franchise system because of the exceptional performer. The best franchise systems not only compile data but also analyze and efficiently distribute the information to franchisees for feedback. Does the contract provide for this informational conduit role?

Field Support

The license agreement should provide for scheduled visits to the franchisee's place of business with prescribed objectives. An efficient agenda might include performance review, field training, facilities inspection, local marketing review, and operations audit. The reality is that some franchisors use their field role as a diplomatic or pejorative exercise. The greater the substance of the field function, the easier it is for the franchisee to justify the royalty cost. Additionally, in a litigious environment a well-documented field support program will mute franchisee claims.

One means of understanding the franchisor's field support motive is to investigate the manner in which the field support personnel are compensated. If field staff is paid commensurate with franchisee performance and ultimate profitability, then politics will play a diminished role. Warning signals are bonuses for growth in the number of stores versus individual store sales growth and pay or bonus for franchisee product usage. Tying arrangements are discussed later. However, the field support system is a part of the practical application of the influence strategy the franchisor has chosen.

Operational Research and Development

An economy of scale in research and development is a principal benefit in franchising. These economies are best achieved through the centralized, monitored, and standardized franchisor. Research of a franchise should track operations-level changes in franchised stores over a period of two to four years. How are changes in the system encouraged, cultivated, harvested, and communicated? A practical mechanism should be referred to or specifically outlined in the license agreement.

This is a difficult and delicate area for the franchisor. The franchisor must ensure standardization but also must encourage change. This paradox is resolved by realizing that change will occur but must be managed. Franchising provides the mechanism for the efficient management of change. Customer needs, the legal environment, competition, and most of all the entrepreneurial fervor of franchisees will stretch the envelope of standardization.

Recognizing this, the franchise must provide rules in the license agreement for optimizing efforts in the search for betterment of the system. In franchise systems where the franchisor does not operate a number of company-owned stores, the existing franchise body or representative group should play a part in reviewing and approving issues of product or operational change. These kinds of changes are sometimes covered in the marketing services section the license agreement.

Marketing, Advertising, and Promotion

This is one of the most sensitive areas in the ongoing franchise relationship. Marketing imprints the trade name and mark in the mind of the consumer. If delivery of the product validates the marketing message, the value of the franchise is enhanced. Store growth increases budgets and spreads marketing costs, optimizing the marketing program for the system.

There are a number of mechanisms to fund and implement a marketing program. Typically, the franchisor controls a national advertising fund. Each franchisee contributes a percentage of top-line sales. The franchisor then produces materials (television, radio, and newspaper ads; direct mail pieces; and point-of-sale materials) and, depending on the size of the fund, buys media time or space. Because it is virtually impossible to allocate these services on an exactly equal basis among franchisees, the license agreement may specify the use of "best efforts" to approximate equal treatment, or some such language.

Best efforts invariably leave some franchisees with a little more and others with a little less advertising. Over time, this should balance but must be carefully monitored.

The second level of marketing, advertising, and promotion in franchising is regional. This is often structured on the basis of an *area of dominant influence* (ADI). All the stores in a given ADI—Greater Hartford, Connecticut, for example—would contribute a percentage of top-line sales to the ADI advertising cooperative. The cooperative's primary function is usually to buy media using franchisor-supplied or approved advertising and to coordinate regional promotions. If the franchise has a regional advertising cooperative requirement in the license agreement, it should also have standardized ADI cooperative bylaws. These bylaws will outline such things as voting rights and define expenditure parameters. A single-store franchisee can be disadvantaged in a poorly organized cooperative. Conversely, a major contributor to the cooperative may find voting rights disproportionately low.

The final level of advertising is typically dubbed local advertising or local store marketing. At this level the franchisee is contractually required to make direct expenditures on advertising. There is a wide spectrum of permissible advertising expenditures, depending on the franchisor guidelines. However, the license agreement will probably not be specific. Franchisors will try to maintain discretion on this issue for maximum flexibility in the marketplace. Company-owned stores should have advertising requirements equal to those for the franchised units to avoid franchisor free riding. Historical behavior is the best gauge of reasonableness.

It is important that the franchisor monitor and enforce marketing expenditures. A customer leaving one ADI and entering another will have been affected by the advertising of adjacent regions. Additionally, advertising expenditures not made are marketing impressions lost to the system. The marketing leverage inherent in franchising is thus suboptimized.

Product Purchase Provision

In many franchise systems, a major benefit is bulk buying and inventory control. There are a number of ways to account for this in a license agreement. Most franchisors will not be bound to best-price requirements. Changing markets, competitors, and U.S. antitrust laws make it impossible for the franchisor to ensure this. The franchise should employ a standard of best efforts or good faith to acquire both national and regional product contracts.

Depending on the nature of the product, regional deals might make more sense than national ones. Regional contracts may provide greater advantages to the franchisee because of shipping weight and cost or service needs. The clever franchisor will recognize this. When this is true and the franchisor does not act, the franchisees will fill the void. The monthly ADI meeting then becomes an expanded forum. The results of such ad hoc organizations can be reduced control of quality and expansion of franchisee associations outside the confines of the license agreement. Advanced activity of this nature can fractionalize a franchise system or even render the franchisor effectively obsolete. In some cases, the franchisor and franchisee-operated buying coops peaceably coexist, acting as competitors and lowering the costs to the operator. However, dual buying coops usually reduce economies of scale and dilute system resources, as well as providing fertile ground for conflict.

For purposes of quality control, the franchisor will reserve the right to publish a product specifications list. The list will very clearly establish the quality standards of raw materials or goods used in the operation. From those specifications, a subsequent list of approved suppliers is generated. This list can evolve into a franchise *tying arrangement*, which occurs when the business format franchise license agreement binds the franchisee to the purchase of a specifically branded product. This varies from the product specifications list because brand, not product content, is the qualifying specification. The important question here is: Does the tying arrangement of franchise and product create an enhancement for the franchisee in the marketplace? If so, then are arm's-length controls in place to ensure that pricing, netted from the enhanced value, will yield positive results? This is impossible to quantify exactly. However, if the tying arrangement is specified in the license agreement, the prospective franchise owner is advised to make a judgment before purchasing the franchise. A franchisor should make a clear distinction of value or abandon the tying arrangement.

Less overt tying arrangements occur when the license agreement calls for an approved suppliers list that ultimately lists only one supplier. If adding suppliers to the list is nearly impossible, there is a de facto tying arrangement. Another tying arrangement occurs when the product specification is written so that only one brand can possibly qualify. A franchisor should disclose any remuneration gained by the franchisor or its officers, directly or indirectly, from product purchase in the franchise system. The market value enhancement test is again proof of a credible arrangement.

The Operations Manual

The business format is documented in a manual or series of manuals. The fact that it is documented should be noted in the license agreement. The operations manual is the heart of the franchise asset, as it delineates the manner in which the trade name and mark are to be delivered to the customer. The franchise purchase should be made on the basis of the business's effectiveness in the marketplace. However, to remain viable, the operations manual must be a dynamic instrument. In 1984, Ray Kroc said, "I don't know what we'll be serving in the year 2000, but I know we'll be serving more of it than anybody else."

The research and development previously discussed must be documented in the operations manual before being implemented. The method of change is crucial to the health of the system, again emphasizing the delicate line between standardization and change. Some license agreements will contain a clause stating that the franchisee must adhere to the operations system as outlined in the "current operations manual," which may change from time to time. Given that the system should change to maintain a competitive advantage, the franchisee must be comfortable that this change will take place for valid commercial reasons and be willing to live with less personal control of the operational techniques.

Specialist Support

The franchisor's organizational design must be congruent with franchisee support needs. If real estate is a system variable, there must be sufficient real estate expertise in the franchisor organization to meet the demand created by the sale of franchises. This should occur in all management disciplines.

Territorial Rights

It is very difficult to establish a protected geographic area that is fair to both the franchisee and the franchisor. Demographics are a constantly evolving factor, and hence the true market area will inevitably change. A territory suitable for one site today may support three sites tomorrow because of a road change or mall development. The newer the franchise system, the more pronounced the problem.

If likely market penetration cannot be judged, then how can geography or customers be allocated? On the sale of a single franchise the address is sometimes the only protected territory. This allows the franchisor to ensure that the market is fully developed, but it provides little protection for the franchisee. When the individual outlet reaches a preestablished market share (measured by sales dollars, customers, or units of output), the franchisor will conclude that customer demand is not being fully met. Its concern is that unfilled customer needs create an opportunity for competition. Because of the market leader's advertising and promotion, a "copycat" operation can propel its startup through the leader's market exposure. Indeed, this is a viable market strategy for some franchisors. Fast-food operators have been known to purposefully locate directly adjacent to the market leader.

One way to handle this problem is to formalize the criteria for market share in an individual location to give the operator the opportunity for a return commensurate with existing franchisees. Penetration within the agreed band of market share for a given period of time triggers the creation of another location for development. The franchisee in the first location has the right of first refusal of the second location. This right may be qualified based on balance sheet and operational standards. This solution allows for the full exploitation of the marketplace, with the performing franchisee having an equally exciting upside.

Related to the territorial issue is the *relocation clause.* This item may be separate or contained within the exclusive territory clause, or operations clause. It may give the franchisor the right to compel a franchisee to relocate the business under specific economic or demographic conditions. Typically, a relocation clause is not found in a franchise contract when the franchisee is required to make a real estate investment.

European franchising has considerably different legal considerations. If the franchise company is large enough to affect trade between nations, the European Community (EC) competition laws may come into effect. These laws were established to regulate contracts or practices that may be anticompetitive. Exclusive territory agreements are generally barred in the EC. However, block exemptions can be granted, and a properly structured franchise exclusive territory will likely qualify for this exemption.

Term of the Agreement

Generally, the franchise relationship is established on a long-term basis. A 15- or 20-year agreement is normal, but some can be as short as 5 years. The key is renewal rights. If the terms of the agreement have been met, the franchisee may reasonably expect the relationship to continue. In some states, the renewal right is legislated, and in others there is legal precedent for court-enforced renewal.

A franchise prospect should be wary of an agreement that does not address renewal. It may be an indicator that the franchisor is predisposed not to grant renewals. Legally enforced renewal will be expensive, or the franchisor may impose substantial renewal fees as a condition for continuing the relationship. Many franchise systems do not have a long history, and renewal is not an easily researched issue. Therefore, it should always be contractually stipulated.

Sale of the Business

The good franchisor spends considerable time establishing the basis for choosing franchisees. It is understandable that they want to have some control over who their partners will be. The franchisee is motivated by the ownership of a business and accruing the benefits of that ownership and, at the end of the experience, a capital gain. All issues regarding control of the sale of the existing franchisee company should be covered in the license agreement. Additionally, the procedure by which the controls are implemented must be clearly defined.

Three other clauses will affect the franchisee's ability to sell the business.

1. *Right of First Refusal:* Some license agreements give the franchisor this right. If so, the price should be equal to or a premium of the bona fide third-party offer. A right of first refusal will typically hinder a sale. The prospective buyer may not be willing to spend time or money on a deal that the franchisor might pull out from under him—hence the premium requirement.
2. *Buyout Formula:* At the beginning of the franchise relationship the franchisor has an advantage in understanding the ultimate value of a successful franchisee company. Franchisors have been known to set a buyout formula in the license agreement.
3. *License Agreement:* Some agreements call for the buyer of an existing franchise to sign the "then current form of license agreement." Of course, the new franchisee has no way of knowing what future changes will be incorporated, and the franchisee is not bound to modify his license. Therefore, a unilateral decision of the franchisor can significantly alter the value of the franchisee company in the marketplace. The value will, of course, be diminished if the new form of agreement changes the fee structure, institutes tying arrangements, or modifies the protected territory or term.

Death or Incapacity of the Franchisee

Most license agreements are signed personally. This generally means that the franchisee must devote all or a majority of her professional life to operating the franchise. Also, the economics of the relationship are guaranteed by the individual(s) who sign the license agreement. Usually, the personal attention of the franchisee is impossible to monitor. However, upon death or disability, the franchisee or his estate may be forced into an uneconomic sale of the company or even the loss of the franchise rights. The proper stipulation is for the franchisor to render short-term assistance in operating the franchise (for a fee) until it is sold or transferred to a qualified heir.

Arbitration

The cost of litigation is often too high for a single-outlet operator to bear. The franchisor will sometimes exclude an arbitration clause because it may afford a small franchisee the opportunity to air a grievance and receive redress she otherwise might not be granted. Conversely, such a clause reduces the likelihood of petty arguments. Arbitration is done in private proceedings with an issue judged by an individual who usually has special knowledge of the subject in dispute. Arbitration can be binding or nonbinding. It is usually to the advantage of the smaller franchisee but is gaining support among franchisors also.

License Agreement Termination

Issues of default must be specifically delineated in this section. Important is a reasonable right to remedy a default, provided the breaches are not recurring. Termination means that the franchisee must cease using the trade name and mark, and other property rights of the franchisor. Practically, this means taking down the sign, changing the name of the operation, and returning all manuals and marketing and promotional materials.

In some cases, the franchisor will tie the property lease to the license agreement. Termination of one can mean voiding of the other. This tie can occur even when the franchisor does not own the property vis-à-vis an *assignment and assumption* agreement. This agreement is signed as an addendum to the lease and states that the termination of the license agreement triggers the right, but not obligation, of the franchisor to assume the franchisee's position in a lease. The lessor must be a party to the assignment for it to be valid.

NONCONTRACTUAL CONSIDERATIONS OF BUYING A FRANCHISE

Financial Analysis

The dream of entrepreneurship can become a nightmare if your financial wellbeing is threatened. An advantage of franchising is a track record that can be scrutinized. The prospect can and should make an in-depth analysis of the offered franchise. The franchisor is wise to package the offering in a manner that assists this due diligence. The franchisor who demonstrates, a keen financial understanding gains a pricing advantage in the franchise sales marketplace, attracts a more sophisticated franchisee, and offers the franchisee an advantage in the capital marketplace.

U.S. law requires franchisors to disclose pertinent details of the offer. However, franchisor earning claims regarding the performance of outlets are optional. The federal requirement is fulfilled through the Uniform Franchise Offering Circular (UFOC), which is filed with the Federal Trade Commission and is a matter of public record. The UFOC must be given to the franchisee the sooner of 10 days before the franchisor's accepting a fee or the first personal meeting. Many states have similar but usually more stringent disclosure requirements.

A vast majority of franchisors adheres to disclosure laws. A franchise search that reveals the slightest deviation from FTC or state rules should be abandoned. The disclosure will have pro forma financials based on actual franchisee experience. These are not designed to apply to any individual investment; they are an average of the composite operations. Assuredly, the new operator will find variances in the actual statements from the disclosure pro forma financial projections. The next sections focus on the areas of likely variance.

Estimating Startup Cost/Initial Investment

If there is a real estate component to the franchise, it is often treated as a lease or rental and not included in the startup calculation. If owning the real estate is a part of the franchisee's strategic plan, it must be accounted for separately from the franchise investment. The basics included in this section are leasehold improvements, furniture and fixtures, machinery and equipment, and tools. Even so-called turnkey arrangements will have some startup expense associated with the leasehold interest. Equipment can sometimes be leased also. This is especially true in restaurant franchises.

Low initial investment may dramatically affect operating expenses. A lease is simply a way to leverage your startup cost. Startup losses should be funded in the initial capitalization but are not always included in the disclosure. Assume a worst-case scenario. Even in franchising, undercapitalization is a major reason for failure.

Calculating Profit and Loss/Income Statement

The prospective franchisee should adjust all the numbers to reflect the realities of the area where their operation is planned. For example, New York City will be more expensive to operate in than Pocatello, Idaho, but income will probably be higher also. Decisions about owner's compensation should be incorporated into the pro forma (or into the cash-flow projections, discussed later). The disclosure will typically show the average manager's compensation, and not any remuneration to the franchisee. The franchisor will assume the franchisee is the manager. If the ownership of the franchised company is spread over more than one individual, the issue of compensation is best answered up front.

Remember the discussion of lease versus buy. If leasing is the leverage decision, its costs should be incorporated here. Also, a disclosure pro forma may not include interest payments. The franchisor takes the position that capitalization methods vary so dramatically as to render an average impractical.

Another item sometimes neglected in pro forma projections is depreciation and amortization. These noncash items represent the cost to the business of the decreasing value of fixed assets. Understanding depreciation and amortization will allow for better pricing decisions and more accurate calculation of profit margins.

Pro forma income statements are often annualized. The ramping up of sales and the accrual of expenses on a *monthly* basis will prove invaluable in the first year of operation. Many financial institutions require 36 months of pro forma statements. Although some franchisors will generate or help generate the additional monthly projections, many will reasonably avoid this out of fear of misleading a franchisee and incurring some liability. What a franchisee sees as help in the startup may be remembered as a promise years later, especially in a courtroom setting.

Constructing a Balance Sheet

Constructing a strong opening balance sheet can significantly aid the long-term health of a franchisee. Too often small businesses focus solely on the income statement and ignore the balance sheet. Business format franchises are heavily weighted in the service and particularly retail segments of the economy. Strong understanding of working capital management in a retail environment, depending on the business, can mean advantageous supplier terms along with cash payments from customers. This may provide you with significant short-term leverage. As with the income statement, franchising gives you the unique opportunity to use pertinent historical data in the balance sheet to lay a sound foundation in your company through proper capitalization.

There is a whole series of financial ratios that should be constructed for the ideally positioned franchisee company. In general, everyone should be aware of liquidity, capital, debt, and trade ratios as they apply to the franchisee requirements. In theory, liquidity is measured to assess a company's ability to generate operating capital or meet sudden credit demands. The lever of optimal liquidity varies dramatically by industry. Franchising allows you to know the details and risks before startup, and the astute franchisor will make this analysis readily available. The Initial Investment section of the UFOC, modified for your specific needs, will define your capital requirement but will not specify the form of capital. Use historical numbers from the franchisor to generate stability ratios to help answer this question. This is particularly important if there is a tying arrangement in the franchise, even if the arrangement is informal. In addition, when the franchisor is a key supplier, inventory estimates will be very precise.

However, the franchisor should carefully avoid conflicts of interest, such as excessive startup inventory requirements.

Cash-Flow Projections

Happiness is a positive cash flow no matter what commercial vehicle you choose. However, profitability does not equate to positive cash flow; a profitable business can suffocate and fail due to insufficient cash flow. Cash-flow projection should also be done on a 36-month basis to match the income statement and balance sheet pro forma. Often omitted in the franchisor's cash-flow projection will be the prospect's franchise search cost, professional consultant expense, and the site search and acquisition costs. Failure to consider these will strangle cash flow even before startup.

Financing a Franchise

Financing requirements for a franchise are no different than for any other business startup. Acquisition or alteration of business premises, fittings and fixtures, machinery and equipment, and working capital are all included in the list. Cash-flow shortages due to business cycle may be added later. The advantage of franchise financing is the added variable of the franchisee. The franchisor packages a proven product and business methods. The franchisee is a "partner" in the deal who brings additional capital and entrepreneurial commitment. This should provide greater comfort to the financing institution. Properly exhibiting the transferability of the success factors is the principle function of the loan request. Existing operations that are profitable make access to a lender's ear easier.

A franchisor will systematically meet with large banks to help build confidence in the concept and clear initial hurdles for franchisees. Structuring a debt proposal should utilize much of the due diligence included in the franchise search. In general, the franchise system and the outlets operating in it should be presented both as an integrated organization and as a stand-alone operation. This will promote the franchisee as one who is independently capable of success but whose prospects are dramatically enhanced by being a part of a system. A banker will likely define the long run as the amount of time debt is outstanding. If the successful operation of the franchise system exceeds the term of the loan, the lender will have a higher comfort level.

From the franchisee's perspective, a franchise is a risk management tool. The increased prospects for success will allow for a more secure loan for the bank. Examples of the franchise system's changing to meet the demands of the marketplace will be helpful in projecting future success. The franchisor's organizational chart and support role is appropriate material to review with a banker. It gives depth to the not-as-yet-operating franchisee organization, an advantage the solo startup doesn't have. Pressing the franchise advantage at startup might yield a more competitive loan and more serviceable debt, compounding the advantage over the nonfranchised competitor. Even with these advantages, the personal commitment of the franchisee in the form of cash invested in the business is inevitably required. The financial analysis done in the investigative stage will be helpful in the search for capital. For the purposes of securing debt, add the proposed loan and subsequent debt service to the projections.

The terms in the loan will vary by specific business, franchisor strength, franchisee strength, and general economic conditions. Loans for the substantiated initial investment can run as high as 80%, but 50% to 67% is more likely. Machinery and equipment will have a 3- to 7-year term with a corresponding amortization. The franchisor can help boost the loan-to-value ratio if a market for used machinery and equipment can be demonstrated. Real estate will likely have a 3- to 5-year term with a 15- to 20-year amortization. A few franchisors will provide some financing, and a few more will assist in placing debt. However, a franchisor should not be expected to be a vehicle for acquiring capital.

A problem the franchisor must be cognizant of is franchisee underinvestment. Many franchisees are required to invest a substantial portion of their wealth in the franchise. Theoretically, this could result in a burdensome risk perspective that might cause the franchisee to pass on a favorable opportunity. Franchisee underinvestment is interwoven with the issue of protected territory and expansion rights. Some franchisors include expansion requirements where rights are given. This is especially true when a geographic territory is sold to a franchisee. Often a development schedule is agreed on in advance. Failure of the franchisee to build out the territory under the terms of the agreement (sometimes called an "area development agreement") results in loss of the exclusivity.

MULTIPLE OUTLET OWNERSHIP

Almost 90% of all franchisees in the United States own a single outlet of a franchise. But some franchisees have developed large companies. A company based in Kansas developed Pizza Hut franchises all over the country and became a publicly traded company. Many Midas franchisees have 10 or more stores. One of the more intriguing aspects of franchising is that you can become a franchisee and still have significant growth potential.

An individual franchisee grows either organically, one or two stores at a time as success in each unit builds, or by purchasing a larger geographic territory with a specified unit growth objective. Let's discuss the latter. Buying a defined market entails projecting the maximum number of potential stores and negotiating a build-out schedule with the franchisor. The conclusions of this negotiation will be memorialized in an Area Development Agreement (ADA). Fast-growing Panera Bread employs the ADA as its main vehicle for adding new restaurants. An ADA usually grants the franchisee and exclusive right to develop and own outlets in a defined geographic space for a specified period of time. The total number of outlets to be developed and the timing of that development is also specified. The franchisee keeps exclusivity only if the development schedule is met. The advantage to the franchisee is a higher degree of freedom in site selection, bigger upside potential and usually a reduced per outlet franchise fee. The disadvantage is higher capitalization requirements, bigger up-front payments and pressure to develop new stores that might make you take your eye off of your operating responsibilities. For the franchisor, an ADA provides higher up-front cash to help fund early capitalization needs and enhances the pace of growth. The downside is that the cash can only be booked as revenue when each outlet is developed and larger franchisees tend to wield more power in a franchise relationship than do individual outlet owners. Also, it can be more difficult to dislodge an underperforming ADA than it would be a single outlet license.

A BRIEF NOTE ON INTERNATIONAL FRANCHISING

The Southland Ice Company opened its first convenience store in 1927 and called it a Tote'm. In 1946, the company changed its store name to 7-Eleven to reflect its operating hours. The company entered franchising in 1964, signed its first U.S. area licensing agreement in 1968, and signed the first international licensing agreement with Mexico in 1971. In 1991, Southland Corporation, the quintessential American company was purchased by its Japanese franchisee. In 2003, almost 80% of 7-Eleven's 24,400 stores are located outside of the United States.

Because franchising is a vehicle for growth, many franchisors ask, "Why stop at U.S. national borders?" International franchising has taken on new meaning in the last ten years. Before 1990, U.S. franchise presence abroad meant a McDonald's in Tokyo or one next to the Spanish Steps in Rome. However even as early as the 1970s, several European based franchises existed, such as Dynorod and Prontaprint. A 1995 report by Arthur Andersen showed that two-thirds of all

U.S. franchisors who decided to expand abroad did so based on first contact from a prospective foreign franchisee.[1] By 2003, thousands of U.S. franchises in food, retail, and services had moved into emerging markets around the globe.

However, the complexities of the franchise relationship increase significantly outside U.S. borders and are beyond the scope of this chapter. Start with a basic understanding of foreign laws that govern franchising. One useful document that summarizes the existing franchise-specific laws in various countries is available for free download from a company called Franchise Consulting. Visit http://www.franchiseconsulting.net and click on "International Franchising" from the main page to find the download called "Compliance with Foreign Country Disclosure."

HOW SELLING A FRANCHISE IS REGULATED

The United States has an extensive statutory regulatory system governing franchising. In essence, the sale of a franchise is subject to the same scrutiny as the sale of a security. On the federal level, the government mandates extensive disclosure through the Uniform Franchise Offering Circular, developed by the American Securities Administrators Organization. The document must include a copy of the license agreement, an area development agreement if applicable, and a laundry list of standard disclosure items.

Details of the costs and ongoing payments and product tying arrangements follow. Typically, the document opens with a narrative description of the franchise. The franchisor must also list details concerning litigation, bankruptcy and store transfer, acquisition, and termination. There is also a summary of the franchisee's responsibilities and the services provided by the franchisor. There is usually a pro forma compilation of financial statements taken from franchise operating histories. If the UFOC does not present financial information, any statement about the economics of the franchise by the franchisor must be disclosed to the prospective franchisee in an *earnings claim document*. If the claims are made in a public fashion, such as in the newspaper, then the earnings claim document is required regardless of UFOC content and use.

The franchisor is required to file the UFOC with the Federal Trade Commission (FTC). Any change to the license agreement or any executory document must be filed at least five days before signing. The prospective franchisee is asked to sign a receipt for the UFOC, which the franchisor keeps on file. Although the FTC dictates disclosure requirements, it does not editorialize or approve the quality of the content.

A number of state governments have passed legislation specific to franchising that also requires a disclosure document. Financial and termination disclosure is often more extensive than under federal requirements. Franchisors face a morass of complicated laws and must be mindful of the legal costs when contemplating a national expansion program.

LIMITATIONS OF FRANCHISING

The franchisor must recognize that *equity* in the business is being sold when a franchise is sold. Rapid growth and a highly motivated management team are born, but a partner, not an employee, is created. That partner, the franchisee, will risk time, energy, and capital and will expect a return. Because of the long-term nature of the license agreement, the franchisor is bound to this partnership for many years. Anyone who considers expansion through franchising must understand that the benefits of a *system* must endure the test of time.

Sources of Conflict

As a part of understanding the implications of franchising, one should note the potential sources of conflict in the relationship. As discussed, the franchisor builds a prototype operation, completes system documentation, establishes support overhead, complies with regulatory requirements, and then sells the first franchise. Typically, a large amount of capital has been used before any franchise fees or royalties are received. Therefore, a high percentage of the franchisor's costs are necessarily fixed. As the system of franchisees and outlets grow, the franchisor's costs are spread over an increasing base. The average cost to the franchisor for providing services per franchisee decreases as the number of outlets increases.

On the revenue side, the franchisor is motivated to maximize system sales. The franchisor's continuing income is derived from franchisee royalty payments, a percentage of top-line outlet sales paid to the franchisor. System growth in terms of the number of outlets and individual outlet sales results in higher franchisor revenue applied against lower per-unit support costs.

The franchisee, on the other hand, aspires to achieve optimal unit sales (not necessarily maximum sales) to maximize profit. An important aspect of optimal sales is the optimal number of outlets in the market (again, not necessarily the maximum). The franchisee's operating model has more variable expense than the franchisors. The implication is that there may be sensitive discussion in the areas of pricing, promotion, and the development of outlets. The potential for conflict is exacerbated by the phenomenon of larger, more sophisticated franchisees. With today's heightened level of competition in the marketplace, franchisees are necessarily more educated, with more capital, entrepreneurial drive, and organizational skills, and are capable of building fully integrated companies.

Inefficient Investment

Especially in single-outlet franchise systems, the franchisee is investing a high proportion of personal wealth in the venture. This is opposed to the large operation, where one additional store does not consume a majority of ownership capital. Therefore, such a franchisee might be excessively risk-averse when facing a large capital outlay. The investment might be forgone, creating an opportunity for the competition or simply suboptimizing the system potential.

CONCLUSION

Franchising might best be described as the combination of a unique association of corporate organizations and a unique form of raising capital. For franchising to work best, the franchisor and franchisee goals must be congruent. The relationship must be highly interactive and dynamic. Although the license agreement is the focal point of franchising, if it is strictly interpreted, the probability of conflict being resolved through litigation is heightened. The franchise system that understands that interdependence is a reality has a higher probability of optimizing return. That interdependence and the inherent economies of scale in franchising lend itself to significant utilization of the Internet and Intranet. The web of branded entrepreneurs in a franchise system can now communicate better among themselves and with partners in the value chain such as suppliers. The potential for wealth creation in franchising now seems even better.

12 ENTREPRENEURS AND THE INTERNET

Julian E. Lange

The impact of the Internet on business and society can hardly be exaggerated. Its presence has become so pervasive so quickly that it is difficult for many people to remember how they previously did without it. What was once a little known communication vehicle for scientists and "techies" has become an essential tool that provides access to a seemingly limitless array of information—ranging from economic data, company reports, product literature, and stock market quotations to breaking news, musical performances, instant messaging, and online courses—and that's just the tip of the iceberg! Perhaps equally important, the Internet has emerged as a worldwide phenomenon, offering the possibility for myriad interactions among businesses, organizations, governments, and people across the globe.

During the 1990s, many entrepreneurs were quick to take advantage of the Internet's possibilities to create exciting new businesses and enhance existing ones, and the word *dot-com* became synonymous with *new economy* success. Venture capital became increasingly plentiful as the IPO market flourished, and many ventures were seemingly funded on the basis of a business idea supported by a dozen PowerPoint® slides. It is well known of course that the dot-com bubble eventually burst and took with it much of the former optimism about the Internet. The IPO market virtually shut down, and venture capital funding decreased dramatically. A few startups like eBay, Amazon.com, and Google prospered, while large numbers of other formerly high-flying startups failed. In addition, new competitors emerged when a number of bricks and mortar "old economy" companies—many of which had been slow to recognize the changes being wrought by the Internet—began to enhance their business models by incorporating the Internet into their operations.

Amidst the chaos of the dot-com failures, the overriding questions for entrepreneurs became: (1) What are the realistic opportunities for entrepreneurs on the Internet? (2) How can they be identified and developed? and (3) How are they likely to change over time? It turns out that a search for answers to these questions can usefully begin with a closer look at the dot-com experience itself. While extremely painful for many of the people and companies involved, the dot-com debacle held many lessons for entrepreneurs. Among them was that the laws of sound business practice had not been repealed in the new economy. It is still true that in order to start and build a successful business, entrepreneurs must pay close attention to the fundamentals. In particular, the business must demonstrate a number of important characteristics including:

1. A product or service that meets a compelling need in the marketplace.
2. A realistic business model providing for actual sales to customers who are delighted with the product/service offering.
3. The capability of achieving a positive cash flow relatively quickly and profitability soon thereafter.
4. An entrepreneurial "A" team which includes people with complementary skills and experience.
5. The ability to gather and leverage sufficient resources.
6. Close attention to operational details.

It should be heartening to entrepreneurs that despite the decline in available investment capital, investors continue to be attracted to businesses that stay close to these principles.

This chapter serves as an introduction for entrepreneurs to the opportunities and challenges afforded by the Internet. We will briefly present an overview of the Internet, its current status and prospects, its history, and some of its basic features. Those readers who are already Internet-savvy may want to turn to the sections on "Internet Business Models" or "How an Existing Business Can Benefit from the Internet," which explore the *why* of being on the Internet and look at how it can be utilized both to further the goals of existing businesses and for the development of new products and services. The Internet is incredibly dynamic and is changing so rapidly that it is challenging to keep up. This chapter offers a way of doing that by providing specific references to Internet sites and institutions that you should visit often.

Although the term *Internet* is familiar to most people, the exact definition may not be. The Internet is a vast array of networks connecting millions of computers around the world. At year-end 2002, there were approximately 666 million Internet users worldwide, and that number was expected to exceed one billion by the end of 2005 (Exhibit 12.1).[1] The United States has by far the largest number of Internet users (estimated to exceed 200 million at year-end 2005 or 20% of worldwide users, Exhibit 12.2). Japan, China, Germany, and the United Kingdom round out the top five users. While increasing at an 8% compounded annual rate, the U.S. growth rate of Internet users has moderated considerably from the 10% to 20% per month hypergrowth of the mid-1990s. The number of Internet users outside the United States is projected to grow at approximately twice the U.S. rate during the next few years.

INTERNET DEMOGRAPHICS

The demographics of Internet usage are constantly evolving. Exhibits 12.3 and 12.4 indicate that while men continue to comprise the majority of Internet users in the overall user category and also in the youngest group of U.S. users (age 11 to 20), women have crossed the 50% threshold in the newest user group (users who have begun to use the Internet during the past year).[2] Seniors (the over-50

EXHIBIT 12.1 Top 15 countries in Internet usage at year-end 2002.

Rank	Country	Internet Users (millions)	Percent of Total
1	United States	160.7	24.13
2	Japan	64.8	9.73
3	China	54.5	6.71
4	Germany	30.4	8.18
5	United Kingdom	27.1	4.08
6	South Korea	26.9	4.04
7	Italy	20.9	3.13
8	Canada	17.8	2.68
9	France	16.7	2.50
10	India	16.6	2.49
11	Brazil	15.8	2.38
12	Russia	13.5	2.03
13	Australia	10.5	1.57
14	Spain	10.4	1.57
15	Taiwan	9.5	1.43
	Top 15 Total	496.0	74.48
	Worldwide Total	665.9	100.00

Source: Egil Juliussen, *Computer Industry Almanac,* Web site (www .c-I-a.com), 2002.

EXHIBIT 12.2 U.S. online users, 2000–2006.

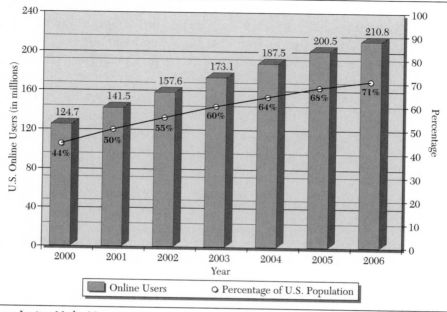

Source: Jupiter Media Metrics, 2001.

EXHIBIT 12.3 Internet use by gender: 1998.

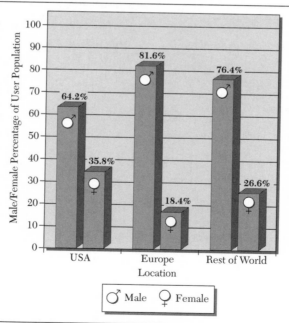

Source: NUA © ComputerScope Ltd. and others, 2001.

EXHIBIT 12.4 Internet use by gender: 2001.

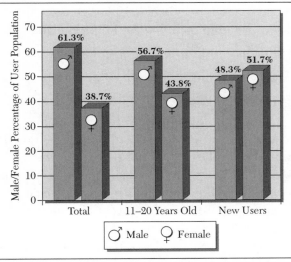

The Web remains a male domain, these figures show. But look at the graph on the right: New Web users are slightly more likely to be women.
(Marco Doelling/ABCNEWS.com)

demographic group) are the fastest growing segment of Internet users, comprising 38% of total Internet users in 2000 (up from 19% in 1998).[3] This group is a highly desirable one to Internet marketers. More than half of these people have not retired, and approximately 30% earn more than $50,000 and have liquid assets greater than $100,000. The great majority of U.S. personal computer-owning households (93%) are connected to the Internet,[4] and most of those users

EXHIBIT 12.5 Internet users: Frequency of use.

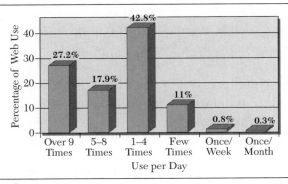

Most users are online often.
(Marco Doelling/ABCNEWS.com)

Source: Michael J. Martinez, *Who are Internet users?* ABCNEWS.com, July 14, 2001, based on Coleen Kehoe, Graphics, Visualization, and Usability Center Survey, Georgia Institute of Technology, 2001.

maintain contact with at least one online user group.[5] Moreover, most Internet users connect several times a day (Exhibit 12.5).[6] Once connected, among other pursuits, 58% play games, and 30% use the PC/online combination to organize their personal finances.

ORIGINS OF THE INTERNET

The Internet began almost 30 years ago as a project sponsored by the Department of Defense. In the depths of the Cold War, it was thought essential to have a network that could connect key military and scientific computers in the United States. Such a network would be useful as a means of exchanging information in the scientific community as well as in the event of a nuclear disaster. To fulfill this mission, the ARPANET was born, funded by the Defense Department's Advanced Research Projects Agency (ARPA). It was initially modest in scope, involving only a handful of scientific sites at major research universities, and it remained the province of academics and the military into the early 1980s. The military portion of the network was split off in the mid-1980s, but there were still significant restrictions on commercial use because the network continued to be funded by the government. Ordinary nontechnical users were discouraged from using the network because of the often-obscure "computerese" commands that needed to be learned to use what was by now known as the Internet. The user interface was also text-based, consisting of line after line of computer jargon, devoid of the point-and-click ease of use of the Apple Macintosh or Microsoft Windows-based personal computers.

That was all changed by the introduction of the World Wide Web. A group of scientists led by Timothy Berners-Lee of CERN, the European Particle Physics Laboratory, decided that it would be desirable to develop a user interface that incorporated graphics, sound, and video as well as text, and that would also link data from various sources around the world on a single screen of information. Subsequently, in the early 1990s, the National Center for Supercomputing Applications at the University of Illinois sponsored the development of the first computer program, called a *browser,* that implemented these ideas and provided nontechnical users with a graphically based tool. This ushered in the age of multimedia on the Internet.

A QUICK OVERVIEW OF INTERNET BASICS

There are a variety of tools and applications available to users that facilitate information acquisition and exchange on the Internet. These tools provide a means to create an Internet presence for an entrepreneurial business that can enhance its growth and effectiveness. Most people today have used the Internet in some fashion, even if it is to exchange e-mail with friends and family. If you are relatively new to business uses of the Internet, you should take some time to get accustomed to the environment. Visit the computer section of a good bookstore (either a physical store or a virtual one like Amazon.com), and you will find a plethora of introductory books about navigating the Internet (Net). Get in the habit of "Net surfing." See what others are doing and get familiar with the territory. Then, you will be better able to assess the possibilities that the Internet offers for your business and, being entrepreneurial, some of you will no doubt invent new capabilities for your business and others.

Web Sites

The immense upsurge of interest in the Internet during the 1990s was no doubt directly related to the growth of the World Wide Web (Web), that part of the Internet that facilitates the use of multimedia—graphics, audio, and video and is most familiar to the vast majority of users. *Web browsers* (i.e., Microsoft Internet Explorer and Netscape Navigator) permit you to view Web documents that have been created especially to incorporate the Web's multimedia capabilities. Another central feature of the Web is its use of hyperlinks that permit the user to view documents that are assembled on a particular Web site from a multiplicity of sources in real time. Hyperlinks transform Web documents into dynamic vehicles for displaying related information in a variety of forms. An important example of the use of hyperlinks are business Web sites, in which companies present information of interest to customers, potential customers, suppliers, employees, shareholders, job applicants, the press, and others. Through the use of hyperlinks, electronic visitors to your company's home page can connect directly to other areas they may wish to explore (and which you may want to encourage them to explore) about your company, such as product descriptions, job responsibilities, bios, and pictures of key employees, tech support information, or a message from the CEO.

Equally important, you can gather data about the visitor that may be useful in gaining feedback about your products or services, both through directly surveying visitors or simply gathering information about the time of their visit, which parts of the Web site they viewed, and how long they stayed. This interactive aspect of the Net is one of its essential features and potentially the most important reason to include the Web in your business strategy. Customer relationship management (CRM) and building brand loyalty continue to be important objectives for businesses large and small. Keeping close to customers and the marketplace has emerged as an important theme for businesses in the new millennium, and the Web and the Net in general provide many excellent oppor-tunities for doing so. (See p. 392.)

Usenet

Another useful Web capability is Usenet, a system of discussion groups centered on a particular topic of interest to its members. There are tens of thousands of such newsgroups in existence involving millions of people. You can access Usenet using your browser software, or, alternatively, using a program called a *news-reader*. There are many such programs available to be downloaded from the Net. You can locate newsgroups on the Net itself (e.g., see http://www.liszt.com) or check out the newsgroup references on your Internet service provider. You can also find newsgroups of interest by consulting references such as the various In-ternet yellow pages compilations published and updated frequently and available in both online (virtual) and physical (brick and mortar) bookstores. After you have joined a newsgroup, you will receive messages posted (i.e., sent to) the newsgroup. Your browser or newsreader software has the ability to filter the messages, and you can follow what are called *threads* (messages related to a par-ticular topic). There are two basic types of newsgroups, *moderated* and *unmod-erated.* In unmoderated groups, all messages posted to the group are forwarded to all members of the group. As the name implies, in moderated groups, posted messages are first reviewed by a moderator for relevance, and some messages are screened out through this process.

While newsgroups vary in content and focus, there are certain unwritten but generally understood rules governing their use. The most important rule from the standpoint of business users is that advertising is not considered ac-ceptable by many newsgroups. Not all groups ban advertising. This is particu-larly true of business-oriented groups, but you should check out the group's policy before posting any advertising-oriented material. Most groups have a file called *FAQ*, which stands for frequently asked questions, that covers the major ground rules of the group. You should read that file before beginning to contribute to the group.

Mailing Lists

Mailing lists are similar to newsgroups but with some important differences. Mailing lists utilize e-mail as the medium for exchanging ideas. You join a mail-ing list by "subscribing" to the list. Subscribing is a simple matter of sending your e-mail address and a request to be included on the list to the list administrator, which usually is a program called a listserver. Canceling your electronic sub-scription is just as easy—simply send a request to the listserver to delete your name from the subscription list. Mailing lists are unmoderated and you do not need any special software to read the postings. Perhaps because of the ubiquitousness of e-mail, there are many more mailing lists than newsgroups. The rules for advertising through mailing lists are similar to those for newsgroups. Be sure to check whether any advertising at all is acceptable, and then follow the custom. If you do advertise, try to include as much content as possible in your posting.

Search Engines

Search engines are software programs that help users locate information on topics of interest. A number of such tools have been developed. Some are available as a feature of a Web site that provides many services (e.g., AOL.com), while other search engines are the main feature of a Web site and the reason that users come to the site. The following sites contain valuable search engines:

google:	http://www.google.com
altavista:	http://www.altavista.com
askjeeves:	http://www.askjeeves.com
lycos:	http://www.lycos.com
yahoo:	http://www.yahoo.com
SearchEngine Watch.com:	http://www.searchenginewatch.com
InterNIC Whois?:	http://www.Internic.net

THE DOT-COM EXPERIENCE

In the latter half of the 1990s, there was a great deal of excitement about the possibilities that were opened up by the Internet and the Web to fundamentally change the way business is transacted. Many young entrepreneurs with new ideas, energy, enthusiasm, and often some unique technical skills set up shop with the objective of changing the world and reaping substantial financial rewards. It was accepted by many that the rules of the so-called "old economy" did not apply in the new dot-com world. Soon many people were declaring that profits were unnecessary and even sales were not important at first. Speed was crucial in being first to market, and the key to success was to capture "eyeballs" or visitors to your Web site. Eyeballs would lead to market share that would eventually result in profits somewhere down the line. Some CEOs even declared that it would be a mistake to make profits early in the life of a dot-com company, because earning profits would mean that the business wasn't spending enough on marketing to capture more eyeballs and build a loyal customer base. Many venture capital investors supported these decisions.

Young Internet firms without a record of profits and sometimes with little revenue were taken public by top underwriters and venture capitalists at often-astronomical valuations.[7]

All of this activity gave rise to what is now referred to as the dot-com or Internet "bubble." While some investors made significant returns through this activity, most did not. After Nasdaq reached a peak on March 10, 2000, Internet stock valuations and those of most of the stocks in the technology sector plummeted, often losing more than 95% of their peak value in a relatively short time. The amount of IPO activity slowed from a torrent to a trickle, and it became extremely difficult to raise any funds for Internet companies from venture capitalists and angel investors. This was not surprising, given the close association between the level of venture capital investment activity and the vibrancy of the IPO markets (which provide the exit mechanism for venture capital investors).

Does the dot-com debacle mean that Internet startups are inherently flawed and likely to be poor investments? Not at all! The dot-com experience has provided entrepreneurs and investors alike with some very important, albeit, painful lessons, the most important of which is that the "laws" of sound business practice have not been repealed in the Internet era. Rather, they must be adapted to the new environment while maintaining their fundamental integrity. Most dot-com companies failed because they lacked a sound business model and didn't follow fundamental business principles. Savvy entrepreneurs have long known that *cash is king*, and the marketplace is very unforgiving of entrepreneurs who have not absorbed that basic business lesson. It is also important to know your customers' needs and pain points well, to seek out customers as early as possible, to keep a watchful eye on expenses, to leverage resources creatively, and to reach breakeven cash flow and profitability as soon a possible.

THE INTERNET BUSINESS ENVIRONMENT AND BUSINESS MODELS

In the midst of an economic downturn in the United States in 2001, Forrester Research published a report entitled *Why E-Commerce Won't Die* and revised upward its e-commerce forecast.[8] Among the reasons cited for optimism were the association of e-commerce with the empowerment of consumers, the convenience of online shopping, and tendency of people who had a satisfying online buying experience to repeat it. Indeed, Forrester and other market analysts continue to predict a rapid growth in the business to consumer (B2C) and business to business (B2B) segments of the e-commerce market despite any weakness in the U.S. economy.[9] A subsequent report attributed the strength in the online

EXHIBIT 12.6 Total e-commerce (billions of U.S. dollars).

	2002	2003	2004	2005	2006
United States	1,610.4	2,527.6	3,759.7	5,296.9	7,091.6
Outside U.S.	683.0	1,351.2	2,441.4	3,943.8	5,745.7
Worldwide	2,293.4	3,878.8	6,201.1	9,240.7	12,837.3

Source: Forrester Research.

B2C marketplace to the combination of consumers' continued purchases of small-ticket items like gifts and large-ticket items like home and entertainment goods, and their increased participation in online auction purchases.

Exhibit 12.6 contains a medium-term forecast for the e-commerce market segments. Expenditures on e-commerce in the United States (including B2C, B2B, infrastructure, and other goods and services) are expected to rise from $1.6 trillion in 2002 to $7.1 trillion in 2006. The comparable worldwide e-commerce numbers are $2.3 trillion in 2002 and $12.8 trillion in 2006. E-commerce in the United States represents 70% of worldwide e-commerce in 2002, but the percentage is expected to fall to 55% by 2006. Thus, e-commerce outside the United States is expected to grow substantially faster than e-commerce in the United States (70%/yr. versus 45%/yr.) during the period from 2002 to 2006. The B2B segment is huge compared to the B2C market (Exhibits 12.7 and 12.8). For example in 2006, worldwide B2B equals $12.3 trillion versus $562 billion in B2C transactions. In both B2B and B2C in 2006, North America accounts for the largest amount of e-commerce (59% and 39%, respectively), followed by the Asia-Pacific and Western European regions with combined shares of 39% and 58%, respectively, and neglible shares for the rest of the world.

EXHIBIT 12.7 B2B market segment projected in 2006.

Region	Online Trade (Billions U.S. Dollars)	Percentage
North America	7,249.2	59.1
Asia Pacific	2,460.4	20.0
Western Europe	2,320.3	18.9
Latin America	93.1	0.8
Eastern Europe	83.9	0.7
Africa and Middle East	68.6	0.6
Total B2B	$12,275.5	100.0%

Source: Forrester Research.

EXHIBIT 12.8   B2C market segment projected in 2006.

Region	Online Trade (Billions U.S. Dollars)	Percentage
North America	219.8	39.1
Asia Pacific	185.2	33.0
Western Europe	138.3	24.6
Latin America	7.0	1.3
Eastern Europe	6.3	1.1
Africa and Middle East	5.2	0.9
Total B2C	$561.8	100.0%

Source: Forrester Research.

Internet Business Models

The E-Commerce marketspace can be divided into three major components: B2B, B2C, and everything else (which includes infrastructure providers, other hardware and software providers, and service providers). The infrastructure providers (e.g., networking companies) were the first to make a profit in the Internet marketplace. The B2B and B2C content and service providers found profits a more elusive goal, particularly during the heady days of the dot-com era.

Following is a list of many of the current revenue models being pursued on the Internet. Remember that the Internet marketplace is moving very quickly, and revenue models and business types are continually being created, modified, and discarded:

- *Transaction Fee Model:* In this model companies charge a fee for goods or services rendered. Examples of such sites are online travel agents like Travelocity that charge a fee for selling airline tickets.

- *Advertising Support Model:* Visitors to the site are attracted by content at the site but pay no fees. Advertisers pay fees to the operator of the site in order to reach the demographic group that frequents the site. A variant of this model combines advertising support with some fees charged to customers, since in most cases the experience of Web firms has been that advertising has not provided sufficient support to make a profit. An example of this sort of site is bluemountain.com, a very popular Web site that consumers visit to send electronic greeting cards to family and friends. There is no charge for sending some electronic cards, but the site does *upsell* customers by offering birthday and holiday cards and companion products for a fee. Another example would be a Web portal like yahoo.com.

  The advertising support model was at the heart of the competition for "eyeballs" in the early days of e-commerce, and it turned out that the eyeballs couldn't be converted into revenue-generating customers at a fast

EXHIBIT 12.9 Top 10 brands, combined home and work unique audience, February 2003.

	Brand	Unique Audience (000)
1	Yahoo!	80,745
2	Microsoft	75,228
3	MSN	74,270
4	AOL	69,721
5	Google	40,310
6	Amazon	34,518
7	Real	34,182
8	Ebay	34,109
9	Lycos Networks	30,116
10	About Network	23,275

Source: Neilsen//NetRatings, 2003.

enough rate for most B2C businesses. Exhibits 12.9 to 12.11 present some interesting data concerning the Web sites that have the greatest number of unique Internet visitors (either home- or work-based) and also concerning those companies that advertise most heavily on the Web. Exhibit 12.11 illustrates that in the February 2003 time frame, AOL Time Warner, Microsoft, and Yahoo had the largest number of unique Internet visitors by a wide margin. In addition, Exhibit 12.10 indicates that Estee Lauder and Amazon.com garnered the largest number of impressions for the same time period. Thus, although the Web was at first considered a level playing field, that is not necessarily the case when it comes to attracting visitors and advertising dollars.

EXHIBIT 12.10 Top 10 online advertisers, February 2003.

	Advertiser	Impressions (000)
1	Estee Lauder Companies	3,472,486
2	Amazon.com	3,239,163
3	NetFlix.com	2,765,256
4	Classmates Online	2,595,426
5	SBC Communications	2,348,631
6	USA Interactive	2,078,961
7	AT&T Wireless Services	1,557,273
8	X 10 Wireless Technology	1,401,316
9	1-800-Flowers.com	1,333,219
10	Florists' Transworld Delivery	1,314,667

Source: Neilsen//NetRatings, 2003.

EXHIBIT 12.11 Top 10 parent companies, combined home
and work unique audience, February 2003.

	Brand	Unique Audience (000)
1	AOL Time Warner	89,898
2	Microsoft	89,187
3	Yahoo!	80,780
4	United States Government	44,885
5	Google	40,340
6	Ebay	35,617
7	Amazon	35,345
8	RealNetworks	34,213
9	About-Primedia	33,512
10	Terra Lycos	31,967

Source: Neilsen//NetRatings, 2003.

- *Intermediary Model:* In this model, the business acts as an intermediary in bringing together buyers and sellers who want to enter into transactions. For example, eBay fits into this category, charging a small commission on each sale.

- *Affiliate Model:* As some Web sites began to draw many more visitors than others, the popular sites developed commission-based models in which they paid commissions to other Web sites that would drive business to their site. Amazon.com uses this model and offers a standard commission to other Web sites who become affiliates.

- *Subscription Models:* Some Web sites charge a fee (e.g., monthly or annually) to visit their site. A good example of this sort of model is a newspaper like the *Wall Street Journal,* which both charges a fixed annual fee for a visitor to enter the site and also a separate variable fee for a visitor to download a copy of an article from its archives.

HOW AN EXISTING BUSINESS CAN BENEFIT FROM THE INTERNET

Three outstanding characteristics about successful entrepreneurs are that they are fast, focused, and flexible.[10] In many ways, the Internet holds out the promise of making the playing field more level for startups and smaller, emerging businesses. An attractive, compelling Web site is often judged on its own terms and can appear to be the work of a larger established company. An Internet presence can also help businesses get closer to customers and other stakeholders like suppliers, investors, and professional service providers. Certain tasks, like requests for product literature, can easily be automated, and thus contribute to a company's reputation for a fast response capability.

Before you commit to setting up an Internet presence, it is important to put the decision into perspective. Utilization of the Internet is one tool in your arsenal, and it is certainly appropriate to consider the Internet as one possible avenue for achieving your company's objectives. At the same time, it is important to specify those objectives clearly and to think through how your Internet strategy is consistent with, and complementary to, your overall business strategy. An Internet presence will cost both money and effort. It is a potentially high maintenance activity and not one to be undertaken lightly. But it also has an intangible benefit as well: that of positioning your business as a cutting edge company conversant with the latest technology. When deciding on a Web presence, the following checklist will be helpful:

- What are your company's business objectives, short term and long term?
- What resources are realistically available?
- Can the company make a long-term commitment to this effort?
- What is the likely benefit/cost ratio of the overall effort or of distinct components?
- What results can be reasonably expected at particular cost and effort levels?
- What is the realistic time frame to accomplish the task?

Some of the traditional business tasks that are being supplemented through an Internet presence include:

- Customer service/support
- Technical support
- Data retrieval
- Public relations and investor relations
- Selling products and services
- Obtaining advice/information

All of the tools and applications we discussed in the previous section are important for deciding on the type and extensiveness of your Web presence. Having downloadable files containing company literature—or even trial product versions in the case of software—can enhance your firm's value to customers. Some companies find it useful to send e-mail announcements about new products or product enhancements, and almost all provide *some* form of e-mail communication with company stakeholders. Many companies provide extensive support services through their Web sites. Let's look at some of these activities in more detail.

Customer Service/Support

There are a number of customer support activities that can be accomplished quickly and efficiently using a Web site including current and new product literature, upgrade information, and short descriptions of common problems and solutions. One of the great strengths of the Internet is that it is an *interactive* medium. While you are expeditiously addressing customers' needs, you can also gather information about your customers. This can be done by tracking the number of customers who visit particular areas of your Web site and by directly surveying visitors. Surveying should be done with caution, however, lest the questions become a nuisance and discourage customers from visiting your site. Survey participation should be optional, and surveys should be short and to the point. One popular feature is a customer feedback capability in which customers can e-mail their comments to the appropriate executive at your company. Not only does this capability empower customers, it also provides a very useful channel for learning more about how your products are being received in the marketplace. Web site support will not completely replace human contact, but it can greatly reduce the number of issues that require the intervention of your staff.

As an example, look at Amazon.com's Web site. If you type in Amazon's address on your browser (http://www.amazon.com), you will see a screen similar to Exhibit 12.12. One of the first things you will notice is that this home page has been customized for the person accessing it. One of the tabs at the top of the page reads "William's Store," and there is a greeting "Hello, William D. Bygrave. We have *recommendations* for you." The word "recommendations" is hyperlinked to another Amazon.com Web page that suggests books, digital photography equipment, and other items similar to ones recently ordered. For example, the latest book by an author whose work has been previously purchased or a book on a similar topic will be suggested for consideration. The Web site lists hyperlinks to a variety of products offered for sale in a column along the left-hand margin. Free shipping for orders over $25 is advertised in the top left-hand corner of the page, and in the upper right-hand corner the Tamrac 5242 is featured because it is on William D. Bygrave's wish list. Finally, also in the top right-hand column, there is (1) another personalized message—"William, check out what's *New for You*" (with an associated hyperlink), (2) a notification of new messages waiting at the message center, and (3) a reminder that the customer's shopping cart has no items in it at present.

EXHIBIT 12.12 Amazon.com web site.

Amazon Exclusive!!
Order a Segway now!
It's only at Amazon

amazon.com.   🛒 VIEW CART | WISH LIST | YOUR ACCOUNT | HELP

WELCOME | WILLIAM'S STORE | BOOKS | APPAREL & ACCESSORIES | ELECTRONICS | TOYS & GAMES | MUSIC | CARS | ◉ SEE MORE STORES

▶ INTERNATIONAL | ▶ TOP SELLERS | ▶ ◉ TARGET | ▶ TODAY'S DEALS | ▶ SELL YOUR STUFF

Save big on reconditioned tools in Tools & Hardware!

SEARCH

All Products ▾
GO!

FREE Super Saver Shipping on orders over $25!
Restrictions apply

WEB SEARCH

GO!
Powered by Google

BROWSE

Featured Stores
- Apparel & Accessories
- Office Products

Books, Music, DVD
- Books
- DVD
- Magazine Subscriptions
- Music
- Video

Electronics & Office
- Electronics
- Audio & Video
- Camera & Photo
- Office Products
- Software
- Computer & Video Games
- Computers
- Cell Phones & Service

Hello, William D. Bygrave. We have recommendations for you. (If you're not William D. Bygrave, click here.)

Get the Versatile Nokia 3650 for Free After Rebates

Equipped with a built-in camera, the Nokia 3650 allows you to take pictures and short video clips and send them to any e-mail address. It also has a dazzling color screen, a built-in speakerphone, Web access, and more. All that and it's yours for free after rebates when you activate a qualifying rate plan.

▶ Get yours today!

Get Ready for More of *The Two Towers*

Pre-order the new, extended edition of *The Lord of the Rings: The Two Towers* now at 35% off and receive immediate access to a special streaming media featurette on the making of the movie.

▶ See more

Get Free Discs When You Buy Easy CD & DVD Creator 6

Order Roxio's Easy CD & DVD Creator 6 Platinum Edition, and you'll not only get the bestselling disc-authoring software, but you'll get a free pack of blank discs to start you on your way!

Answer the following question correctly and

You Know You Want It

Tamrac 5242 Adventure 2 Photo Backpack (Black) beckons from your Wish List.

29 NEW FOR YOU

William, check out what's **New for You**:

(If you're not William D. Bygrave, click here.)

Your Message Center

🔴 You have 5 new messages.

Your Shopping Cart

🛒 You have 0 items in your Shopping Cart.

Your New Releases

Under the Banner of Heaven by Jon Krakauer

More Categories
- Religion & Spirituality
- Travel
- Biographies & Memoirs
- Reference
- Nonfiction

▶ **More New Releases**

The Web site is visually attractive and relatively easy to navigate. Amazon has also designed a simple and intuitive shopping cart and payment system, and the cart is always one click away using the tab at the top of the page, as is the customer's account, which is accessible by clicking on another nearby tab. Customer service is also one click away with a link at the bottom of the page (just out of view in Exhibit 12.12). In addition, Amazon pioneered the formation of communities of reader-customers who exchange comments about various books and authors. Amazon also adheres to what is perhaps the most important rule of Web site design: new content is being added at frequent intervals to give users a reason to return to the site often.

Technical Support

Tech support is another fruitful area to be considered for inclusion on your Web site. If your company sells technology-based products, customers will frequently have questions concerning installation and proper product functioning. A word processor document file or pdf file[11] describing the problem and solution in detail can handle many such questions. This Web site feature means that your company is open 24 hours a day, 7 days a week (24/7) to solve customer problems. This procedure can also save dollars by reducing the amount of time tech support representatives spend on simple questions, and allows your staff to focus their efforts on more complex problems.

Many companies maintain tech support capabilities on forums offered by some of the online services in addition to their own Web sites. These provide for the downloading (and sometimes uploading) of software, e-mail discussions by users, and a facility for asking questions of company tech support reps and receiving answers by e-mail.

Data Retrieval

There are many types of information that can be useful in growing your business. These include data concerning:

- Customers
- Competitors
- Industry trends
- Suppliers
- Economic conditions
- Financial results
- Forecasts

The Internet is a vast repository of such information. The challenge is in discovering how to find the data you want.

We have discussed how a Web presence offers opportunities for useful interactions with customers. Feedback from customers about products and the observation of what product information they are requesting provide useful data on customer preferences. Data on competitors is readily available by visiting their Web sites. Often, there is much to be learned about competitors' positioning of products and approach to marketing by thoughtful analysis of the content and structure of their Web sites.

There are many sources on the Internet for gathering traditional data on industry trends and economic conditions. Among the best places to look are the Web sites of academic libraries. For example, the Babson College Library Web site (http://fusion.babson.edu/html/library) contains lists of sources (both online and otherwise) for industry analyses, overviews, and forecasts, industry statistics, brokerage house reports, trade association data, and market research reports. Babson students, faculty, staff, alumni, and distance learners can access information both on and off campus at no charge. Visitors can access much of the information at on-site terminals for a small fee. The FedWorld Web site (http://www.fedworld.gov) is a central source of U.S. government data maintained by the Commerce Department and is a good place to find information supplied by the U.S. Small Business Administration. The Securities and Exchange Commission's (SEC) EDGAR database (http://www.sec.gov/edgar .shtml) is a good source for any filings that public companies are required to make with the SEC, including such items as annual and quarterly reports and initial public offerings. Additionally, you can check on the constantly changing environment for Initial Public Offerings (IPOs) by visiting Nasdaq's home page (http://www.nasdaq.com) or cnnfn's site (http://money.cnn.com). If you want to check on the progress of legislation, you can find the full text of pending bills at http://thomas.loc.gov (named for Thomas Jefferson, a champion of public education and dissemination of information). Many daily newspapers can be accessed online without charge. A large number of business newspapers and periodicals are also online, with some of their content being supplied gratis and some—particularly their archives—for a fee. For example, the *Wall Street Journal* online edition (http://www.wsj.com) features in-depth coverage of topics from the regular paper edition. The full online service requires a paid subscription, with a discount for current subscribers to the paper edition. The use of hyperlinks simplifies the location and retrieval of data from all of these sources.

Much data are available through the online services. Easy access to a variety of proprietary databases is one of the strengths of the online services, but in most cases you can connect directly through your Internet service provider. See, for example, the following data sources:

- Global Access databases (http://www.primark.com/ga/): Annual reports and SEC filings on more than 10,000 companies which must file with the SEC.
- Ebsco Host (http://ebscohost.com): Provides full-text of articles on business and management topics.
- Hoovers Online (http://hooversonline.com): Provides basic information on more than 14,000 public and private companies.
- ProQuest (http://www.proquest.com): Includes over 700 trade publications for trade and industry information on a wide variety of industries.
- Thomson Research (http://research.thomsonib.com): Provides access to research reports on public companies written by investment banking analysts.

Public Relations and Investor Relations

It is just a small jump from customer service and tech support activities to the realm of public and investor relations. CEOs often use the Web site home page as a vehicle for conveying the company culture and leadership position (or hoped-for leadership position) in an industry. Product literature and public statements on company vision can easily be read by securities analysts as well as the company's other constituencies. The Internet provides a very inexpensive way to distribute product announcements and collateral marketing materials, and its instantaneous availability is a plus for analysts and investors seeking the information.

Selling Products and Services

The potential for selling goods and services on the Web is one of its great fascinations for entrepreneurs. It was originally thought that Internet companies could level the business playing field by being on the Web; since the Web is a virtual world, the argument went, to paraphrase the movie *Field of Dreams*, "if you build it they will come." Unfortunately, in many instances that did not turn out to be the case. Exhibit 12.10 illustrates the concentration of Web advertising in just a few companies.

At its base, the decision involves whether your company wants to open its own Web site store-front (using an Internet Service Provider's server as a host or the company's own server), open a store on another company's Web site or virtual mall, or develop an affiliate arrangement with another Web site in which you pay a commission to those sites for customers "driven" to your site. Each strategy involves up-front costs. Having your own Web site involves both development and maintenance costs. Affiliate relationships involve less front-end and continuing maintenance expense, but you will incur some advertising expenses and also have to cede a certain amount of control to the company with which you are partnering. Your decision rests partly on whether you think that a stand-alone site will attract sufficient traffic or whether you will benefit from the spillover traffic from other Web sites. The decision depends very much on the characteristics of your affiliated Web site or on the design of the virtual mall by the developer. Ideally, you would want the demographic profile of virtual mall shoppers or the affiliated site to be very similar for as many of the sites as possible, thus encouraging virtual shoppers to follow the hyperlinks to your site.

An Example: The Internet Fashion Mall

Ben Narasin was the founder and CEO of the Boston Prepatory company, a manufacturer of high quality affordable men's sportswear. From his vantage point in the fashion industry, Narasin saw an opportunity to develop a virtual mall centered on the industry. Targeting both the mass market and the fashion trade, the Internet Fashion Mall (IFM) afforded visitors access to leading fashion houses, magazines, and stores. Within a year of its startup, the Internet Fashion Mall had demonstrated that it was very popular with its customers and potential customers. IFM is a classic example of a knowledgeable entrepreneur seizing an opportunity to apply new technology to a field with which he or she is already familiar. Like many other Internet companies, IFM was affected by the dot-com bubble. Ben changed the company's business model to adapt to the changing business environment and also took the company public. Unlike many dot-com ventures, IFM managed to keep hold of a large amount of cash while its stock price and those of most other Internet companies declined precipitously. At this juncture, IFM's story continues to be written.[12]

Factors to Consider in Designing Your Commercial Web Site

Because Web sites are an electronic and software creation, a potential customer is just a click and a split second away from leaving your site for another. Consequently, you should follow a few simple principles in implementing your Web site to make it more "sticky":

- Make sure your Web site is content-rich with content and products geared to pique the interest of your target customer(s).

- Make sure the content changes frequently so that your customers and potential customers will want to return to your site often.

- Design your hyperlinks to keep the customers at your site, particularly at the beginning of their visit. It does not make sense to fill your first Web page with hyperlinks to an area of their interest at some other site. They may never return.

- Be sure to encourage a means of interaction with your site visitors. You can accomplish this in the context of the products and services you offer. An example of this technique is Amazon.com's setting up a convenient means for their customers to comment on the books that they have purchased.

- Include an e-mail response mechanism so that you can obtain timely feedback from your customers.

- Install some form of tracking software, so that you will be able to determine which areas of your site hold the most interest for your customers and which areas might need improvement.

- Consider redesigning and updating the user interface periodically, in order to add novelty to your customers' experience.

Security and Payment Issues

During the early days of the popularization of the Web, many people were reluctant to send private payment data over the Internet (e.g., credit card and bank account numbers), and some still are. Part of this apprehension is based on the inherent openness of the Internet, deriving from its origins as a medium for the free exchange of information. Additionally, there have been numerous instances in which computer hackers have broken into systems, and the proliferation, and sometimes rapid, spread of computer viruses have gained much public attention. Fortunately, these issues are being dealt with in a number of ways by government and industry. However, despite claims to the contrary, someone skilled and determined enough to do so can defeat most security systems. The real question is what level of security is necessary to maintain the public's confidence in entering into transactions using the Internet, both from the standpoint of maintaining the privacy of personal information and financial integrity.

Consumers have in general overcome their initial reluctance to transact business over the Net. This has been accomplished by advances in technology and Internet merchants' attention to their sales procedures. One of the simpler methods of facilitating the ordering of products from Web sites is to have customers call an 800 number and give their payment information over the telephone. Companies also post their privacy policies prominently on their Web sites to make clear how customers' personal data will be protected. The use of

SSL (i.e., Secure Sockets Layer) technology in browsers has provided an added layer of transactions security. Additionally, some companies have developed alternative payment systems for facilitating Internet transactions.[13] The dramatic increase in consumer purchases over the Internet in recent years demonstrates that a large number of consumers have become comfortable with this mode of transacting business, just as consumers' early resistance to telesales transactions was eventually eliminated.[14]

Cutting Costs

Revenue-increasing activities are not the only way to use the Internet to enhance your business. Reducing the costs of providing essential support services will also improve the bottom line. As an example, consider FedEx's experience with package tracking.

As part of its operations strategy, FedEx installed a system of bar-coding packages and entering them into portable devices which would convey the information to its data-processing system. A customer could then call a support line to check on whether a package had been delivered and if not, what its estimated time of arrival was. In 1996, FedEx instituted a Web-based tracking system. Using a browser, a customer could go to FedEx's Web site (http://www.fedex.com), enter the tracking number, and observe the progress of the item through the various steps on the way to its ultimate destination. It has been estimated that FedEx initially saved more than $10 million a year through this system, since each tracking inquiry cost approximately $6 and the volume of inquiries exceeded 140,000 per month. The beauty of the system was that FedEx effectively transferred the majority of the cost of the transaction to the customer (who supplied the computer and browser software) while improving the quality of its customer service at a negligible incremental cost. And the savings dropped right to the bottom line.

Another development in the category of cost cutting and improving efficiency has been the growth of *intranets* and *extranets.* Intranets are internal networks which help to facilitate communication within your company, including the exchange of documents, schedules, customer information, and product data. Extranets are restricted Web sites for the coordination of the activities of your company and one or more other companies. Extranets are most often used to coordinate interactions with vendors and customers. Extranet Web sites are typically password protected and for purposes of security are maintained separately from your intranet. Extranets usually require a more substantial investment than intranets. Hence, the benefits of increased efficiency in interacting with suppliers, customers, and strategic partners must be weighed carefully against the cost of setting up and maintaining the extranet.

Obtaining Advice/Information

In addition to the data sources that we have explored in this chapter, the Internet offers a number of opportunities for entrepreneurs to obtain advice and practical know-how about management and general business issues. Through online forums, newsgroups, mailing lists, and dedicated Web sites, entrepreneurs have many resources available to them. The following list represents a sample of these resources:

- Babson's Arthur M. Blank Center for Entrepreneurship Web site (http://www2.babson.edu/babson/babsoneshipp.nsf/public/homepage). Babson College has long been a leader in entrepreneurship, and the Web site describes the various programs, courses, outreach activities, research, and teaching initiatives being undertaken at Babson. As mentioned previously, the Babson College Library Web site (http://fusion.babson.edu /html/library) is an outstanding source of materials helpful to entrepreneurs in starting and growing their businesses.

- The Ewing Marion Kauffman Foundation Web site (http://www.emkf.org) is a very useful Web address for entrepreneurs. In addition to the on-going programs described on its home page, the Kauffman Foundation's *Entre-World* Internet Web site has been designed to provide a wealth of useful information for both practicing and aspiring entrepreneurs (http://www .entreworld.org). Its search engine is an outstanding tool for locating a wealth of practical information for entrepreneurs.

- The U.S. Small Business Administration Web site (http://www.sba.gov) contains a great deal of information concerning SBA loans and other available programs, as well as general resource materials for small businesses.

- The Center for Entrepreneurial Leadership Clearinghouse on Entrepreneurship Education (www.celcee.edu) is a very useful online source for accessing diverse materials on the subject of entrepreneurship education, including syllabi, videos, books, government publications, journal articles, and software. This site is funded by the Ewing Marion Kauffman Foundation.

- The MIT Enterprise Forum (http://web.mit.edu/entforum/www/) and the MIT Entrepreneurs Club (http://web.mit.edu/e-club/WWW /e-club-home.html) are sites with a number of hyperlinks to information about starting new businesses, venture capital, and business plans.

- The Lowe Foundation Web site (http://www.lowe.org) has as its objective the providing of information, research, and educational experiences to help entrepreneurs to grow their businesses.

- Newsgroups and mailing lists are an additional source of entrepreneurship information. The Topica Web site (http://www.topica.com) contains a search engine through which you can locate both mailing lists and usenet newsgroups focused on entrepreneurship. Once having subscribed to a few mailing lists or having joined some newsgroups, those discourses will lead to further sources elsewhere on the Net. In addition, when you first set up newsgroups on your browser, you can join a few newsgroups for new users (e.g., news.announce.newusers and news.newusers.questions) that can point you in the direction of newsgroups of interest.

- Various forums and resource sites on the commercial online services (e.g., CompuServe and America Online) cater to entrepreneurs' interests. For example, on America Online, take a look at the area "Careers and Work: Startup Businesses."

- Additional Web sites of interest to entrepreneurs include:
  - Wall Street Journal Online Edition (subscription): http://www.wsj.com
  - Library of Congress: http://www.loc.gov
  - Ziff-Net (computer magazine, news, and software source): http://www.zdnet.com
  - Online bookstore: http://www.amazon.com
  - CNN: http://www.cnn.com
  - AT&T 800 Directory: http://www.tollfree.att.net/index.html
  - Telephone directory: http://www.switchboard.com
  - Real Networks (source of streaming video/audio): http://www.real.com
  - White House: http://www.whitehouse.gov
  - Postal rates: http://www.usps.gov/consumer/rates.htm
  - Land's End (mail order retailer): http://www.landsend.com
  - Travelocity.com (online travel agent): http://www.travelocity.com
  - CNET.com (technology and computer news): http://www.cnet.com

INTERNET-RELATED OPPORTUNITIES FOR THE CREATION OF NEW BUSINESSES

The rapid growth of the Internet has resulted in an environment where opportunities abound for entrepreneurs to create software and hardware products and goods and services to meet market needs.

Amazon.com is one of the most dramatic examples of the achievement of enormous success by an Internet software entrepreneur. Jeff Bezos, the founder, saw an opportunity to create a business around a product that he thought people would be willing to buy without inspecting it first, and also one that seemed relatively uncomplicated to work with. The company has had enormous success and, despite some trials and tribulations, has survived the excesses of the dot-com period. Amazon.com is also emblematic of another important Internet trend—the gradual merging of the business models of the "old-economy" bricks-and-mortar companies and the "new-economy" Internet firms. In the early days of the Web, it was often said that the old-economy companies "didn't get it" in terms of understanding the changed paradigms of the new Internet world. In fact, that was true in some cases. But what has actually transpired is far more interesting. It turned out that many of the new-economy companies didn't get it either, in terms of understanding the importance of cash flow, cost and operational control, and the need for revenues and profits. Companies like Barnes and Noble (Amazon's bricks-and-mortar competitor) have moved to integrate their operational strength and network of stores and warehouses with the advantages of the Internet. At the same time, companies like Amazon.com have realized the importance of operational considerations in the physical world as a critical success factor and have taken actions to remedy their shortcomings in those areas.

Eventually, e-commerce will become just "commerce" or business as usual. Both Internet and traditional firms are rapidly realizing that the new B2B and B2C models really represent the application of cutting edge tools to existing business processes in order to make them more efficient and effective. In the new millennium, no one brags about using the telephone or the automobile as essential business tools, but there was a time when the use of both of these innovations fundamentally changed the way business was transacted. The integration of the Internet into existing business practice will likely take a similar course.

The Internet continues to evolve rapidly. In this chapter, we focused attention on the Web using the terms *Web* and *Internet* almost interchangeably. But the Internet is far more than the Web. One of the next steps in using the Internet will be the proliferation of "smart" devices that communicate with each other without user intervention. Tiny devices will be embedded in clothing to communicate with your washer and dryer to make sure that the water and dryer temperature are appropriate. Companies' computers will communicate with each other much more effectively than at present in order to maintain appropriate inventories and production processes. In short, we have just seen the tip of the iceberg, and entrepreneurial opportunities will be plentiful and exciting.

A short list of some of the opportunities that exist in the Internet marketplace for entrepreneurs follows, but you will no doubt think of many more:

- There are numerous opportunities for software applications relating to the Internet, including the development of new plug-ins—programs that provide additional video and sound capabilities for your computer.
- The creation of tools for Internet software developers.
- The development and refinement of increasingly powerful, automated, and specialized search engines.
- The implementation of enhancements to compression technology.
- The creation of security products, both hardware and software, including the creation of advanced security and encryption techniques.
- The development of improved telephony capabilities for the Net.

Opportunities also exist in creating advances in the hardware necessary to provide Internet capabilities to companies and individuals. Advances in multimedia capabilities demand accompanying hardware improvements in the throughput of data. Areas where creative entrepreneurs can make significant contributions include:

- The development and refinement of high-speed communication devices between computers and also between computers and peripheral equipment.
- The improvement of battery life and operational capability.
- The development of ever smaller and more powerful computer chips, based on materials other than silicon.
- Advances in network technology.
- Improved cable technology.
- Improved satellite technology.

A third area of opportunity lies in providing services to Internet users. Among those services are:

- Providing technical and design services in developing effective distance learning systems.
- Creating and maintaining Web sites.
- Providing consulting services to help businesses utilize and integrate new technologies.
- Providing business process consulting services.

CONCLUSION

The Internet is truly changing the way people live, work, learn, and do business at a rapid and relentless pace. For creative entrepreneurs with limited resources, the Internet offers significant opportunities to build new businesses and enhance existing enterprises. New businesses will be developed to exploit technological advances by providing, among other capabilities, new services and innovative hardware and software solutions to enhance the Internet user's experience. Existing businesses will also benefit from a variety of Internet applications in the areas of customer service and support, sales and order processing automation, data retrieval, investor relations, purchasing, and the like. The dot-com bubble provided a painful but useful lesson for entrepreneurs, that is, that successful businesses must be built on sound business principles. It remains to be seen how Internet business models will evolve and which ones will ultimately succeed. But it is clear that many talented entrepreneurs already view the challenges posed by the Internet for what they are—opportunities to delight customers and create exciting entrepreneurial ventures.

13 MANAGING A GROWING BUSINESS

Donna Kelley and Ed Marram

Caught up in its phenomenal early success, the J. Peterman Company found itself with an organization ill equipped to handle its rapid growth. Lacking sufficient management structures, internal controls, and resources to manage its burgeoning operations, the company struggled with internal chaos while boundaries rose between work units and friction developed between the original employees and the new management team.

The company's vision, clear to the early hires, became obscured as the company grew. Its product line multiplied without clear strategic guidance, diminishing the consistent and unique message needed to compete in the increasingly crowded catalog market. John Peterman commented after the company's failure in 1999, "There comes a time in the life of a growing business when you, as its founder and top manager, realize the company has taken on a momentum of its own. You influence it, certainly, but more and more you are swept along by it."[1]

John Peterman's experience is not uncommon among entrepreneurs. In fact, as Chapter 1 states, the eight-year survival rate for incorporated startups is about 50%. This suggests that startups surviving their initial phase cannot rest on their laurels, but must continually face the critical challenge of creating organizations able to sustain themselves.

Every business today faces a globally competitive, frequently changing and complex environment. More and more we see shorter product lives, less stable and more diverse customer preferences, and rapid advances in knowledge. This provides continuous opportunities for new firms to start up and enjoy initial success, even in industries long dominated by well-established and well-resourced incumbents. Yet at the same time, it creates a short-term window for these small, growing companies to capture the value of their early advantage. Entrepreneurial firms must build organizations that can operate effectively in these dynamic environments. They must make decisions to ensure they can sustain themselves over the long term, while building the foundation for future new businesses.

Numerous challenges face the growing entrepreneurial business. The purpose of this chapter is to identify these challenges and help entrepreneurs understand key elements of managing and sustaining growth. The chapter is relevant to a range of businesses, from small to large enterprises, from those managed by founders or outside hires, and from those in rapidly growing versus more slowly growing industries or markets.

STAGES-OF-GROWTH MODELS

Stage models depict an entrepreneurial firm as passing through a sequence of stages, each with its own particular characteristics and challenges. The problems facing a company at an early stage of growth are not those it faces in later stages, and therefore the decisions and solutions will change. By knowing where the organization stands in the life cycle, an entrepreneur can tell which problems are normal and which require special attention. For example, while direct involvement in all activities is typical in the startup stage, the entrepreneur should not be so involved in later stages.

The focus of this chapter is on an entrepreneurial business' growth stages that fall just after the startup stages and before the mature stages, as illustrated by Exhibit 13.1.

During startup stages, the business opportunity is taking shape but significant sales have not yet been made. The founders are acquiring resources and organizing initial operations—and they do everything. These critical early tasks are covered in other chapters of this book. This chapter is concerned with how entrepreneurs operate once they've started and the companies have reached a point of initial success with their opportunity. The primary task beyond this startup stage is to create an organization capable of managing this growth.

At the other end, in the mature stage and beyond, the business must deal with conditions of a well-established organization. Systems and structures can become entrenched and the culture can impede efforts to grow further, leading

EXHIBIT 13.1 Growth stages of an entrepreneurial firm.

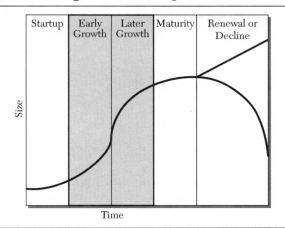

to decline. On the other hand, if the company is able to continually renew itself, or undertake transformation efforts when needed, it will continue to grow.

The primary task for entrepreneurial firms in their growth phase is to ensure the organization can sustain growth into this mature stage. To do so, it needs to create a professional organization that is both responsive to external change and entrepreneurial enough to continually create new businesses through innovative thinking.

Exhibit 13.2 introduces five stage models. It summarizes the main focus of each model and then identifies, first, the main challenges and characteristics of the early and later growth stages in the model, and then the key tasks the entrepreneur must undertake in managing the firm during these stages. This review provides a broad understanding of what entrepreneurs experience as they grow their companies, and what they must do to manage and sustain this growth. We incorporate this understanding into our discussion and prescriptions for managing growth in the entrepreneurial firm.

Managing and Sustaining Growth

Activities associated with managing growth involve building an organization that can handle its burgeoning growth. Key concerns are the organization's *people, controls,* and *financing.* Efforts aimed at ensuring sustained growth involve creating an organization that can plan for the future. This includes *delegating, professionalizing,* and *strategic planning.* These challenges should be addressed in the growth stages. To do so too early impedes the entrepreneurial flexibility and

EXHIBIT 13.2 Review of stage models of new firm growth.

	Focus of Model	Characteristics and Challenges of Early Growth Stages	Characteristics and Challenges of Later Growth Stages	Key Tasks for Managing during Growth Stages
Adizes	Characteristics and normal versus abnormal problems encountered during organization lifecycles. Analyzing organizations and treating problems at different stages.	Tendency to over commit, pursue many diverse opportunities. Sales orientation, but less attention to profitability. Inadequate structure, systems, and planning. Company outgrows founders' capabilities.	Company finds life apart from founders, establishes its own vision, and becomes more focused with priorities and goals. Emphasis on profits, not just sales. Systems and structure developed. Management training becomes necessary.	Delegate, transition to professional management, and decentralized structure. Develop effective processes, while maintaining balance between control and creativity. Develop and maintain strategy that focuses objectives, and leads to new momentum and long-run effectiveness, not just capitalizing on past momentum.
Churchill	Describes five management factors impacting each stage: managerial style, organizational structure, extent of formal systems, strategic goals, and owner's involvement.	Has at least average profits and sufficient cash flow. Owner increasingly spends less time doing and more time managing. Functional managers and first professional managers come on board. Basic systems and some planning (budgets). Strategy oriented toward maintaining status quo.	Generating cash and securing financing for growth. Ensuring cost control and profitability. Hiring higher quality managers for growth. Implementing systems and planning for future needs. Strategic planning shared with key managers and operational planning delegated. Decentralized, even divisionalized structure.	Get good people, planning, and systems in place before they are needed. Move toward increased delegation and professional management. Manage cash to grow.

(continued)

Sources: Adizes, Ichak. (1999). *Managing Corporate Lifecycles.* Prentice Hall Press: Paramus, NJ.

Churchill, Neil C. (1997). "The Six Key Phases of Company Growth." In S. Birley and D. Muzyka, *Mastering Enterprise.* Pitman Publishing: London.

Flamholtz, Eric G., and Randle, Yvonne. (2000). *Growing Pains: Transitioning from an Entrepreneurship to a Professionally Managed Firm.* Jossey-Bass: San Francisco.

Greiner, Larry E. (1998). *Evolution and Revolution as Organizations Grow.* Harvard Business Review, Reprint 98308.

Harper, Stephen C. (1995). *The McGraw-Hill Guide to Managing Growth in Your Emerging Business.* McGraw-Hill: New York.

EXHIBIT 13.2 Continued.

	Focus of Model	Characteristics and Challenges of Early Growth Stages	Characteristics and Challenges of Later Growth Stages	Key Tasks for Managing during Growth Stages
Flamholtz	Characteristics, problems, and challenges at major stages. Developmental emphasis at each stage. How to manage transition from one stage to the next.	Rapid expansion in sales and employees. Rapid growth creates resource constraints and overwhelms operational systems.	Transition to professional management. Goals, responsibilities, systems, and planning become more formalized.	Develop operational systems and acquire resources. Build professional organization while maintaining entrepreneurial orientation. Institute adequate planning and controls.
Greiner	Each period is characterized by the dominant management style used to achieve growth, and the dominant management problem that must be solved before growth can continue.	Move toward delegation. Functional organization structure introduced, jobs become more specialized. Systems and standards are introduced. Communication more formal as hierarchy grows.	Increased delegation with less direct communication with top levels: management by exception. Incentive systems to motivate employees. Difficulties of coordination and control as decentralization increases.	Be aware of stages and recognize when change is needed; solutions differ at different stages. Revolutions provide platform for change and new practices. Prepare management and structures that not only solve problems, but fit the next phase of growth.
Harper	Management characteristics and challenges. Evolution of management structure and how entrepreneur achieves it.	Generating cash flow and profits. Sales orientation with less attention on efficiency, quality, controls. Delegation may begin as span of control exceeds entrepreneur's time. Internally promoted managers often lack adequate skills. Problems with interdepartmental coordination and turf battles.	Size and complexity requires a higher level of managerial sophistication. Tension between professional management and entrepreneur, employees, customers. Competitive pressures require sharpening competitive offering. Evolves beyond one product/service. Proactive planning replaces reactive approach.	Delegate authority to supervisors, then invest in key professional management talent. Establish competitive uniqueness with offering and move beyond 'one-product' orientation. Develop proactive planning and ensure all functional areas are in sync. Develop strategic orientation to complement operating systems (requires fully-functioning board of directors).

energy needed to launch the business. Waiting too long creates an organization unable to function efficiently and effectively as the company grows, and one unable to plan effectively for the future.

As Exhibit 13.1 shows, we divide the growth phase into early and later growth. The early phase starts as the company's growth is starting to ramp up, then accelerates to a rapid rate. The later phase starts during accelerated growth, which starts to level off as the company becomes more established.

Meeting the challenges of both managing and sustaining growth requires considerable time and resources. During growth, however, time and resources are scarce commodities. While the entrepreneur should be thinking about how to best manage as well as sustain growth early on, the reality is these efforts will need to be prioritized. Given this, the bulk of the entrepreneur's early efforts should be directed toward managing growth. It is imperative to get people, controls, and financing into place early. It does no good to plan for the future if the organization fails because it can't handle its current operations.

During later growth, the company can focus more intently on looking ahead. With an organization capable of managing rapid growth, the entrepreneur can put in place mechanisms to ensure the company continues to grow. As the company works on sustaining growth, however, its efforts will need to work in concert with the management of growth, as Exhibit 13.3 illustrates. As the company professionalizes and engages in strategic planning, it will need to modify its operations and people, and therefore engages in a continual effort to create new forms of growth while ensuring its organization is capable of managing this effectively.

MANAGING GROWTH

To prepare the organization to most effectively manage accelerating growth, entrepreneurs should address three key elements: people, controls, and financing.

People

Two common people mistakes an entrepreneurial firm makes are preparing its people inadequately and maintaining the wrong people as the organization grows. Early in the business' life, organization members do their jobs and pitch in wherever needed. It is more important for the lean team to maintain the flexibility and broad skills needed to accomplish a lot with a little. This early in the game, it is not yet apparent these employees lack the skills needed to scale up the organization. It is difficult to think about training to develop future skills when growth is consuming everyone's time.

EXHIBIT 13.3 The process of managing and sustaining growth in entrepreneurial organizations.

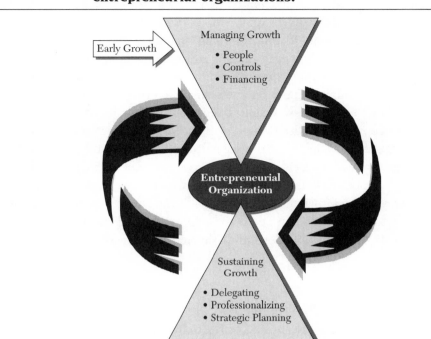

As the need for specialists and managers arises, some employees may be able to rise to the challenges presented and assume these new functions and responsibilities. The process of adapting to these new roles takes time, however. And as the company's growth accelerates, time is a precious commodity. To succeed, the company often needs to hire from the outside.

Most entrepreneurs have a sense of loyalty to these early hires. Indeed, they may have worked side by side with these employees many long hours. They may have continually asked them to assume more responsibilities. They may recognize the dedication and sacrifice they made to get the business to where it is. But there comes a time when the task expected of these employees exceeds their abilities. And when this happens, entrepreneurs need to make tough decisions. They have to recognize a responsibility to the stakeholders of the company that is greater than any one employee's needs. These stakeholders include investors, lenders, customers, suppliers, and others.

Loyalty to early employees versus the commitment to give the company what it needs to grow and succeed can be in conflict. This conflict is usually accompanied by increasing distance between the entrepreneur and many of the employees. This distance increases as the organization adds new employees, diminishing the cohesiveness and motivation around the goals that made the company a success initially. The organization will have to deal with reduced motivation from setbacks or crises at the same time its employees struggle with adapting to employees and higher level managers coming from the outside, both of which lack the shared experiences gained through the organization's history.

The growing company needs to develop a culture that motivates and guides employees through these changes and continues to motivate and guide them as the entrepreneur's initial vision is replaced by an organizational vision. Stonyfield Farms, for example, instituted a culture based on sharing information openly, enhancing communication through regular meetings, and allowing teams to pursue employee-based initiatives. They motivated employees through profit sharing and stock ownership, and through internal training and promotion. As the organization grows it needs to be in touch with the appropriate internal culture for its people and determine the actions necessary for reinforcing this culture.

Controls

When operations first start, the company typically has informal systems for internal activities such as collecting payments, paying bills, and tracking inventory. In early growth, the company struggles with accelerating cash demands as increased sales require more cash to support the operating cash cycle that extends from the time payment must be made for inventory to the time cash is received from sale of product.

Effective control systems include the following actions:

- Institute and continually assess accounts receivable and collection policies.
- Develop an inventory system that minimizes the risk of both stock outs and overstocks.
- Establish a payables policy that balances desire to pay as late as possible with the need to maintain relationships with vendors through on-time payments.
- Determine effectiveness of expenditures.
- Use metrics to track trends in receivables, inventory, payables, and financial performance.

A growing organization's policies and the accompanying controls have a large impact on its cash position. An accounts receivable policy has to weigh the desire for cash as soon as possible with the need to maximize revenue by offering attractive payment terms. A typical way of obtaining early payments from customers is to offer them discounts for paying early. But the most important impact on accounts receivable involves something often lacking in the entrepreneurial firm: constant attention to a collections policy that both ensures on-time payment and reduces losses due to uncollectible accounts. An accounts receivable policy should include dates for:

- When communication is made relative to account balances or payment reminders
- When/how contact is made for past due accounts
- When/how collection efforts are undertaken

Inventory controls need to balance both the threat of stock outs and the threat of overstocks. Stock outs can mean lost sales. Overstocks not only tie up cash until the items are sold, but carry the risk of total loss due to obsolescence, theft, damage, or spoilage.

Accounts payable policies should allow for payment as late as possible, while managing payables in a way that maintains good relationships with vendors. Vendors may have required more strict payment terms when the firm was just starting. As the company grows, it may be able to negotiate for more favorable payment terms.

To detect inefficiencies or a need for policy changes in the company's cash management practices, the company can identify a set of metrics that can track and reveal trends in receivables, inventory, and payables: the number of days it takes on average, for example, to collect receivables, turn over inventory, and make bill payments.

Managing costs requires both making decisions on expenditures and instituting controls that monitor spending. A growing firm's selling and administrative costs often expand rapidly with its escalation in sales. This is often justified because marketing is needed to generate sales, and administrative overhead is needed to support the burgeoning organization. Yet these areas need to be monitored to determine effectiveness and detect overspending. For example, certain advertising approaches may be more effective than others, or they may work in one region, but not another.

As the company begins to sell more and more products into multiple markets, it is useful to analyze performance in different product or market segments, along with an examination of the effectiveness of expenditures. Entrepreneurs need to understand what each product costs and whether a profit is truly being made. All the costs going into each product are those that would disappear if the product were discontinued. The remaining overhead costs need to be covered with the margins generated by the company's product mix.

Along with metrics for controlling cash, companies can develop performance metrics to aid in decisions about investments and expenditures. Performance measurements in an early stage company are designed less for evaluation of actual outcomes against a plan, as they would be in a more stable established organization, and more for entrepreneurial decision making. As the company's operations expand, managers can develop metrics to help them answer the following questions:

- Which products or markets generate the highest revenues and margins?
- Which customers or customer groups are reliable accounts (make timely payments, are at low risk of default)?
- How effective are our expenditures in areas such as marketing and sales, and does this differ across markets?

How does a company determine what's good or bad when examining key metrics? For some financial ratios, published sources can provide industry averages for comparison. Entrepreneurial firms, however, often adopt policies differing from more stable established firms, such as the need to spend on marketing while building brand awareness. It may be more useful to look at trends in metrics over time: For example, an increase in collection period for receivables could indicate a relaxing of collections policy, or a decrease in inventory turns could indicate increasing risk of stock outs. Shifts in metrics may reflect prior policy changes, but other than that, significant changes should be accompanied by a search for causes and an examination of the need for adjustment in policy.

One way that entrepreneurial firms track controls and performance is through an informal set of "hot buttons" to help them understand where their business is and where they need to devote their time and attention. Here are some examples of entrepreneurial hot button metrics at work:

- One very successful consulting firm measured performance through its B Report (Exhibit 13.4). They had an Excel spreadsheet with every consultant's name in the rows, and columns representing every week of the year.

EXHIBIT 13.4 Example of the B-report.

Consultants	1	2	3	4	5	6	7	8	9	10	11	12	13	14	.	.	.	.	52
John Doe	B	B	B	B	B	B	B												
Donna Kelley	B	B	B																
Ed Marram	B	B	B	B	B	B	B	B	B	B	B								

If consultants expected to bill in a given week, they put a B in the column. If they did not, they left it blank. If the entrepreneur did not see a lot of Bs, he knew he had a problem.

- Another company developed the "Red-Line/Green-Line" approach. Every time they spent money, they would add to the Red Line. Every time they received money, they would add to the Green Line. Whenever the Red Line was longer than the Green Line, they knew they had to examine the cause.

- Another consulting company had a "Client Unbilled" category on their time sheet where consultants could enter time spent at the client site that was not billed for. If they saw a high amount of unbilled time for a particular client, they knew they had a service quality issue.

Over time, as the business matures and has more resources, it will develop and benchmark itself against a formal plan. In the early stages of a business, however, the entrepreneur can develop the business' own set of hot buttons that helps it figure out where it needs to be to help the business succeed.

Financing

Experienced entrepreneurs understand that *Cash is King*. Growing companies need cash, not only to handle current growth, but to prepare for future growth. By improving its cash flow, the growing company can better avoid a crisis of being out of cash and at the mercy of reluctant or expensive lenders or investors. The company may even be able to self-finance some of its future growth, reducing reliance on more expensive sources of funding.

Entrepreneurs can increase the amount of growth they can finance internally by reducing the operating cash cycle or increasing margins. To reduce the operating cash cycle entrepreneurs adopt a "collect early, pay late" focus. As mentioned in Chapter 7, a few examples of how this can be achieved include:

- Obtain at least partial prepayment from customers.
- Provide discounts to customers for early payment.
- Maintain a stringent collections policy.
- Sell or factor receivables.
- Negotiate better payment terms with suppliers.

As the company grows and its products and services expand, entrepreneurs should increasingly look for opportunities to value price—determine what a customer will pay for a product—rather than set a price based on covering costs and an allowance for profit. Growing companies should always seek ways to increase margins, even when cash flow is healthy. It enables the organization to preempt problems associated with inefficient operations. Efforts to internally finance growth therefore go hand in hand with controls.

Once controls are in place, however, generating financing internally is not just a matter of effective controls, but finding creative ways to generate cash. One computer hardware company, for example, found it cheaper to have suppliers perform some subassembly work, than to do this internally. Entrepreneurs should constantly ask themselves questions such as: What does my product cost and how can this be reduced? How can overhead be minimized?

Another way to conserve cash is to reduce inventory levels and minimum cash balances—taking care not to run out of cash or inventory, as the previous section suggested. If cash fluctuates, it can be put into short-term interest generating investments or a line of credit can cover temporary cash shortfalls. There is also the lease, not buy, option that many entrepreneurs take advantage of. But if prior fixed asset purchases have been made, there may be opportunities to sell or lease out underutilized assets.

Conserving cash should optimally be done before there is a cash crisis and with an eye to the potential impacts on the future of the business. Will reducing head count in engineering constrain the company's ability to generate new products and get them to market quickly? Will reducing inventory levels create stock outages and dissatisfied customers? Proactive cash management is not always possible but avoids reactiveness that can lead to unfavorable outcomes.

Shortening operating cash cycles and increasing margins are vital efforts for conserving cash. They essentially represent costless financing. The rapidly growing organization, however, will likely need to tap additional sources to finance its growth. Not only will financing be needed to support accelerating sales, but new policies, such as granting customer payment terms or taking on bulk orders, as well as investments in new products or services, will create a drain on cash.

Despite its success and future prospects, however, a company in its growth cycle may have only certain options available. For example, early in a company's growth, a bank would not typically extend credit. But a computer manufacturer who is motivated to sell computer equipment might. After a company has been established for a year, if its typical customer is a well-established company, a bank might be willing to loan monies against a portion of the receivables provided the founders have good credit and will co-sign the receivables line personally.

Thinking in terms of stages can be useful when considering financing during growth. Sources closed to the firm earlier in its life may open up later. It is therefore worthwhile to undertake periodic surveys of what the firm currently has for financing and changes that have occurred that may open up new and cheaper financing sources. In this respect, the firm may recognize new opportunities for refinancing at lower rates.

Sources of financing for growing organizations include:

- Investment from key management
- Founder loans
- Family and friends
- Angel investors
- Loans on assets, such as receivables, inventory, or equipment
- Equipment leases
- Credit cards

As the company undertakes expansion efforts, such as selling internationally or launching new products or services, financing needs to come from sources more appropriate for higher risk and longer term investment. Banks will typically not loan substantial funds, unsecured, for riskier expansion efforts that won't generate returns for quite some time. The firm will likely need to rely on equity sources.

But there are other ways to finance future growth. A company can look to strategic partners who, in return for nonfinancial benefits, are more likely to provide favorable financing terms. The company may also decide to expand by franchising. The risks of these financing modes must be taken into consideration. For example, potential customers that also compete with a strategic partner may view a relationship with the firm as too risky because the partner has some control over the firm or has greater access to information that could impact the customer.

SUSTAINING GROWTH

To sustain growth, the company needs to address three key issues: delegation, professionalizing the organization, and strategic planning

Delegation

As John Peterman states, "It's tough to balance your own instincts as a founder and top manager with the desire to let the people you've hired do their thing. Managing managers wasn't something I set out to do; it was a job requirement that was incorporated by default into my position because my original idea for a business was a good one."[2]

When an organization is founded, the entrepreneur is directly involved in most tasks of the business. But as the organization grows, the entrepreneur must shift from doing to managing, and increasingly leave more and more responsibilities to others.

The following symptoms reveal the need to delegate:

- The volume of decisions multiplies. The entrepreneur is working hard, but accomplishing less.

- Decisions become harder to make: more complex and specialized. The entrepreneur increasingly wonders whether he or she has made the right decision.

- Everyone is still pitching in and doing everything, but more and more, something critical slips by, or mistakes are made.

- If the entrepreneur is not directly involved in the task, no progress seems to be made.

Faced with these challenges, the entrepreneur may revert back to what he or she does best and ignore tasks they don't feel comfortable or capable dealing with. A technical entrepreneur may retreat to developing new products, while ignoring the company's inability to pay bills on time. What's so bad is not the entrepreneur doing what he does best—it's having no one pay attention to the company's most critical problems.

Employees may not have a problem with the lack of delegation because they feel comfortable going to the entrepreneur for everything and then carrying out orders. Because the entrepreneur makes decisions, they don't need to take responsibility for outcomes. By allowing employees to take responsibilities for decisions, the entrepreneur needs to allow them to make mistakes and learn from their mistakes—circumstances neither the employees nor the entrepreneur may feel comfortable with.

Delegation, while necessary for surviving the entrepreneurial growth phase, is typically difficult for the entrepreneur to accomplish. He may continue to attempt to do everything himself while he becomes frustrated when he is unable to do so. The entrepreneur cannot continue to be the "go-to" guy when the volume of decisions mushrooms and he becomes increasingly less qualified to provide direction in many areas.

The typical path to delegation is shown in Exhibit 13.5. As this figure shows, the entrepreneur starts by assigning specific tasks to others. As delegation proceeds, the entrepreneur passes responsibility for achieving objectives to specialists, then managers, without needing to understand or know about the underlying mechanics. Then, the setting of objectives moves to others: experienced managers and teams close to the activity. This process enables the

EXHIBIT 13.5 Hierarchy of delegation in an entrepreneurial firm.

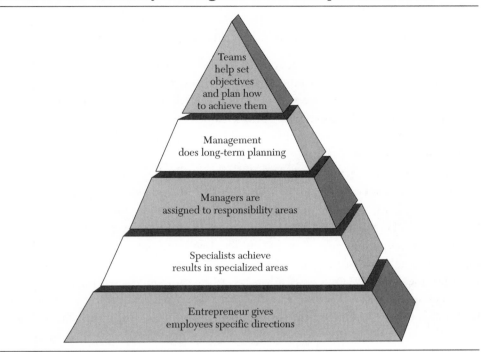

entrepreneur to spend less time on the day-to-day details of everything and focus on what he does best, while at the same time having decisions made by those most qualified to make them.

To start the delegation process, the entrepreneur can do the following:

- Identify the organization's major activities and the skills required to perform them.
- Assess the skills of organization members and identify gaps to be filled through internal development or external hiring.
- Assign groups of employees and managers to activity areas.
- Determine objectives and performance goals for these activities, increasingly leaving their achievement to those with the experience and closeness to that activity.
- Periodically review progress. Reset objectives and goals as needed, with input from managers.

Professionalizing the Organization

Delegation does not happen on its own; it needs to be accompanied by a conscious organization-building effort. The entrepreneur should take the following steps:

- Assemble an effective leadership team.
- Create a network of outsiders playing advisory roles.
- Structure the organization to allow thinking in terms of activity areas.

The leadership team must be balanced in all the critical areas important to advancing the firm toward continued growth. While a startup's goals reflect those of its founder, these will change to reflect the evolving goals of the owner/manager. Yet as the organization grows and assumes an identity of its own, its goals and the founder's goals often diverge. On top of that, goals may also diverge among the many founders.

As a company grows, it is the entrepreneur who must change the most. What made him successful at one stage is not what will make him successful in a later stage. This is perhaps the most difficult thing for an entrepreneur to come to grips with. He must examine his own goals and abilities with the requirements needed to lead the organizations to the next level. He must be willing to, if necessary, either leave the organization or take a position where he can focus on what he does best.

The leadership team needs to work in concert with a qualified board of directors. The composition of the board changes as it emerges from start up. Initially the board may be informal, occupied by those likely to lack high-level experience, but able to be supportive to the entrepreneur in his early endeavors. In early growth, boards typically evolve to include those able to provide operational guidance, for example, retired bankers, investors, and lawyers.

As the company professionalizes, the board should be more useful for strategic purposes, with members having a broader and visionary view of the market and industry, for example, other CEOs, industry experts, and senior executives in related businesses. While many investors require representation on the board of directors, it is advisable to avoid stakeholders who can control the firm for their benefit through board positions, such as: suppliers, customers, and the company's lenders.

The skill and experience of the company's leadership and board of directors can be supplemented with the skill and experience of advisory boards and consultants. For example, to examine industry technological trends, the company may assemble a group of technology experts from universities, government labs, and corporations. In addition, the company may bring in a marketing consulting firm to determine tactics for expanding into overseas markets.

As the company builds its leadership capabilities and its effectiveness through delegation, it needs to accompany these actions with an appropriate organizational structure. This effort entails segmenting the organization in a manner that allows groups to focus attention on critical tasks and report results to the entrepreneur/leadership team. In addition, information by segment can be used to assess performance and help decision making.

An organization will naturally divide into functions, such as:

- Research and development
- Administration
- Sales and marketing
- Operations

The organization can also segment based on other factors, such as:

- Geographic regions
- Product lines
- Customer groups

Entrepreneurial organizations adding a layer of middle management may feel they're becoming bureaucratic, that they're moving away from the notion that decentralization is the key to remaining entrepreneurial. Yet, by separating into divisions, each division can act as a smaller, entrepreneurial unit.

At the same time, the firm needs to be careful that organization-wide communication and responsiveness isn't stymied. Structuring the organization must always be done with an eye toward maintaining balance with the entrepreneurial side. The organization's culture, as previously discussed, can be designed and reinforced in a manner that communicates vision, allows for risk taking and failure, encourages members to interact and share ideas, and motivates employees to do their best.

Strategic Planning

In the beginning stages, planning is informal in the entrepreneurial firm—everyone knows why the company was started, and its purpose is largely self-evident. Strategy is dynamic and responsive to new knowledge but is basically informal and owner/manager driven. The company's strategy may not be clearly articulated during startup, but may be evident in the pattern of decisions made by the entrepreneur over time. Mintzberg and Waters described a startup's initial strategy as "justifying, elaborating, and making public a strategy it already had, the one based on the leader's vision."[3]

There comes a point in the company's growth phase, however, where strategic planning needs to be formalized. The company needs to think of itself as a business, not a product. Unfortunately, many companies "approach growth management with no strategy other than to do what they did when they were new."[4] Yet customer needs will evolve; markets will shift; and competitors, existing and new, will introduce new products and services. The growing business will need to rethink, over and over, how it can compete in a changed environment.

An unfavorable consequence of a lack of long-term planning is an eventual slowing of growth. This is often blamed on ineffective sales. But without new products or new strategies, revenues from existing solutions are bound to level off. There may be two dimensions of a startup's success: a gap in the market and a product that fills that gap. The startup may very well enjoy initial success because a market needs something in which there are few competing substitutes. Whether the product is initially less than adequate, or can easily be improved on, it will later become apparent it's not enough to simply fill a gap. Competition will inevitably come in with a product that meets these needs better.

Osborne (1994) compared 20 privately held firms experiencing initial success followed by stalled growth with 6 that were able to sustain growth beyond the entrepreneurial phase. Factors such as inadequate resources, poor managerial capabilities of the entrepreneur, and bureaucracy were minor factors in the growth stall. The main factor was the inability to perceive and respond to changing opportunities and conditions in their environment.[5]

Exhibit 13.6 shows the process of strategic planning and opportunity capture in the growing organization. The organization's strategy is depicted as emerging from knowledge of both conditions and changes in the external environment and awareness of internal capabilities. This strategy can therefore outline areas where the company has the capabilities to pursue opportunities that will create advantage in the external environment. Intuit, for example, followed its initial success with Quicken personal finance software by creating

EXHIBIT 13.6 Strategic planning and opportunities capture in the growing organization.

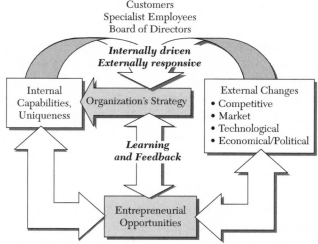

new products for their existing customers, such as Quicken Deluxe, by introducing its existing products into foreign markets, and by creating new products for new markets, such as Quick Books for small businesses. These all leveraged Intuit's strategy for providing easy-to-use, affordable, customer-driven solutions for personal and business finance.

Although strategy may be consciously formulated, it may not evolve as intended. Strategic planning therefore needs to allow for learning and feedback and the interplay between internal capabilities and the firm's dynamic environment, likely resulting in a modification of original intentions.[6] It needs to be both internally driven and externally responsive.

The growing company also needs to be responsive to impending environmental shifts, maintaining the ability to transform its strategy in a way that establishes a new source of uniqueness in a changed environment. Crunch Fitness enjoyed tremendous success as a startup in the competitive aerobics studio market in New York City by offering innovative aerobics classes, creating a unique brand image, and employing creative marketing techniques. While other aerobic studios fell victim to the decline of the aerobics craze and the emergence of multiactivity health clubs, Crunch shifted its strategy by transforming to a full-service facility while maintaining the uniqueness it was founded on.

As the company grows, its strategic planning efforts benefit from the input of others inside and outside the company with critical knowledge that can influence the company's direction. Customers have information about market needs, and specialist employees are close to important information, such as with markets and technologies. The firm can institute a function that gathers and monitors external information, examining the trends and opportunities in the outside environment. Carefully selecting members of the board of directors—including experts from outside the firm—and making them key participants in the strategic planning process can provide alternative perspectives. What's important for both internal and external modes is the firm takes a proactive, rather than reactive, approach to seeking ways to extend and build value.

The strategic planning process is not just about planning; it's also about effective implementation. Entrepreneurs need to address the following to ensure planning can be put into action:

- Strategic objectives are set and communicated throughout the organization.
- Management is capable of implementing and overseeing the effective execution of strategy.
- Each functional area or unit is aligned with the objectives, and performance measures are developed to help decision making.

- Leaders and managers are flexible enough to change plans based on feedback, to allow for experimentation with new opportunities, and to use information to modify strategy.

All too often, entrepreneurial firms pursue strategies where the various functions impacting the strategy are out of alignment. One software company, for example, financed its operations using only internally generated cash, and they employed only a few people. They successfully developed a high quality product and introduced it at an entry-level price to the mass market. The demand for the product was overwhelming, as one would hope, but their financial strategy prohibited the company from fulfilling most of the orders, and they were unable to hire and train employees fast enough. Eventually, they were forced to sell the entire product with its intellectual capital, at a significantly low valuation.

INTEGRATING AND BALANCING THE MANAGING AND SUSTAINING OF GROWTH

Exhibit 13.3 shows managing and sustaining growth as interactive, yet parallel processes. As the company puts in place the mechanisms necessary for sustaining growth, it needs to revisit the actions it took to manage growth. It needs to ensure its efforts to grow are consistent with its mechanisms for managing this growth.

For example, strategies focusing on geographic expansion versus new product development may have different implications for R&D and marketing expenditures. As it considers its growth options, the company will need to reevaluate its people and control systems, as well as its financing strategy.

There may be times when a slowing in the pursuit of new growth is called for to give the company room to improve its ability to manage growth. Joel Kolen, president of Empress International Ltd., a seafood distributor emphasizes that "By taking a break from growth and putting in controls such as those at a large company, an entrepreneur can ease the growth transition and ensure that the qualities that helped build the company don't get lost in the rush to fill new orders."[7]

CONCLUSION

Starting a business is a risky endeavor, but staying in business can be just as challenging. As the entrepreneurial firm grows beyond founding, it needs to ensure its organization is capable of managing growth. In addition, it needs to prepare for long-term survival and growth.

We reviewed three key tasks associated with managing growth—people, controls, and financing—and three key tasks associated with sustaining growth—delegating, professionalizing, and strategic planning. While these are by no means exhaustive, they represent critical areas where otherwise busy entrepreneurs should direct their attention. To manage and sustain a growing organization, entrepreneurs need to understand the challenges they face during these stages, build an effective plan for meeting these challenges, and revisit this exercise as circumstances change.

These efforts, however, must not distance the company from its entrepreneurial roots. Growing companies struggle with, not only having fewer resources than big companies, but with creating an organization that can become a bureaucracy that inhibits entrepreneurship. They must continually work on being entrepreneurial at a time when this is their biggest challenge. They have to consciously work on preserving and maintaining their entrepreneurial spirit; and if lost, they have to rejuvenate the company and rekindle entrepreneurship before it's too late.

14 HARVESTING YOUR VENTURE: A TIME FOR CAPTURING VALUE

William Petty

SO WE CREATED VALUE—WHAT DO WE DO NOW?

Harvesting: A Tale of Two Entrepreneurs

Bill Waugh started his business with a single restaurant establishment in Texas, largely with borrowed money. After 15 years, the business consisted of 84 restaurants throughout the Southwest, under the umbrella of the Casa Bonita Corporation. The firm's annual revenues eventually exceeded $50 million.

On several occasions, Waugh had been approached by prospective buyers. He was always willing to listen, but he had no desire to sell, at least not until Unigate, Ltd. offered $32 million for his firm, allowing him to stay on as president for five more years. After some thought, Waugh decided to sell the firm. The date was set for the closing in London at the Unigate headquarters. Waugh attended the closing, signed the papers, and received the money for the sale. But on the return trip to the United States, Waugh began having second thoughts about selling the business. By the time he arrived in New York, he was convinced that he had made a big mistake. Instead of continuing the trip home to Texas, he stayed in New York for the night and returned to London the next day to attempt to repurchase the company. He offered Unigate $1 million to cancel the contract, but to no avail. He returned to Texas sorely disappointed. In his eyes, he had lost his "base." To make matters even worse, he soon discovered he had significant philosophical differences with the Unigate management in terms of how to run the business.

Ed Bonneau, founded the Bonneau Company, a successful sunglass firm, with $1,000. From that meager beginning, he grew the company to a sales level of $50 million. On one occasion, he had the opportunity to sell the company for $28 million, but he declined the offer. It was some six years or so later that he again had the opportunity to sell the firm. By then the industry was experiencing fierce competition and consolidation; consequently, the firm value had decreased. Realizing that he probably could not do with the firm what was needed in the new environment, he decided to sell for $21 million.

What may we conclude from these two case studies? For one thing, harvesting the value created in a company may prove to be difficult, and even disappointing, compared to expectations. Certainly understanding the important issues is absolutely essential to the eventual success of the entrepreneurial journey.

Harvesting can be thought of as the third and final phase in the wealth creation process: building, growing, and harvesting. Harvesting is the process entrepreneurs and investors use to exit a business and liquidate their investment in a firm. While all three phases are important pieces of the entrepreneurial process, building and growing have received far more attention than harvesting—despite the fact that many entrepreneurs who fail to execute a successful harvest never realize the full benefits of their labors.

During the 1990s, a large host of entrepreneurs exited businesses, many of which were founded in the 1950s and 1960s. In fact, a national survey estimated that 48% of family owned businesses will have changed hands by 2003.[1]

From a purely financial perspective, harvesting is capturing or unlocking value, reducing risk, and creating exit options. However, to the entrepreneur, harvesting is about more than money; it involves personal and nonfinancial considerations as well. As a consequence, even upon realizing an acceptable monetary value for the firm, an entrepreneur who is not prepared for the lifestyle transition that accompanies the harvest may come away disappointed with the overall outcome of the harvest. Thus, crafting a harvest strategy is as essential to the entrepreneur's personal success as it is to his or her financial success. The message to the entrepreneur is this—the time to develop an effective harvest strategy is now, not later.[2]

As a firm moves toward the harvest, two questions regarding value are of primary importance: First, are the current owners/managers creating value? You can harvest only what you have created. Value is created when a firm's return on invested capital is greater than the investors' opportunity cost of funds, which relates both to the firm's operating profit margins and its efficient use of total capital invested. Second, could a new set of owners create more value than the current owners? If so, then the firm would have greater value in the hands of new owners. Growing a venture to the point of diminishing returns and then selling it to others who can carry it to the next level is a proven way to create value. How this incremental value will be shared between the old and the new owners depends largely on the relative strengths of each party in the negotiations—that is, who wants the deal the most or who has the most leverage.

In this chapter, we look at the harvest options available to owners and investors in privately held companies. We then describe the two primary methods for valuing a firm at the time of the harvest. Finally, we summarize lessons learned about creating an effective harvest strategy, as expressed by a group of entrepreneurs and investors who have been involved in harvesting a business.

HARVESTING OPTIONS: HOW DO WE CAPTURE THE VALUE CREATED?

There are three commonly used ways to harvest an investment: (1) selling the firm, (2) releasing the firm's free cash flows to its owners, or (3) offering stock to the public through an initial public offering (IPO) or a private placement of the stock.

Option 1: Selling the Firm—The Road Most Traveled

Unquestionably, selling the firm is far and away the most common approach for entrepreneurs and investors to execute the harvest. The financial issues arising from the sale of a firm—like any harvest strategy—involve questions of how to value the firm as well as how to structure the deal. Previous research, however, has shown that financial considerations are not the only important issues and may not even be the most important ones. Petty, Bygrave, and Shulman (1994) interviewed a sample of owners of privately held companies (valued between $5 million and $100 million) that were sold between 1984 and 1990, and made the following observations:

- The most common reason for selling a company related to estate planning and the opportunity to diversify the owner's investments.
- Entrepreneurs were frequently disappointed after selling their firms. They subsequently came to realize that the firm served as the base for much of what they did, both in and out of the business arena. Their disillusionment with the results of the sale was particularly evident when they continued managing the company under the supervision of the acquiring owners. Then the differences in corporate culture frequently became a significant problem for both parties involved in the transaction—but usually more so for the selling entrepreneur.

- The harvest did provide the long-sought-after liquidity, but some entrepreneurs found managing money more difficult, and less enjoyable, than they had expected—and less rewarding than operating their own company.

- A number of the selling owners were disappointed in the advice they received from so-called experts. After the fact, they wished they had talked to other entrepreneurs who had experience in selling a company.

- Most entrepreneurs relied on their staff and advisors to determine a fair price for their company. However, many of the entrepreneurs felt they had a sense of what they would accept for the firm, and that instinct probably had a greater influence than did the supporting computations. Furthermore, while price was an important issue, it was *seldom* a primary point of contention.

- There is considerable downside risk if the acquisition is not consummated. During the negotiations, management shifts its focus from operating the company to completing the sale. Members of the existing management team may be promised that after the acquisition they will receive promotions—which do not occur if the negotiations fail. Hence, if the sale falls through, it may take several months to regain the firm's focus and momentum. Furthermore, the upheaval brought about by the attempted sale may result in the loss of important members of the management team.

When selling a firm, an entrepreneur, for all practical purposes, has three options: a strategic sale, a financial sale, or a sale to employees. The strategic buyer is interested in synergies, the financial buyer is interested in existing business cash flows, and the employee buyer is interested in preserving employment. We will consider each in turn.

Strategic Sale

From the seller's perspective, the key point in a strategic acquisition is that the value strategic buyers place on the business depends on the synergies that the buyers think they can create. Since the value of the business to the buyers derives from both its stand-alone characteristics and its synergies, strategic buyers often pay a higher price than purely financial buyers, who value the business only as a stand-alone entity. For strategic acquisitions, we need to look for strategic fit between the company to be harvested and potential buyers. If the potential buyer is a current rival, and if the potential acquisition possesses long-term, sustainable competitive advantages over the potential buyer (such as lower cost of production or superior product quality), the buyer may be willing to pay a premium for the acquisition.

Financial Sale

Financial buyers, unlike strategic buyers, look primarily to a firm's stand-alone cash-generating potential as the source of value. Often the source of value that the financial buyer hopes to tap relates to stimulating future sales growth, reducing costs, or both. This fact has an important implication for the owner of the firm being purchased. The buyer often will make changes in the firm's operations that translate into higher pressures on the firm's personnel and may result in decisions that the original owner was unwilling or unable to make, which frequently levies a high cost on the firm's employees.

During the 1980s, leveraged buyouts (LBOs) became synonymous with financial acquisitions—and they were often the so-called *bust-up LBOs* that entail very high levels of debt financing to be paid down rapidly as the new owners sell off the acquired firm's assets. In the 1990s, however, the bust-up LBO was replaced by the *build-up LBO*. As the name suggests, the build-up LBO involves constructing a larger enterprise that is then taken public via an IPO. During the 1990s, private equity capital investors successfully refined the build-up LBO and tapped the public capital markets at unprecedented levels. This practice begins with acquiring a platform company (which may have been a publicly traded corporation or division of a larger firm). Next, the platform company acquires a number of smaller companies that in some way complement it. These subsequent acquisitions may expand capacity into related or new businesses. The newly formed combination is operated privately for five to seven years to establish a track record of success and then is taken public. While popular in the 1990s, more recently, build-up LBOs have declined in popularity, in large part due to the demise of the IPO markets.

LBOs may at times include the firm's top management as significant shareholders in the acquired firm—referred to as a *management buyout* (MBO). There is evidence that MBOs can contribute significantly to a firm's operating performance by increasing management's focus and intensity, and that they offer long-term benefits.[3]

An MBO is a potentially viable means for transferring firm ownership. If the managers have a strong incentive to become owners but they lack the financial capacity to acquire the company, an MBO may be the best answer, provided that the managers can tolerate the stress of living with the heavy debt financing.

Employee Stock Ownership Plans

Employee Stock Ownership Plans (ESOPs) are a way for a firm to be sold either in part or in total to its employees. A wide variety of companies have used these plans for many reasons. As a method of selling an entrepreneurial company, though, an ESOP appears to be the last resort, behind strategic and financial sales.

The basic ESOP arrangement is depicted in Exhibit 14.1. There are three principal participants in the arrangement: the employer corporation, the lender, and the ESOP. An ESOP trust borrows from the lender on behalf of the ESOP and buys common stock from the employer corporation. The trust subsequently services the debt from dividends and contributions that the employer pays into it. Such dividends are fully tax deductible, and other contributions are deductible up to a maximum of 25% of payroll.[4] In effect, it is possible for principal as well as interest payments to be tax deductible for the employer corporation. As the debt is retired, shares of stock are taken out of the trust and credited to the participants' accounts in the ESOP.

As far as the employer corporation is concerned, it has equity financing and will be making tax-deductible payments to service it. If the employer is unable to make sufficient payments into the trust to service the debt, the lender would have recourse only to the assets held in trust for the ESOP.

EXHIBIT 14.1   Using the leveraged ESOP.

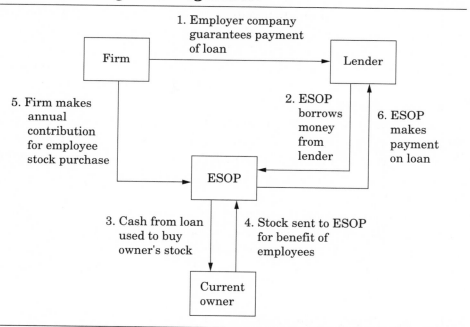

Source: Adapted from Daniel R. Garner, Robert R. Owen, and Robert P. Conway, *The Ernst & Young Guide to Raising Capital* (New York: John Wiley & Sons, 1991), p. 282.

Employee ownership is not a panacea, and it should not be prescribed indiscriminately. Selling all or part of the company to the employees, works only when it resolves conflicts that otherwise would exist between the owners and employees in such a way that both groups are better off. While advocates argue that employee ownership improves motivation, leading to greater effort and reduced waste, the value of any greater employee effort that might result from improved motivation could vary significantly from firm to firm.

Option 2: Releasing the Firm's Free Cash Flows— Only Patient Entrepreneurs Should Apply

The second harvesting strategy involves the orderly withdrawal of the owner's investment. The withdrawal process might be immediate if the owner simply sells off the assets of the firm and ceases business operations. However, for a value-creating firm—one that earns attractive rates of return for its investors— such would not make economic sense. By the mere fact that a firm is earning rates of return that exceed the investors' opportunity cost of funds indicates that the company is worth more as a going concern than a dead one. Thus, we would not want to rationalize the company; instead, we could simply not continue to grow the business; and in so doing, increase the *free cash flows* that can be returned to the investors.

Free cash flow represents the amount of cash that can be distributed to its investors—debt and equity—after all operating needs have been met. Specifically,

$$\text{Free cash flows} = \frac{\text{Operating profits}}{\text{after tax}} + \text{Depreciation} - \frac{\text{Investments required to}}{\text{grow the firm}}$$

In a firm's early years, all its cash flow is usually devoted to growing the firm. As a consequence, the firm's free cash flow during this period is zero or even negative, requiring its owners to seek outside cash to finance its growth. As the firm matures and the opportunity to grow the business declines, sizable free cash flows frequently become available to its owners. Rather than reinvesting all the cash flows in the company, the owners can begin to withdraw the cash, thus harvesting their investment. If they do so, only the amount of cash that is necessary to maintain current markets is retained and reinvested; thus, there would be little if any effort to grow the present markets or expand into new markets.

Harvesting by withdrawing the firm's cash outflow has two primary advantages: The owners can retain control of the firm while they harvest their investment, and they do not have to seek out a buyer or incur the expenses entailed in consummating a sale. There are disadvantages, however. Reducing reinvestment when the firm faces valuable growth opportunities results in lost value creation and could leave the firm unable to sustain its competitive advantage while the owners are harvesting the venture. If so, the end result may be an unintended reduction in harvestable value, compared with the potential value of the firm as a long-term going concern. There may also be tax disadvantages to an orderly liquidation compared with other harvest methods. For example, if a corporation simply distributes the cash flows as dividends, the income may be taxed both as corporate income and as personal dividend income to the stockholders. (This would not be a problem for a proprietorship, partnership, or S-corporation.)

Finally, for the entrepreneur who is simply tired of day-to-day operations, siphoning off the free cash flows over time may require too much patience. Unless other people in the firm are qualified to manage it, this strategy may be doomed to failure.

Option 3: The IPO—Is It Really a Method for Harvesting?

Many entrepreneurs look to the prospect of an IPO as the "holy grail" of their career. However, in reality, an IPO is used primarily as a way to raise additional equity capital to finance company growth, and only secondarily as a way to harvest the owner's investment. Lisa D. Stein, vice president, Salomon Smith Barney, offered the following reasons for going public:[5]

- To raise capital to repay certain outstanding debt
- To strengthen the company's balance sheet to support future growth
- To create a source of capital that can be selectively accessed in the future to fund the company's continuing growth
- To create a liquid currency to fund future acquisitions
- To create a liquid market for the company's stock
- To broaden the company's shareholder base
- To create ongoing interest in the company and its continued development

While these motivations for going public exclude the entrepreneur's eventual need for exiting a business, there is evidence that IPOs do eventually lead to a harvest. The median ownership percentage of the officers and directors declines from 68% to 18% in the 10 years following an IPO.[6] In addition, startup firms tend to go public to finance expansion, while established companies go public to liquidate the shareholdings of owners. Similarly, the original owners retain a high ownership stake at the time of the IPO, but high turnover in control occurs following the IPO.[7] There is evidence that IPOs are undertaken to maximize the founding owners' value from an eventual sale of the company.[8] Thus, although an IPO is not primarily a harvest mechanism for the entrepreneur, going public does provide the owners with increased liquidity—which facilitates their eventual exit.

In very general terms, the steps in the IPO are as follows:[9]

- The firm's owners decide to go public.
- If not already completed, the last three years of financial statements are audited.
- An S-1 Registration Statement is drafted.
- The Registration Statement is subject to an SEC review period of approximately 30 to 35 days.
- Management responds to suggested comments by the SEC and prints a Red Herring/Prospectus describing the firm and the offering.
- The firm spends the following 10 to 15 days "on the road" explaining its investment attributes to potential investors, including institutional, middle market, and retail investors.
- On the day before the offering is released to the public, the actual offering price is decided on. Based on the demand for the offering, the shares will be priced to create constructive trading of the stock in the aftermarket.
- Months of work come to fruition in a single event—offering the stock to the public and seeing how it is received.

The IPO Process: An Entrepreneur's Perspective

The IPO process may be one of the most exhilarating—but frustrating and exhausting—experiences of an entrepreneur's life. Managers frequently discover that they do not like being exposed to the variability of public capital markets and to the prying questions of public-market investors. In a survey of the *Inc.* 100, the CEOs who had participated in public offerings indicated that they spent 33 hours per week for four and a half months on the offering.[10] To many, the cost of the IPO process seemed exorbitant. They found themselves being misunderstood and having little influence in the decisions being made. There was frequent disillusionment with investment bankers and much of the entire process. At some point, they wondered where they had lost control of the process—a feeling shared by many entrepreneurs involved in a public offering.

To understand the IPO process as seen by the entrepreneur, it is necessary to consider the shift in power that occurs during the IPO process. When the chain of events begins, the company's management is in control. They can dictate whether or not to go public and who the investment banker will be. After the prospectus has been prepared and the road show is under way, however, the firm's management, including the entrepreneur, is no longer the primary decision maker. The investment banker is now in control. Finally, the marketplace, in concert with the investment banker, begins to take over, and, ultimately, it is the market that dictates the final outcome.

In addition to the issue of who controls the events and decisions in the IPO process, it is important that the entrepreneur understand the investment banker's motivations in the process. Who is the investment banker's primary customer here? The issuing firm is rewarding the underwriter for its services through the fees paid and participation in the deal. But helping with an IPO may not be as rewarding for the investment banker as other activities, such as involvement with corporate acquisitions. The investment banker is also selling the securities to its customers on the other side of the trade.

While the entrepreneurs may generally be pleased with the outcome of going public, they dislike the feeling of powerlessness over the firm's stock price and the perception that the market price may not reflect the true value of the firm (a concern shared widely by managers, regardless of firm size). The perception is that the capital markets are myopic, that management is under pressure for short-term performance and can no longer look to the shareholders' long-term best interests.

Jones, Cohen, and Coppola (1992) describe this perception:

> In a closely held company, management has the flexibility to focus attention on long-term goals, even if earnings in the near term suffer. In a public company, the investor's return depends on the company's performance, as well as the overall market's performance. Shareholders expect steady growth in areas such as sales, profits, market share, and product innovation. . . . Management must weigh the potential long-term benefits against shareholder reaction, the effect on the market value of the stock and the risk that the long-term sales goal may not be achieved. (p. 398)

Private Equity Placements: An Alternative to the IPO

Up to this point we have considered public IPOs, in which a portion of the firm's equity is sold in the public equity markets. There is an alternative form of equity, in which private equity capital is infused into the company. This option is especially attractive for family-controlled firms as a way to help a firm make the transition of ownership from one generation to the next and at the same time provide growth capital.

Trying to finance liquidity and growth while retaining control is perhaps the most difficult task facing family-controlled firms. The difficulty is compounded when the family is attempting to transfer ownership and leadership to the next generation. The situation can be further complicated by the capital and liquidity needs of estate planning and the fact that most family business owners hold their primary assets within the business.

When transferring ownership within a family-owned firm, trade-offs among three factors are of primary importance—the objectives of providing liquidity for the exiting family members, continued financing for company growth, and maintenance of family control of the firm. One study provides evidence of the relative importance of these three factors for a sample of entrepreneurs who had transferred or were planning to transfer ownership of their businesses.[11] Of the respondents, 85% stated that maintaining control of the company was "very important." About 45% considered providing capital for the firm's future growth and meeting the personal liquidity needs of family members "very important." When asked how the transition would be financed, the responses were as follows:

Gift	38%
Seller financing	24%
Acquirer's personal financing	14%
Third-party financing	12%
Other	12%

In addition, the owners indicated that their financing of choice involved debt more often than equity. The right to convert from debt to equity on the part of the investor, either through conversion rights or warrants, was essentially nonexistent in the transitions that had already occurred. For the planned transfers, 23% of the respondents expecting to use third-party financing thought such features would be part of the financing arrangement. Also, 67% of the owners acknowledged that their investors had a planned exit strategy. Two-thirds of the owners who had not experienced a transition, however, were uncertain what they should expect concerning the timing of the investors' exit.

Family-owned firms used a limited number of alternatives to finance a transition.[12] The ownership generation exiting the firm in many cases apparently had sufficient personal liquidity not to require external financing. Others financed the transition from the firm's operating cash flows, but that can be done only at the expense of limiting the firm's growth opportunities. For those who did seek third-party financing, the primary source of financing was the traditional banker.

The Private Placement

Selling a company's stock to private equity investors represents an alternative to taking the firm public, but only for economically attractive companies with growth potential. Furthermore, as with IPOs, the entrepreneur will most likely be required to retain a partial—and significant—investment in the company.

Heritage Partners in Boston provides a good illustration of a private equity investor that provides capital for mature, successful family businesses that are not "in play." Heritage has what it calls its "Private IPO."[13]

To illustrate the Private IPO, consider a company that could be sold for $50 million as an LBO. The sale would most likely be financed through 80% debt, consisting of about $28 million in senior debt, $12 million in subordinated debt, and 20% equity. For many entrepreneurs, such an arrangement would be intolerable, even though the owners would have cashed out. They simply would not want their company subjected to a high-leverage transaction.

An alternative approach provides less cash but allows the family to retain control. In this process, the firm described above would be sold for $45 million—10% less than the LBO price assumed above. The sellers would receive $38 million in cash, not the full $45 million. Instead of relinquishing all or most of their ownership, however, the family owners would receive 51% of the equity in exchange for the $7 million retained in the company. The remaining $38 million of the purchase price would be financed from two sources: $24 million in senior debt and $14 million provided by a private investor, consisting of $7 million in common equity for 49% of the firm's ownership and $7 million in preferred stock. The preferred stock would have an annual dividend (to be paid in additional shares of stock in the first years of the transaction), as well as warrants for additional common stock to bring the private investor's economic—not voting—ownership up to 65%, but only if management does not make its projections. For instance, management might predict that the current earnings will increase 60% over the next five years. If this goal is realized, then management keeps the 51% economic share of the firm when the eventual exit occurs. If the goal is not realized, then management's economic ownership is scaled down depending on how far the target is missed, but not below 35%. This deal structure is represented in Exhibit 14.2.

The differences in the two capital structures are clear. The debt ratio in the latter structure allows for a lower interest rate on the debt than an LBO and permits the firm's cash flows to be used to grow the firm rather than being so heavily focused on paying down debt. The arrangement allows the senior generation of owners to cash out while the next generation retains control and the cash to grow the firm—a win-win situation. The younger generation

EXHIBIT 14.2 Illustration of a private equity financing.

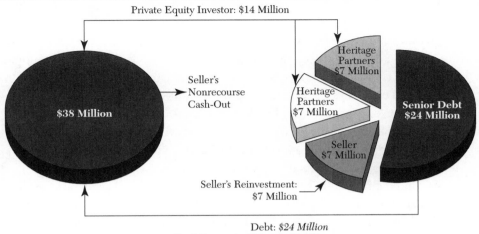

Private Equity Investor: $14 Million

Seller's Nonrecourse Cash-Out

$38 Million

Heritage Partners $7 Million

Heritage Partners $7 Million

Senior Debt $24 Million

Seller $7 Million

Seller's Reinvestment: $7 Million

Debt: *$24 Million*
Total Enterprise Value: *$45 Million*

also has the potential to realize significant economic gains if the firm performs well.

In summary, there are three primary ways to harvest a business venture: company sale, distribution of free cash flows, and the infusion of new equity, either through a public offering (IPO) or a private placement. Many entrepreneurs seek to take their firms public through an IPO. Company sales are perhaps the most common method of harvest. These sales can be classified into one of three basic categories depending on the nature of the buyer: strategic sale, financial sale, or sale to the firm's employees through an ESOP.

FIRM VALUE: HOW LARGE IS THE HARVEST?

A significant part of the harvest strategy involves determining a firm's value. As we said earlier, only if value has been created can there be a harvest of any significance. While there is a host of valuation techniques, there are two methods that are most common: (1) market comparables and (2) present value of discounted cash flows.

Market Comparables

More often than not, buyers and sellers base the harvest value of a firm on some observed market value of a comparable company relative to its earnings.

The observation of the market value of a comparable firm can be the market price of a publicly traded security or an actual transaction involving the sale of a comparable company.

Earnings may be measured by net income, operating income, or earnings before interest, taxes, depreciation, and amortization (EBITDA). For example, a buyer might try to acquire a company's equity for about four times EBITDA, plus the firm's cash, less the outstanding debt—but the price could reflect substantially lower or higher multiples depending on how badly the buyer wants the company and how willing the seller is to part with the business.

Different procedures are used in capitalizing a company's earnings to find value, but the underlying concept is always the same: Determine a "normalized earnings" and capitalize it at some rate of return, called a capitalization rate—or alternatively at some multiple of earnings. Typically, this rate or multiple is determined by some rule of thumb, based on conventional wisdom and the experience of the person doing the valuation. However, in doing so, we are making implicit assumptions about the firm's riskiness and its expected future growth in earnings. The greater the firm's risk, the lower the multiple should be, and the greater the expected growth in earnings, the higher the multiple to be used. The multiples will also vary based on competitive conditions. For example, a high-potential venture in the late 1990s that sold for six or seven times EBITDA might sell in 2003 for four or five times EBITA, where the decrease was largely due to the changing market conditions.

To illustrate a firm valuation based on a multiple of earnings, consider the Visador Corporation. Robert Hall, the CEO at Visador, a family-owned company, received an offer for his firm that was based on a multiple of EBITDA. The offer was presented to him in the following format:

Net income	$ 4,676,267
Plus:	
Income taxes	3,167,992
Interest expense	115,098
Depreciation and amortization	1,176,648
EBITDA	$ 9,136,005
Multiple of EBITDA	5X
Firm value	$45,680,025
Less long-term debt	1,350,000
Equity value	$44,330,025

Hall rejected the offer and indicated he would accept no less than $54 million for the firm's equity, which translated to a multiple of six times EBITDA. The buyer accepted Hall's terms.

The appropriateness of using earnings to value a firm is the subject of ongoing debate. Some contend that the markets value of a firm is based on future cash flows, and not its reported earnings. Moreover, they argue that there are simply too many ways to influence the firm's reported earnings within generally accepted accounting principles that lead to material differences in the valuation estimate but no difference in the intrinsic value of the firm. For these individuals, a firm's value is the present value of the firm's free cash flows.

Free Cash Flow Valuation

Free cash flow valuation defines the value of the firm to be the present value of its expected future cash flows. More specifically, a firm's *economic* or *intrinsic* value is equal to the present value of its free cash flows discounted at the company's cost of capital, plus the value of the firm's nonoperating assets. Examples of nonoperating assets include such items as excess investments in marketable securities and the amount by which the firm's pension fund is overfunded. We then compute shareholder or equity value as firm value less the value of outstanding interest-bearing debt.

A firm's free cash flow is calculated as follows:

Operating income + Depreciation and amortization

> = Earnings before interest, taxes, depreciation, and amortization (EBITDA)
>
> − Tax payments
>
> = After-tax cash flows from operations
>
> − Investment (increase) in net operating working capital
>
> − Investments in fixed assets (plant and equipment) and other assets
>
> = Free cash flows

We compute the present value of the firm's free cash flows as the sum of the present values of the free cash flows for a *planning period* plus the present value of the cash flows beyond the planning horizon (the residual value), that is,

$$\begin{matrix} \text{Intrinsic or} \\ \text{economic value} \\ \text{of the firm} \end{matrix} = \text{Present value} \begin{pmatrix} \text{Planning period} \\ \text{cash flows} \end{pmatrix} + \text{Present value} \begin{pmatrix} \text{Residual} \\ \text{value} \end{pmatrix}$$

The present value, PV, of the free cash flows (FCF_t) for the planning period (year one through year T) is computed as follows:

$$PV = \sum_{t=1}^{T} \frac{FCF_t}{(1+k)^t}$$

where k is the discount rate, which corresponds to the firm's cost of capital. For instance, if you expect to receive $400 in year one and $450 in year two and your required rate of return is 15%, the present value of these cash flows would be determined as follows:

$$PV = \frac{\$400}{(1+0.15)^1} + \frac{\$450}{(1+0.15)^2} = \$347.83 + 340.26 = \$688.09$$

The value of residual cash flows in year T, which begins in year $T+1$ can be calculated as follows:

$$RV_T = \frac{FCF_{T+1}}{k-g}$$

Here we assume that the residual cash flows will grow at a constant rate, g (which must be less than k) forever. To illustrate, assuming your required rate of return is 15%, the value at the end of year two of a $500 cash flow stream beginning in year three and growing at 5% in perpetuity would be calculated as follows:

$$RV_5 = \frac{\$500}{0.15-.05} = \$5,000$$

We then find the present value of the residual value as follows:

$$RV_0 = \frac{RV_T}{(1+k)^T}$$

For our example,

$$RV_0 = \frac{\$5,000}{(1+.15)^2} = \$3,780.72$$

Then the present value, PV, of the combined planning period free cash flows and the residual cash flows can be expressed as follows:

$$PV = \sum_{t=1}^{T} \frac{FCF_t}{(1+k)^t} + \frac{RV_T}{(1+k)^T}$$

For our example, the total present value of cash flows would be $2,853.81:

$$PV = \$688.09 + \$3,780.72 = \$4,468.81$$

Illustrating the Free Cash Flow Model

In the previous section, we described the valuation of the Visador Corporation based on a multiple of earnings. Let's now value the firm based on its free cash flows. To do so requires the following information about Visador:

- Sales for the most recent period, which were $45,452,000 last year for Visador
- Estimated sales growth rate, both for the planning period and beyond
- Expected operating profit margins
- Income tax rate
- The projected relationship of operating assets to sales—the ratio of net working capital to sales, fixed assets as a percentage of sales, and other long-term assets relative to sales
- The firm's cost of capital

These variables have come to be known as *value drivers* because they represent the primary factors that drive a firm's economic or intrinsic value.

In projecting the free cash flows for the Visador Corporation, we made estimates for each of the firm's value drivers. As already noted, the most recent annual sales were $45,452,000. The remaining assumptions were based on the company's historical performance and management's assessment of the situation at the time. One set of assumptions—there could have been others—is as follows:

	Years		
	1–5 (%)	6–10 (%)	11 and Beyond (%)
Sales growth	12	8	5
Operating profit margins	16	14	10
Income tax rate	35	35	35
Net working capital (percentage of sales)	13	13	13
Fixed assets (percentage of sales)	18	18	18
Other assets (percentage of sales)	1	1	1

Exhibit 14.3 on page 445 presents the projected free cash flows for the Visador Corporation, based on the assumptions shown above. For instance, the free cash flow in the first year is computed as follows:

	(in millions)	
Sales:	$50,906	[$45,452 last year's sales × (1 + 12% growth rate)]
Operating profits:	8,145	[$50,906 sales × 16% operating profit margin]
Taxes	2,851	[$8,145 operating profits × 35% tax rate]
After-tax profits	$ 5,294	[operating profits − taxes]
Net working capital	709	[(change in sales $50,906 − $45,452) × 13% net working capital to sales]
Plant and equipment	982	[(change in sales $50,906 − $45,452) × 18% fixed assets to sales]
Other assets	55	[(change in sales $50,906 − $45,452) × 1% other assets to sales]
Total investments	1,745	[total of investments in working capital, fixed assets, and other assets]
Free cash flows	$ 3,549	[After-tax profits − total investments]

Note that free cash flows are found by computing after-tax operating profits and subtracting the *incremental* investments, where the incremental investments are determined by computing the *change in sales for the year* multiplied by the percentage of the particular asset-to-sales relationship.

Also, note that we did not add back depreciation expense as is usually done in computing free cash flow. Instead, it is common practice in a free cash flow model to assume that the depreciation expense equals the cost of replacing fixed assets. That is, accounting depreciation is assumed to equal the economic depreciation—the actual cost of replacing depreciating assets. Therefore, we do not add back any depreciation expense, but neither do we show a cash outflow for the cost of replacing already existing fixed assets. Additions to fixed assets only occur when sales increase.

Taking the free cash values shown in Exhibit 14.3, we estimate Visador's equity value to be $39.6 million:

		(in millions)
Present value of free cash flows for:		
Years 1 to 10 (planning period)		$25,789
Years 11 and beyond (residual)		
As of year 10	$61,496	
As of today		15,201
Total firm present value		$40,990
Less: Debt value (book value)		(1,350)
Shareholder value		$39,640

The present value of the cash flows for years 1 through 10 is found by discounting each year's cash flows back to the present and summing the results.

EXHIBIT 14.3 Visador free cash flows (in millions).

	Years										
	1	2	3	4	5	6	7	8	9	10	11
Sales	$50,906	$57,015	$63,857	$71,520	$80,102	$86,510	$93,431	$100,905	$108,978	$117,696	$123,581
Operating profit	8,145	9,122	10,217	11,443	12,816	12,111	13,080	14,127	15,257	16,477	12,358
Taxes	2,851	3,193	3,576	4,005	4,486	4,239	4,578	4,944	5,340	5,767	4,325
After tax profits	5,294	5,930	6,641	7,438	8,331	7,872	8,502	9,182	9,917	10,710	8,033
Less investments:											
Working capital	709	794	889	996	1,116	833	900	972	1,049	1,133	765
Plant and equipment	982	1,100	1,232	1,379	1,545	1,153	1,246	1,345	1,453	1,569	1,059
Other assets	55	61	68	77	86	64	69	75	81	87	59
Total invested	1,745	1,955	2,189	2,452	2,746	2,051	2,215	2,392	2,583	2,790	1,883
Free cash flow	3,549	3,975	4,452	4,986	5,584	5,822	6,288	6,791	7,334	7,921	6,150
PV of FCF	3,086	3,005	2,927	2,851	2,776	2,517	2,364	2,220	2,085	1,958	

The residual value (value of all future cash flows beginning in year 11 and beyond) as of year 10 was found as follows:

$$RV_{10} = \frac{FCF_{11}}{k-g} = \frac{\$6,150}{.15-.05} = \$61,496 \text{ (small rounding difference)}$$

Discounting the residual value in year 10 back to the present gives us a value of

$$RV_0 = \frac{RV_{10}}{(1+k)^{10}} = \frac{\$61,496}{(1+.15)^{10}} = \$15,201$$

Combining the two present values gives us a firm value of almost $41 million; and subtracting debt of $1.35 million yields an equity value of about $39.64 million. Notice that the free cash value is essentially the same as the original offer made by the buyer. Moreover, the higher value paid by the buyer, $54 million, proved with hindsight to be more than the firm was worth.

DEVELOPING AN EFFECTIVE HARVEST STRATEGY

As already emphasized, developing an exit or harvest strategy is important in the entrepreneurial process, despite the tendency of many entrepreneurs to ignore it until some crisis or unanticipated event comes along. We have described the methods for harvesting the investment in a privately held firm and the two primary means used to value a firm in this process. In the sections that follow, we offer some insights for developing an effective harvest strategy. What we present is based on in-depth interviews with entrepreneurs, investors, and investment bankers located across the United States who have been part of one or more company exits.[14]

When Designing the Terms of the Harvest, Cash Is King

Other things being the same, cash is generally preferred over stock and other forms of remuneration—at least by the entrepreneurs. Entrepreneur Bill Bailey, the founder of a telecommunications firm, Cherokee Corporation, encourages prospective sellers to be conservative—take the cash. He noted that one could be tempted to go for half cash and half stock in the hopes that the stock will run up in value. But Bailey believes such a temptation is to be avoided, and most entrepreneurs agree. Robert Hall, former CEO of the Visador Corporation, put it this way: "The $20 per share selling price we received in cash was the key, but the cash was even more important than the $20." Ed Cherney (CMI Corporation) agreed with Bailey and Hall, unless there is a specific reason. As Cherney explains,

> Every entrepreneur would like to get all this money up front, and in a perfect world I would ask for that. However, I wanted to stay with the business. I was more interested in having access to money in the future at a reasonable cost. The strategic partner that would lend me money and have an unlimited amount of money was more important to me than how fast I got my money. I didn't focus on getting anything at closing. The buyer, however, sensed that I would enjoy having some personal liquidity. So he restructured the deal so that I received $500,000 at closing, even though it was not part of the original agreement.

From an investor's viewpoint, Pat Hamner and Tim Smith at venture capital firm, Capital Southwest Corporation, believe that cash is best except for the tax consequences. Their advice: "Start with cash and work down from there." The problem comes when there are competing offers and the entrepreneur must compare cash offers with security-based offers and various combinations of the two.

There are exceptions to any rule. Some venture capitalists do not have a preference between being paid with stock or cash. William Unger and George Pavlov at Mayfield Fund were indifferent between cash and stock; this indifference they said reflects the preferences of their limited partners, which are large pension funds. Their concern was more with any restrictions on the future sale of the stock.

Plan for the Harvest but Manage for the Long Term

Investors are always concerned about how to exit, and entrepreneurs need to have a similar mind-set. Peter Hermann, general partner at Heritage Partners, a private equity investment group, notes, "People generally stumble into the exit and don't plan for it." However, for Hermann, "The exit strategy begins when the money goes in." Similarly, Gordon Baty at Zero Stage Capital, Inc. enters each investment with a clear understanding of its investment horizon and exit strategy. In his words, "We plan for an acquisition and hope for an IPO." Jack Kearney formerly at Rauscher Pierce Refsnes Inc. indicates that an exit strategy should be anticipated in advance, unless "the entrepreneur expects to die in the CEO chair. . . . The worst of all worlds is to realize, for health or other reasons, that you have to sell the company right now." Jim

Knister at the Donnelly Corporation advises entrepreneurs to start thinking two or three years ahead about how they are going to exit so that they can correctly position their companies.

This type of advice is particularly important when the entrepreneur is planning an IPO. Running a public company requires information disclosures to stockholders that are not required of a privately held firm. Specifically, this means (1) maintaining an accounting process that cleanly separates the business from the entrepreneur's personal life, (2) selecting a strong board of directors that can and will offer valuable business advice, and (3) managing the firm so as to produce a successful track record of performance. These requirements, along with others, have become critically important given the Sarbanes-Oxley legislation aimed at improving the governance of publicly traded firms.

Having an exit plan in place is also very important, because the window of opportunity can open and close quickly. The opportunity to exit is triggered by the arrival of a willing and able buyer, not just an interested seller. From the perspective of an IPO, hot markets may offer very attractive opportunities, as they did in the 1990s; so a seller must be ready to move when the opportunity arises.

Furthermore, entrepreneurs frequently do not appreciate the difficulties encountered in harvesting a private company investment. One investor commented that exiting a business is "like brain surgery—it's done a lot, but there are a lot of things that can go wrong." Exiting, whether through a sale or a stock offering, takes a lot of time and energy on the part of the firm's management team and can be very distracting from day-to-day affairs. The result is often a loss of managerial focus and momentum, leading to poor performance.[15]

Uncertainties accompanying an impending sale often lower employee morale. The stress can affect the whole organization, as employees become anxious about the prospect of a new owner. Lynn Baker at Sutter Hill Ventures offers this advice: "Don't start running the company for the liquidity event. Run the business for the long haul." Jim Porter at CCI Triad describes the situation in Silicon Valley during the days when high tech startups were the rage and IPOs were easy to sell:

> Some people don't think in terms of long-term value as much as short-term returns. This carries over into developing an IPO exit strategy. I saw a growing number of people who were already planning their next company before they were even finished with the first company. They were looking to exit the first one, get the money out and start the second one, get the money out, and pyramid their return. In a hot market, you could do that and get away with it.

So, while an entrepreneur should not be caught unaware, there is also the risk of becoming so attentive to "playing the harvest game" that you forget to keep first things first.

SOME FINAL THOUGHTS

An entrepreneur should anticipate the exit. In the words of Ed Cherney, an entrepreneur who has sold two companies, "Don't wait to put your package together until something dramatic happens. Begin thinking about the exit strategy and start going through the motions, so that if something major happens, you will have time to think through your options." On the other hand, an entrepreneur should keep one eye on the ball, lest the firm lose focus in its operations.

Expect Conflict—Emotional and Cultural

Having bought other companies does not prepare entrepreneurs for the sale of their own company. Entrepreneurs who have been involved in the acquisition of other firms are still ill prepared for the strains and stress associated with selling their own businesses. Jim Porter, who has been involved in a number of acquisitions, says "It's definitely a lot more fun to buy something than it is to be bought." One very real difference between selling and buying is the entrepreneur's personal ties to the business that he or she helped create. A buyer can be quite unemotional and detached, while a seller is likely to be much more concerned about nonfinancial considerations.

For this reason and many others, entrepreneurs frequently do not make good employees. The very qualities that made them successful entrepreneurs can make it difficult for them to work under a new owner. In fact, an entrepreneur who plans to stay with the firm after a sale can become disillusioned quickly and end up leaving prematurely.

Lynn Baker observes, "There is a danger of culture conflict between the acquiring versus the acquired firm's management. The odds are overwhelming that somebody who's been an entrepreneur is not going to be happy in a corporate culture." When Ed Bonneau sold his firm, the Bonneau Company, he was retained as a consultant, although the buyer never sought his advice. Bonneau recalled that he "could not imagine that someone could or would buy a company and not operate it. The people who bought the firm had no operations expertise or experience whatsoever and, in fact, didn't care that much about it."

These conflicts occur to varying degrees whenever an entrepreneur remains with the company after the sale. Although the nature of the conflict varies, the intensity of the feelings does not. An entrepreneur should expect culture conflict and be pleasantly surprised if it does not occur.

Get Good Advice

Entrepreneurs learn to operate their businesses through experience gained in repeated day-to-day activities. However, they may engage in a harvest transaction only once in a lifetime. Thus, they have a real need for good advice, both from experienced professionals and from entrepreneurs who have personally been through a harvest. Bill Dedmon formally at Southwest Securities advises, "Don't try to do it alone, because it's a demanding process that can distract you from your business." Jack Furst at Hicks, Muse, Tate, & Furst believes that advisors can give entrepreneurs a reality check. He contends that, without independent advice, entrepreneurs frequently fall prey to thinking they want to sell unconditionally, when in fact they really want to sell only if an unrealistically high price is offered.

It is also wise for an entrepreneur to talk to other entrepreneurs who have sold a firm or taken it public. Professional advice is vital, but entrepreneurs stress the importance of talking with someone who has exited a company. No one can better describe what to expect—both in events and in emotions—than someone who has had the experience. This perspective nicely complements the advice given by professional advisors.

IPO Fallacies

Perhaps the greatest misconception among entrepreneurs is that an IPO is the end of the line. They often feel that taking their firm public through an IPO means they have "made it." The fact is that going public is but one transition in the life of a firm. Many entrepreneurs are surprised to learn that a public offering is just the beginning, not an end. For one thing, an entrepreneur will not be able to cash out for some time after the completion of the IPO. In a sense, investors in the new stock offering have chosen to back the entrepreneur as the driving force behind the company—that is, they have invested in the entrepreneur, not the firm. While the daily stock price quotes will let the management team keep score, the business will have to reach another plateau before the founder can think about placing it in the hands of a new team and going fishing. When considering an exit from his business, Ed Bonneau talks of being surprised in this matter:

> The question of an IPO was put to me a number of times over the years. I had some investment bankers come and look at our company to talk about going public; they said, "Yeah, you can go public." Then they asked me why I wanted to go public. I said, "For one thing, I want some money out of the company. I have every dime I've got stuck in here." They responded that I couldn't do that. I asked what they meant. They responded, "Getting money out it not the purpose of going public."

Lynn Baker describes the typical entrepreneur's thinking about an IPO as "the Bride Magazine syndrome in which the entrepreneur is like the bride-to-be who becomes fixated on the events of the wedding day without thinking clearly about the years of being married that will follow. Life as head of a public corporation is very different from life at the helm of a private firm. Major investors will be calling every day expecting answers—sometimes with off-the-wall questions." Under these circumstances, getting good advice is a must.

Most of All, Understand What You Want

For an entrepreneur, exiting a business that has been an integral part of life for a long period of time can be a very emotional experience. When an entrepreneur invests a substantial part of his or her working life in growing a business, a real sense of loss may accompany the harvest—as was the case in our opening study of Bill Wangh. Thus, entrepreneurs should think very carefully about their motives for exiting and what they plan to do after the exit. Entrepreneurs who exit their investment frequently have great expectations about what life is going to be like with a lot of liquidity, something many of them have never known. The exit does provide the long-sought liquidity, but some entrepreneurs find managing money—in contrast to operating their own company—less rewarding than they had expected.

Entrepreneurs may also become disillusioned when they come to understand more fully how their sense of personal identity was intertwined with their business. While Jim Porter understands that a primary purpose of exiting is to make money, watching a number of owners cash out led him to conclude that the money is not a very satisfying aspect of the event:

> The bottom line is that you need more than money to sustain life and feel worthwhile. I see people who broke everything to make their money. They were willing to sacrifice their wives, their family, and their own sense of values to make money. I remember one person who was flying high, did his IPO, and went straight out and bought a flaming red Ferrari. He raced it down the street, hit a telephone pole, and died the day his IPO money came down. You see these guys, including a few of the people involved in the first Triad IPO, go crazy. They went out and bought houses in Hawaii, houses in Tahoe, new cars, and got things they didn't need.

Peter Hermann believes that "seller's remorse" is definitely a major issue for a number of entrepreneurs. His advice is "Search your soul and make a list of what you want to achieve with the exit. Is it dollars, health of the company, your management team or an heir apparent taking over?" The answers to these and similar questions determine to a significant extent whether the exit will prove successful in all dimensions of one's life. But there can be conflicting emotions, such as those expressed by Bill Bailey, founder of the Cherokee Corporation:

> There is a period in your life when you get up in age and you begin thinking more about your family. For me, it became important for the first time in my

life to have money available to do some long-range personal planning for myself, and for my family. But if there is any one thing to be understood when you are selling a business or anything else, it is the excitement of the journey and the enjoyment for doing what you're doing that matters.

Entrepreneurs are also well advised to be aware of potential problems that may arise after the exit. There are stories about people selling a firm or going public and then losing everything. Ed Cherney says, "It is more difficult to handle success than it is to handle struggling. People forget what got them the success—the work ethic, the commitment to family, whatever characteristics work for an entrepreneur. Once the money starts rolling in, . . . people forget and begin having problems."

And for the entrepreneur who believes that it will be easy to adapt to change after the exit, even possibly to start another company, William Unger at the Mayfield Fund quotes from Machiavelli's *The Prince:* "It should be remembered that nothing is more difficult than to establish a new order of things."

BIBLIOGRAPHY

Arthur Andersen/MassMutual, *American Family Business Survey 1997* (Houston, TX: Arthur Andersen Center for Family Business, 1998).

L. Brokaw, "The First Day of the Rest of Your Life," *Inc.* vol. 15, no. 5 (1992): 144.

S. R. Holmburg, "Value Creation and Capture: Entrepreneurship Harvest and IPO Strategies," *Frontiers of Entrepreneurship Research,* eds. N. C. Churchill, W. D. Bygrave, J. C. Covin, D. L. Sexton, D. P. Slevin, K. H. Vesper, and W. E. Wetzel Jr. (Wellesley, MA: Babson College, 1991), pp. 191–204.

H. Hyatt, "The Dark Side (of Going Public)," *Inc.* vol. 12, no. 6 (1990): 46–56.

S. Jones, M. B. Cohen, and V. V. Coppola, "Going Public," *The Entrepreneurial Venture,* eds. W. A. Sahlman and H. H. Stevenson (Boston: Harvard Business School Publications, 1992), pp. 394–416.

S. Kaplan, "The Effects of Management Buy-Outs on Operating Performance and Value," *Journal of Financial Economics* vol. 24 (1989): 217–254.

S. Kaplan, "The Staying Power of Leveraged Buyouts," *Journal of Financial Economics* vol. 29 (1991): 287–313.

W. H. Mikkelson, M. Partch, and K. Shah, "Ownership and Operating Performance of Companies that Go Public," *Journal of Financial Economics* vol. 44 (1997): 281–308.

M. Pagano, F. Panetta, and L. Zingales, "Why Do Companies Go Public? An Empirical Analysis," *Journal of Finance* vol. 53 (1998): 27–64.

J. W. Petty, W. D. Bygrave, and J. M. Shulman, "Harvesting the Entrepreneurial Venture: A Time for Creating Value," *Journal of Applied Corporate Finance* vol. 7, no. 9 (1994): 48–58.

J. W. Petty, J. Martin, and J. Kensinger, *Harvesting Investments in Private Companies* (Newark, NJ: Financial Executive Research Foundation, 1999).

J. Timmons, *New Venture Creation* (Chicago: Irwin, 2001).

N. Upton and J. Petty, "Venture Capital Funding of Transition in Family-Owned Business: An Exploratory Analysis," *Proceedings of the International Family Business Program Association* vol. 3 (1997): 44–61.

M. Wright, S. Thompson, K. Robbie, and P. Wong, "Management Buy-Outs in the Short and Long Term," *Frontiers of Entrepreneurship Research,* eds. N. C. Churchill, J. Katz, B. Kirchhoff, K. H. Vesper, and W. E. Wetzel Jr. (Wellesley, MA: Babson College, 1992), pp. 302–316.

L. Zingales, "Insider Ownership and the Decision to Go Public," *Review of Economic Studies* vol. 62 (1995): 425–448.

GLOSSARY

Agency theory: A branch of economics dealing with the behavior of principals (e.g., owners) and their agents (e.g., managers).

American Stock Exchange (AMEX): Stock exchange located in New York, listing companies that are generally smaller and younger than those on the much larger New York Stock Exchange.

Angel: An individual who invests in private companies. The term business angel is sometimes reserved for sophisticated angel investors who invest sizable sums in private companies. (See *invisible venture capital* and *informal investor*.)

Antidilution (of ownership): The right of an investor to maintain the same percentage ownership of a company's common stock in the event that the company issues more stock. (See *dilution*.)

Asked: The price level at which sellers offer securities to buyers.

Asset acquisition: Means of effecting a buyout by purchase of certain desired assets rather than shares of the target company.

Audited financial statements: A company's financial statements prepared and certified by a certified public accounting firm that is totally independent of the company.

Balance sheet: Summary statement of a company's financial position at a given point in time. It summarizes the accounting value of the assets, liabilities, preferred stock, common stock, and retained earnings. Assets = Liabilities + Preferred stock + Common stock + Retained earnings. (See *pro forma statements*.)

Basis point: One-hundredth of a percent (0.01%), typically used in expressing yield differentials (7.50% − 1.15% = 0/35%, or 35 basis points). (See *yield*.)

Bear: A person who expects prices to fall.

Bear market: A period of generally falling prices and pessimistic attitudes.

Best efforts offering: The underwriter makes its best effort to sell as much as it can of the shares at the offering price. Hence, unlike a firm commitment offering, the company offering its shares is not guaranteed a definite amount of money by the underwriter.

Bid: The price level at which buyers offer to acquire securities from sellers.

Big Board: See *New York Stock Exchange.*

Blue sky: Refers to laws that safeguard investors from being misled by unscrupulous promoters of companies with little or no substance.

Book value (of an asset): The accounting value of an asset as shown on a balance sheet is the cost of the asset minus its accumulated depreciation. It is not necessarily identical to its market value.

Book value (of a company): The common stock equity shown on the balance sheet. It is equal to total assets minus liabilities and preferred stock (synonymous with net worth and owners' equity).

Break-even point: The sales volume at which a company's net sales revenue just equals its costs. A commonly used approximate formula for the break-even point is Sales revenue = Total fixed costs/Gross margin.

Bridging finance: Short-term finance that is expected to be repaid quickly. It usually bridges a short-term financing need. For example, it provides cash needed before an expected stock flotation.

Browser: A computer program that enables users to access and navigate the World Wide Web.

Burn rate: The negative real-time cash flow from a company's operations, usually computed monthly.

Business model: The way in which a business makes a profit. As an example, here is IBM's definition of its business model: "IBM sells services, hardware and software. These offerings are bolstered by IBM's research and development capabilities. If a customer requires financing, IBM can provide that too." Southwest Airlines' business model is to provide inexpensive fares by keeping costs low through being more efficient than its major competitors.

Business plan: Document prepared by entrepreneurs, possibly in conjunction with their professional advisors, detailing the past, present, and intended future of the company. It contains a thorough analysis of the managerial, physical, labor, product, and financial resources of the company, plus the background of the company, its previous trading record, and its market position. The business plan contains detailed profit, balance sheet, and cash flow projections for two years ahead, and less detailed information for the following three years. The business plan crystallizes and focuses the management team's ideas. It explains their strategies, sets objectives, and is used to monitor their subsequent performance.

Call: A contract allowing the issuer of a security to buy back that security from the purchaser at an agreed-on price during a specific period of time.

Capital gain: The amount by which the selling price of an asset (e.g., common stock) exceeds the seller's initial purchase price.

Capitalization rate: The discount rate K used to determine the present value of a stream of future earnings. PV = (Normalized earnings after taxes)/(K/100), where PV is the present value of the firm and K is the firm's cost of capital.

Carried interest: A venture capital firm's share of the profit earned by a fund. In the United States, the carried interest (carry) is typically 20% of the profit after investors' principal has been repaid.

Cash flow: The difference between the company's cash receipts and its cash payments in a given period.

Cash-flow statement: A summary of a company's cash flow over a period of time. (See *pro forma statements.*)

Chattel mortgage: A lien on specifically identified property (assets other than real estate) backing a loan.

Collateral: An asset pledged as security for a loan. Common stock: Shares of ownership, or equity, in a corporation.

Compensating balance: A bank requires a customer to maintain a certain level of demand deposits that do not bear interest. The interest forgone by the customer on that compensating balance recompenses the bank for services provided, credit lines, and loans.

Conversion ratio: The number of shares of common stock that may be received in exchange for each share of a convertible security.

Convertible security: Preferred stock that is convertible into common stock according to a specified ratio at the security holder's option.

Corporation: A business form that is an entity legally separate from its owners. Its important features include limited liability, easy transfer of ownership, and unlimited life.

Cost of capital: The required rate of return of various types of financing. The overall cost of capital is a weighted average of the individual required rates of return (costs).

Cost of debt capital: The interest rate charged by a company's lenders.

Cost of equity capital: The rate of return on investment required by the company's common shareholders (colloquially called the hurdle rate).

Cost of goods sold: The direct cost of the product sold. For a retail business, the cost of all goods sold in a given period equals the inventory at the beginning of the period plus the cost of goods purchased during that period minus the inventory at the end of the period.

Cost of preferred stock: The rate of return on investment required by the company's preferred shareholders.

Covenant: A restriction on a borrower imposed by a lender. For example, it could be a requirement placed on a company to achieve and maintain specified targets such as levels of cash flow, balance sheet ratios, or specified capital expenditure levels in order to retain financing facilities.

Cumulative dividend provision: A requirement that unpaid dividends on preferred stock accumulate and have to be paid before a dividend is paid on common stock.

Current ratio: Current assets/Current liabilities. This ratio indicates a company's ability to cover its current liabilities with its current assets.

Deal flow: The rate at which new investment propositions come to funding institutions.

Debenture: A document containing an acknowledgment of indebtedness on the part of a company, usually secured by a charge on the company's assets.

Debt service: Payments of principal and interest required on a debt over a given period.

Deep pockets: Refers to an investor who has substantial financial resources.

Default: The nonperformance of a stated obligation. The nonpayment by the issuer of interest or principal on a bond or the nonperformance of a covenant.

Deferred payment: A debt that has been incurred and will be repaid at some future date.

Depreciation: The systematic allocation of the cost of an asset over a period of time for financial reporting and tax purposes.

Dilution (of ownership):   This happens when a new stock issue results in a decrease in the preissue owners' percentage of the common stock.

Discounted cash flow (DCF):   Methods of evaluating investments by adjusting the cash flows for the time value of money. In the decision to invest in a project, all future cash flows expected from that investment are discounted back to their present value at the time the investment is made. The discount rate is whatever rate of return the investor requires. In theory, if the present value of the future cash flows is greater than the money being invested, the investment should be made. (See *discount rate, internal rate if return, net present value,* and *present value.*)

Discount rate (capitalization rate):   Rate of return used to convert future values to present values. (See *capitalization rate, internal rate of return,* and *rate of return.*)

Doriot, General Georges: Founder of the modern venture capital industry, Harvard Business School professor, and one of the creators of INSEAD.

Double jeopardy: The case where an entrepreneur's main source of income and most of her/his net worth depend on her/his business.

Due diligence: The process of investigation by investors into a potential investee's management team, resources, and trading performance. This includes rigorous testing of the business plan assumptions and the verification of material facts (such as existing accounts).

Dun & Bradstreet (D&B):   The biggest credit-reporting agency in the United States.

Early-stage financing: This category includes seed-stage, startup-stage, and first-stage financing.

Earnings: This is synonymous with income and profit.

Earnings before interest and taxes (EBIT):   See *operating income.*

Earnings per share (EPS):   A company's net income divided by the number of common shares issued and outstanding.

Elasticity of demand: The percentage change in the quantity of a good demanded divided by the percentage change in the price of that good. When the elasticity is greater than 1, the demand is said to be elastic, and when it is less than 1, it is inelastic. In the short term, the demand for nonessential goods (e.g., airline travel) is usually elastic, and the demand for essentials (e.g., electricity) is usually inelastic.

Employee stock ownership plan (ESOP):   A trust established to acquire shares in a company for subsequent allocation to employees over a period of time. Several possibilities are available for structuring the operation of an ESOP. Essentially, either the company makes payments to the trust, which the trust uses to purchase shares; or the trust, having previously borrowed to acquire shares, may use the payments from the company to repay loans. The latter form is referred to as a leveraged ESOP and may be used as a means of providing part of the funding required to effect a buyout. A particular advantage of an ESOP is the possibility of tax relief for the contributions made by the company to the trust and on the cost of borrowing in those cases where the trust purchases shares in advance.

Employment agreement: An agreement whereby senior managers contract to remain with the company for a specified period. For the investing institutions, such an agreement provides some measure of security that the company's performance will not be adversely affected by the unexpected departure of key managers.

Equity: See *owners' equity.*

Equity kicker (or warrant):   An option or instrument linked to the provision of other types of funding, particularly mezzanine finance, which enables the provider to obtain an equity stake and hence a share in capital gains. In this way, providers of subordinated debt can be compensated for the higher risk they incur.

Exit: The means by which investors in a company realize all or part of their investment.

Expansion financing: Working capital for the initial expansion of a company that is producing and shipping products and has growing accounts receivable and inventories.

Factoring: A means of enhancing the cash flow of a business. A factoring company pays to the firm a certain proportion of the value of the firm's trade debts and then receives the cash as the trade debtors settle their accounts. Invoice discounting is a similar procedure.

FAQ: Frequently asked questions—a computer text file that contains answers to common questions about a topic.

Filing: Documents, including the prospectus, filed with the SEC for approval before an IPO.

Financing flows: Cash flows generated by debt and equity financing.

Firm commitment offering: The underwriter guarantees to raise a certain amount of money for the company and other selling stockholders at the IPO.

First-round financing: The first investment made by external investors.

First-stage financing: Financing to initiate full manufacturing and sales.

Five Cs of credit: The five crucial elements for obtaining credit are character (borrower's integrity), capacity (sufficient cash flow to service the debt), capital (borrower's net worth), collateral (assets to secure the debt), and conditions (of the borrowing company, its industry, and the general economy).

Fixed and floating charges: Claims on assets pledged as security for debt. Fixed charges cover specific fixed assets, and floating charges relate to all or part of a company's assets.

Flame: A highly negative electronic message objecting to the actions of or opinions expressed by another user, often in response to a breach of Internet etiquette.

Floating lien: A general lien against a group of assets, such as accounts receivable or inventory, without the assets being specifically identified.

Flotation: A method of raising equity financing by selling shares on a stock market, and often allowing management and institutions to realize some of their investment at the same time. (See *initial public offering.*)

Forum: An electronic discussion group of computer users on an online service (e.g., America Online or Compuserve) that is centered around a particular subject area of interest to the participants.

Four Fs: Founders, family, friends, and foolhardy persons who invest in a person's private business—generally a startup. (See *angel* and *informal investor.*)

Franchising: An organizational form in which a firm (the franchisor) with a market-tested business package centered on a product or service enters into a continuing contractual relationship with franchisees operating under the franchisor's trade name to produce or market goods or services according to a format specified by the franchisor.

Free cash flow: Cash flow in excess of that required to fund all projects that have a positive net present value when discounted at the relevant cost of capital. Conflicts of interest between shareholders and managers may arise when the organization generates free cash flow. Shareholders may desire higher dividends, but managers may wish to invest in projects providing a return below the cost of capital. (See *cost of capital* and *net present value.*)

FTP: File transfer protocol—an Internet tool that allows you to upload and download files from other computers on the Internet.

Future value: The value at a future date of a present amount of money. $FV_t = PV \times (1 + K/100)^t$, where FV, is the future value, PV is the present value, K is the percentage annual rate of return, and t is the number of years. For example, an investment of \$100,000 must have a future value of \$384,160 after four years to produce a rate of return of 40%, which is the kind of return that an investor in an early stage company expects to earn. (See *net present value, present value,* and *rate of return.*)

Gearing: British term of leverage. (See *leverage.*)

Going concern: This assumes that the company will continue as an operating business as opposed to going out of business and liquidating its assets.

Golden handcuffs: A combination of rewards and penalties given to key managers to dissuade them from leaving the company. Examples are high salaries, paid on a deferred basis while employment is maintained, and stock options.

Goodwill: The difference between the purchase price of a company and the net value of its assets purchased.

Gross margin: Gross profit as a percentage of net sales revenue.

Gross profit (gross income, gross earnings):   Net sales revenue minus the direct cost of the products sold.

Guarantee: An undertaking to prove that a debt or obligation of another will be paid or performed. It may relate either to a specific debt or to a series of transactions such as a guarantee of a bank overdraft. For example, entrepreneurs are often required to provide personal guarantees for loans borrowed by their companies.

Harvest: The realization of the value of an investment. (See *exit.*)

High-potential venture: A company started with the intent of growing quickly to annual sales of at least $30 to $50 million in five years. It has the potential to have a firm-commitment IPO.

Home page: A document on the World Wide Web that serves as the introductory menu for that Web site.

HTML: Hypertext markup language—a computer language that enables the construction of documents that can be viewed on the World Wide Web.

Hurdle rate: The minimum rate of return that is acceptable to investors. (See *return on investment.*)

Hyperlinks: Dynamic references to other computer-based documents that facilitate the rapid movement between documents.

Income statement: A summary of a company's revenues, expenses, and profits over a specified period of time. (See *pro forma statements.*)

Informal investor: An individual who puts money into a private company—usually a startup or a small business. Informal investments range from micro loans from family members to sizable equity purchases by sophisticated business angels.

Initial public offering (IPO): Process by which a company raises money, and gets listed, on a stock market. (See *flotation.*)

INSEAD: The European Institute of Business Administration located in Fontainebleau, France.

Interest cover: The extent to which periodic interest commitments on borrowings are exceeded by periodic profits. It is the ratio of profits before the deduction of interest and taxes to interest payments. The ratio may also be expressed as the cash flow from operations divided by the amount of interest payable.

Internal rate of return (IRR): The discount rate that equates the present value of the future net cash flows from an investment with the project's cash outflows. It is a means of expressing the percentage rate of return projected on a proposed investment. For an investment in a company, the calculation takes account of cash invested, cash receipts from dividend payments and redemptions, percentage equity held, expected date of payments, realization of the investment and capitalization at that point, and possible further financing requirements. The calculation will frequently be quoted in a range depending on sensitivity analysis. (See *discount rate, future value, present value,* and *rate of return.*)

Internet: The vast network of networks connecting millions of individual and networked computers worldwide.

Inventory: Finished goods, work in process of manufacture, and raw materials owned by a company.

Investment bank: A financial institution engaged in the issue of new securities, including management and underwriting of issues as well as securities trading and distribution.

Investment flows: Cash flows associated with purchases and sales of both fixed assets and business interests.

Invisible venture capital (informal venture capital): Venture capital supplied by wealthy individuals (angels), as opposed to visible venture capital, which is supplied by formal venture capital firms that make up the organized venture capital industry.

ISP: Internet Service Provider—a company that provides direct connections to the Internet for computer users.

Junior debt: Loan ranking after senior debt or secured debt for payment in the event of a default.

Junk bonds: A variety of high-yield, unsecured bonds tradable on a secondary market and not considered to be of investment quality by credit-rating agencies. High yield normally indicates higher risk.

Key person insurance: Additional security provided to financial backers of a company through the purchase of insurance on the lives of key managers who are seen as crucial to the future of the company. Should one or more of those key executives die prematurely, the financial backers would receive the insurance payment.

Lead investor: In syndicated deals, normally the investor who originates, structures, and subsequently plays the major monitoring role.

Lemons and plums: Bad deals and good deals, respectively.

Leverage: The amount of debt in a company's financing structure, which may be expressed as a percentage of the total financing or as a ratio of debt to equity. The various quasi-equity (preference-type shares) and quasi-debt (mezzanine debt) instruments used to fund later-stage companies means that great care is required in calculating and interpreting leverage or gearing ratios.

Leveraged buyout (LBO): Acquisition of a company by an investor group, an investor, or an investment/LBO partnership, with a significant amount of debt (usually at least 70% of the total capitalization) and with plans to repay the debt with funds generated from the acquired company's operations or from asset sales. LBOs are frequently financed in part with junk bonds.

Lien: A legal claim on certain assets that are used to secure a loan.

Limited liability company: A company owned by "members," who either manage the business themselves or appoint "managers" to run it for them. All members and managers have the benefit of limited liability, and, in most cases, are taxed in the same way as a subchapter S corporation without having to conform to the S corporation restrictions.

Line of credit (with a bank): An arrangement between a bank and a customer specifying the maximum amount of unsecured debt the customer can owe the bank at a given point in time.

Line of credit (with a vendor): A limit set by the seller on the amount that a purchaser can buy on credit.

Liquidation value (of an asset): The amount of money that can be realized from the sale of an asset sold separately from its operating organization.

Liquidation value (of a company): The market value of the assets minus the liabilities that must be paid of a company that is liquidating.

Liquidity: The ability of an asset to be converted to cash as quickly as possible and without any price discount.

Listing: Acceptance of a security for trading on an organized stock exchange. Hence, a stock traded on the New York Stock Exchange is said to be listed on the NYSE.

Listserver: A computer program that handles the administration of subscriptions to electronic mailing lists by computer users.

Loan note: A form of vendor finance or deferred payment. The purchaser (borrower) may agree to make payments to the holder of the loan note at specified future dates. The holder may be able to obtain cash at an earlier date by selling at a discount to a financing institution that will collect on maturity.

Management buyin (MBI): The transfer of ownership of an entity to a new set of owners in which new managers coming into the entity are a significant element.

Management buyout (MBO): The transfer of ownership of an entity to a new set of owners in which the existing management and employees are a significant element.

Market capitalization: The total value at market prices of the securities in issue for a company, a stock market, or a sector of a stock market, calculated by multiplying the number of shares issued by the market price per share.

Mezzanine financing: Strictly, any form of financing instrument between ordinary shares and senior debt. The forms range from senior mezzanine debt, which may simply carry an interest rate above that for senior secured debt, to junior mezzanine debt, which may carry rights to subscribe for equity but no regular interest payment.

Middle-market company: A company that has sales revenue of $5 to $20 million and modest growth. In contrast to a high-potential company, it does not have the potential to float an IPO, but it may be a candidate for an acquisition, LBO, MBI, MBO, or ESOP.

Multimedia: The combination of text, graphics, audio, and video within a single computer application or presentation.

Multiple: The amount of money realized from the sale of an investment divided by the amount of money originally invested.

Murphy's Law: What can go wrong, will go wrong. An unexpected setback will happen at the most inconvenient moment.

National Association of Securities Dealers (NASD): Organization for brokers and dealers in OTC stocks.

National Association of Securities Dealers Automated Quotation (Nasdaq): An electronic system set up by NASD for trading stocks. It is commonly referred to as the OTC market.

Net income (net earnings, net profit): A company's final income after all expenses and taxes have been deducted from all revenues. It is also known as the bottom line.

Net income margin: Net income as a percentage of net sales revenue. In a typical year an average U.S. company has a net income margin of about 5%.

Net liquid value: Liquid financial assets minus callable liabilities.

Net present value: The present value of an investment's future net cash flows minus the initial investment. In theory, if the net present value is greater than 0, an investment should be made. For example, an investor is asked to invest $100,000 in a company that is expanding. He expects a rate of return of 30%. The company offers to pay him back $300,000 after four years. The present value of $300,000 at a rate of return of 30% is $105,038. Thus, the net present value of the investment is $5,038, so the investment should be made. (See *free cash flow, future value, present value,* and *rate of return.*)

Net profit: See *net income.*

Net worth: See *book value.*

New York Stock Exchange (NYSE):   The largest stock exchange in the world, located in New York. Also known as the Big Board.

Offering circular: See *prospectus.*

Operating cash flows: Cash flows directly generated by a company's operations. The cash flow from operating activity equals net income plus depreciation minus increase in accounts receivable minus increase in inventories plus increase in accounts payable plus increase in accruals. (See *financing flows* and *investment flows.*)

Operating income: Earnings (profit) before deduction of interest payments and income taxes, abbreviated to EBIT. It measures a company's earning power from its ongoing operations. It is of particular concern to a company's lenders, such as banks, because operating income demonstrates the ability of a company to earn sufficient income to pay the interest on its debt. (See *times interest earned.*)

Out of cash (OOC):   A common problem with entrepreneurial companies. The OOC time period is cash on hand divided by the burn rate.

Over the counter (OTC):   The purchase and sale of financial instruments not conducted on a stock exchange such as the New York Stock Exchange or the American Stock Exchange. The largest OTC market is the Nasdaq.

Owners' equity: Common stock plus retained earnings. (See *book value of a company.*)

Pain point: A potential customer's problem that a business can relieve with its product or service.

Paid-in capital: Par value per share times the number of shares issued. Additional paid-in capital is the price paid in excess of par value times the number of shares issued.

Partnership: Legal form of a business in which two or more persons are co-owners, sharing profits and losses.

Par value: Nominal price placed on a share of common stock.

Piggy-back registration rights: The right to register unregistered stock in the event of a company having a public stock offering.

Pledging: The use of a company's accounts receivable as security (collateral) for a short-term loan.

Portfolio: Collection of investments. For example, the portfolio of a venture capital fund comprises all its investments.

Postmoney valuation: The value of a company's equity after additional money is invested.

Pratt's Guide to Venture Capital Sources: Annual sourcebook for the venture capital industry.

Preemptive rights: The rights of shareholders to maintain their percentage ownership of a company by purchasing a proportionate number of shares of any new issue of common stock. (See *antidilution, dilution,* and *pro rata interest.*)

Preference shares: A class of shares that incorporate the right to a fixed dividend and usually a prior claim on assets, in preference to ordinary shares, in the event of a liquidation. Cumulative preference shares provide an entitlement to a cumulative dividend if in any year the preference dividend is unpaid due to insufficient profits being earned. Preference shares are usually redeemable at specific dates.

Premoney valuation: The value of a company's equity before additional money is invested.

Prepayment: A payment on a loan made prior to the original due date.

Present value (PV):   The current value of a given future cash flow stream, FV_t, after t years, discounted at a rate of return of $K\%$ is $PV = FV_t/(1 + K/100)^t$. For example, if an investor expects a rate of return of 60% on an investment in a seed-stage company, and she believes that her investment will be worth $750,000 after five years, then the present value of her investment is $71,526. (See *discount rate, future value, net present value, present value,* and *rate of return.*)

Price-earnings ratio (P/E ratio):   The ratio of the market value of a firm's equity to its after-tax profits (may be calculated from price per share and earnings per share).

Prime rate: Short-term interest rate charged by a bank to its largest, most creditworthy customers.

Private placement: The direct sales of securities to a small number of investors.

Profit: Synonymous with income and earnings.

Pro forma statements: Projected financial statements: income and cash-flow statements and balance sheets. For a startup company, it is usual to make pro forma statements monthly for the first two years and annually for the next three years.

Pro rata interest: The right granted the investor to maintain the same percentage ownership in the event of future financings. (See *antidilution* and *dilution.*)

Prospectus: A document giving a description of a securities issue, including a complete statement of the terms of the issue and a description of the issuer, as well as its historical financial statements. Also referred to as an offering circular. (See *red herring.*)

Put: A contract allowing the holder to sell a given number of securities back to the issuer of the contract at a fixed price for a given period of time.

Rate of return: The annual return on an investment. If a sum of money, PV, is invested and after t years that investment is worth FV_t the return on investment $K = [(FV_t/PV)^{1/t} - 1] \times 100\%$. For example, if $100 is invested originally, and one year later $108 is paid back to the investor, the annual rate of return is 8%.

Rationalize: Reduce a company's asset base.

Realization: See *exit.*

Redeemable shares: Shares that may be redeemable at the option of the company or the shareholder or both.

Red herring: Preliminary prospectus circulated by underwriters to gauge investor interest in a planned offering. A legend in red ink on its cover indicates that the registration has not yet become effective and is still being reviewed by the SEC.

Registration statement: A carefully worded and organized document, including a prospectus, filed with the SEC before an IPO.

Retained earnings: The part of net income retained in the company and not distributed to stockholders.

Return on investment: The annual income that an investment earns.

Running returns: Periodic returns, such as interest and dividends, from an investment (in contrast to a one-time capital gain).

SBA: Small Business Administration.

SBDC: Small Business Development Centers (supported by the SBA).

SBI: Small Business Institutes, run by universities and colleges with SBA support.

SBIC: Small Business Investments Companies.

SBIR: Small Business Innovation Research Program.

Schumpeter, Joesph A.:   Moravian-born economist whose book *The Theory of Economic Development,* written in Vienna in 1912, introduced the modern theory of entrepreneurship, in which the entrepreneur plays the central role in economic development by destroying the static equilibrium of the existing economy. Excellent modern examples are the roles played by Steve Jobs, Bill Gates, and Dan Bricklin in creating the microcomputer industry in the late 1970s. By the beginning of the 1990s, microcomputers (personal computers) were the principal force shaping the computer industry, and the old companies manufacturing mainframe and minicomputers, which dominated the computer industry until the mid-1980s, were in distress, ranging from outright bankruptcy to record-breaking losses.

SCORE: Service Core of Retired Executives, sponsored by the SBA to provide consulting to small businesses.

Search engine: A computer program that facilitates the location and retrieval of information over the Internet.

Second-round financing: The introduction of further funding by the original investors or new investors to enable the company to grow or deal with unexpected problems. Each round of financing tends to cover the next period of growth.

Securities and Exchange Commission (SEC):   Regulatory body for investor protection in the United States, created by the Securities Exchange Act of 1934. The supervision of dealers is delegated to the self-regulatory bodies of the stock exchanges and NASD under the provisions of the Maloney Act of 1938.

Seed financing: A relatively small amount of money provided to prove a concept; it may involve product development and market research but rarely involves the initial marketing of a product.

Sensitivity analysis: Examination of how the projected performance of the business varies with changes in the key assumptions on which the forecasts are based.

Short-term security: Generally, an obligation maturing in less than one year.

Sole proprietorship: A business form with one owner who is responsible for all the firm's liabilities.

Spamming: The simultaneous sending of the same advertising message indiscriminately to a large number of Internet users—a practice viewed very negatively by the Internet community and which often results in retaliatory "flames" directed at the offending message sender.

Startup financing: Funding provided to companies for use in product development and initial marketing. Companies may be in the process of being organized or may have been in business a short time (one year or less), but have not sold their product commercially. Generally, such firms have assembled the key management, prepared a business plan, made market studies, and completed other preliminary tasks.

Stock option plan: A plan designed to motivate employees, especially key ones, by placing a proportion of the common stock of the company under option at a fixed price to defined employees. The option may then be exercised by the employees at a future date. Stock options are often introduced as part of the remuneration package of senior executives.

Subchapter S corporation: A small business corporation in which the owners personally pay the corporation's income taxes.

Subordinated debt: Loans that may be unsecured or, more commonly, secured by secondary charges and that rank after senior debt for repayment in the event of default. Also referred to as junior debt or mezzanine debt.

Sweat equity: Equity acquired by the management team at favorable terms reflecting the value to the business of the managers' past and future efforts.

Syndicate: A group of investors that act together when investing in a company.

Term loan: Debt originally scheduled to be repaid in more than one year, but usually in 10 years or less.

Term sheet: Summary of the principal conditions for a proposed investment by a venture capital firm in a company.

Times interest earned: Earnings before interest and taxes, divided by interest (EBIT/I). The higher this ratio, the more secure the loan on which interest is paid. It is a basic measure of the creditworthiness of a company.

Underwrite: An arrangement under which investment banks each agree to buy a certain amount of securities of a new issue on a given date and at a given price, thereby assuring the issuer of the full proceeds of the financing.

Underwriter: An institution engaged in the business of underwriting securities issues.

Underwriting fee: The share of the gross spread of a new issue accruing to members of the underwriting group after the expenses of the issue have been paid.

Unsecured loans: Debt that is not backed by a pledge of specific assets.

URL: Uniform (or Universal) Resource Locator—the unique address through which users can be located on the Internet.

Valuation (of a company): The market value of a company. (See *market capitalization.*)

Value-added (by investors): Many venture capital firms claim that they add more than money to investee companies. They call it value-added, which includes strategic advice on such matters as hiring key employees, marketing, production, control, and financing.

Value proposition: The value of a businesses products and services to its customers.

Venture capitalist: A financial institution specializing in the provision of equity and other forms of long-term capital to enterprises, usually to firms with a limited track record but with the expectation of substantial growth. The venture capitalist may provide both funding and varying degrees of managerial and technical expertise. Venture capital has traditionally been associated with startups; however, venture capitalists have increasingly participated in later-stage projects.

Vesting period: The time period before shares are owned unconditionally by an employee who is sold stock with the stipulation that he must continue to work for the company selling him the shares. If his employment terminates before the end of that period, the company has the right to buy back the shares at the same price at which it originally sold them to him.

Virtual mall (cybermall): The electronic equivalent of a physical shopping mall, in which stores consist of Web pages that display goods and services that can be purchased over the Internet.

Visible venture capital (formal venture capital): The organized venture capital industry consisting of formal firms, in contrast to invisible venture capital or informal venture capital.

Vulture capital: A derogatory term for venture capital.

Waiver: Consent granted by an investor or lender to permit an investor or borrower to be in default on a covenant.

Warrant: An option to purchase common stock at a specified price. (See *equity kicker.*)

Warranty: A statement of fact or opinion concerning the condition of a company. The inclusion of warranties in an investment agreement gives the investor a claim against the company if it subsequently becomes apparent that the company's condition was not as stated at the time of the investment.

Web pages: The menus and information offered for users to browse through and interact with at a World Wide Web site. (See *home page.*)

World Wide Web: The part of the Internet that enables the use of multimedia-text, graphics, audio, and video.

Yield: Annualized rate of return on a security.

NOTES

Chapter 1: The Entrepreneurial Process

[1] P. D. Reynolds, W. D. Bygrave, E. Autio, and M. Hay, *Global Entrepreneurship Monitor—2002 Summary Report,* www.gemconsortium.org.

[2] *MIT: The impact of innovation* (Bank of Boston, 1997).

[3] http://www.census.gov/Press-Release/www/2001/cb01-54.html.

[4] *Inc. 500* vol. 22, no. 15 (2000).

[5] Ibid.

[6] Ibid.

Chapter 2: Opportunity Recognition

[1] Keynote address at the 1984 Babson Entrepreneurship Research Conference, co-sponsored by the School of Management, Georgia Institute of Technology, April 23–25, 1984, Atlanta, GA.

[2] Joline Godfrey, *Out Wildest Dreams: Women Entrepreneurs, Making Money, Having Fun, Doing Good* (New York: Harper Business, 1992), p. 27.

[3] Herbet A. Simon, "What We Know about the Creative Process" *Frontiers in Creative and Innovative Management, 1985,* ed. R. L. Kuhn (Cambridge, MA: Ballinger Publishing Co.), pp. 3–20.

[4] Keynote address at the first annual Entrepreneur's Night of UCLA Graduate School of Business, April 18, 1984, Westwood, CA.

[5] William J. J. Gordon, *Synectics* (New York: Harper & Row, 1961), p. 6.

[6] Michael Gordon, "Why Personal Power?" Presented at the Price Babson College Fellows Program REFLECT sessions, May 1992. Reprinted with permission from Michael Gordon.

[7] See Jeffry A. Timmons, *New Business Opportunities* (Acton, MA: Brick House Publishing, 1989).

[8] Barrie McKenna, "More than the Sum of Its Parts," *The Globe and Mail* (February 23, 1993), p. B24.

[9] Amar Bhide, "Bootstrap Finance," *Harvard Business Review* (November–December 1992): 112.

[10] Edward B. Roberts, *Entrepreneurs in High Technology: Lessons from MIT and Beyond* (New York: Oxford University Press, 1991), p. 144; Table 5.2.

[11] Teri Lammers and Annie Longsworth, "Guess Who? Ten Big-Timers Launched from Scratch," *Inc.* (September 1991): 69.

[12] Financial data from Dow Jones Interactive: http://www.djnr.com.

[13] Ibid.

[14] Robert A. Mamis, "The Secrets of Bootstrapping," *Inc.* (Setpember 1991): 54.

[15] See J. A. Timmons, D. F. Muzyka, H. H. Stevenson, and W. D. Bygrave, "Opportunity Recognition: The Core of Entrepreneurship" *Frontiers of Entrepreneurship Research, 1987,* ed. Neil Churchill et al. (Babson Park, MA: Babson College, 1987), p. 409.

[16] Comment made during a presentation at Babson College, May 1985.

[17] Scott W. Kunkel and Charles W. Hofer, "The Impact of Industry Structure on New Venture Performance," *Frontiers of Entrepreneurship Research, 1993* (Babson Park, MA: Babson College, 1993).

[18] J. A. Timmons, W. Bygrave, and N. Fast, "The Flow of Venture Capital to Highly Innovative Technology Ventures," a study for the National Science Foundation, reported in *Frontiers of Entrepreneurship Research: 1984* (Babson Park, MA, Babson College, 1984).

[19] For a more detailed description of free cash flow, see "Note on Free Cash Flow Valuation Models" by William Sahlman, HBS 9-288-023 (Boston: Harvard Business School).

[20] William A. Sahlman, "Sustainable Growth Analysis," HBS 9-284-059 (Boston: Harvard Business School, 1984).

[21] R. Douglas Kahn, president, Interactive Images, Inc., speaking at Babson College about his experiences as international marketing director at McCormack & Dodge from 1978 through 1983.

[22] This point was made by J. Willard Marriott, Jr., at Founder's Day at Babson College, 1988.

[23] See also David E. Gumpert and Jeffry A. Timmons, *The Encyclopedia of Small Business Resources* (New York: Harper & Row, 1984).

[24] Leonard M. Fuld, *Competitor Intelligence: How to Get It: How to Use It* (New York: John Wiley & Sons, 1985), p. 9.

[25] Ibid. See also "How to Snoop on Your Competitors," *Fortune* (May 14, 1984): 28–33; and also information published by accounting firms such as Sources of Industry Data, published by Ernst & Young.

[26] Fuld, *Competitor Intelligence,* pp. 12–17.

[27] Ibid., p. 325.

[28] Ibid., pp. 46, 48.

[29] Fuld, *Competitor Intelligence,* pp. 369–418.

Chapter 3: Entrepreneurial Marketing

[1] Robert J. Dolan, "Note on Marketing Strategy," Harvard Business Schools (2000), 9-598-061.

[2] Leonard L. Berry, *Discovering the Soul of Service* (New York: Free Press, 1999), pp. 100–101.

Chapter 4: Writing a Business Plan

[1] Special thanks to Matt Feczko, Michael DiPietro, and Dan Goodman for their assistance in writing this chapter.

[2] P. Thomas, "Rewriting the Rules: A New Generation of Entrepreneurs Find Themselves in the Perfect Time and Place to Chart Their Own Course," *Wall Street Journal* (May 22, 2000): R4.

[3] Running sidebar is a visual device that is positioned down the right hand side of the page that periodically highlights some of the key points in the plan. Don't overload the sidebar, but one or two items per page can draw attention to highlights that maintain reader interest.

[4] J. Timmons and S. Spinelli, *New Venture Creation,* 6th ed. (New York: Irwin McGraw-Hill, 2003).

[5] B. Joseph Pine II and James H. Gilmore, *The Experience Economy: Work Is Theatre and Every Business a Stage* (Boston, MA: Harvard Business School Press, 1999).

[6] O. Sacribey, "Private Companies Temper IPO Talk," *The IPO Reporter* (December 18, 2000).

[7] Burn rate is how much more cash the company is expending each month than earning in revenue.

Chapter 5: Building Your Pro Forma Financial Statements

[1] Special thanks to Matt Feczko, Michael DiPietro, Dan Goodman, Michael Collins, and Jeff Greenstein for their assistance in writing this chapter.

[2] By minimum wage, I mean that the money the entrepreneur can take out of the business is less on an hourly basis than the minimum wage.

[3] J. Tracy, *How to Read a Financial Report,* 5th ed. (New York: John Wiley & Sons, 1999).

[4] We discussed The History Shoppe (THS) in the Business Plan chapter. THS is a retail concept specializing in history books and artifacts.

[5] *1999 ABACUS Financial Study.*

[6] Look for publicly traded companies on your favorite database, such as SEC.gov.

[7] http://bizstats.com/otherretail.htm.

[8] Exhibit 5.9 is a reprint of Exhibit D from John Tracy, *How to Read a Financial Report,* 2nd ed. (New York: John Wiley & Sons, 1983).

[9] As of the writing of this chapter, you could download the template at http://leeds.colorado.edu/bplan/html/spTools.html. Hit the financials hotlink.

Chapter 11: Franchising

[1] Charles L. Woolweaver, "International Franchising Checklist: Short- and Long-term Considerations," *FranchiseConsulting.net.* http://www.franchiseconsulting.net /?source=overture. 2002.

Chapter 12: Entrepreneurs and the Internet

[1] Estimated by Egil, Juliussen, Computer Industry Almanac, Inc. Available from www.c-I-a.com. 2002.

[2] NUA/ComputerScope Ltd., 2001, and Michael J. Martinez, *Who Are Internet Users?* ABCNEWS.com, July 14, 2001, based on Coleen Kehoe, Graphics, Visualization, and Usability Center Survey, Georgia Institute of Technology, 2001.

[3] The Media Audit, 2000. Available from www.nua.ie/surveys.

[4] Yankee Group, October 2001. Retrieved November 2001, from nua.ie.

[5] The Pew Internet Project, 2001. Retrieved November 2001, from nua.ie.

[6] Michael J. Martinez, *Who Are Internet Users?* ABCNEWS.com, July 14, 2001, based on Coleen Kehoe, Graphics, Visualization, and Usabilty Center Survey, Georgia Institute of Technology, 2001.

[7] Julian E. Lange, William Bygrave, Sakura Nishimoto, J. R. Roedel, and Walter Stock. "Smart Money? The Impact of Having Top Venture Capital Investors and Underwriters Backing a Venture." *Venture Capital* vol. 3, no. 4 (2001): 309–326.

[8] Forrester Research, 2001.

[9] Forrester Research, 2001; and Jupiter Media Metrics, 2001.

[10] Jeffry A. Timmons, *New Venture Creation,* 5th ed. (New York: McGraw-Hill, 1999).

[11] pdf is the "universal" file format developed by Adobe, Inc. which allows users to view a document in its original form without having to deal with formatting problems. Adobe supplies a free downloadable program called *Acrobat Reader,* which enables a user to view pdf files virtually automatically. *Adobe Acrobat Reader* is available on Adobe's Web site at http://www.adobe.com.

[12] For further information on IFM, see the case *Internet Fashion Mall, LLC,* Babson Park, MA 02457-0310: Arthur M. Blank Center for Entrepreneurship, 1997.

[13] For example, see VeriSign at http://www.verisign.com.

[14] This brings up an interesting question of just how secure traditional telesales transactions are. In fact these transactions are only as secure as the honesty and care with which the payment information is treated. In the early days of mail-order selling,

similar security concerns were raised about this process, but over time the public has become comfortable with it despite the occasional problem.

Chapter 13: Managing a Growing Business

[1] John Peterman, "The Rise and Fall of the J. Peterman Company," *Harvard Business Review* (September–October 1999).

[2] Ibid.

[3] Henry Mintzberg and James A. Waters, "Tracking Entrepreneurial Strategy in an Entrepreneurial Firm," *Academy of Management Journal* vol. 25, no. 3 (1982): 495.

[4] Georg Von Krogh and Michael A. Cusumano, "Three Strategies for Managing Fast Growth," *Sloan Management Review* (January 2001): 53–61.

[5] Richard L. Osborne, "Second Phase Entrepreneurship: Breaking through the Growth Wall," *Business Horizons* vol. 37, no. 1 (1994).

[6] Henry Mintzberg, "Patterns in Strategy Formation," *Management Science* vol. 24, no. 9 (1978): 934–948.

[7] Joel Kolen and Susan Biddle Jaffe, "Knowing When to Take a Breather: Controlling Company Growth," *Nation's Business* vol. 83, no. 11: 6.

Chapter 14: Harvesting Your Venture: A Time for Capturing Value

[1] Arthur Andersen/MassMutual, *American Family Business Survey 1997* (Houston, TX: Arthur Andersen Center for Family Business, 1998).

[2] There is evidence that entrepreneurs do plan for the harvest. Holmburg (1991) surveyed CEOs at computer software firms that went public between 1980 and 1990 and found that 15% had a written harvest strategy as part of the original business plan; 5% developed a formal exit strategy subsequent to preparing the business plan; 40% had given some "thought" to the harvest; and 40% did not give any consideration to the harvest beforehand. Hyatt (1990) also found that 40% of the CEOs surveyed did not consider the harvest at the outset of the venture. Thus, it appears that a majority of firms (60%) give some advance thought to the harvest, either informally or formally. S. R. Holmburg, "Value Creation and Capture: Entrepreneurship Harvest and IPO Strategies," *Frontiers of Entrepreneurship Research*, eds. N. C. Churchill, W. D. Bygrave, J. C. Covin, D. L. Sexton, D. P. Slevin, K. H. Vesper, and W. E. Wetzel Jr. (Wellesley, MA: Babson College, 1991), pp. 191–204.

[3] See Kaplan 1989 and 1991 for an analysis of the operating effects of large-firm MBOs; and see Wright, Thompson, Robbie, and Wang, 1992, for a discussion of smaller-firm MBOs. S. Kaplan, "The Effects of Management Buy-Outs on Operating Performance and Value," *Journal of Financial Economics* vol. 24 (1989): 217–254. S. Kaplan, "The Staying Power of Leveraged Buyouts," *Journal of Financial Economics* vol. 29 (1991): 287–313. M. Wright, S. Thompson, K. Robbie, and P. Wong, "Management Buy-Outs in the Short and Long Term," *Frontiers of Entrepreneurship Research*, eds. N. C. Churchill, J. Katz, B. Kirchhoff, K. H. Vesper, and W. E. Wetzel Jr. (Wellesley, MA: Babson College, 1992), pp. 302–316.

[4] Internal Revenue Code, Section 415, paragraph 19,566.

[5] Presentation at the National Forum for Women in Finance, sponsored by the Financial Women's Association of New York, *Fortune,* and the Financial Executive Institute, New York, NY, September 16–17, 1998.

[6] W. H. Mikkelson, M. Partch, and K. Shah, "Ownership and Operating Performance of Companies That Go Public," *Journal of Financial Economics* vol. 44 (1997): 281–308.

[7] M. Pagano, F. Panetta, and L. Zingales, "Why Do Companies Go Public? An Empirical Analysis," *Journal of Finance* vol. 53 (1998): 27–64.

[8] L. Zingales, "Insider Ownership and the Decision to Go Public," *Review of Economic Studies* vol. 62 (1995): 425–448.

[9] See note 5. Adapted from Stein, National Forum for Women in Finance.

[10] L. Brokaw, "The First Day of the Rest of Your Life," *Inc.* vol. 15, no. 5 (1992): 144.

[11] N. Upton and J. Petty, "Venture Capital Funding of Transition in Family-Owned Business: An Exploratory Analysis," *Proceedings of the International Family Business Program Association* vol. 3 (1997): 44–61.

[12] Ibid.

[13] Heritage Partners, a Boston venture capital firm, obtained a registered trademark the "Private IPO®."

[14] J. W. Petty, J. Martin, and J. Kensinger, *Harvesting Investments in Private Companies* (Morristown, NJ: Financial Executive Research Foundation, 1999).

[15] We use the term "exit" interchangeably with "harvest."

ABOUT THE AUTHORS

Jeffry A. Timmons is known internationally for his research, innovative curriculum development, and teaching in entrepreneurship, new ventures, entrepreneurial finance, and venture capital. Timmons has held simultaneous professorships at Babson and Harvard Business School. He returned to Babson full time, and in 1995 was named the first Franklin W. Olin Distinguished Professor of Entrepreneurship. Timmons' friends and supporters endowed the Jeffry A. Timmons Professorship in the mid-1990s in recognition of his contributions to Babson College and to the field of entrepreneurship.

Timmons has authored several books including the leading textbook *New Venture Creation,* 6th ed. (2003); *Venture Capital at the Crossroads,* with Babson colleague William D. Bygrave (1992); and the groundbreaking *The Entrepreneurial Mind* (1989). He has published more than 100 articles and papers in publications such as *Harvard Business Review* and *Journal of Business Venturing,* as well as numerous teaching cases.

Timmons has earned a reputation for "practicing what he teaches." For nearly 30 years, he has been immersed in the world of entrepreneurship as an investor, director, or advisor in private companies and investment funds including Cellular One in Boston, New Hampshire, and Maine; the Boston Communications Group; BCI Advisors, Inc.; Spectrum Equity Investors; Internet Securities, Inc.; Chase Capital Partners; and others. He served as a trustee at his alma mater, Colgate University, from 1991 to 2000. He lives on his farm in New Hampshire with his wife and partner of 37 years, Sara, and winters at Bray's Island Plantation near Savannah, Georgia.

Abdul Ali, PhD, is an associate professor of Marketing and currently serving as chair of the Marketing Division at Babson College. He earlier taught at University of Maryland, College Park, and Syracuse University.

Ali has worked at Ciba-Geigy (India) Ltd. (currently known as Novartis Co.). Ali received an engineering degree from Indian Institute of Technology, Kharagpur;

an MBA from Indian Institute of Management, Ahmedabad; and a doctorate from Purdue University.

Ali's teaching and research interests include entrepreneurial marketing, new product management, marketing research methods, marketing strategy, and marketing high-tech products. His work has appeared in *Management Science, Journal of Product Innovation Management, Managerial and Decision Economics, Journal of Business Research,* and *Marketing Letters.* Ali and his two co-authors published a book entitled, *A Casebook for Business Statistics: Laboratories for Decision Making.*

Kathleen Seiders, PhD, is an associate professor of Marketing at Boston College. She received her doctorate at Texas A&M University, where she was affiliated with the Center for Retailing Studies, and previously taught at Babson College.

Seiders had a 10-year career in food retailing, with a focus on operations management. Her research has been published in *Organizational Dynamics, Journal of Marketing, Sloan Management Review, Marketing Management, Academy of Management Executive,* and *Journal of Retailing.* Seiders' research interests include retailing strategy, services marketing, and food marketing.

Seiders' comments on retailing and marketing have been published in the *New York Times, USA Today, Los Angeles Times, Inc. Magazine, Economist, Christian Science Monitor, Supermarket Business, Women's Wear Daily,* and *Boston Globe.* She has been a guest on BBC Radio, National Public Radio's *Marketplace, All Things Considered, CBS' This Morning, CBS' 60 Minutes,* and *CNBC Evening News.* Her current research focuses on service convenience.

William E. Wetzel Jr. is professor emeritus of Management at the Whittemore School of Business and Economics, University of New Hampshire, and director emeritus of the Center for Venture Research. Prior to his retirement in 1993, he held the Forbes Professor of Management Chair at the Whittemore School. During the 1987/1988 academic year, he served as the Paul T. Babson Visiting Professor of Entrepreneurial Studies at Babson College.

Wetzel's professional and research interests include the role of the entrepreneur in economic development, the financial management of high-growth private companies, and the informal venture capital markets. He has authored articles published in *Business Horizons, Sloan Management Review, New England Journal of Business and Economics, Black Enterprise, Journal of Business Venturing, Technovation, Pratt's Guide to Venture Capital Sources, Entrepreneurship and Regional Development,* the *Financier, Journal of Applied Corporate Finance, McGraw-Hill Encyclopedia of Economics, Encyclopedia of Entrepreneurship, The Portable MBA in Entrepreneurship,* and *The Art and Science of Entrepreneurship.* Prior to retirement, he served on the editorial boards of the *Journal of Business Venturing, In Business, Frontiers of Entrepreneurship Research,* and the *Journal of Small Business and Entrepreneurial Finance.*

Wetzel was a founding member of the New Hampshire High Technology Council and is a past president of the Council. In 1993, he received the Council's Lifetime Creative Vision Award. He founded the Center for Venture Research in 1983 and the Venture Capital Network, Inc. (VCN) in 1984. VCN is now the Technology Capital Network at MIT. Wetzel was a member of the Small Business Association of

New England (SBANE) where he served as chairman of the Academic Liaison Committee and as a member of the board of directors from 1983 through 1986. In 1998, Wetzel was named Ernst & Young New England Entrepreneur of the Year for his work as a supporter of entrepreneurship.

Joel M. Shulman is a Chartered Financial Analyst, a Certified Management Accountant, and a Certified Cash Manager. He directs the Shulman CFA Review Program that provides training for investment professionals throughout the world. He is author or co-author of numerous academic articles and books including *Encyclopedia of Business, Leasing for Profit, Alternatives to Conventional Financing, Planning Cash Flow, How to Effectively Manage Corporate Cash, A Manager's Guide to Financial Analysis, The Job of Corporate Controller,* and *How to Manage and Evaluate Capital Expenditures.*

Shulman has consulted for small entrepreneurial firms and large corporations, including Coldwell Banker, Ford Motor Company, Freddie Mac, Kmart, Merrill Lynch, Salomon Brothers, Sears, and UNISYS. He is also an active consultant for the World Bank, assisting with the development of capital markets in Central Asia and republics of the former Soviet Union.

Elizabeth J. Gatewood, PhD, is the Jack M. Gill Chair of Entrepreneurship and director of The Johnson Center for Entrepreneurship & Innovation at Indiana University. She directs Center activities, teaches MBA students, and conducts research on entrepreneurial topics. Gatewood holds a BS in psychology from Purdue University and an MBA in finance and PhD in business administration with a specialty in strategy from the University of Georgia. She taught at the Nijenrode Institute of Business in the Netherlands.

Gatewood's work has appeared in the *Journal of Business Venturing,* the *Journal of Venture Capital, Entrepreneurship Theory and Practice,* the *Journal of Small Business Management,* and *Entrepreneurship and Regional Development.* She is a member of the editorial review board of *Entrepreneurship Theory and Practice.* She serves on the National Advisory Board for Entrepreneurship Education of the Kauffman Foundation. Gatewood also serves on the advisory board for Spring Mill Ventures, a venture capital firm of the Village Ventures network. She is a past chair of the Entrepreneurship Division of the Academy of Management. She received the 1996 Advocate Award for outstanding contributions to the field of entrepreneurship from the Academy of Management.

Gatewood was named the Texas Woman in Business Advocate of the Year by the U.S. Small Business Administration. Her work in entrepreneurial cognition received the National Foundation of Independent Business Award for best paper at the 2001 Babson-Kauffman Foundation Entrepreneurship Research Conference. She is a member of the "Diana" project, a research study of women business owners and equity capital access, funded by the Kauffman Center for Entrepreneurial Leadership, the U.S. Small Business Administration, and the National Women's Business Council.

Richard P. Mandel serves as dean of undergraduate curriculum at Babson and has been a member of the Babson faculty since 1985. He teaches in the undergraduate, graduate, and executive education programs delivering a variety of courses. In addition to the Honors Foundation of Business Law, Professor Mandel currently teaches Commercial Law, Federal Taxation, American Constitutional Law, and Strategic Business and Tax Planning for the Entrepreneurial Venture. He also teaches Corporate Restructuring in the Finance Division and Introduction to Meteorology in the Math/Science Division.

Mandel also served as chair of the Finance Division from 1995 through 1998.

In addition to his teaching responsibilities, Mandel is a partner in the law firm of Bowditch and Dewey, specializing in the corporate, tax, and securities issues facing small, growing companies. His research and writing parallels his law practice, concentrating in entrepreneurial law. He is a contributing author to the Portable MBA series published by John Wiley and Sons, Inc. Mandel is a member of the bar of the Commonwealth of Massachusetts and the United States Supreme Court. In addition to practicing law for over 25 years, he has previously taught at a variety of colleges including Clark University.

Joseph S. Iandiorio is the founding partner of Iandiorio and Teska, a law firm specializing in intellectual property. He has been engaged in the private practice of law since 1965. Mr. Iandiorio lectures regularly and his writings are published widely in the field of intellectual property. He is a co-author of *The Portable MBA in Entrepreneurship* and is the author of the section on intellectual property in the new *Encyclopedia of Electrical and Electronics Engineering* also published by John Wiley & Sons. He also has written and published a newsletter, *Decisions & Developments,* since 1980, on issues relating to intellectual property and writes and publishes "New Ideas, Methods, and Products," a series of primers in brochure format on the same topics.

Iandiorio is actively involved in fostering the creation and growth of small businesses and high-technology companies. He was chosen as the SBA's Lawyer Small Business Advocate of the Year. He has been a director and treasurer of the Massachusetts Technology Development Corporation, a venture capital fund, since 1980; chairman and a longtime director of the Smaller Business Association of New England; chairman of the governor's advisory council on small business; chairman of the Small Business Development Committee; a member of the Massachusetts Small Business Advisory Council and the Science and Technology Advisory Board. He is a member of the Advisory Board on Intellectual Property at the Franklin Pierce Law School and was a founding member of the steering committee and a sponsor of the Worcester Polytechnic Institute Venture Forum. He is a recipient of the IEEE United States Activities Board Regional Professional Leadership Award and was a co-founder of the IEEE Entrepreneur's Network.

Kirk Teska aided Joseph Iandiorio with his chapter. He is a patent attorney, specializing in patents; trademarks; copyrights; trade secrets; licensing; and litigation of intellectual property matters, employee and consultant contracts, confidential disclosure agreements, and other related areas of intellectual property. He is actively involved in fostering the creation and growth of small businesses and high-technology companies. Teska was co-chairman of the IEEE Entrepreneurs' Network and is a columnist for *Mass High Tech,* authoring the monthly column *Patent Watch,* which features a review of selected patents issued to New England companies and changes in the laws concerning intellectual property. He also publishes many articles and delivers numerous lectures each year on topics in intellectual property law. Teska is a volunteer "Lawyer for the Arts" and an adjunct Professor of Law at the Suffolk University Law School and also at the Franklin Pierce Law Center, Concord, New Hampshire—ranked the number 1 patent law school by *U.S. News and World Report* in 1997, 1998, and 1999.

Teska has experience with the U.S. District Court for the District of New Hampshire as an intern/clert for Judge Norman Stahl (now of the 1st Circuit Court of Appeals). Prior to law school, Teska worked as an engineer for the U.S. Department of Defense, Naval Weapons Station, Seal Beach, California. He has a BSME, a Master of Science degree, and a Juris Doctor degree.

Teska's published works include: "Problems Are Our Business," *Proceedings of the U.S. Naval Institute,* October 1998; "Computer Software Quality Assurance Meets Computer Software Copyright Litigation," *Computer Law Reorter,* August 1993; "Federal Court Jurisdiction over Settlement Agreements," *Trial Magazine,* June 1994; and "Re False Security of Continuation-in-Part Applications," *JPTOS,* March 2001, Vol. 83, No. 3, p. 223.

Stephen Spinelli, PhD, began his entrepreneurial career when, three years after graduating from college, he was a founder of Jiffy Lube International in 1979. The Jiffy Lube team believed that rapid growth was essential to success in the newly created "quick lube" business and focused their efforts on franchising. Three years later, Spinelli left the founding management team to become a franchisee. Ultimately, he became Jiffy Lube's largest franchisee with stores in Massachusetts, Connecticut, and New York. Thirteen years after founding Jiffy Lube, Spinelli sold his founding shares and pursued a career in academia.

Moving to England in 1992, Spinelli earned a PhD in economics from the University of London's Imperial College, studying with world-renowned scholar Professor Sue Birley and writing his dissertation on the franchisor-franchisee relationship. He then joined the faculty at Babson College where he is the director of the Arthur M. Blank Center for Entrepreneurship and the chair of the entrepreneurship division.

Spinelli is the creator of Babson's MBA course in franchising, has published several academic studies on the subject, and has written a number of teaching cases about franchising. His is the co-author of a book titled *Franchising: Pathway to Wealth.*

Julian E. Lange, PhD, is an sssociate professor of entrepreneurship and the Benson Distinguished Entrepreneurship Fellow at Babson College. He has also previously served as an assistant professor of finance at Harvard Business School. Lange is known internationally for his teaching and research in entrepreneurship and for the practical application of the principles of entrepreneurship to business and government.

An accomplished entrepreneur, Lange was CEO of Software Arts, the company that created VisiCalc—the world's first electronic spreadsheet. Lange is also founder and president of Chatham Associates, a management consulting firm to business and government. He has more than 25 years of experience advising a wide variety of businesses and organizations including startups, mid-size, and *Fortune* 500 companies, and government agencies.

Lange has published articles in leading journals including the *Journal of Applied Corporate Finance, Venture Capital, Frontiers of Entrepreneurship Research,* and *International Management.* He has also co-authored a book on the construction industry and has contributed chapters on entrepreneurship to leading texts. Lange's commentary on entrepreneurship topics has appeared on National Public Radio, in television interviews, and in the American and international press. Lange is a Phi Beta Kappa, Magna Cum Laude graduate of Princeton University. He also holds an MBA from Harvard Business School, and an AM and PhD in Economics from Harvard University.

Donna Kelley is an assistant professor of entrepreneurship at Babson College, where she holds the Paul T. Babson Term Chair in Entrepreneurship. She teaches courses across the range of an organization's life cycle: starting new ventures, developing business plans, managing growing businesses, and corporate entrepreneurship. After an early career as a chemist, Kelley cofounded a health fitness business and later joined the management team of a computer hardware start-up. She received her doctorate from Rensselaer Polytechnic Institute in 1999.

Kelley has studied the entrepreneurial efforts of firms in both growth and mature phases. This research has been published in the *Journal of Business Venturing, Entrepreneurship Theory and Practice, Journal of Small Business Management, Small Business Economics, R&D Management,* and *Frontiers of Entrepreneurship Research.* She has studied the efforts of technology-based firms to sustain growth beyond founding by leveraging and building technological capabilities; this research focused on the patent, alliance, and product innovation activities of computer hardware and telecommunications firms. Kelley has also published research on the early stage evaluation of radical technologies in large established organizations. She is currently researching the corporate entrepreneurship process through in-depth interviews with managers in 12 multinational organizations, taking a special interest in how organizations create systems for managing entrepreneurial projects.

Edward P. Marram, PhD, has been an entrepreneur in the high-technology sector for more than 35 years. He is the founder, president, and CEO of GEO-CENTERS, INC., a high-technology, professional services firm. The company excels in a number of critical technological areas including biomedical research, toxicology, environmental remediation, technology transfer, human factors, and defense and civilian scientific policy. GEO-CENTERS has twice been recognized by *Inc.* magazine as one of the fastest growing, privately held companies in the United States.

Marram has developed a reputation for outstanding technical and academic accomplishments during his long years of scientific, industrial, and academic careers. In 1999 and 2000, he was appointed to the National Defense Science Board, which deals with strategic planning for our nation's defense. In addition to his professional activities, Marram is entrepreneur-in-residence at Babson College where he has developed entrepreneurship cases. He is also an adjunct professor at Flanders Business School in Belgium. He regularly lectures on entrepreneurship and issues facing high growth companies in both graduate level and executive education programs. Marram was named a Price Babson College Fellow and received the Edwin M. Appel Prize for Bringing Entrepreneurial Vitality to Academia.

Marram serves as a member of both public and private boards. He is a member of the Health and Educational Financial Authority (HEFA) of Massachusetts and the

MIH Power Options (a Massachusetts nonprofit energy-purchasing consortium). He serves on the College Advisory Council, College of Natural Sciences and Mathematics at the University of Massachusetts, Amherst. He is a member of the National Association of Corporate Directors, and he serves on the boards of several privately held companies.

J. William Petty is professor of finance and the W.W. Caruth Chairholder of Entrepreneurship at Baylor University. He currently serves as the director of the Entrepreneurial Studies Program at Baylor University. His research interests include valuation and acquisitions of privately held companies, the financing of entrepreneurial firms, and shareholder value-based management. He has served as the co-editor for the *Journal of Financial Research* and as the editor of the *Journal of Entrepreneurial and Small Business Finance.* Petty has published in numerous finance journals and is the co-author of two leading corporate finance textbooks, *Basic Financial Management,* and *Foundations of Finance,* and co-author of a widely used text, *Small Business Management.* He recently completed a study for the Financial Executive Institute on exit strategies in privately held companies ("Harvesting Investments in Private Companies," 1999). He has also co-authored a book, *Value-Based Management: Corporate America's Response to the Shareholder Revolution.*

Wang Chao, the chairman and CEO of ChinaEquity Advisory, Inc., aided Petty in his research for this chapter. Wang's "niche business" raises between $5 and $50 million in venture capital for high-tech companies and introduces strategic partners to small businesses. He is the largest individual venture capitalist in China, offering online financial consulting service and providing an incubator service that mainly targets Chinese returning home from foreign studies. Wang studied at Tsinghua University in Beijing, where he was a member of the first MBA graduating class at the university. He was then sponsored by Zhu Rongji, China's Prime Minister, to study in the United States. Coming to the United States, he studied finance at Rutgers University. He returned home 14 years later, leaving his position as vice president, Morgan Stanley Asia, to pursue his dream—to create "something extraordinary" in his homeland.

Jiahe Zhao, the chairman of International Finance and Trade in the School of Economics and Management at Tsinghua University in Beijing, also aided Dr. Petty. Zhao has published extensively during his academic career in the area of international finance, and he is frequently a guest lecturer regarding the Chinese business environment. After retiring from Tsinghua University, Zhao founded an investment banking and consulting firm, where he is heavily involved in international business, participating in joint venture negotiations and project feasibility studies. He has worked as a senior consultant with foreign firms, such as Andersen Consulting. He has also served as a visiting professor at the University of Texas at San Antonio.

INDEX